Alive 5 times
An Autobiography of Past Lives

Allen Eastman

Lightrise Press

Alive 5 times

An Autobiography of Past Lives
by Allen Eastman

Copyright © 2003 by Lightrise Press.
All rights reserved.
Published 2003.

Lightrise Press
Scottsdale, AZ 85259
Email: info@lightrise.com
Website: www.lightrise.com

ISBN: 0-9741303-0-3

Editing, design, and cover design by
Tony Stubbs
[www.tjpublish.com]

Printed in the United States of America

Table of Contents

Introduction

Flashback to the Past vi

How it All Began x

What's Inside? xi

Brief Overview of Reincarnation xiv

Reincarnation and Religion xv

How Past Life Regression Works xviii

Recurring Themes xx

Life #1: Meera: Makah Shaman-Woman (1693-1733) 2

Group-Link: Indians & the Environmentalists 76

Lessons Learned 77

Life #2: John Hogans: Fighting the Un-Civil War (1831-1865) 78

Group-Link: Abraham Lincoln & John F. Kennedy 131

Group-Link: Robert E. Lee & Martin Luther King 144

Lessons Learned 145

Life #3: Sorrel Horse: At the Little Bighorn (1863-1876) 146

Group-Link: Indians & the Vietnam War 215

Group-Link: Indians & WWII 216

Group-Link: Custer & Marc Antony 218

Lessons Learned 219

Life #4: Louis St. Jacques: Drinking with van Gogh (1870-1914) 220

Group-Link: France & Buffalo Bill Cody 304

Group-Link: France & Texas Tea 306

Lessons Learned 307

Appendices

A. Resources: Three Techniques for "How to Do It"

A1. The Sedona Method: letting go of the past................................309
Lester Levenson's "Amazing Story"

A2. Meditation & Yoga; retreat & community 315
Autobiography of a Yogi: "Resurrection & the Astral World"
Autobiography of a Yogi: "Cosmic Consciousness"

A3. Reflection: hypnotic regression reading 332
"Definitions of Reincarnation": soul mates and more.
"God and Life": descriptions of the afterlife and more.

B. "Waking Up" and other Realizations 344

C. Table of Soul Group Relationships 350

D. Bibliography 353

Index 358

*"Change yourself,
and the whole world
will change before your eyes."*

Figure 0-1. "Suddenly, a huge medieval fort appears before my eyes." *[Engraving reprinted from Jewett (1887).]*

Introduction: Flashback to the Past

With a flash and a shimmer, my living room disappears, and a bizarre scene unfolds before my eyes. I am standing about 30 feet above the ground on the stone parapet of an old medieval fort. It is a moonless overcast night. Torches placed in stands help light the area, revealing moss-covered, mottled gray stone walls. All around me, I smell the intense aromas of mold, fire oil, and smoke.

Staring out over the fort walls, I see more torches burning furiously. Men, whom I recognize as soldiers, are moving about. Nearby, horses stomp nervously at the soft earth, breathing so hard that great plumes of steam shoot from their nostrils.

On my head, I wear a heavy conical iron helmet with a long extension to protect my nose. I recognize it as a Norman battle helmet. A thick, blue-green leather cloak drapes from my shoulders to my ankles. Around my waist hangs a sword in a thick scabbard that must weigh 15 pounds.

Somehow, I know that the year is 1066 and that I am part of the Norman Invasion of England by William the Conqueror. It is late October, and this is the Battle of Hastings. Having defeated King Harold and the Saxons in a fierce fight today, we are consolidating our gains after the battle.

Figure 0-2. Norman soldiers in armor. *[Reprinted from Jewett (1887).]*

Unexpectedly, through the stillness, I hear shouts coming from the road leading to the fort. Next, I hear the clanking of heavy steel as the clash of swords and axes rises above the shouting. The Saxons are mounting a counterattack, although it sounds as if only eight to ten men are fighting.

I am now fully engaged in the persona of a captain. No longer viewing the scene as if I were watching a movie, I view it through the eyes and soul of the soldier who now shouts orders to the guards below. I am that soldier. I see and understand everything from his perspective. Cautiously, I peer over the parapet, straining to see the fighting below through the darkness. I can see little save for the occasional flash as one blade strikes another.

As I turn to call for more soldiers to join in the skirmish, I hear the muffled grunt of a man concealed in the darkness below. Alert and straining my eyes, I see nothing, but now there is a rapid whirring noise – whup, whup, whup. I recognize this sound immediately as that of a heavy weapon being hurled into the air. In a heartbeat, before I can react, a 3-foot long Saxon battle-axe comes into view, spinning up and out of the darkness. I see a flash of the lethal weapon reflected from the fires below. Time is standing still. I am in a slow-motion scene. Anything that would take seconds to occur in real time now seems to last minutes. My senses are so acute that my eyes catch every gold and red flicker of firelight reflecting off the edge of the axe, honed to razor sharpness. The details are intricate. Even the indentation of wood grain in the handle is perfectly clear. The initials "RL" are carved deeply into the wood. With one last somersault, the heavy crescent-shaped blade reaches my head.

Figure 0-3. Battle-axe used at the battle. *[Engraving reprinted from Jewett (1887).]*

Continuing in ultra-slow-motion, the axe slices through my helmet with the grating sound of metal tearing metal. Though the scene should be horrifying, I am somehow completely detached, feeling no pain. The blade continues through one layer after another – through my skin and the muscles of my face. As it slices deeper, I taste the sharp flavor of iron on my tongue. It cuts into the bone of my cheek, jaw, and forehead, and now, it carves into the soft, fleshy meat of my brain. Suddenly, there is a bright flash of light. It is all over.

Standing outside my body, I see my life as the captain rapidly fading away. Brain activity ceases, and I watch as my knees buckle, the momentum of the heavy axe throwing my body violently backwards, lifeless and now merely under the law of gravity. It tumbles slowly backwards off the parapet and drops headfirst onto the ground below like a heavy bag of sand. I am dead as I hit the hard stone walkway, all in the blink of a real-time eye. The impact breaks loose the axe, which clatters loudly on the stones. In spirit, I hover over the scene, viewing my body, now crumpled like an old rag doll.

In this spirit state, I feel no shock, surprise, or sadness. As a soldier in the army of William the Conqueror, I long ago accepted that this would most likely be my fate. Having seen so many men die violently in brutal battles, death no longer moves me. Nevertheless, I am relieved that it is all over.

There is nothing more for me here, so I move gently into the light.

As this vivid scene ended, my consciousness returned to my living room, and I opened my eyes. My "flashback" had lasted all of about 20 seconds. Now, it was over, and I was no longer back in the year 1066. The year was 1996, and I was enjoying a quiet evening at home with a good book. Andrea, my wife, was in the family room, quietly working with her gemstones.

Collecting myself, I took a few moments to meditate on what had just happened. It had started as a delightful relaxing moment, one in which I felt at peace with everything. As I had looked down at the book in my lap, the soft light behind me had spilled over the pages. Then suddenly, while reading a passage about a battle around an ancient castle, I had been struck with an excruciating pain behind my right eye. I rarely have headaches, but when I do, they are usually similar to this one. Still, I was surprised with the severity of the pain. The searing ache throbbed in my eye, extending deep through my brain and down behind my right ear.

I was startled and then worried. Almost instantly, the pain grew stronger as the vivid battle scene unfolded before me. At first, it appeared as a full-color still picture, then more like the individual scenes in a slide show. Immediately, I recognized the lifetime as having been one with William the Conqueror. I already had seen several other flashbacks of this life but never this particular scene. The experience was as real as the hair standing up on the back of my neck or the chair I was sitting in. As the drama played out before my inner vision, I was caught up in the experience so deeply that I could not even call out to Andrea. *[See inset.]*

When it was over, after I had relived the source of the pain, a past life experience that ended long ago, the headache disappeared, never to return. Somehow, the terrible pain and pressure in my head caused by that battle-axe had been bottled up inside of me as if in a pressure cooker. Bringing the incident to my conscious awareness was like lifting the lid and releasing the force.

In spite of having to watch the violent death of a former body, I came out of the experience feeling very relaxed. After all, even though my body had died violently, here I was hundreds of years later watching it all over again as if in a movie. True, my body died but the *real me* is still around. Bodies come and go. The spirit lives on.

Experiences such as this one have convinced me that we all have lived many times before. This book recounts four of my own past lives, as experienced through the fifth, my present one.

Flashback Experiences

Flashbacks such as this one are set into motion by what I call "triggers," which are simply ordinary events from my daily life. These triggers almost invariably produce an emotion, a smell, taste, sound, or touch, or they can create something like my headache or some other physical pain.

The trigger that caused this experience was a passage in my book that described a castle much like the one in my past.

Later in the Appendices, there is a list of resources, including web sites, organizations, and books that will help you learn how to revisit your own past lives and how to use that information to make your current and future lives more fulfilling.

How it All Began

Born in Florida in 1946, my early childhood was typical and uneventful. As I was growing up, experiences such as this one at the Battle of Hastings never happened to me. However, starting at the age of 15, I began to have odd experiences that led to revelations about the relationship between body and soul – insights that defied conventional thinking about reality. As time went on, such experiences have become commonplace, until now I consider them to be as normal as the sunrise.

In particular, several of these experiences set me off on a lifelong journey in search of answers. Appendix B includes a detailed discussion of these experiences and others. The following is a short summary of two of them:

- *Life after Death:* While studying for college exams in 1965, I stayed with an aunt who put me up in her Civil War era guest cottage. There, I had an astounding encounter with a family of ghosts, visible to me as blue shapes through which I could see the walls of the cottage. I realized for the first time that there was life after death and that body and spirit are separate. *[The full story is in Appendix B.]*
- *Soul Travel:* During an experiment with self-hypnosis in college, I vividly imagined visiting my girlfriend at home, walking down her hall, and sitting on the foot of her bed. Later, to my astonishment and without my asking her about it, she described the exact event happening at exactly the same time as I had experienced it. This event was my first conscious out-of-body experience. In it, I learned that the spirit is separate from the body and that the spirit can move in and out of the body at will, much like getting in and out of a car. *[The full story is in Appendix B.]*

In 1967, these unusual experiences led me to cancel plans to attend Harvard Medical School; instead, I began a sabbatical to find answers my professors could not provide. Driven by a powerful "need to know," I became deeply involved in the study of reincarnation and past life regression. Finally, in 1968, I was satisfied that I had found in the world's religions some satisfactory explanations for the spiritual experiences that were happening to me.

From 1965, when I started this journey into spirit, until the present day, I have been involved in many things that deepened my spiritual understanding. Among other things, I have lived in a Zen Buddhist monastery; trained in California with a gifted psychic; studied with several highly advanced spiritual teachers; completed training to become an ordained minister; and worked off and on for 30 years with several international spiritual groups, serving in many roles from cook to carpenter to CEO.

For all of these last 34 years, I have remained a student, continuing to experience and to live the truths contained in the world's great religions and philosophies. Now 56 years old and semiretired, I have spent the last two years researching and writing this book. It is intended both for those who accept reincarnation and for those who just have a curiosity about past lives. For those looking for some new answers, please suspend your current beliefs for the brief time that it takes to read this book. Imagine, if only for a few hours, that anything and everything is possible, and then reach your own conclusions.

Whether or not you ultimately consider this book to be fact or fiction, the recall techniques that I have used have led me on a path of extraordinary self-discovery and understanding. As a result, I am more at peace with myself and with the world around me, and I believe that I am a better person for having gone through the experiences you will read about in these pages.

I have not found all the answers – I am still searching and studying, too. However, I have stumbled across a few things that may be of interest to you. You will find some of them in these pages.

What's Inside?

The Stories: This book is a journey through four of my past lives, all encountered from within the fifth, my current one as Allen Eastman. Each account begins with a brief background of the era in which the life took place and is followed by the vivid details of the lifetime, reported in the first person. Collectively, these four lives span 220 years, from 1693 to 1914, although I have lived more than 40 other times that I can recall in high detail.

Each of these stories recalls the highlights of a particular lifetime, with sidebars interweaving real events of my past physical life on this earth with the real events from the world of spirit. Each of these worlds is different, but we exist in both of them at the same time, so they are integral and inseparable parts of our nature.

Western culture mostly has overlooked the spiritual aspect of our existence, preferring instead to insist that each of us is only a physical body. Most people accept as true such slogans as, "What you see is what you get" and "It doesn't get any better than this."

The stories you will read here, however, offer a different viewpoint. If we make the effort to become aware of our past lives and if we integrate that wisdom into our current life, then we will have gone far towards understanding our soul's grand purpose. When we do so, then we understand that "You get *much* more than what you see" and that "It does get better than this – a *whole lot* better!"

Putting these stories together, one piece at a time, has taken years. The scenes and experiences tend to come to me in a seemingly unrelated fashion, one layer upon another until finally, at some point, an entire story becomes clear. The four past lifetimes described here are quite dramatic; some are peaceful, others painful, a few humorous, and still others horrifying. However, the one common thread they all share is that they have all affected my current life in some manner, including my work habits, relationships with others, my physical and emotional health, and even the way I dress.

Following each story are two sections of Life Review for the life. The first is a section on my soul's Group-Links, showing how I and other souls have interacted as a group across time. The second section deals with Lessons Learned, covering the themes and insights that have helped me to improve my current life.

The Appendices contain useful information about reincarnation:
- *Appendix A,* the Techniques Section, is a "How to" section that describes three proven, hands-on, learn-through-your-fingertips techniques that will help you explore your past lives. The section contains Internet links and phone numbers for three of the very best techniques that have worked for me and for many others over the years. Some of these techniques have been used and refined continuously for many thousands of years. Also in the section are first-person accounts from two spiritual teachers about the startling realizations that turned their lives around and brought them deep peace and understanding.
- *Appendix B,* as mentioned above, covers a few of the major realizations and events that helped shape my own journey into spirit.
- *Appendix C* is a chart showing the interrelationships between twelve of the various souls that have incarnated with me in the lifetimes in this book and my current lifetime as Allen.
- *Appendix D* offers a Bibliography of the books I consulted for background notes on the four lifetimes and for my studies in reincarnation.

If you have a personal interest in developing past life recall, then Appendix A may be very useful. However, just knowing about your other lifetimes will be of little use other than to amuse your friends. In fact, you already may have heard your friends, associates, or others claim to have lived as some famous person, perhaps as Cleopatra, George Washington, or Napoleon.

Sorry to say, but most likely, these people do not have it quite right. Usually when people have a past life memory indicating they were someone famous, they do not examine it thoroughly. In most cases, those people might have been close to a famous person like Cleopatra, such as having been a servant or a bystander in the crowd during a procession, as many thousands were. Because of seeing Cleopatra in their flashback, they assume that *they* were the Queen of the Nile, when, in fact, they only saw her in that lifetime. True, they have had a past life recall; only they have not remembered it from the correct viewpoint.

Figure 0-4. Who *really* was Cleopatra? *[Drawing reprinted from North (1906).]*

They were not the person they think they were … although, in fairness, some soul somewhere out there actually *did* incarnate as Cleopatra.

Putting aside the entertainment value of these memories, if you are interested in recalling past lives in order to make your life better, then the information you uncover can be vitally useful. For instance:

- Are there people in your life who hurt you or upset you a lot?
- Do you have bad habits that you just cannot seem to change?
- Are you having emotional problems, such as depression, grief, fear, greed, anger, or pride?
- Do you have some physical problems that cannot be explained?

If you answer "Yes" to any of these questions, then any of the three techniques described in Appendix A might help. With them, you can identify the actions and attitudes from your past lives that are influencing you now, in an unconscious way, without your knowledge, and against your will.

The overall process is simple and is the same for all three:
- Identify the problem or feeling in the present moment.
- Locate where the problem or feeling came from in the past.
- Undo it and let it go, so that it affects you no more.

If you follow this simple process, almost invariably your problems will at least get better, leaving you happier each time you repeat the process. At best, the problem will vanish completely and never bother you again.

None of these three simple techniques requires any special understanding or ability. Each of them has worked extremely well for me and for thousands of others just like you and me. If you would like to change your life for the better, they can work for you, too.

Brief Overview of Reincarnation

Have you ever had vague feelings that you lived before this lifetime? Have you ever experienced *déjà vu*? If so, you are not alone. A Harris Poll conducted in 1998 found that 23 percent of all American adults believe in reincarnation – that is nearly 40 million people.

To understand this phenomenon of past lives better, let us look briefly at the concept. Under reincarnation, portions of the soul are reborn into a series of physical bodies over time. This process is rarely instantaneous; sometimes there are gaps that can extend for years, decades, or even millennia. And, as you will read in my case, lifetimes can sometimes overlap by a few years. In between lives, the soul continues learning and growing on the soul plane.

What is the purpose of all this? In a word: *understanding*. For, to the soul, each body is simply another vehicle for spiritual growth. *Most importantly, the thoughts, actions, and events of each lifetime influence future lifetimes.*

Reincarnation makes clearer such seeming tragedies as being born with serious handicaps or, for example, when a child might die within a few moments of birth. Reconciling such apparent injustices in the world is possible only in the context of reincarnation.

In such cases, reincarnation offers several very simple and compassionate answers: either (1) that particular soul desired to experience the especially difficult lesson of dying young or (2) the soul did something in the past that it needed to balance. In any event, an early death is not the end; the soul will get other chances to incarnate. With reincarnation, there are no victims.

With reincarnation, no matter how many chances we need, each one of us will get many opportunities. Every soul will make it through all the problems; no one will be left behind. Everyone will reach the ultimate goal, which I believe, is fulfillment, happiness, and a deep unshakable peace of mind with no hint of sorrow. As the Apostle Paul said, we all eventually will find the "peace of God, which surpasses all understanding."

Reincarnation and Religion

Christianity

Most of the world's religions, with the exception of mainstream Christianity and Judaism, believe in some form of reincarnation and the influence of past lives on current lives. Even Christians, as suggested by the Bible, perhaps have referred to it. For example, certain passages about Jesus in the New Testament's Gospel According to Mark, Chapter 9, seem to hint at reincarnation.

Figure 0-5. Jesus said, "This man has not sinned." *[Courtesy NARA.]*

1. "As he walked along, he saw a man blind from birth."
2. "His disciples asked him, 'Rabbi, who sinned, this man or his parents, that he was born blind?'"
3. "Jesus answered, 'Neither this man nor his parents sinned; he was born blind so that God's work might be revealed in him.'"

How could the man, who was blind from the moment of birth, have sinned in the womb before he was born? Perhaps the disciples meant that he did so in a former incarnation.

Early church leaders, such as Justin Martyr (100-165 AD), St. Clement (150-220 AD), and Origen (185-254 AD), referred to the "preexistence of the soul" and "reimbodiment," or reincarnation, but these concepts were suppressed in 553 AD by the Roman emperor Justinian. After that, even talking about the existence of the soul before birth was declared *anathema* and was punishable by death.

Buddhism and Hinduism

The majority of the world's population freely believes in reincarnation. Hinduism and Buddhism, which together account for more than two billion people, have accepted the concept of reincarnation for many thousands of years. The concept is discussed in some of the oldest written texts ever discovered anywhere on the planet.

One part of Eastern philosophy that is widely accepted in our society is the concept of "karma," the idea that "what comes around, goes around." Some religions interpret karma as operating blindly and irrevocably. In other words, if you have wronged someone in a past life – injured, robbed, killed, etc. – then in some future life, you will have to experience that same level and intensity

Figure 0-6. Buddha is on the left. *[Reprinted from Foucher (1917).]*
Shiva is on the right. *[Reprinted from Havel (1920).]*

of pain. Some say that the Bible contains the same concept in the Exodus passage, "an eye for an eye, and a tooth for a tooth."

On the other hand, some Hindu teachings emphasize that karma is a learning opportunity and is not predetermined. Different situations offer different karmic opportunities. In other words, you have choices about how to handle the difficult situations that arise in your life. Furthermore, deep introspection that leads to the understanding of a problem may eliminate the need to experience that situation outwardly. This means that correcting the problem through *thought* rather than through *action* can result in much faster spiritual growth.

Once we understand karma, the universal system of checks and balances, then many of the world's seeming injustices become clearer. One example is the "Beltway Sniper" killings in 2002 by Muhammad and Malvo. Most everyone agrees that it was a terrible, horrible crime, and that those two were brutal, heartless killers who gunned down innocent victims. However, what if there were more to the story? Are the facts as clear as they appear to be? Maybe there are some hidden karmic threads running through these events. What if there were no "victims" after all?

I decided to find out and sat down to meditate one day. After I got quiet, I asked, "Is there a past life connection between the shooters and the victims?"

Suddenly, I saw a mental vision of a small town after the Civil War in the rural South in Virginia, near where most of the shootings took place. Most of the townspeople, maybe 20 or 30, were gathered around a large oak tree outside of town. With terror in their eyes, two black men had their hands tied and

Figure 0-7. Like this man, Muhammad was trained to shoot in the military. [Courtesy of the National Archives.]

were being hauled up on benches under the tree. The other men roughly looped nooses over their heads. Then, to cheers, curses, and laughter from the townspeople, the two black men were lynched.

Unfortunately, the two men were killed for something they did not do. Little or no effort was made to see if they were, in fact, guilty. They were lynched mainly because the townspeople hated all black slaves who had been set free.

The two black men would later incarnate as Muhammad and Malvo. Nearly every one of their modern-day "victims" had been standing around that oak tree, cheering loudly as the two innocent men were hanged. Later, as victims of the sniper shooting, they experienced the same feelings of terror that the two black men had felt a century earlier. Each got to experience being a victim and being killed, even though innocent of any wrongdoing.

Knowing the karma of the situation makes the blame much less clear. Who were the "real" victims? The people who were shot or the two black men who were hanged? Neither action was right or justifiable in a worldly sense. However, understanding the karma puts things in a very different light.

When something bad unexpectedly happens to someone, we often hear the person cry, "Why me? I didn't do anything to deserve this?" Far from being an innocent victim, that person can usually find the roots of the problem in some past life. The truth is that the "innocent victim" probably *did* do something to deserve it – only it happened long ago, and in a different body.

The last 30 years of the twentieth century have witnessed an enormous expansion of interest in reincarnation and karma, both in the United States and around the world. Today, reincarnation is becoming widely accepted as the model for the world to use to interpret "reality."

We are undergoing a radical shift in which our view of the nature of reality is changing profoundly. Eventually, everyone may come to accept that spirit and body are separate entities and that the spirit can leave the body at will.

How Past Life Regression Works

Rather than just tell these stories in a flat monotone, I have tried to convey the emotions as I experienced them in the past moment. In fact, one of the "triggers" that brings these memories to life is strong emotion. It has been my experience that five steps have been involved in my own recall process:

Step #1: Triggers

Invariably, the first thing that happens is that something in my daily life triggers a past life recall. These include the five senses:

- *Sight* – seeing a newsreel of Werner Von Braun and a V-2 rocket reminded me of my life as a German woman and saboteur in World War II.
- *Sound* – the crack of a black-powder musket recalled scenes from my life as a soldier while I lay dying during the Civil War.
- *Smell* – unusual-smelling cigarette smoke reawakened memories of a turbulent life as a young friend of Vincent van Gogh.
- *Touch* – the feel of sealskin recalled memories of surviving a devastating earthquake and tsunami as a Native American medicine woman in the 1700s.
- *Taste* – eating venison stew once reminded me of life as a young Lakota warrior before the Battle of the Little Bighorn.

Step #2: Flashbacks

Next, the triggers set off flashbacks that involve one or more of the following elements:

- *Déjà vu* – a powerful indefinable feeling of "I've been here before," or "I've done this before."
- *Strong sensory impressions* – usually some sensation, such as an aroma or taste, but which comes from the past, not from the present.
- *Strong emotions* – the easiest memories to recall are those that contained strong emotions. If I am experiencing a strong feeling in the present day and a past life contained a similar feeling, it will quite likely trigger a flashback.
- *Waking vision* – when this happens, I see the memory faintly superimposed over the physical reality of the moment.

Step #3: Meditation

Once I have had a flashback, I use one of the techniques described in Appendix A (either meditation or the Sedona Method©) to go deeper into the experience by focusing on the triggers or emotions that brought it about.

Step #4: Intuitive writing

Once I have recalled enough information (this process may take years and many layers of experiences), I put it down in writing. As I do this, I place myself into a meditative state, which tends to make the experience clearer and more vivid, allowing me to write in richer detail.

Step #5: Deep-trance hypnosis

This is usually the final step, and I use it to check validity and enhance the memories that have come up. This is not a do-it-yourself process for me, so I go through it with Steve and Donna Kinniburgh, deep-trance hypnosis experts. Steve is the facilitator for Donna, who goes into deep trance and communicates with a group of astral souls whom she calls "Reflection."

Some of these souls are friends from my former lives, some are my own spiritual guides, and some are guides that work regularly with Donna and Steve. Some have never incarnated on a physical planet; others have been here often.

Being in the astral worlds, the guides often can see karmic connections that are hidden from us; knowing these connections can be invaluable. Because of that, I consider them valued advisors, much as I would an expert health professional or an experienced lawyer. However, they are not right all the time; just because souls are in the astral world does not mean that they are omniscient or infallible. Using facts that I can check on, in my experience, even the best guides are wrong about 25 percent of the time. However, this means that they are right for the other 75 percent, which is extremely good. So I ask the same questions in different ways in later sessions when I want to double-check.

The narrative of the four lifetimes in this book contains a wealth of information that has been provided by or verified by the Reflection group. Their comments and revelations have helped clarify many details that were not clear to me from my own meditations or that I did not personally witness in a given lifetime. (More about the Kinniburghs and Reflection in Appendix A3.)

Just one note about the process of recalling past lives: the stories that follow are highly personal journeys through actual events, but they are not news documentaries; memory is just too subjective for that. We are all familiar with the quirks of memory from eyewitnesses. For example, two witnesses of a bank robbery may give widely varying accounts: one may say the brown-haired gunman wore a red jacket, while another says he had black hair and a brown coat. One person says the getaway car was a Chevy; another says it was a Ford, and so on. All of them definitely agree, however, that a robbery took place.

My memories are no different. In fact, past life memories are much more difficult to recall since they happened long ago in different bodies, often using different languages. Some memories I recall with startling clarity, while others are fuzzy and indistinct. Overall, I am confident of the main events of these life stories, but I am less certain of the finer details. Where possible, I have cross-checked my memories against historical records. However, in the final analysis, this is only a single viewpoint of the events as I recall them. Just like the robbery witnesses, others who were there might remember some things differently.

Some Recurring Themes in this Book

Understanding your past lives can be a powerful healing force in your life. Several themes throughout this book will guide you in using this knowledge to heal yourself both mentally and physically. They include:

(1) The essential "you" will survive, no matter how difficult life gets.

The body dies, but the spirit lives eternally. If you want to experience limitations, disease, pain, and misery, then just go on believing that you are only just a body and cease to exist at death. If you want greater happiness and freedom from the fear of death and from physical pain, then start to accept that the "essential you" is an eternal soul.

This concept can be especially reassuring for those left behind when a loved one's soul leaves the body and passes on. You can take comfort from knowing that you will most certainly meet your friends and loved ones again on the soul plane and in other lifetimes. Furthermore, if you develop your intuition, you can learn to see them right now, to see how they are doing. Instead of being lost to us, our loved ones are always only a thought away.

Another important point: since you will also meet your "enemies" in the future, it might be a good idea to try harder to settle your differences and to turn them into friends right now, if possible.

(2) The purpose in living many lives is to learn and to gain experience.

Life is much like school: the goal is to gain knowledge, experience, and wisdom. If you fail a class in school, you may repeat the year, and when you finally pass all your classes, you can go on to higher levels. Having incarnations is like that, too, except that unlike school, it doesn't really matter whether someone is "slow" or "fast," and it doesn't matter if someone fails along the way. Eventually everyone graduates. No one is left behind.

Furthermore, the goal is not necessarily to have a pleasant, peaceful life. We may choose to experience a lifetime that may be very unpleasant. Sometimes we get to play the role of the villain in order to learn a valuable lesson. As I look back over my various past lives, I realize that some of my greatest revelations have come, not when things were pleasant, but when I have been in the greatest trouble. The good news is that by successfully overcoming the trouble, it cannot bother us again.

In addition, growth and understanding come from tackling and overcoming challenges. A life without challenge may seem like a vacation, but from the soul's perspective, not much may be gained. So if your current life seems full of challenges, honor yourself for having set up a major opportunity for spiritual growth.

(3) Reincarnation allows us to balance our actions in the past.

A more popular word for this balancing is "karma," as we discussed earlier. You will see how it may take several lifetimes to achieve a balance in harmony with this universal law. For full understanding of the dynamics of any situation, a soul must be on both the giving *and* receiving ends. So, if in one lifetime, a soul's actions impact other people (for better or worse), then in some other lifetime (or even the same), the soul must experience that same impact. Therefore, it will arrange to be on the receiving end in a similar situation. There is no element of "punishment" in this, but just the desire of the soul to fully understand the energy of exchange.

You must become aware of the past in order to change it, since many of our present-day problems have roots far into the past. This can include everything from troubling relationships to painful headaches.

(4) You can use past life recall to clarify some of history's mysteries.

As an example, recalling my life as a Lakota Indian helped me fill in many of the gaps in the story of Custer's Last Stand. Since none of Custer's soldiers survived, exactly what happened that day has been shrouded in mystery. The story presented here will add some previously unrevealed facts and insights to the history of that event. As I relived the battle, I saw that it did not happen the way that history claims.

(5) Many of our past life connections are affecting us now in the present.

At the end of each story is a section entitled: "Group-Links" which shows some of my soul's past life relationships. Over the course of several lifetimes, the same group of souls incarnates together, but in varying roles. A wife in one lifetime may be a daughter in another, and a close friend in a third.

Why do souls stay together like this? So that we can experience the deep and complex relationships that are possible when we meet someone with whom we are certain that we can trust and bond, either as a mate, friend, or business partner. Rather than being surrounded by "complete strangers" with whom we must start at the very beginning, our relationships with soul group members can progress very quickly. This allows for more intense and meaningful relationships faster, and hence, fosters more learning, understanding, and growth.

By understanding what happened to me in these stories, you can see what you might accomplish by using past life recall. This is important, because one of the main ways that you can gain insight from a past life is to use, in your current life, the knowledge and understanding gleaned from the past. Having recalled the memories, you can use them to identify your past mistakes and to change things for the better in the present. These past mistakes are linked together like beads on a string. Once you "grab" the end of one of these memories and "pull" it into your consciousness, the beads of similar incidents from other lifetimes often will pop into view. Undoing these with proven techniques, such as those in Appendix A, will allow you to eliminate these problems from your present lifetime. This process is one of the simplest and fastest methods for spiritual growth.

For example, as a Roman legionnaire, I was in a position to be compassionate to another soldier and allow him an honorable death, but I chose to end his life in a way that gave him an ignominious death without honor. That soul later incarnated as Gen. Custer, and he was indirectly responsible for the deaths of two of my incarnations. This was a major soul lesson in compassion.

Knowing that your life is like one pearl on a string of pearls cannot help but change that life. In your current lifetime, your personality, skills, and interests are a function of all the other lifetimes your soul has lived, and this will color the future lives your soul will fashion.

Look at the times in history that fascinate you, and chances are that your interest is bleeding through from a lifetime in that era. People who devote their weekends to Civil War reenactments are not fighting those battles for the first time, but at least this time they'll only get muddy, not bloody.

As I look at the four lifetimes in this book, and the 40-odd others of which I'm aware, I see the common thread is soul, like the string joining the pearls. Each pearl is unique – a masterpiece of creation in its own right – but they all have soul, linking and joining them so that each enhances the whole. I suggest that it behooves us to become more aware of the common thread that all our pearls share.

I am not special or different from you, so if what you are about to read is true for me, it is also true for you. If you can accept that you have lived before in dozens, if not hundreds, of lives, then how will that change your life today? And if you know that you have incarnated in the past with many of the people in your present life, will that change how you deal with them today?

First, you will see your current lifetime as a vital element in a rich, vibrant tapestry of lives across time. You will also know that you incarnated with specific objectives, goals, and an agenda of learning and understandings to achieve. This will make you more mindful of your purposes and lead to the realization that your life didn't "just happen." Your soul carefully planned it in terms of circumstances, events, and relationships.

The purpose of our relationships is to serve as mirrors in our individual explorations of who we are and who we could be, all within the vast enterprise of exploring unconditional love. But the amnesia of birth allows us to forget this while incarnated, so we are free to explore fear, greed, shame, jealousy, and the full spectrum of other human traits, as well as striving to express our true soul nature – pure unconditional love.

Hopefully, reading this book will help alleviate some of the fears that beset us humans – fear of not having enough, fear of not being good enough, and "the biggie" – fear of death. Obviously, the four lifetimes in this book ended in four deaths, and each one was a blessed release to something far more wonderful, an event to be eagerly anticipated, not feared.

If you are troubled in this lifetime by any circumstance, this book should put things into perspective. In some past life, you may have starved to death, drowned, been struck by lightning, died suddenly in battle or slowly from battlefield injuries, been trampled to death by stampeding woolly mammoths, been eaten by saber-toothed tigers, died of plague, malaria or in childbirth, been burned at the stake during the Inquisition, etc., etc. When you have gone through all that, *what can be so bad right now?*

The bottom line is, then, that lifetimes are carefully planned forays, where we can forget who we really are as soul, and explore a reality very different from that on the soul plane. And when our foray is over, we return to the magnificent splendor of our natural state – soul – having gained valuable understanding of the larger reality in which we all exist.

Compared to the eternity of soul, these Earth experiences are brief episodes that allow us to treasure our co-travelers, relish the opportunities life presents, and maximize the understandings we glean to take back with us to the soul plane. And at the end of the day, that is all we *can* take back – what we have learned and the love we have allowed to flow through us.

In summary, I offer you these thoughts:
When you confront and dissolve patterns from past lives, profound changes will happen quickly in your current life. As you eliminate the old patterns, attitudes, and feelings that make you unhappy, you will become steadily happier.

These last two statements are at the heart of this book. It is my sincerest wish that you take what you read and use this information to transform your life, to help you in the healing process of your heart, mind, and soul.

In any event, whether you use this information to gain more peace and understanding or whether you just want to be entertained for a few hours … fasten your seat belts. **Here we go!**

Alive 5 times

The Lifetimes

Life #1: Meera: Makah Shaman-Woman (1693-1733)

In the Pacific Northwest, 7-year-old Meera barely survived a massive earthquake and tsunami. Afterward, a female spirit guide trained her to be the tribe's shaman-woman. Later, after devastating personal tragedies and a terrible accident, the entire tribe met in council to decide her fate.

MEERA PHOTOS: To add to the realism of these stories, they are illustrated with more than 250 photos. Many in this shaman story are by E.S. Curtis, world-famous for his rich authentic photo portraits of Native Americans during the late 1800s and early 1900s.

Life #2: John Hogans: Fighting the Un-Civil War (1831-1865)

In 1865, as a Confederate lieutenant, John retreated with Gen. Lee ahead of the pursuing Union forces. After a week of exhausting battles, they marched into Appomattox only to find themselves surrounded. Wounded in this last desperate battle, John had a remarkable experience with the spirit world.

HOGANS PHOTOS: Dozens of 140-year-old photos from the Civil War era illustrate this story. Most were taken during Hogans' lifetime and some are of actual places visited by him before and during the war.

Life #3: Sorrel Horse: At the Little Bighorn (1863-1876)

When Gen. Custer attacked the huge village on the Little Bighorn, Sorrel Horse, eager to earn his first warrior's feather, fought desperately to stop the troopers from overrunning the village. Early in the battle near the river, he saw something happen to Custer that instantly changed the course of the battle.

SORREL HORSE PHOTOS: Most of the Plains Indians photos in the story are by E.S. Curtis. Some stunning black-and-white landscape photos are by world-famous photographer Ansel Adams. The dramatic drawings and paintings of Frederic Remington also are used to illustrate the battle scenes.

Life #4: Louis St. Jacques: Drinking with van Gogh (1870-1914)

In the 1880s, as a young aristocrat in Paris, living the bohemian lifestyle, Louis frequented the Paris cafes, where Vincent van Gogh, Paul Gauguin, and Henri Toulouse-Lautrec befriended him. After a nearly fatal drug overdose, Louis had an astounding vision that changed the direction of his life.

LOUIS PHOTOS: Many photos in this story are of paintings by van Gogh, Gauguin, Manet, Degas, and Toulouse-Lautrec. During the lifetime described, Louis would have seen many of these paintings and, indeed, personally would have witnessed some of them in the process of being painted.

Alive 5 times

Meera: Makah Shaman-Woman (1693-1733)

Background.

After an exciting and dangerous lifetime as an English buccaneer in the 1600s, my soul chose a more peaceful, spiritual lifetime ... as Meera, a shaman-woman of the Makah Nation in the Pacific Northwest, west of today's Seattle, Washington.

For thousands of years, the Makah have continuously inhabited their villages along the Pacific coast near Cape Flattery at the extreme northwestern point of the contiguous United States. Their way of life includes hunting whales and fishing in the cold waters of the Pacific Ocean. Neighboring tribes gave them the name "Makah," which means "Generous with food." The tribe members use that name for themselves today, but they also call themselves the "People-who-live-among-the-Cliffs-and-Seagulls." They were one of the very few oceangoing tribes, renowned for using fifty-foot-long dugout canoes in the extremely dangerous hunt for the great whales. *[See Figure 1-1.]*

Born into the Makah tribe, Meera lived in Tsues village, one of five main Makah villages. *[See map, Figure 1-3.]* The story opens with Meera, at age seven, walking not far from her village ...

Figure 1-1. Like some other Native American tribes on the Northwest Coast, the Makah traveled in very large oceangoing canoes such as this one. *[Detail from a photo by E.S. Curtis, ca. 1915. Courtesy of the Library of Congress.]*

Figure 1-2. At the age of seven, Meera would have looked like this young Makah girl. *[Detail from photo by E.S. Curtis, ca. 1915. Courtesy of the Library of Congress.]*

Winter in the Pacific Northwest

As the afternoon sun fades, I turn a corner on the trail through the thick coastal forest. Suddenly, I freeze in my tracks. Ahead of me, a large doe stands in the bulrushes, drinking from the river. She does not see me yet. I crouch down and watch her in silence, entranced by her breathtaking beauty. Even as she drinks, she swivels her big ears around to catch the slightest sound of danger. Thinking she hears something, she pops her head up and looks around cautiously, sniffing the air for strange scents. Reassured, she lowers her head to drink again, all the while flicking her white tail side to side. I creep closer to see her better, keeping downwind so she cannot smell me.

As I get about fifty paces away, suddenly she jerks up her head and snaps it around in my direction. She has heard me! I hold my breath and freeze in place. Eyes wide, nostrils flared, she is tense with fear. She stamps her foot several times in warning – but she is not looking at me. Something else has caught her attention.

With a loud noise, a cascade of small boulders rattles and clatters down the cliff face. The doe springs into action, lunging through the shallow water in great bounding leaps that send water splashing in all directions. Within a few heartbeats, she races wildly away from the unseen danger to the safety of the distant trees.

As I watch her bounding away, I hear a deep, faint rumble like thunder, but it does not come from the sky; it comes from beneath my feet. Suddenly, the ground heaves, causing the trees and bushes to sway back and forth around me, shaking the leaves with a rustling noise. The ground rolls up and down violently and, losing my balance, I grab onto a small sapling for support. Large

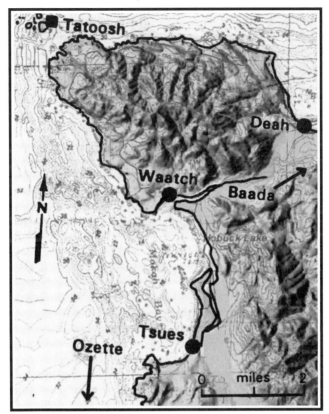

Figure 1-3. Washington: The Makah flourished in a community of five villages: Baada, Deah, Waatch, Ozette, and Tsues (pronounced "Soo-Yes"). This last village, where Meera lived, was located on the Pacific south of Vancouver Island and Juan de Fuca Strait. *[Map is a composite of three maps courtesy of (1) Washington State Univ. and the National Park Service (1991); (2) the USGS; and (3) Washington State Dept. of Ecology (2003).]*

Figure 1-4. "The doe hears something!" *[Detail from a photo courtesy of the National Archives.]*

boulders roll down the cliff, crashing through the trees and knocking some of them down, leaving a swath of flattened plants behind. *[See inset.]*

> **Earthquake Fault**
> This part of Washington is located on one of the world's most seismically active fault systems, extending from South America to Alaska. A very high percentage of all the world's earthquakes occur along this fault system.

Frozen with fear, I should run like the doe, but I cannot move. I search around anxiously for rolling rocks that might smash into me, but they are all far enough away. Gradually, the shaking stops; it lasts only a few dozen heartbeats, but I hug the tree a little longer just to be safe.

Still trembling, I take a deep breath and race quickly back upstream to the village. While passing a few uprooted trees and piles of rubble that spill across the trail, I have to dodge an occasional rock bouncing down the cliff.

Almost out of breath, I finally reach the village. Many of my People are outside their lodges, fearfully looking up at the sky or peering at the bluffs nearby. Babies are crying, and dogs are barking or hiding under cover. Sprint-

Figure 1-5. Deah Village: The Makah lived in cedar-planked houses that were about 30 by 60 feet long with 15-foot ceilings. The planks were hand-hewn from huge cedar trees that grew in ancient old-growth forests along the coast. Each house could hold about four families of 30-40 people total. *[Photograph by E.S. Curtis, ca. 1915. Courtesy of the Library of Congress.]*

ing to our longhouse, I see Mother standing outside gazing at the sky with both hands cupped above her eyes. "Mother! Mother! What was that?" I cry. I have never felt such a thing before.

Looking down briefly, she puts her hand on my shoulder. Now staring up again, she replies, "It was the Thunderbird Spirit. Sometimes, when it heads out to sea to hunt whales, it flies over the clouds very low and makes the ground shake."

Figure 1-6. According to Makah oral tradition, earthquakes and tsunamis were caused by the occasional struggles between the Thunderbird Spirit and Whale Spirit, as depicted in this native painting. *[Photograph by E.S. Curtis, ca. 1914. Courtesy of the Library of Congress.]*

"Did you see it?" I ask in amazement.

"I have never seen it," she replies, "No one but a shaman can. Even so, we all know when it goes by. Sometimes, if it looks down as it passes, lightning flashes from its eyes."

"You mean like in a big storm?"

"Except then, the ground does not shake. Only the lightning flashes."

I shudder, shaking my head, "It makes me want to hide."

Mother kneels down to put her arms around me. Her clothes carry the faint, pleasant aroma of cedar branches and smoked salmon. "I know. All of us are frightened. The Thunderbird is very powerful." I enjoy Mother's hug, and I feel safe for the moment. She continues, "Sometimes in the old days, around the fires, the old ones would tell of when the Thunderbird struggled fiercely with the Whale Spirit. They both rolled around so much that they broke the land into pieces, kicked up big waves, and knocked the whole top off of Big Mountain."

I tremble a little at the thought, and Mother strokes my head. "Then dark clouds shot up, and flaming rocks flew out of the mountain. Then fiery rivers flowed out and covered the land. The People were very afraid."

I respond, "I would never want to see that."

She says, "But that was long ago before I was born, so do not worry. The Whale Spirit stays in the deepest ocean now. It does not go near the mountain anymore. It is too afraid of the Thunderbird."

"Good," I say with relief, feeling a little better at last. I look up at her again, asking, "Has it gone now?"

She nods her head. It is late afternoon, and the sun has almost set over the ocean. I finished all my duties earlier, so I ask, "Can I go down to the beach and play?"

She looks at me for a moment, hesitating because of the danger, but finally says, "All right, Meera, but keep near the river and stay a safe distance away from the cliffs." I nod in agreement as she adds, "It will be dark soon, so do not wander too far." When I do not respond, she says, "Do you hear me, daughter?"

Figure 1-7. View north from Ozette along Washington coastline toward Tsues. *[Courtesy Washington State Univ. and National Park Service (1991).]*

"Yes, Mother," I say happily. I give her one last big hug, and hurry off, running through the village, dodging in and out among the cedar-plank lodges. Several of the village dogs happily chase after me. Mother calls out something more to me, but I cannot hear her clearly and decide not to risk finding out what she said. Giddy with my freedom, I race out of the village before she can call out again, running headlong towards my favorite place in the entire world – the long, curved, sandy beach at the south end of Makah Bay.

After racing beyond the village, I grow short of breath and slow to a fast walk. Looking back one last time, satisfied that I have "escaped," I turn down the village trail alongside Tsues River. The path leads to the place where the river empties into the Great Ocean. I could have brought a friend or one of our family dogs, but I am happy to be alone, exploring the seashore, free from my duties.

In a short time, I turn a bend of the river, and there is the beach, glistening in the fading sunlight. It is exhilarating! I never tire of it. All around me are the wonderful smells, sounds, and sights of the Great Spirit's world: the salty aroma on the sea breeze; the chatter of gulls soaring on the wind; the barking of sea lions on the gray-brown rocks offshore; and the brilliant flickering sparks of sunlight, dancing on the rolling waves of a gentle sea. Trying to take it all inside, I draw in a deep breath until my lungs hurt. I hold it until I start to see little sparks of light dancing before my eyes. Finally, feeling dizzy, I gulp in several big breaths of sea air. I am so happy to be here.

Now suddenly, I am aware of the cold air, although it is warmer than usual for midwinter. The early evening sea air is moist, and as I step onto the broad beach, I am glad to be wearing a thick, warm dress.

Figure 1-8. This photograph shows where Tsues River meets the Pacific Ocean. Meera spent a lot of time exploring this beach. The original site of Tsues village was located on high ground upstream along the river to the right. *[Courtesy of Washington State Dept. of Ecology.]*

Figure 1-9. "A misty plume rises over humpback whales as they break the surface." *[Photograph courtesy of the NOAA / Dept. of Commerce.]*

Slowly turning my head, I dreamily scan the whole vista of sky, ocean, and forest, shimmering in the radiant golden-orange glow of sunset. Above me and out over the ocean, the sky is a brilliant, clear blue, while a few thin, wispy low-lying clouds cover the tops of the coastal mountains. From the cloud-capped mountains down to the sea, a dense forest covers the land.

Offshore, a passing pod of gray whales swims north towards Tatoosh Island, named for the Thunderbird. They surface, one by one, blowing tall spouts of misty breath from their blowholes, and now they dive again, leaving their breath-plumes to shimmer and glow in the light of the setting sun. I tremble with happiness, glad to be alive on an afternoon such as this.

I wander down the beach south towards the Point *[now called Anderson Point – see Figure 1-10]*, a sharp rugged cliff nearly ten times my own height that plunges down steeply to meet the narrow crescent of sandy shore. Dense spruce, gray-green firs, red cedars, and hemlock cover the cliff top, growing over the edge down to the base of the cliff. Some have even toppled down the steep face. The damp air provides constant moisture to the cliff, so that between the trees, rich green clumps of thick grass, ferns, and moss partially cover the rocky ground. Tough bunches of sharp-leafed salt-grass grow back from the water above the high tide line.

Figure 1-10. One of Meera's favorite spots was on the Point at the base of the cliff (lower left corner). *[Courtesy of Washington State Dept. of Ecology.]*

A jumble of large surf-smoothed rocks lies near the base of the cliff, so I choose a flat one as a seat and lean against a taller one behind it. This gives a perfect view of the ocean waves breaking ceaselessly on the shore, surging in and around the rounded boulders. Watching the waves, my mind begins to drift, and I imagine that I am watching a great battle, a struggle between the Water Spirit and the Stone Spirit – fighting each other and wrestling to see who is strongest. Will the Water win and smash the Stone into sand? Or can the Stone hold back the Water and remain unbroken? Imagining this timeless battle, I feel small in comparison and shiver a little. Both the Water Spirit and Stone Spirit are much more powerful than I am. As I close my eyes and feel the coolness of the rock beneath me, these thoughts slowly fade away. I focus on my breath as it flows rhythmically in and out like the waves ... in and out ... as my cares and worries ebb away as well. Happy and drowsy, I fall into a half-waking, half-dreaming sleep-state.

After what seems only a few moments, I awaken from this strange but peaceful sleep to find that the sun has already set and that its light has faded completely. I must have slept for a long time. Above me, the moon clearly has been up for a while. It has already moved past straight up and now shines out over the ocean. Almost half-full, its silvery-blue light flickers and dances across the ocean surf and faintly lights up the forest and shore. The whole world seems so quiet, lovely, and peaceful.

For a moment, I worry about what Mother will say. She will wonder where I am, but for some reason, I am not worried. I feel that, somehow, everything will be all right. Still dreamy, I close my eyes and think again about the Rock-and-Water battle. I listen to the waves rolling in, surging around the rocks, and now withdrawing again. Roll in and withdraw. Roll in and withdraw.

As my mind follows the ebb and flow of the surf, my breathing slows to match it. Waves come in, and I breathe in. Waves go out, and I breathe out. In and out. As this rhythm repeats over and over, I gradually sense a subtle shift. I am still sitting on the rock, but somehow my body seems to blend with it, to melt into it. I can no longer tell where my dress stops, where my body ends, and where the rock begins. As my breathing slows even more, the feeling of being small gradually disappears. I am somehow part of this rock, this cliff, this sandy beach ... and the Great Ocean. I am part of something enormous – not small. My sense of separation flows away, replaced by a feeling of deep peace, a feeling that everything is exactly as it should be, just as the Great Spirit intended. Instead of a constant struggle, I see this as a have-fun game, endlessly played by these two spirits. There will always be the Water Spirit to wear down the stone. And there will always be the Stone Spirit to make more stones.

"Hah!" I laugh aloud, "It is all just a game!" Happily, I call to the sea lions dozing out on the moonlit rocks, "It is just a fun-forever game. Do you know that?"

Startled, they look over at me and bark in response. I laugh with the rocks and waves, with the wind and the sand. A few seagulls, probably startled by my voice, circle overhead in the dim moonlight, peering down at me, making loud calls that sound like laughter, too. Joining in with the laughing gulls, I wave to them and shout, "I know! I know! It is just a have-fun game."

Figure 1-11. "Startled, the sea lions bark in response." *[Courtesy of NOAA/ Dept. of Commerce.]*

I understand the sea and the shore more clearly than ever before. I am eager to run back and tell Mother, tell her about the Rock-and-Water game. Surely, she will understand. And the shaman, too. He will know.

As I jump up to run for home, the seagulls suddenly become silent, flapping away from the beach out over the water – and the sea lions also grow quiet. Surprised, I look up and down the darkened beach; maybe a bear has come – or an orca *[killer whale]*. Everywhere along the beach, in the dim moonlight, shorebirds and seagulls are taking flight.

Suddenly, a deep, low-pitched rumble rises from the earth. It grows louder and louder, like some great wounded beast. It is so powerful that it makes my bones and teeth ache – and my skin crawls. The sound is horrible, like dragging a huge rock across another rock – grinding, groaning, and rumbling – high-pitched and low-pitched at the same time. I clap my hands over my ears, but it does not help. The sound comes at me from all directions.

Now I stare in disbelief to the north – foot-high sand waves ripple down the beach towards me faster than storm-driven waves. Before I can run away, the first ground-wave rolls under me, throwing me violently onto my back and nearly cracking my head on the rocks. *[See inset.]*

Stunned, I lay on the ground, covering my ears and shielding my face with my forearms. The shaking becomes stronger and, now, even stronger still. I am terrified that the force will break my bones or maybe even kill me.

In panic, I roll over on my stomach and start to crawl, but I can barely balance as the rolling, bucking earth throws me sideways first one way and now another.

Suddenly to my horror, the sand starts to liquefy, and I begin to sink. *[See inset.]* I scurry ahead as fast as I can on all fours like a crab, but the

Huge Earthquake

Geological research indicates that the Pacific Northwest was struck by a mega-quake on the evening of January 26, 1700.

USGS studies suggest that it was one of the most violent earthquakes to occur anywhere on the planet during the last 400 years. The quake, which lasted from 3-5 minutes, is estimated to have been about magnitude 9.

By comparison, the 1906 San Francisco earthquake was only about magnitude 7.8. Thus, this NW Pacific quake was over 30 times more powerful than the one the devastated San Francisco *(Atwater (1998))*.

Liquefaction

Sand often liquefies when an earthquake violently shakes water-soaked earth.

'Sand volcanoes' occur when the liquefied mud or sand appears to erupt from the ground and flow out across the surface.

When this occurs, the ground can, like quicksand, swallow up rocks, trees, people, and even whole buildings.

wet, soupy sand sucks at my hands, my feet, and my knees, pulling them down. The entire beach has turned to quicksand. Gurgling, slow-motion spouts of muddy water and flowing beach sand shoot up all around me, splattering me with wet, muddy gobs. I struggle mightily to crawl to safety.

The moonlit world is a moving mirage of constant jerky motion. Trees are shaking wildly and toppling down the cliffs with loud crashes, followed in slow motion by flowing masses of mud, rocks, and giant boulders. The ground continues to shake relentlessly with a powerful jerking and rolling motion. It is hard to focus my eyes, as everything is a wild blur of movement.

Near me, the liquefied sand is slowly flowing out towards the ocean in wide rivulets, carrying along rocks, driftwood, roots, and stumps. The nearby boulders, on which I sat just a few minutes ago, are slowly toppling over in a thick river of mud, sinking gradually deeper.

Yanking my feet and arms out of the mud, I struggle with all my might to keep from being sucked down into the sand. Using a final burst of strength, I manage to get a handhold on a firmer gravelly section of the shore, and I drag myself up on the bedrock bench above the shoreline. Legs and arms dripping with mud, gasping for breath and terrified, I rest for a moment hiding my head in my arms. With the earth still pitching and rolling, I pray repeatedly for help.

Now, after one more powerful twitch, the earth becomes still again. Except for an occasional rockfall and the gurgling flow of mud, it is quiet all around. Even the ocean has gone silent. Surprised not to hear the surf, I raise my head to glance out to sea. It is hard to see in the dim light, but finally my eyes adjust. Stunned, I realize that the ocean is *gone*! Where once there were waves, there is now only a great glistening mudflat, hundreds of paces wide. Dozens of fish flop around in shallow pools of water, and out by the rocks, groups of stranded sea lions scrambling clumsily towards deeper water. In the distance, highlighted with silvery moonlight, I can make out small waves breaking on the new shoreline. I sit up in wonder. Where has the ocean gone? I begin to get very uneasy.

As I sit catching my breath, a voice exclaims, "Meera!"

Startled, I swivel around to see who spoke, but there is no one. "Meera!" The voice is louder now and appears to come from all around and from within me. I stand up, spinning around dizzily, searching for the speaker.

"Run, Meera! You must not delay! Hurry! Run for the cliffs! *NOW*!" The voice is commanding and persistent.

Fearing that there is some great danger, I spin around and race towards the tallest part of the cliff, dodging mudflows and soft spots as best I can. Scrambling through the bushes and tough salt-grass, I cut my legs on the sharp blades. The wounds sting and small streams of blood ooze down my legs, but I pay no attention. My mind focuses only on the words "Run!" and "Hurry!" which still ring loudly in my ears. *[See inset.]*

Approaching the cliff, I find a narrow cleft that runs all the way to the top. I rush up, grabbing rocks and roots, pulling myself up with all my strength. My feet and hands slip on the muddy rocks, scraping skin off elbows, fingers, toes, and shins. Thin red blood covers my arms and legs, but they never stop moving, constantly grabbing, pushing, gripping, and scrambling up the rocky cliff face.

At last, when I think I cannot go on, I pull myself over the top edge of a cliff ledge and lie panting with exhaustion. I am not fully to the top, but surely, this is far enough from whatever might be chasing me. I collapse on the flat ledge.

Gradually, as I regain my composure and my breathing slows down a bit, I raise my head to look around. I squint to see down the coast in each direction. Straining my eyes, I do not see any bears, wolves, or any other danger.

Relieved not to see any danger, I begin to think that my fear made me imagine the voice. Maybe it was not real. Mad at myself for such foolishness, I sit up with my legs dangling over the ledge and gingerly inspect my cuts and bruises. How will I explain these cuts to Mother?

"Look!" the voice speaks again, and my head is moved as if by invisible hands, so that I am forced to stare out to sea. There is something out there in the dim moonlight. Squinting, I try to make it out, but the light is too dim. Something is glittering out in the ocean beyond the shore. Puzzled, I slowly stand up to get a better view.

"MEERA!" The voice startles me out of my trance. "Move higher! *NOW!*"

Obeying the mysterious voice, that "Voice-with-no-Body," and powered by fear, I feel a new burst of energy suddenly surge through me. Turning, I race up the rest of the slope climbing from rock to rock, from one foothold to the next. My body leaps, turns, and balances in ways I never thought possible. I let out one short nervous laugh, enjoying the powerful fear-born energy that flows through my body. I feel very alive and incredibly focused.

Exhilarated and breathing heavily, I reach the top and lean over, hands on knees, to catch my breath. As I do, I feel a growing wind at my back. As I turn my head, my eyes become wide with terror; a speeding shimmering silver band

---

Getting Help

If we are receptive, we can receive Spirit warnings like this during times of great danger.

The help may come in various ways, including hearing voices or other sounds, seeing a suddenly visible spirit who can warn us, or in many other ways.

Unfortunately, when the help comes, we are often too upset to recognize it. Knowing how to meditate and to quiet the noisy mind can help us to listen when trouble comes. There is always help if we will listen for it.

is racing closer and closer to me. Faster than a deer can run, faster than the storm winds, faster than *anything* I have ever seen, a gigantic blue-green wave rolls silently in towards shore. The moon glimmers on its leading edge, making a shimmering silver-blue trace along it.

My knees grow weak, and I am frozen with fear, like a seal caught by an orca. I cannot move. I can only stare at something that is beyond belief.

As it surges in over the shallows, the terrifying wave grows rapidly in height, leaving behind a churning mass of moon-dappled foam and muddy water. At first, it was silent, but now I begin to hear a low moaning roar, like some giant wounded bear. The wave rolls over the sea lions, and they disappear. It rolls over the fish in the tidal pools and swallows them, too. It rips through the exposed stone beds, and they vanish. *[See inset.]*

Mesmerized with fascination, with eyes fixed onto that monstrous wave, I slowly begin backing away, but my back is to the sheer cliff, and I can go no higher. The rock cliff hums and trembles as the wave approaches; the trees and bushes around me vibrate, and small rocks clatter down the hillside below me. The roar of churning water grows louder. The wind, pushed ahead of the Great Wave, increases until my hair streams out behind me. I have to brace against the growing wind, and the wild force of it strips leaves and branches from the trees. Flying sand stings my face.

Finding a low depression in the flat ledge, I drop down quickly, keeping my head up to see the wave. I jam my fingers and toes in among the rocks, locking myself in as best I can.

Seeming to move in slow motion, the giant wave crests over the shore, arches its top, and tumbles forward. With a horrible crash, it smashes into the base of the cliff, violently rocking the entire hill. Following the curve of the cliff, the water roars straight up towards me.

Shaking with panic, I am terrified with facing death. Unable to close my eyes, I stare wide-eyed at the Great Wave heading towards me. Rising with furious speed now, foaming and boiling, it shoots up past my head with a

> **Mega-tsunami**
> The earthquake in 1700 A.D. produced a massive tsunami that is recorded in the geological record of the northwestern U.S. and Canada. Scientists estimate that the tsunami along Washington's coast may have been as much as *33 feet high*.
> According to Japanese scientists, the tsunami was so powerful that it crossed the entire Pacific Ocean. When it struck Japan 10 hours later, it still had enough remaining force to destroy many homes along the coast *(from Atwater (1998))*.
> In the open ocean, tsunamis can travel as fast as 400 m.p.h. Their speed slows down considerably as they reach shallow water, but they still travel very fast, often catching coastal residents by surprise.

Figure 1-12. Photograph of a massive wave heading toward shore in 1975. *[Courtesy of NOAA/ Dept. of Commerce.]*

ground-shaking roar. The monster wave slows its climb in a few heartbeats and now seems to hang in midair.

For a moment, I can see the moon flickering and shimmering through the body of the wave. Gradually, the wind almost stops, and light mist and water spray begin to rain down around me.

Staring helplessly at the terrible giant wall of water in front of me, I inhale deeply and hold my breath. Slowly at first, now gaining speed, the wave reverses direction, falling back down to the sea. I lower my head at the last minute, closing my eyes and digging my fingers and toes tighter into every possible crevice in the rock. With the force of falling rock, the descending wall of water crashes into me, knocking the breath from my lungs, banging my head sharply onto the stone, and pinning my body against the rock.

As the water cascades back down the cliff, it pulls with it bushes, logs, rocks, trees – and me. The water surges over and around me, dragging me down, down, down. Losing my grip on the rock, I scratch and claw at the rough surface, breaking fingernails and trying to find the tiniest fingerhold to slow my descent. Tree branches, small rocks, and debris crash into my head, shoulders, and hands, knocking me ever closer to the cliff edge.

With growing panic, I clutch desperately at everything as I slide helplessly toward certain death. At the last moment, my left arm hooks around the big arched root of a spruce stump, anchored deeply into the bedrock. Frantically, I grab it with my right arm, locking both arms fiercely around the root.

The suction of the ebbing water swings my body around, scraping my thighs, knees, and toes over the rough rocks. As the torrent forces me closer to the cliff edge, the rocks disappear first from under one foot – now the other – now my knees – now my thighs. There is nothing under my legs but air; they dangle out over open space. Only a single tree root separates me from certain death, from drowning or being smashed on the rocks below. With my eyes tightly shut, I hang there for what seems to be an eternity, desperately clutching the root, while dirty foaming water surges past me trying to suck me down.

Slowly, the streaming water begins to ease its pull on me, and the noise subsides a little. I am afraid to look up – afraid to breathe – afraid to hope – but the water is slowing its relentless pull. Shaking my head back and forth to clear the water and dirt from my eyes, ears, and nose, I cautiously open my eyes. Painfully, I drag my bruised body away from the cliff edge. **[See inset.]**

> ### Drowning
> For most of my current lifetime, I have had an irrational fear of water and of drowning. As I re-lived this incident of nearly drowning as Meera, the fear lessened considerably and now has disappeared.
>
> Memories like this one affect us all on a subconscious level, causing us to fear some situations in the present that are not dangerous. Releasing these irrational fears leaves us freer to function in the present moment.

Down below, water swirls angrily around the base of the cliff. Hundreds of small rivulets pour off the rocks in miniature waterfalls. The muddy water has completely submerged the beach, hiding it from view. Water is everywhere – dirty, churning, ugly water. Broken trees float all around, scattered like jumbled grass straws. Dead and injured orcas, sea lions, and gray whales float in the surf, their bodies mangled and crushed.

Turning my bruised head to look north, I see that the swirling waters have traveled upstream far along the Waatch River. Most of our sister village of Waatch is gone. Vanished! Some of my friends are surely dead, swallowed up by the Great Wave. Tears well up in my eyes, and I choke back my grief.

Now, I search further up the Waatch valley. Even in the dim moonlight, it is clear that the angry water has rushed far inland. I can see nearly all the way to Neah village, three miles away on the other coast. Only churning water is visible, faintly reflecting the silvery moonlight. Much of that village must be gone, too. The peak on the Cape has become an island surrounded by a sea of rolling water. I am stunned.

From where I stand, I cannot see my own village on the Tsues River. With a growing sense of despair, I scramble north over the cliff top until the basin comes into view. The village is *gone!* The water has surged far up the riverbed, stopped only by the foothills of the tall peaks back from the ocean. The entire river basin and most of the coastal lowlands are underwater for as far as I can see. I strain hard to see where my Mother's house used to be, but I cannot. My heart grows heavy. I could be the only one left alive. Has the Great Spirit spared me only to drown all others in the surging sea? Is this a cruel joke played by Voice-with-no-Body? To save me when all the others are dead? Grief and anger overwhelm me.

I break down and sob uncontrollably, thinking to jump off the cliff and to end my own life, too. I no longer wish to live in such a world without Mother and my family. I sob and sob until I am out of breath. I am heartbroken for the loss of my tribes-people. I grieve for all the dead animals, and I am sad for myself, left alone, surrounded by a sea of churning water. I lie face down on the cold, damp rock. Cradling my head on my arms, I cry uncontrollably again, overwhelmed by all that has happened. Exhausted from fear and grief, I curl up among some fallen trees and drift into a troubled fitful sleep.

A Few Hours Later

"Meera," Voice-with-no-Body says softly. The voice awakens me, but I try to ignore it. Stiff, cold, and aching, I wonder how long I have slept. Off to the east, the sky is beginning to show a little color from the coming sunrise. I must have slept for hours. Everywhere I look, the wet, muddy earth is littered with debris left behind by the Great Wave.

Figure 1-13. Olympic coastline: "The sun rises over a wet and muddy world."
[Photo courtesy NOAA/ Dept. of Commerce.]

As I awaken fully, my grief for Mother and the others returns. I begin to cry again.

"Meera, it is not as you think," the Voice says. I wipe my eyes with my hands, but say nothing. "Your mother lives … and others, as well."

I raise my head and look around again, my eyes blurry from sleep and from crying. For a few moments, I still do not say anything. Now, I try to speak, but I can only manage a harsh squeak. Clearing my throat, I try again. "Mother is alive?" I ask, doubtfully. My voice is raspy.

"Yes. She is worried about you," the Voice says.

I nod. I am worried about her, as well. I look around once more. "I cannot see you. Where are you?" I ask.

"Closer than you think," the Voice says. "Your tribe will continue. All were given a warning, just as you were. Many did not listen, but some did and escaped to high ground."

I nod, feeling a little better. "I can hear you … but where are you? Are you really a 'Voice-with-no-Body,' or do you have a body, too?"

The Voice says lightly, "Oh, yes, I have a body, but you cannot see it because your 'sight' is not yet strong enough." The sound of the Voice has a beautiful, soothing, almost musical quality, like a slow gentle chant, rising and falling on the breeze. It is full of compassion, and I am fascinated by it, drawn to it.

Slowly sitting up, I wince with the pain of my cuts and bruises. "What do you mean about my 'sight'? Is there something wrong with my eyes?" I ask, getting worried again.

"Oh, no!" the Voice laughs gently. "Not your physical eyes, just your inner eyes."

Thoroughly puzzled, I say, "How can I have eyes inside?"

The Voice laughs again softly, "Well, not actually inside you. You see, you have eyes to see the physical world, but there is a different way to see the Spirit World, with what I call 'inner eyes.' The Spirit World is my own home, and it is the world of our Ancestors. One day, when your body dies, it will be your home, too. With practice, you will be able to see my world just as easily as you see your own."

Thinking about this hurts my head. I have heard the elders talk about this, but I am not quite sure I understand, so I change the subject. "You sound like a woman. Are you?"

"For you, I am," the Voice says, hesitating for a moment, "though ideas like 'man' and 'woman' are not quite the same over here. In the Spirit World, we do not make babies the same way you do." She pauses for a moment. "It is more correct to say that I have a feminine energy."

I think I understand, so I nod. "What shall I call you? Do you have names, too, in the Spirit World?"

She speaks again gently, "You may call me 'Sings-on-the-Wind.'"

What a perfect name, I think. Her voice rises and falls just like a song. *It is a very lovely name.*

"Thank you," she says quietly.

Startled, I say, "You heard that? You hear me when I speak in my head?"

She says, "That is where you are hearing me right now – in your head." I shake my head in surprise and disbelief. She continues, "You will become used to it in time."

She pauses for a moment and says, "Meera, the Great Spirit and the Thunderbird have sent me to you not just to save you from the Great Wave. I have come to ask a question."

I look up in silence, and she continues, "The Great Spirit has looked into your soul and sees that you can become a great healer – a shaman-woman. The Great Spirit wishes me to ask you: Would you like to follow that path?"

I am dumbfounded, and sputter, "But ... but, I am just a little girl."

"That is true," answers Sings-on-the-Wind with a musical laugh, "but little girls have been known to grow up."

"Well, I have done a lot of growing up for one day," I respond.

"Indeed, you have." There is silence between us, but my head races with a whirlwind of thoughts: of wanting to become a shaman-woman, but of being afraid to try, and of fearing that I am not good enough. I moan inwardly, *I do not wish to think anymore!*

Hearing my thoughts, she says, "I know. Perhaps it is too much for you today. You do not have to answer. I can go now, and we can talk again later."

"NO!" I blurt out but hurriedly add, "Please do not leave. Please. I would like to talk about this now. Do not go. I have dreamed of this, but I did not think I could do it. I mean, the tribe more often chooses a man as shaman – and I thought I would have no chance – because I am a woman. Well, what I mean is, I am a girl right now, but soon I will be a woman. Well, maybe not soon. But someday. I mean –"

Sings-on-the-Wind laughs and says soothingly, "Slow down, Meera. Slow down. The windy gusts of your excitement are blowing me off this cliff."

"I am s ... sorry," I stutter. "I am truly sorry."

"There is no need to apologize," she continues. "It is understandable that you would be excited."

She is silent again for a few moments, allowing me to calm down. "Now, about my question from the Great Spirit. Am I to understand that your very long answer can be shortened to a simple 'Yes'?"

"Yes! Yes! YES!" I reply excitedly.

She chuckles, "All right, so we will shorten it to three 'Yeses!'"

As she pauses again, I can hear only the wind. "And now you are probably wondering what comes next. Am I right?"

I nod my head eagerly.

"Well, we will start right away – but slowly – if that is all right with you."

After I nod, she continues, "Good, the sun is rising over a troubled world, and many people and creatures need our help. I am here to work with you closely … but only you and I will know of it for now."

She pauses to give me time to understand. "I will always be around when you need me during your training. You have only to call me inwardly, and I will come to you instantly. Do you understand what that means? Is everything clear to you so far, Meera?"

"Yes, very clear," I answer, my excitement building again.

She continues, "Good. But you must work hard on your part to become aware of me. Sometimes, if your thoughts are noisy, you will not see me or hear me. I will be there, but you may think I am not. If that happens, just take a few moments to quiet your mind, and you will sense that I am there beside you." She pauses again for a few moments, and I am eager to hear what comes next. In spite of the growing light of sunrise around me, I think I am beginning to see a faint bluish glow in front of me. Could that be her? I am not sure. I open and close my eyes several times, but the glow is still there.

"Yes, Meera, you *are* beginning to see me. Just a glimpse," she says, "as you open your awareness. You will do very well indeed!" She pauses as happiness wells up inside me. Now she continues solemnly, "Meera, this is my promise to you. It is a promise that I will never break. I will always come to you when you genuinely need me. That does not mean I will come whenever you call; but I will be with you whenever you *truly* need me. Do you understand what my promise means?"

I nod my head gratefully; "Thank you, Sings-on-the-Wind, and thanks to the Great Spirit, also. This is my dream come true." My eyes mist up in gratitude. "And in return, to you and the Great Spirit, I promise always to do my best and to try never to let you down."

"No one can ask more than that, Meera," she says tenderly. "Come. Many cry out for healing. Let us go down to ease their suffering. I will show you some ancient secret ways that you can use to heal all creatures. Are you ready?"

I nod, and feel a faint pressure as she takes my hand. Beside my blue-light-clad friend, under a brilliant deep-blue sky, with the golden light of dawn on my face, I climb down into the valley of destruction.

The Mega-quake and Tsunami of 1700 A.D.

This seismic event devastated many areas along 500 miles of the Pacific coast from California to Canada. One of the largest quakes ever known to hit the Pacific Rim, it was so powerful that it permanently lowered parts of the coastal land as much as 6 feet, submerging and killing lowland forests.

Coastal villages of many tribes, besides the Makah, were destroyed by the earth tremors or by the tsunami, and to this day, the rich oral traditions of the area refer to the catastrophe. Undoubtedly, thousands, perhaps tens of thousands, of Native Americans died in this disaster.

Archaeological proof for the event is widespread, coming from dozens of sites along the coast of Washington and Oregon *(see Atwater (1998))*. The evidence includes widely distributed thick layers of sand, covering many low-lying areas along the coast. At Ozette, about 15 miles south of Meera's village, the earthquake caused sudden liquefaction of the ground, producing a sudden mud slide that buried many lodges, entombing the inhabitants. Since the 1960s, archaeologists have uncovered over 55,000 priceless artifacts of Makah life at Ozette.

Rebuilding the Villages

As Meera moved down from the top of Anderson Point, she discovered, as predicted by Sings-on-the-Wind, that some people of her tribe had listened to the warnings from spirit and had survived. Most of their homes had been demolished, so they began the difficult task of putting their lives back together. The event made a powerful impression on the people's consciousness, bringing them closer together, and giving them a stronger appreciation for spiritual values.

Figure 1-14. Photo taken of offshore island and rocks from the Ozette site. *[Courtesy of Washington State Univ. and the National Park Svc. (1991).]*

Figure 1-15. This is a sweat lodge used by the Hupa tribe along the Pacific coast. *[By E.S. Curtis, ca.1923. Courtesy of Library of Congress.]*

Three Winters Later

The cedar-planked sweat lodge is cramped, and the air is heavy with the aroma of burning cedar bark, fir needles, and hemlock branches. For three days and nights, I have fasted and prayed continuously, spending every hour awake, waiting for a vision. I have decided to ask the Great Spirit for guidance about becoming a shaman-woman.

Sings-on-the-Wind has been with me the entire time. For about the last year, I have been able to see her spirit body clearly, not just talk to her, and now, she sits cross-legged in the far corner without moving. She keeps silent, respecting my spiritual quest, promising that she will speak only if I need help. I have spent the entire time with no food and with no sleep. Even so, after three full days, nothing has happened. I have had no visions and no guidance, and I feel very bad. I am beginning to fear that I will never get an answer, that I am not worthy enough to be a healer, and that the Great Spirit is no longer pleased with me.

Now, on the evening of the third day, I am ready to admit defeat, and I struggle to stand up. Immediately I feel dizzy, and my legs grow weak and shaky. I lean forward to grab the center pole with one hand for support. Suddenly, the lodge fills with a dim, greenish-blue glow that flickers and ripples eerily. The light floods in as if someone were pouring a great bowl of water into the sweat lodge. The smoky air becomes thick, and I labor to breathe, trying hard to draw the liquid-like air into my lungs. At first, I am fearful, but now I become elated as realization dawns on me. *Finally, a vision is coming.* Excited, I sit down again on the floor as the vision sweeps over me.

A booming voice, not from Sings-on-the-Wind, announces, "It is time to find your Totem." I nod without answering. I am ready. Before my heart can beat one more time, the entire lodge flickers and dissolves from view. Another scene slowly comes into focus, an underwater panorama. No longer fearful, I relax and just slide into the vision. I have plunged under the ocean about three times as deep as I am tall, and now, I look up at the underside of the surface waves rolling by overhead. The brilliant sun appears as a blurred, shimmering patch of light, sending long ghostly silver beams flashing briefly down all around me. Small patches of seaweed and tiny specks of vivid green plankton drift languidly around me, driven endlessly back-and-forth by the power of the passing waves.

Suddenly, I see a flash of movement from behind, and the head of a Chinook salmon wiggles into view, now another, and another still. I am surrounded by them, first hundreds and now thousands, all swimming along peacefully in a huge school. I realize, with a rush of excitement, that I have entered the body of a great Chinook salmon with a belly full of eggs! Our school is heading for the river's mouth to spawn.

Filled with happiness, I realize that, at last, the Great Spirit has shown me my totem animal! This is a very good omen, for the salmon is highly prized by my people. I look with pride at my new body, which is longer than one arm of a human body and is plump, powerful, and sleek. My long angular jaw moves rhythmically up and down, pumping seawater past my gills. I stare out through huge glassy eyes at the cold ocean around me.

The school moves in a flowing, coordinated, rhythmic dance, first swimming in one direction, and now, fluidly changing slightly to follow another course. Even though each of us is a separate fish individual, we move as one unit, as if parts of a larger organism. We are much like the scales on my fish-body. Each scale is distinct and separate when viewed up close, but from a distance, with the right perspective, all the scales blend into one organism. The same is true with our school, each fish is part of the larger whole. We swim, breathe, and eat almost as one body – and there is safety in these great numbers.

Off to the left, just within my range of vision, I detect a rapid flash of white. Now, I see it again – far out where the dim light vanishes, and the water turns dark green. With a faint sense of danger, I begin to swim away from it. My brother and sister salmon have sensed it, too, and the entire school veers to the right. Now, I see it again, closer now, along with the rush of bubbles bobbing away to the surface. The danger is stronger now; we all sense it, drawing close to one another, packing in to feel the safety of our neighbors' fins brushing against our sides.

Alive 5 times

Figure 1-16. "In a feeding frenzy, the Orca slashes through the school of salmon." *[Courtesy of NOAA and the Department of Commerce.]*

White flash! There it is again, moving fast, faster than we are swimming. Some ancient part of my brain recognizes this as a primeval enemy of salmon, some destroyer of our peace. Our swimming takes on a greater urgency now.

Get away from it! Some prehistoric memory is compelling us now. *Move away. Faster. Get away now!* The school is overcome with a rising panic that I can feel rippling out through all of us.

Suddenly, I hear it – a screeching whistle – and I know. *Orcas! Sea-wolves! Killers! The Enemy!* Their whistling calls grate on my nerves and spur the school into a frantic flight, trying to escape the huge monsters that prowl just beyond the light. *Swim faster! Swim away! Swim for safety!*

We turn to the right, instinctively knowing that shallow water will be safer, allowing us to maneuver freely, while hindering the orcas. *Swim for shore!* The unspoken thought ripples through the school, giving us hope, as we turn and race eastward.

Flash of white! Closer now. Panicked, the school turns to the right again, fleeing the danger, but moving south now along the shore. Flash of white again, streaking along the flanks of the school. *Turn again! Escape as fast as you can! Flee to safety!* All along our left flank now, there are constant flashes of white and those dreadful whistling calls. Flashes of white below us now. They are herding us!

In a panic, the school moves up towards the surface, continuing to the right in an ever-spiraling ball of darting, wriggling terrified fish. We swim faster and tighter together. The ball collapses in on itself. We pack together next to each other, a huge, swirling mass of fish bodies. My fins slap and crash into my neighbors as we all struggle to stay alive.

Orcas are all around us now, below and on all sides, surrounding us in our ball. Their dim shapes are clearer now, dark bodies with patches of white that make them look small, but I know that they are huge. Their dark eyes watch us intently without blinking, staring coldly at us, seeing us only as their next meal.

Suddenly, a huge black and white shape slashes through ahead of me, sending salmon fleeing in terror. The orca tears a great empty gash in the ball of packed fish, its monstrous jaws snapping shut repeatedly, leaving swirling eddies of scales, blood, and body parts.

I try to flee the carnage ahead of me, while still keeping close to my brothers and sisters. Wriggling deeper into the writhing mass, I seek greater safety, when suddenly, the fish on my right scatter in panic. With blazing speed, faster that my brain can comprehend, a set of great gaping jaws accelerates straight towards me.

Flee! Get away! But it is too late.

In the split second before the jaws close around me, I see the pink mouth and huge tongue of the orca. Now, filling my vision, paralyzing me with fear, the jaws snap shut around me. Hundreds of dagger-like teeth mesh as the lower jaw closes, trapping me inside the huge mouth. Other salmon are not so lucky. A headless tail and part of a head twitch spasmodically next to me.

I am wedged into the soft flesh of the mouth, but now the giant tongue wiggles a few times, and I slide headlong into the belly of the orca. I expect it to be as dark as a moonless night, but a dim reddish-pink light pervades everything. It is just barely bright enough for me to see. All around me are the sloshing noises of other fish. There is water around us, but it burns my eyes and skin.

Despair floods over me. *This is the end. I am inside an orca. Dead! Nothing but supper for a whale!* Gradually, I feel my life force slipping away. My thoughts slow down, my energy ebbs, and I cease struggling against the impossible. Soon, it will be over.

"Meera! Meera!" a voice calls. I am dimly aware it is someone called Sings-on-the-Wind.

"Go away!" I answer feebly. "Leave me alone. I am dead."

"You are talking, so how can you be dead?" she says.

"Well, I might as well be dead," I respond testily. "I have been *eaten* by a whale!" I have grown accustomed to speaking my mind to Sings-on-the-Wind. Now, she really annoys me.

"Yes," she says gently, "but do you *want* to live?"

"Are you paying attention, Sings-on-the-Wind?" I remark acidly. "I am a whale's dinner."

She continues patiently, "You can only be a dinner for a whale if you can be eaten."

I have little patience for such riddles, "Tell me something useful."

She says gently, "I can help you out of there if you like."

Peeved about the whole thing, I respond, "Do you think I *want* to be whale-food?"

She continues patiently, "You can be food for this Orca right now only if you are a fish. Are you?"

Shocked a little, I am reminded by her question that this is only a vision, "Hmmm … well, yes and no. I mean, I appear to be a fish now, but I was *not* one when we started."

"All right, so what are you?" she asks.

Feeling exasperated, I answer, "Sings-on-the-Wind, you *know* who I am!"

She chuckles, "True, but do *you* know who you are? A moment ago, you thought you were a salmon. Before that, you thought you were a girl called Meera. So, who were you before you became Meera?"

Getting a little confused again, I answer, "Just … just 'me,' I guess."

"Oh," she says, "so then you were called 'Mee,' rather than 'Meera?'"

Exasperated again, I snap, "You *know* what I mean. Stop asking questions, and help me get out of this whale!"

She continues evenly, "I am trying to do that, so pay attention, 'Whoever-you-are.'" Now she chuckles a little. "This next part is important." She pauses to see if I want to argue some more, but I keep quiet. "Look at your fish body. Do you see it?"

"Of course, though it is hard to see anything in an Orca's belly!" I say sarcastically.

Ignoring my remark, she says, "Now, close your eyes, and tell me what you see."

I do as she asks, and after a short pause, I say, "Nothing."

"Very good!" she responds. "Now, keep your eyes closed and pay attention to this 'nothingness' and to the one who sees it. That observer, the part of you that is looking at 'nothing,' is the *real* you."

She pauses while I think about this for a moment and now continues softly, "So, you-who-looks-at-nothing, exactly how big are you?"

Surprised at the question, I stammer, "I … I … Well, I do not know. I do not have any size. I just *am*."

She continues patiently, "Are you smaller than your fish body?"

I say, "I do not have any size at all. I am more like a point – a *tiny* point of awareness."

She continues, "So, are you saying that you have no size – no length and no width?"

"Not that I can tell," I respond.

"Well, if that is the case, how can an orca eat you?" she asks.

I begin to see her point, "Hmm ... well, I guess it cannot! It can eat my *body*, but not the *real me*."

"Very good!" she says.

I almost shout, "I see what you mean, Sings-on-the-Wind! I understand now! I am *not* this fish-body!"

"So do you, who are not that fish-body, have to stay in an orca's belly?"

"No! No, I do not!" I say forcefully. Opening my eyes, I am still able to maintain my new viewpoint, and I slip easily out of my fish-body. It is so simple, now that I understand!

I could move straight out through the sidewall of the Orca's body, right through muscle and bone, and be free. Instead, I decide to have a little fun and go out a different way. Leaving my fish-body behind, I move slowly up the orca's throat, reaching its mouth. Viewing the clenched jaws and knife-sharp teeth, I am curious to see if I feel any fear, but I do not. Those teeth cannot harm me now. I am "nothing!"

Turning my attention to the back of the whale's cavernous mouth, I move down the throat a little until I come to the fleshy blowhole running upwards. As I move rapidly up through this tube toward the ever-increasing light, the orca crests the surface and breathes out with a noisy, powerful blast of air. Streaming out through the orca's blowhole, surrounded by fine, misty, swirling spray, I burst out into the open ocean air. I am finally free! No Orca ever can eat me again!

Falling like a drop of mist, I settle back down onto the ocean surface. Below me, spikes of shimmering sunlight dart down through the water. What a beautiful sight! A deep sense of relief floods over me, and I bask joyfully in the warm sunlight, rocking gently with the waves. I drift along, enjoying

Figure 1-17. "Like a drop of mist, Meera shot out through the Orca's blowhole into the open air." [*Courtesy NOAA and the Dept. of Commerce.*]

not having a body, savoring my new understanding of nothingness, floating along with no cares and no worries. I am nothing ... I am everything!

Drifting along on the waves, I am content just to stay this way forever. I turn my awareness to the sun and just feel the warmth become a part of me. As I do, the sun gets brighter until it fills my entire vision. I have no other thoughts but peace and enjoyment.

With a slight shimmer, I see the sweat lodge appear faintly around the edges of the light. My spirit-vision has changed,

> **Out-of-Body Experience**
> In this vision, Meera had her first conscious out-of-body experience. After being transformed into a salmon in the vision, she saw that she was neither a fish nor a girl called Meera. With great clarity, she realized that she was spirit.
> This experience opened up the spirit worlds for her, and greatly speeded up her spiritual growth.
> All people go out-of-body when they sleep, but each soul must master the process consciously in order to gain the greatest benefit.
> The greatest test of all is to leave the body consciously at the moment of death. This alone shows mastery over death; this alone demonstrates conclusively that the soul can never die.

and I see the familiar, though indistinct outline of the body that others call Meera. The brilliant white light shines easily through my body and through the walls of the lodge. I see the luminescent, translucent body of Sings-on-the-Wind, who nods with a smile.

Figure 1-18. "Seeking guidance from the Great Spirit, Meera bravely undertook her vision-quest alone." [Photograph by E.S. Curtis, ca. 1913. Courtesy of the Library of Congress.]

Now, I begin to sense another presence, in the light itself, almost as if the light were alive and full of a joyous vitality. A deep sense of joy floods over me. The Great Spirit has come!

A deep, resonant rumbling sound gradually forms into words. The voice is captivating and full of love and compassion. It sounds not quite masculine, not quite feminine, but both at the same time. Not being sure which it is, I decide to think of it as the voice of a woman. Her voice comes from all around me, gentle, yet powerful, "You have done well, Reflection-on-Water, very well indeed. Today, you have found your totem animal, not the Salmon, as you first thought, but the Orca, and you should merge with the nature of that animal, for it is powerful, goes wherever it wishes in the vast ocean, and fears no creature. That will become your nature, as well.

"Best of all, you have grown from being 'something' to becoming 'nothing.' Today, because of your inner journey, I give you a new spirit name, known only to you and to Sings-on-the-Wind, in honor of what you have done. Do not tell it to others, for it is your secret medicine name. From today, your name shall be She-who-was-Swallowed-and-became-Nothing.

"So many people struggle to be 'something' in their lives, when the truth is just the opposite; they would do well not to concern themselves with *things* and be content to live as *spirit*. If you accept that truth, you will be able to heal others, for most disease is sickness of spirit. Your hands are blessed with the gift of healing, Reflection-on-Water. Use your gift for all creatures; turn away no living thing. Give of yourself to all."

Next, she touches my forehead. A great, glowing light fills my vision. Whether I close my eyes or open them, I see it all around me. It surrounds me, engulfs me, washes over me, and fills me with deep peace and happiness. Overcome with joy, I know that I will never be the same as I was. The Great Spirit Herself has blessed me. Trying to take it all in, it is too much for me, and I fall into a deep dreamless trance-sleep.

Training as a Shaman

After receiving her totem-vision, Meera turned her attention enthusiastically to her training as a shaman-woman. With the blessing of Meera's family, the tribal shaman accepted her for initiation, and at the same time, she continued her inner training with Sings-on-the-Wind. While many of Meera's young girlfriends engaged in chatter and play, dreaming of being married and having a family, Meera thought only about her life as a shaman-woman, learning all she could, as fast as she could, about the rich tribal lore of natural healing and sacred chanting.

Six Winters Later -- Meera is 16 Winters Old

Because the wind has been blowing hard, and it has been drizzling all morning, many from the three families that share our lodge are inside staying dry. It is spring and still chilly, so there are two fires burning in fire pits along the centerline of the lodge, one at our end and one in the middle. Most of the Otter clan family has gone fishing at the big pool on Tsues River, so at the far end, near the door, there is no fire, just glowing embers.

The women of the Otter clan sit around the fire of the family next to them, talking noisily as they work, one at a loom making a blanket, and several others mending a fishnet.

As I try to help Mother make some cattail cloth, I feel annoyed with them, as usual. I like to concentrate on what I am doing, while keeping centered in spirit, but that is not possible with that flock of chattering crows inside the lodge. I glance over at Mother, making a face and shaking my head in disgust. Mother only laughs quietly, seeming to be sympathetic, but I think that, secretly, she likes to listen to them. Now, I am upset with her, too.

Today, Father is home, mending the barbed tip on his long salmon spear. Yesterday, while tossing it at a fat fish in the shallows, he broke the tip on the river boulders. Now, he is carving a new one of better wood. After he has finished carving it, he will polish it with rough sharkskin and harden it in the fire, so it will be less likely to break.

Life was Wet

The Japanese Current flows off the Washington coast, bringing warmer waters from Asia. Because of this, the climate along the coast is mild and very wet. Warm, moist air rises off the ocean, producing frequent thick fog and rain, lots of rain. The area gets an average of about 150 inches per year, or nearly a half-inch per day.

Because of the mild climate, food was abundant and richly varied; perhaps more so than for any other place on the continent.

Suddenly, the lodge door flies open, framing the silhouette of a man. A strong gust of rain and wind swirls in to settle on the people who are closest to the door. *[See inset.]* Several of them complain loudly to the man. Even at our end of the lodge, the fire flickers wildly in the wind, throwing up a cloud of sparks, as a tongue of fire reaches over and licks the bottom of my bare foot. Yelping in pain, I jerk my foot back, rubbing it vigorously.

With a scowl, I start to scold the man for his carelessness, thinking that one of the men of the Otter clan has come back from fishing. Glaring over at him, I suddenly choke back my words with a stifled squeak. There, in the doorway to the lodge, I see the tribe's chief harpooner, carrying a thick bundle.

Figure 1-19. "Whale-Slayer was the very best harpooner that anyone could recall." *[Photo of a Nootka Whaler by E.S. Curtis, ca. 1915. Courtesy of the Library of Congress.]*

As he steps inside, the wind catches the door and slams it closed behind him with a loud bang, shaking the entire lodge. I jump nervously, but the harpooner does not flinch. Instantly, everyone else stops talking and looks up.

With a grim, serious look on his face, he approaches our family area. The wind has blown his hair around giving him a wild, unkempt look. Involuntarily, I slide sideways towards Mother. Water still drips off his sealskin coat, so he shakes himself quickly, like a bear climbing out of a stream. Drops of water fly off a few paces in all directions. He is tall, muscular, and powerful, good qualities in a hunter of whales. He is the best harpooner in anyone's memory, so his father named him, simply, Whale-Slayer.

Father looks up, too, when the door slams, and now, the harpooner walks directly over to Father with powerful strides and stands silently in front of him. Father does not get up or look up at him. He does not like the harpooner or his family, who often oppose our family in tribal council. Even though they are an influential and wealthy family and even though the harpooner is the son of the chief of their clan, Father does not show him any respect. Father, as the chief of our clan, ranks above him.

Whale-Slayer opens the bundle and then bends over to place long smoked salmon filets in front of Father. Standing up, he says matter-of-factly, "I have come to pay my respect to you and your family and to ask for your daughter in marriage."

His words are like a dagger in my heart. I am stunned and shaken. My hands tremble as I hold the cattail cloth.

Father looks down at the salmon and, without a word, flicks his wrist towards the door, signaling the harpooner to leave, that his offering is not enough. Silently, without emotion, the man turns and stalks out of the lodge. The wind catches the door again, slamming it behind him. All the people in the lodge, who have been watching this drama, are still shocked into silence, and the only sound is the faint moaning of the wind, whistling through the cracks in the cedar planks. After a few moments, everyone starts talking excitedly at once, that is, all except our family.

Bursting into tears, I slide over beside Mother and bury my head on her shoulder, sobbing as quietly as I can. I welcome his proposal like the bite of a snake, and finally, I manage to complain, "Mother, I wish to be a shaman-woman!" Silent, Mother rocks me gently for a few moments before I continue, "I do not want to be married. I wish only to be a healer."

Finally, Mother speaks, "I know that is your first choice, Meera, but you can do both. Many have done so in the past." She continues to rock me gently.

"I do not care what others have done," I protest. "I am afraid of him, Mother. He will stand in the way of my training. I know it! He only wants a wife who will cook his food and make his babies. Oh, Mother, please say 'No!' He has the wisdom of a rock! He will kill my spirit, like he kills the whales!"

"Daughter!" Mother says sternly. "Control yourself. You are letting your feelings run away. He is from a fine family, and he will care for you well. Do not dismiss him so lightly."

Wiping my eyes a little and sniffing, I admit that maybe I am being a little unfair, but only a little. On the other hand, I do feel an attraction. Since I reached womanhood, my urges have been growing. A few weeks ago, I walked past the harpooner on my way back from the river. Though he did not know I was watching, I saw him testing his new harpoon by thrusting it into a large sheaf of dry grass stuffed into a deerskin. As he drew back the heavy harpoon with his powerful arms, I held my breath in anticipation. Then, he snapped his powerful arm forward, bending his head and chest to increase the power. I felt a great surge of excitement, watching his rippling muscles, as he plunged the harpoon deep into the target. As the harpoon vibrated and hummed for a moment, rocking back and forth, I stared with admiration at his dark hair and his chiseled features. I will admit that the sight stirred me and thrilled me. He struck me as a sleek, powerful bull elk that had somehow taken human form. He seemed more than just a man.

Within moments, the thrill passed, as I recognized the other side of him as well, the dark side. I wish to be a healer, and he is, to put it bluntly, a killer. When he came into our lodge today to ask for me as his wife, he eyed me like a hungry shark eyes a salmon. He is cold, powerful, unfeeling, and not to be denied. Like a shark, he destroys without conscience and without remorse, and this lack of feeling disturbs me deeply.

As I think about the harpooner's destructive side, Father approaches us, and I begin crying quietly again. Without a word, Father nods once to Mother, asking for her opinion. She is often wiser than he is in such matters, and he respects her opinion greatly.

Mother says, "He is from a powerful family and will provide for her well, but I have doubts that this is a good match in other ways." Mother is sensitive to my feelings and presents my concerns to Father. "Meera has been chosen by Spirit to be a shaman-woman, and that is a family honor that we must not refuse. If this match is to occur, his family must understand that and allow it."

Father nods, "I agree, my wife. However, it is acceptable for a shaman to marry and have a family. There is not any conflict of duty in doing so. Should Meera be any different? Is it not possible for her to be a fine healer and a good wife at the same time?"

"Of course, it is," Mother answers. She and Father talk as if I were not there, and in truth, my own opinion matters little in such marriage negotiations. Marriage is a family decision for adults in our tribe. It always has been so.

Reflecting my own worries, Mother continues, "And yet there is something about Whale-Slayer that I fear, as a deer fears the wolf. I still worry about Meera's calling."

Father counters, "Wife, those are foolish fears. A wolf seeks food, but he does not eat his mate. True, Whale-Slayer is forceful, but she can get used to that, and you can get over it, too, my wife." He pauses and becomes thoughtful for a moment before continuing, "In any event, I hear your concerns, so I say, 'Let us wait.' We do not have to decide now, so let us see what happens. If he is not serious, he will lose interest, and then, he will have made the decision for us."

With this faint glimmer of hope, I silently pray for the Great Spirit to cause Whale-Slayer to lose his memory so completely that he will never remember having come here today.

The next day is clear and sunny, but my disposition is gloomy. Thinking about the harpooner, I have trouble concentrating on helping Mother. We are hanging freshly sliced salmon over the drying racks and removing the smoked strips from the smokehouse. Mother is constantly scolding me about not paying attention, until finally, becoming exasperated, she tells me to go away and let her finish it. Glad to be alone with my misery, I retreat to the lodge to work on decorating one of my dresses.

As I am sitting in the lodge, the door opens and Father enters, followed closely by Whale-Slayer. Both look stern, and neither of them is talking. This time, Whale-Slayer holds an armload of furs – marmot, weasel, otter, and beaver. As Father sits down cross-legged on his mat, the harpooner places them in front of him, remaining standing without a word.

Father leans forward casually to inspect the top fur by the light of the fire, running his fingers over the otter pelt, just as if he were bartering for it with a trader from another tribe. The pelts, which are of exceptional quality, are a substantial and valuable gift. However, it is apparent that Father is unconvinced, so Whale-Slayer reaches into his belt pouch and takes out two long strands of dentalium shells, each strand of which is nearly as valuable as the entire pile of furs. Without touching the shells, Father looks them over with only mild interest. Next, he shakes his head sharply and firmly from side to side, while waving his hand toward the door, telling the harpooner to go away once again. *[See inset.]*

> **Dentalium**
> Dentalium is a marine mollusk with a tusk-shaped shell that is open at both ends. From the larger end, a long foot appears that the animal uses to move around.
> It lives in muddy sand and sometimes at great depths of the sea along the U.S. Northwest Coast. The shell is smooth, opaque, white, thick-walled, and large in diameter.
> Dentalium shells were highly prized by many North American tribes, who used them for barter and exchange as a form of money.
> In addition, the shells were commonly used for decorating wall coverings and ceremonial clothing.

At first, Whale-Slayer's eyes harden a little, as he tries to remain impassive, but he cannot. Emotion flashes across his face, showing his displeasure with Father's rejection. He did not expect this; he has brought a small fortune in gifts, and Father has turned him away again. Beginning to tremble a little, he backs up to go, almost stumbling over the edge of a

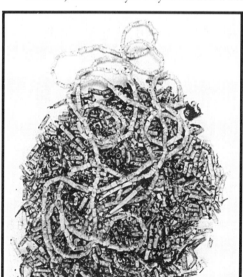

Figure 1-20. "Whale-Slayer offers a small fortune in Dentalium shells." *[This photo from the excavations at Ozette. Courtesy of Washington State University and the National Park Service (1991).]*

seating mat. He leaves the furs and shells, turns, and goes out of the lodge in frustration for the second time.

Mother hurries over to Father. "What are you doing?" she scolds him. "You wanted to see if he was determined, and now he has brought us more fine gifts. You cannot keep taking these things from him and turning him away."

Smiling a little, obviously enjoying himself, Father gathers up the pelts and tosses them onto a pile of blankets, saying, "Meera is unusual and has much to offer, and we will see if he is aware of that. We will see how much he will be devoted her."

With a strand of shells in his hand, he studies it closely, thumbing the shells one by one through his fingers, "I am only looking out for her interests, my wife."

Shaking her head angrily, Mother is upset, "Your only interest, husband, is in extracting more furs and shells from him!"

As they argue quietly back and forth, I become dejected, despairing for my unmarried status. It is out of my hands now. I must accept the will of my parents in this. It is their duty to make a good match for me and for the family. Whale-Slayer is wealthy and well respected, even though others criticize him for his sullen ways. Father and Mother could find worse matches, but probably not one that is better for our family. Though my preference is for *no* match, I must accept the will of my family in this matter.

At mid-morning of the next day, Father returns from talking to some of his clan friends, people whose opinion he respects. Much to my relief, he is leaning against the match. Whale-Slayer's family has voted against us many times in council, and there is little indication that they would vote any better after our families are allied by marriage. I say a silent prayer of thanks to the Great Spirit. There is hope again now!

By noon, the rain starts falling again heavier than in the past few weeks. It is so intense that the drops make a constant pecking noise on the roof. Peeking out of the door, I stare in wonder as the heavy rain pours off the roof in torrential sheets. Curved, bleached whalebone ribs, sunk into the ground just outside the line of the roof eaves, catch the water like gutters and guide it away from the lodge. The wide village path has turned into a shallow creek full of muddy water, rippling and rushing towards the river. Leaves, twigs, and bits of village debris ride along on the current. People from our tribe are outside rapidly repairing the low banks that guide the water away from their lodges.

Inside our lodge, the overlapped cedar planks shed water fairly well, but here and there, thin streams of water pour through the roof into the living area. Using sharp sticks, several of us scratch little grooves into the earth to channel the water around the fires, mats, and working areas over to the outer walls. There, the water flows out of the lodge under the raised sleeping-benches that line the walls.

After a while, Mother, who has been away visiting family, comes back into the lodge. Without taking off her large drenched rain hat, she calls to us excitedly, "Come quickly!" All the while, she points with an upraised arm through the open lodge door.

Thinking that the rain has caused some serious problem, Father and I rush to the door. To our stunned surprise, there, where Mother is pointing, sits Whale-Slayer. He is cross-legged by the side of the village path on a low bank just beyond the rushing water, with no hat and with no rain gear. As water streams down his face, he stares at our lodge with a determined look. Occasionally, as water runs into his eyes, he blinks a few times, but other than that, he sits motionless.

Realization sweeps over me, as Mother whispers, "Death vow!" He has taken an oath to sit until Father says "Yes." Otherwise, he will remain there until he dies. For him, the humiliation of Father's refusal would be just too great to bear.

Angry at the sight, Father grabs us both by the arms, pushing us back inside. "Pay no attention to him," he says sternly. "He will give up by tomorrow and leave us alone."

When I awaken in the morning, the rain has stopped, and just as it is getting light out, I peer outside. I hope to see that Whale-Slayer has gone home, but he is still there. *Please, Great Spirit, make him go away!* I plead. After a moment, I get angry. *He has no right to do this! I belong to Spirit — I can never belong to a man!*

By noon, the sun is out and the world has turned into a huge sweat lodge. Steam rises off the ground, the trees, and the bushes in thin wispy clouds, but Whale-Slayer has not moved from his seat. He has closed his eyes, but sweat rolls off his face, flowing into his eyes just as the rain did yesterday. Occasionally, he rubs his eyes to wipe away the salty sweat, but mostly, he just sits. He has taken no food for two days, and he appears not to sleep.

In spite of this, I am confident that he will fail and hope that, like a whipped dog, he will run home soon and leave me alone. Nevertheless, some part of me is in awe of what he is doing. It reminds me of my three-day vision quest in the sweat lodge. Perhaps he, too, will come out of this with some spiritual vision. If the worst comes and I must marry him, then, I pray that he will gain some spiritual understanding from this ordeal.

It is the morning of the fourth day now, and the entire village is murmuring about the harpooner. Four days in the hot sun and in the rain. Four days without food. Four days without rising from his seat. No matter whether or not they like him, most people agree that he has proven himself and that Father should give in.

Father, however, has now become adamant. "Let him die," he says harshly, having hardened his heart against the alliance between families. "I cannot accept him into the family. I would accept a mad wolf first," he says.

Over the course of the day, I check on him several times, hoping that he will be gone, but he is not. The heat and humidity become oppressive. Now, a crowd gathers around Whale-Slayer, some urging him to continue, some pleading with him to quit. He is so weak that he does not respond.

Now, while keeping his eyes constantly closed, he has begun to sway almost uncontrollably. Sometimes, he moves his lips and whispers as if talking to unseen spirits. Sometimes he argues, and sometimes he moans softly as if in great pain. Other times, he shouts in a hoarse voice as if riding in a great canoe, chasing a whale. Occasionally, he twitches and jerks like a sleeping dog as if watching some inner vision hidden from the rest of us.

Finally, as the sun begins to set on the fourth day, he topples over. Others try to support him and prop him up, but he waves them off silently. Struggling back into a sitting position, we see a long gash in his left temple. A thin stream of blood runs down his cheek and drips off his chin. At first, he does not seem to notice, but finally, he raises a trembling hand to feel the cut. Without opening his eyes, he reaches down for a handful of dirt, moss, and grass and smears it several times across the cut, pressing with his hand until the bleeding stops. When it does, he returns to sitting silently, but he still sways erratically, looking as if he will fall again.

Seeing this, Mother storms into the lodge, ordering everyone out except Father. Standing outside, entranced by the endurance of this man, never taking my eyes off him, I can only hear part of what they are saying. Mother shouts a while, and Father shouts a while. Now, Mother shouts louder and longer, and Father talks less. Finally, only Mother is talking, and Father is silent. Now everything is quiet.

After a few moments, Mother comes out of the lodge, carrying a carved wooden bowl filled with water, berries, and pieces of salmon. Thin wisps of steam rise from the bowl. Visibly tense but smiling tightly, she glances at me and nods. I feel my chest tighten. The Great Spirit is not granting my wish.

Mother kneels in front of Whale-Slayer with her head level with his and touches him lightly on the arm, speaking his name softly. Shaking a little as if startled, he returns from the dreamworld, slowly opening his eyes to look at Mother. She extends the bowl out to him with both hands in a ceremonial manner. Slowly, she smiles and nods her head once. A faint smile flashes across his face, and he nods back to her. In ritual fashion, he extends two shaking fingers, dips them into the bowl, and touches them to his lips. With that one motion, I am betrothed.

He is too weak to drink any more. Putting down the bowl, Mother grabs him under one arm and helps him to stand. He stumbles feebly, almost falling again, until one from his own family grabs the other arm to support him. Slowly, the three of them move away to his lodge at the end of the village.

It is over. Sadly accepting my fate, I turn away and return to my lodge.

About a Year Later ... Marriage

Time for a Potlatch

For the Makah, major ceremonies, such as marriages, took place at elaborate events called "potlatches." Held in the family lodge of the bride's father, potlatches were organized by the families of the bride and groom. They could last for days and take months to prepare.

Typically, many people were invited, both from the couple's own tribe, as well as from other tribes. Because of this, a lot of food was needed. The feast included such things as salmon stew with clams and seaweed, cooked in a large dugout wooden log, as long as a small canoe. The stew was heated by placing red-hot rocks into the log-container, causing the stew to boil. Generous host families also might serve salmon eggs, venison, as well as fresh strawberries or raspberries.

A potlatch was very expensive for the host families because of the long-standing Makah tradition that the hosts should give extremely lavish gifts to the guests, according to their social standing. Sometimes, the hosts would borrow from friends in order to give more generously, becoming temporarily poor in the process. However, they gained great prestige, and so, because of their increased status, they would receive expensive gifts when they became guests at the next potlatch.

Mother and Father have been planning the wedding for many moons, expecting to fill the great community lodge. They sent out special invitations, painted on thin slabs of cedar bark, and now, we have family and friends from many tribes here today, all dressed in their finest clothes. Riding in great canoes, with fifteen to twenty people in each one, they have come from the big island far away across Whale Strait and from villages to the south. Putting aside any disagreements and grudges, everyone is here today to have a good time – even me, although reluctantly.

At first, I was determined to be an unwilling bride, but as I meditated on it, Sings-on-the-Wind helped resolve my misgivings. She pointed out that having a family is simply a matter of caring for others, which is what a shaman-woman vows to do. Marriage will be a good way to start caring, first for a husband and then for the young ones as they arrive. After a short time, Sings-

Figure 1-21. When attending a potlatch, guests wore their finest clothing. *[Photo by Edward S. Curtis, ca. 1914. Courtesy of the Library of Congress.]*

on-the-Wind convinced me that I was being selfish in not wanting to be married. Now, I feel much better about it, though not completely, of course.

Father, known as a great and generous man, is beside himself with excitement over this potlatch because he gets to give many lavish gifts to the guests. In a friendly competition, he and Whale-Slayer's father are competing to see who can be the most generous parent. By the time the wedding is over, they both will have nothing left, but they will be so proud of their generosity that they probably will be unable to sleep for days!

As the ceremony begins, I watch excitedly but have to stay hidden from view. Our guests are sitting, chattering, and singing happily in the great lodge.

Now, starting softly and rising to a loud crescendo, the village drummer beats on his four-foot-high carved box drum. The crowd gradually settles

Figure 1-22. Many people from neighboring tribes came to attend this Makah potlatch on Tatoosh Island around 1895. *[Courtesy of MSCUA, Univ. of Wash. Libraries, NA703.]*

down, but several guests continue to chatter along. After a stern glance from Father, everyone becomes quiet.

Sitting next to the box drummer, two other drummers join in, pounding rhythmically on smaller log drums. The powerful, hypnotic rhythm fills the lodge, making the walls vibrate slightly. The people begin to move and sway in time with the drumming. As it gets louder, some of the guests begin shaking rattles made of turtle-shells or carved hardwood.

Entering through the lodge door, four of the tribe's most skilled dancers make a dramatic entrance. Wearing elaborate costumes with carved wooden masks of the Bear, Raven, Orca, and Whale, they circle wildly around the dance fire in the center of the lodge. There are "ahhs" of pleasure from the crowd. The fierce-looking Bear-Man, having fun, gives a loud roar and makes a clumsy grab for one of the little girls sitting near the circle. She squeals happily and

Figure 1-23. Kwakiutl wedding party dancing inside the community longhouse. *[Photo by E.S. Curtis, ca. 1914. Courtesy of the Library of Congress.]*

scrambles to safety behind her young mother, who smiles and puts on a brave face, scarcely concealing her own desire to hide behind someone, too.

Accompanied by loud chanting and music, the dancers sing and act out the legends and stories that hold the rich traditions of our tribes, especially those of Orca, my totem, and Whale, totem of my husband-to-be. After a while, the

Figure 1-24. Dancers in elaborate costumes make a dramatic entrance. *[Photograph by E.S. Curtis, ca. 1914. Courtesy of the Library of Congress.]*

dancers whirl and shout as they leave the lodge much to the disappointment of the crowd, who I believe, would prefer more dancing rather than a wedding.

Next, my father calls several times for quiet, and now, he and other family members ceremoniously lay out for me a long bridal path, made of beautiful skins from ermine, marmot, and mink. When they are through, they stand, lining the path, looking expectantly toward the lodge door. The crowd becomes silent. This is my signal.

Taking a deep breath, I enter and walk solemnly over to where Whale-Slayer sits. Dressed in the finest clothes that Father can afford, I wear a beautiful finely woven cape and dress, covered with beads, furs, shells, and amulets. At first, I feel shy being the center of attention, but the rich furs feel wonderfully

Figures 1-25 & 26. Dancers in carved masks acted out stories for the guests. *[Photos by E.S. Curtis, ca. 1914. Courtesy of the Library of Congress.]*

Figure 1-27. Kwakiutl bride and wedding party prepares for the ceremony. *[Photo by E.S. Curtis, ca. 1914. Courtesy of the Library of Congress.]*

relaxing on my bare feet. After a few moments, I begin to feel euphoric, and I smile with happiness, as does my husband-to-be.

Whale-Slayer rises from his seat, extending a hand to me. Taking it, I move to stand alongside him, facing our family and the shaman. The ceremony is filled with glowing speeches by both of our fathers, but it is short, because the important part of the ceremony is the feasting and continued gift-giving that is to follow. The merging of our two families, rather than the joining of two people, is what is important. With a final blessing by the shaman, we are married.

When it is over, I glance at my husband shyly, and he looks at me with bright eyes and a wide smile. I feel a warmth come over me for this man. Perhaps, we will learn to love each other in time, but for now, I certainly like him and respect him very much. Few men would have been capable of his four-day vigil to win my hand, and few people have successfully changed Father's mind once he has decided on something, though Mother had a lot to do with that.

Now, for the two of us, there is one more tradition, a fun one. To seal the bond and to win the right to consummate the marriage, Whale-Slayer must show his whaling skills. Solemnly he stands. As his brother and father carry in a huge plank of red cedar, an "ooh" ripples through the crowd. The board is very large, much larger than anyone has seen at such a ceremony. It is taller than the tallest man and a hand's width in thickness. The grain is fine and tight, without a single knot in it. The two of them lean it against the central lodge pole, setting it firmly in the earth so that it will not move.

Figure 1-28. "Whale-Slayer grips his harpoon." *[Photo by E.S. Curtis, ca. 1914. Courtesy Library of Congress.]*

Next, Whale-Slayer removes his wedding shirt, allowing his mother to rub whale oil on his body until he glistens in the light. Now, his father, with great ceremony, hands his son the ritual harpoon of his clan. Twice the length of a man, the harpoon has two sharp elk horn barbs lashed to a jagged opalescent clamshell tip that gleams in the firelight with the reflection of many colors.

Whale-Slayer, who is about five paces from the cedar plank, takes the harpoon, hefting it carefully in his right hand, balancing it perfectly with just the right feel. After

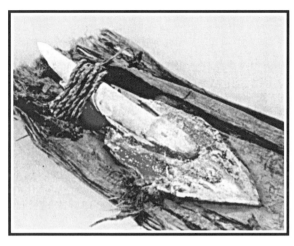

Figure 1-29. Ancient Makah shell harpoon tip and carrying case excavated from Ozette. *[Courtesy of Washington State University and the National Park Service (1991).]*

extending his left arm straight at the plank, without the slightest hesitation, with one fluid, powerful sinuous motion, he draws the harpoon back and pauses. Now, with a loud growl, he launches it powerfully at the plank faster than a snake can strike.

Speeding toward the wood slab, the harpoon hits with a mighty crack and splits the plank cleanly into two pieces. As the crowd roars with approval, the two cracked slabs somersault off to either side among the nearby guests who scramble out of the way.

The harpoon tip buries deep into the heart of the lodge pole, and the shaft vibrates with an audible hum. Whale-Slayer walks up to the pole, grips the harpoon, and tugs it with a great yank. The entire lodge roof rocks and sways. With a jerk, the shaft pulls free from the tip, leaving it stuck deep in the pole. Whale-Slayer walks closer to admire his handiwork.

Turning to the crowd, he proudly announces, "I leave the harpoon tip here as a reminder of the wedding of Meera and Whale-Slayer." Now, looking at me with a wide smile, he says, "I have split the plank. Now, I claim my bride." There are cheers and shouting all around.

Handing the headless shaft to his brother, Whale-Slayer approaches me with a smile. Picking me up as if I were only a child, he carries me towards the lodge door on the way to the marriage hut. As we leave, the crowd cheers once again and offers congratulations, but neither of us hears it. We are intent only on each other.

He tosses open the door to the hut, and we enter. The women of our clan have prepared it for us, and it is warm and comfortable. Off to the back, I see the marriage bed, strewn with soft, warm blankets made from the wool of mountain sheep. Fragrant leaves, berries, and flowers cover the floor and bed. The delightful aroma of burning fir needles, cedar, and hemlock fills the air.

Figure 1-30. "Family members have prepared the marriage lodge." *[Photograph by E.S. Curtis, ca. 1912. Courtesy of the Library of Congress.]*

Mother has prepared me well, explaining the mating ritual to me, and of course, I have seen animals mating as well, so I know how it is done. Still, I am a little fearful. Will I be pleasing to him? Will it be enjoyable for me or painful?

Still smiling but without a word, my husband lowers me gently to the bed. Now, he turns me face downward, raises my hips to a kneeling position, and folds my soft skirt up over my back. As I look back to watch him, he is gazing at my well-rounded bare bottom with obvious admiration. I giggle a little, as he loosens his pants. As he moves to enter me, I turn my head away.

I feel a brief, sharp twinge of pain that makes me want to cry out, but I hide my face in my hands to muffle it. Rocking my body back and forth, my husband thrusts about ten times and, with a powerful convulsion, plants his seed. As his powerful back muscles arch, he pulls me tightly towards him, pressing his body firmly against mine. Now, he releases a deep, resonant, powerful growl, like some wild bear snarling in the woods. It does not sound human. I am thrilled and fearful at the same time.

We remain locked in our mating embrace for a few moments, until his spasms subside. Now, slapping me playfully on my bottom, he grins, yawns, stretches out on the bed, pulls up the goat-hair blanket, and within ten heartbeats, falls asleep.

I lie beside him, staring at the ceiling. Mother warned me both that mating might be painful and that some men are not considerate of a woman's pleasure. Knowing my husband's nature, I did not expect too much of him, yet still I am disappointed. Mating is all right, but it is not as pleasant for me as some of the older women have said. Perhaps, in time, it will get better.

Slipping under the covers next to my new husband, I savor the new experience of having his massive male body next to me in bed. Relaxing, I enjoy his pleasant masculine scent and listen quietly to his deep, rhythmic breathing. Gently, I put one arm over his arm to be close to him as he sleeps. I think that, in time, I shall come to love my slayer of whales, but for now, I am content just to lie beside him.

Before long, I fall into half-sleep, that warm relaxing place between waking and sleeping. As I do so, I see a young girl standing at the end of our bed, watching us silently. She looks to be about four or five winters old, with long, dark hair and large eyes that sparkle in the dim light. As she smiles at me, I call out, "Hello. Who are you?"

"I am your …" she starts to say, but I fall into deep sleep before I can hear her full answer.

One Cycle of Seasons after the Wedding

Motherhood
Nine months later, Meera delivered a daughter to Whale-Slayer. The birth was simple and easy with no complications, and Meera was back at her duties within a day or so. Though Whale-Slayer was happy with his new daughter, it was clear he would have preferred a son, one who could follow him in the hunt for the great whales.

Meera continued with her training as a shaman-woman under the guidance of the tribal shaman, a man who was in his sixties. Wise and well versed in the ways of the mysteries of healing, he taught her much. Sings-on-the-Wind also continued her lessons from the spirit world.

It is almost light as I relax in bed before rising. I hold our daughter, Morning-Song, to my breast, nursing her quietly. Whale-Slayer snores noisily next to me. He is determined to have a son, so we have just finished mating again. We have been doing so frequently for about a week.

Though mating is more pleasurable for me than it was at first, it still puzzles me. Why is it that so many men are so driven by it and that it seems to be so enjoyable to them? It is not so for me. While the act itself feels good, I am more attracted to the feeling of closeness with my husband. I love to feel his powerful body next to mine, to sense his enjoyment with my body, and to be close to him. However, the act itself is not important to me, except for the making of children.

He is still not very open with his feelings, but I sense that he loves me in his own way, as I do him. In spite of his gruffness and toughness, I sense the inner nature of his spirit, and it is not nearly as hard as his outer nature. His family molded his character, so that sadly, he is little interested in things of the spirit himself, but he does not interfere with my calling. With that, I am satisfied. Some husbands are not so tolerant of their wife's interests.

Morning-Song is finished feeding and has fallen asleep, so I gently put her aside. Now, as I lay in bed, thinking of our lovemaking, I wonder how long it will be before I bear him a son; having one is so important to Whale-Slayer.

As I drift between wake and sleep, I feel a vision come over me. The light grows brighter, coming from all directions. Sings-on-the-Wind, who always appears during my visions, walks through the wall of our lodge, carrying a baby boy. My heart jumps as I see it, so small and helpless in her arms. *Perhaps I am pregnant!* I am elated, but Sings-on-the-Wind is wearing a frown and is not smiling. A growing sense of foreboding comes over me.

"What is wrong?" I ask her in a worried tone.

Without a word, she shakes her head slowly back and forth, turns, and walks back out through the wall, carrying away the baby.

In a panic now, I call out to her in spirit, "Wait! Sings-on-the-Wind, wait! What is the matter? What is wrong?" She does not answer.

I start to get out of bed to go outside after her, when suddenly a powerful force holds me down in bed. At first, I struggle, but now, sensing that the vision is not over, I wait. The entire lodge shimmers

Figure 1-31. "The great whale's fluke comes close as it swims past." *[Detail of photo courtesy NOAA/ Dept. of Commerce.]*

Figure 1-32. "The whale sends water and foam flying in all directions." *[Photograph courtesy NOAA/ Dept. of Commerce.]*

and disappears. I am in the ocean again, staring close-up at the rough barnacled jaw of a great whale. It is so close that I could reach out to stroke the creased rubbery hide of the massive animal. I sense that I am in no danger, so I wait as the huge whale glides slowly past me. At last, its great eye comes into view. Larger than my head, its eye is deep black, and it stares into my own eyes without blinking.

With a tremble, I sense the full nature of the whale, its great power, and the peaceful way that it views the world. I also feel its concern that our men come to hunt it in the deep ocean. I feel remorseful for the actions of my husband; for I am a healer and prefer to help living things continue to live.

Following my inner intuition, I grab the whale's powerful fluke as it glides past, so that now I travel with it. With a powerful flip of its tail, the whale moves faster, rushing towards the surface. From below, I can detect the black silhouette of a large whaling canoe above us. With ever-increasing speed, the whale carries me directly toward the boat on the surface. I feel a rising panic.

It flexes its tail powerfully at the last second, opening its great mouth to take in the canoe. Propelling its giant body out of the water, surrounded by swirling foam and crashing waves, the whale grips the canoe and closes its mighty jaws around it.

As its skyward momentum is spent, the whale slowly turns on its side to crash back into the ocean. Trapped by its sharp knife-like teeth, the boat shatters with a loud bone-chilling crack into hundreds of pieces, some flying end-over-end far away from us. Just as the powerful animal crushes the canoe with its jaws, I see in a flash, to my great relief, that the canoe is empty.

As the whale reenters the ocean, water, foam, and bubbles surge crazily all around us, almost ripping me off the fluke. Crunched and splintered pieces of the canoe spill out of the whale's mouth, banging against me as they flow past.

Suddenly, with a growing horror of recognition, I stare at two large, long pieces coming right towards me. Paralyzed with fear, I watch as they spin around dangerously – the broken pieces of my own husband's harpoon. In a heartbeat, the pieces smash into my arm, gashing my flesh and drawing blood. Spinning wildly, the broken harpoon drifts away behind me. In its wake are thin, red streamers of my own blood, twisting and turning in the powerful currents pouring along the side of the whale.

In a panic, I am jarred out of the vision and sit up in bed, screaming "No!"

Startled, Morning-Song begins wailing, and Whale-Slayer, who had been sleeping peacefully, awakens with a start. "What is it?" he asks, looking around quickly for some danger.

Still in a panic, I grab him by the arm, saying, "Do not go, husband! I have had a vision of the whale hunt. It is a bad omen. Do not go."

Whale-Slayer eyes me sleepily for a moment, before saying, "The hunt will go fine, Meera. It is just a bad dream. We have fasted, prayed, and performed all of the ceremonies to insure good fortune. I am prepared, and all of the omens are good. Do not be afraid. Go back to sleep." As he finishes saying this, he turns over and pulls the cover back over him.

Still moved by the graphic images of the vision, I plead with him, "Listen to me, husband, please, for I know of these things. It is *not* well. Do not go, for the Whale Spirit is angry. Wait for another day."

Now, he is beginning to look irritated. "You may know visions, wife, but you do not know whales. They are none of your business. They are mine. So be silent."

Overcome with fear and frustration, I turn away from him and hide my head on the bed. Crying silently, I fall quickly into a fitful nightmare-filled sleep.

It seems like only a short time has passed before I awaken again. Rising up on one elbow, I look around the lodge. Whale-Slayer has gone.

Figure 1-33. "Whale-Slayer and his crew head out to hunt for whales."
[Photograph by E.S. Curtis, ca. 1915. Courtesy of the Library of Congress.]

Figure 1-34. "Whale-Slayer plunges the harpoon into the whale."
[Courtesy of MSCUA, Univ. of Wash. Libraries, NA740.]

Later that Day

Still depressed from what I have seen, I sit outside our lodge. While Morning-Song watches from her basket nearby, I use a grindstone to pulverize some black cherry leaves to use as medicine. I rock back and forth, pushing the grinding stone rhythmically with both hands. The grinding noise is comforting, helping to hide my thoughts. Right now, I wish to think of nothing at all.

Hearing many people talking by the water, I look up briefly but cannot see them. After a while, my uncle, who was hunting with Whale-Slayer, comes walking up the path from the beach. His head is down, and his shoulders are slumped.

Approaching me, he stands silently for a few moments. "Speak," I say quietly without looking up. "I know why you have come."

He nods and says almost in a whisper, "Meera, Whale-Slayer is gone." He pauses, but I do not stop rocking back and forth, continuing to grind the leaves.

Perhaps my uncle is just a vision, I think idly. *Perhaps he will leave, and I will awaken soon.* But he does not go away.

"Soon after we began the hunt, we came upon a huge whale, one of the biggest I have ever seen. Whale-Slayer harpooned him cleanly, but as the whale began to dive, the rope played out so wildly that it looped around the prow of the canoe. In a heartbeat, the great animal began to pull the canoe down under the ocean. Water poured over the side of the canoe. We were very afraid."

I continue rocking, as he stops to clear his throat and wipe his eyes. "We were far out to sea and would have drowned. Instantly, Whale-Slayer leaped with his knife to cut the rope and free the canoe. As he did, the rope snapped back and coiled around his arm. In a heartbeat, the whale jerked him overboard and pulled him down into the deep ocean depths. We did not see him again."

I stop grinding in mid-stroke, staring vacantly at the grindstone. My uncle pauses again, turning away to gaze out at the open ocean for a moment. "Your husband was very brave. His actions saved the rest of us. Because of him, many wives and children will not weep tonight … all except for you, Meera. I am sorry." He touches me gently on the shoulder and quietly moves away.

I had hardened myself for this before my uncle came. Now, I am only sad that I could not have made Whale-Slayer listen. Perhaps my warning caused him to act faster, saving the rest of the men, but I could not save him.

Distressed and numb with pain, moving as if in a dream, I put away the grinder, turn, and gather up Morning-Song. She sleeps quietly. *Maybe if I sleep, too, the pain will go away.*

Returning to the lodge, I reach into my medicine pouch and pull out a small deerskin bag of powdered herbs. Taking a large pinch, I place it into my mouth. It is bitter and burns my tongue, so with a shudder, I quickly swallow a mouthful of cold water. I know that I will sleep within a few minutes. After checking on Morning-Song, I lie down on our bed and close my eyes to wait, trying to forget my pain. The others in the lodge know enough to leave me alone. I will be all right before long. Life will go on.

Before I drift off to sleep, I drop into vision again. To my complete surprise, my husband appears before me, wet and dripping. His face is pale. I am excited and happy to see him, for we did not get to say good-bye.

Before I can speak, he says, "Meera, I am sorry that I did not listen. So very sorry. Can you forgive me?" he asks.

I say gently, "Husband, you do not need to ask my forgiveness, but you may have it if you wish. You made your own choice, as is your right. I am only sorry that we could not have lived to old age together." I smile at the man that I have come to love. "I have grown accustomed to sharing your bed."

"Well, that may still be possible, so that is why I am here," he continues excitedly, more so than when he was in a body. "I am here to ask you to take me back, to ask you to train me in the ways of spirit. Now that I am on this side, things are clearer. I wasted my life while I was with you, and now I wish to make up for it."

Shaking my head, I look at him sadly, "Husband, it is too late. Have you forgotten that your body sleeps with the whales? We cannot change that now?"

"But we can!" he insists. "As your son, Meera – actually, as *our* son!" he answers eagerly. "You are pregnant, my wife, with a boy! I can see it from over here. And if you will accept me, I wish to return to be your son." He pauses for my answer, but I am too stunned to speak.

"Well?" he asks with a pleading voice.

I am still speechless, but in my vision, I see Sings-on-the-Wind appear alongside my husband. She says to me, "Meera, now you know why I showed you the child in the vision and then took him away. Now, your son has returned to you. You may take him if you wish." *[See inset.]*

Shaking my head in amazement, I look back at my husband, who is staring at me expectantly. Finally, I laugh aloud wholeheartedly. He looks at me with total puzzlement, so I add, "Husband, can you

Rebirth into Same Family
This is most likely to happen when a family member dies an early or accidental death. Because of unfulfilled desires, the soul may choose to return to the same family almost immediately.

Following most wars, there is a jump in the birth rate, for example. This is often because many of the casualties of war reincarnate quickly, sometimes like Whale-Slayer, into the same families that they left behind.

not see the humor in what you ask? My husband wants to become my son! This is *not* what I meant when I said I wanted you back in my bed."

He gazes at me intently, still looking puzzled by my laughter. With a sigh, I realize that being dead has not improved his sense of humor. "Let it be as you wish, husband. I consider it an honor to have you back both as son and as student. Let it be so."

My husband, so recently dead, now my son-to-be, smiles broadly, as he slowly fades from view.

Sings-on-the-Wind remains, saying, "Meera, he must not know it until he is older, but there is a price he must pay for this to happen. In order to move ahead spiritually, he must balance out his refusal to listen to your warning. Even more, he must balance out his destruction of other life forms. If he had revered and respected the great whales more and thanked them for allowing one of them to be taken, he would have been all right. However, he did not do so fully enough. He enjoyed far too much the glory and power of his destructive acts. He became puffed up with pride." I listen intently to what she is saying.

"Later, in his life as your son, after you have crossed into spirit, he will have to pay, but by then, you will have had time to work with his spirit. He truly wishes to learn from you, and he has agreed to a difficult test. With your help, Meera, he will do well."

A little bit worried, I ask, "How must he pay?"

Sings-on-the-Wind looks at me for a moment, before asking, "Are you sure you want to know." I nod without hesitation.

"As you wish," she says.

With a flash, I stand by the edge of a deserted strand of beach along the great ocean. There are no villages or people to be seen anywhere, except for a man I recognize as Whale-Slayer, standing with his back to the sea, gazing inland. Suddenly without warning, unseen by Whale-Slayer, the sea begins to boil and churn, as a huge green sea turtle crawls slowly out of the depths. It is bigger than our village, even bigger than the mountain on the cape. Great cascades of water, sand, and seaweed pour off its back as it rises from the ocean. It wears a shiny gray covering over its head that looks like the strange shiny knives *[made of iron]* from the traders, and its shell is made of the same material. Whale-Slayer does not see it coming. Cawing and screaming with a terrible noise, dozens of ravens glide down and land on its back.

With a growing sense of danger, I watch the giant turtle stretch its long neck and head out towards my son. I scream, "Look out! Run!" but before Whale-Slayer can move, the turtle opens its great sharp jaws, grabs him, and with my son struggling in its mouth, backs slowly into the sea.

Overwhelmed with despair, I cry, "No, do not take him. Please!" Bursting into tears, I plead, "I have lost him once already. Please, do not take him again!"

Figure 1-35. Seeing photos of the beautiful, rugged Washington-Oregon coastline, particularly the jagged sea-stacks, helped me to recall memories of this past lifetime. *[Courtesy of MSCUA, Univ. of Wash. Libraries, Pickett-4373.]*

Submerging under the waves, my son disappears. I collapse onto the beach, and I am still crying as the vision ends. Sings-with-the-Wind stands there quietly. She speaks softly, "I hesitated to show you, Meera, but do not lament for what must be. The test will be hard, but your son will gain great strength from what is to come. You will be proud of him."

Gathering my composure, I ask, "I am confused about the vision. I do not fully understand. Am I allowed to know what it means?"

Sings-with-the-Wind looks at me lovingly, "After you are gone from his life, your son will meet a powerful tribe from the south. Some will call them demons, but they are men, with thick, dark, bushy hair on their faces *[the Spaniards]*. They will ride on the back of a great oceangoing canoe that will be thick and hard like the shell of a turtle *[Spanish galleons]*. These demons also will wear hard shells *[armor]*, just like the turtle, and like the raven, they will be cunning and deceitful. They will steal from anyone whenever they can, and they will steal your son."

Shuddering a little, I ask, "Will they kill him?"

"They will not," she replies, "but they will carry him to a foreign land [Mexico], where he will learn things that no one else in the tribe has ever seen. He will never return to this village, but he will develop great spiritual power by going through this. Do not despair for him. Just prepare him well, Meera, and he will be fine."

Still upset, I gradually begin to let it go. I have come to trust Sings-on-the-Wind in such things. Finally satisfied that the Great Spirit will protect him, I nod solemnly and say softly, "Because of what you speak, I will choose his name now. He shall be known as 'Travels-Far.'"

Sings-on-the-Wind smiles and nods in return.

Four Years Later

> **Many Changes for Meera**
> Shortly after the death of Whale-Slayer, when Meera was 22 winters old, the tribal shaman also died, elevating Meera to that position. Thus, within a short time, the two most important men in Meera's life, other than her father, were dead. Meera never remarried, choosing instead to concentrate on raising her two children and on performing her duties as shaman. Her focus gradually grew from caring only for the smaller circle of her family to caring for the larger circle of the entire tribe.

Today, hand-in-hand with my young daughter, Morning-Song, I walk along Hobuck Beach near Tsues Village, enjoying the sea, the sand, and the sun. I walk very slowly so that her little legs can keep up. My young son, who was once my husband, is still too young and too impatient for long walks, so Mother cares for him today.

Ahead of us, just out from the shore in shallow water, there are dozens of sea-stacks, huge, jagged, gray-brown, moss-covered, standing stones, some of them ten times my height. They look as if the Great Thunderbird dropped them from the sky, maybe during a game with the Water Spirit or maybe in battle with the Whale Spirit. They stand in the shallow water with their ends pointing upward towards the sky. Around the larger rocks, jumbles of smaller stones break the surf into constantly shifting patterns of green-blue water spray and gray-white foam.

On some of the smaller rocks that are close to the water, sea lions enjoy the warm rays of the sun. As we approach them, we can hear them barking loudly to each other. Morning-Song says, "Listen, Mother. They are having talks with each other."

Figure 1-36. "All the sea lions are talking at once." *[Photo courtesy NOAA, Dept. of Commerce.]*

"Well, almost," I reply, amused. "They are not exactly having talks *with* each other ... since they are all talking at once. It is hard to have a real conversation when no one is listening."

We both laugh and stop to watch them for a while. Now, as we continue, she chatters on brightly, talking about what the sea lions might be having for lunch, wondering what the seagulls are "saying" to each other, and any other thoughts that wander into her young head. As she talks, I scan the steep cliffs along the shore for medicine herbs and mushrooms. Here where the sea meets the land, under the harshest conditions, some of the most powerful healing herbs grow. Besides collecting them for my work, I am teaching my young daughter some of the secrets of healing ... when she is not talking. I have been a shaman-woman for so long that I always search for useful things automatically now, even when someone, like my daughter, talks to me as we walk.

Morning-Song notices that I am searching the shoreline intently. She stops, puts her hands on her hips, and says "*Mother!*" with that indignant tone only a young daughter can use. "You are just like the sea lions. You are *not* listening."

I squat down on the beach and look at her, smiling; "But I *am* listening, daughter. I find it possible to walk, to listen, and to search for herbs at the same time."

She cocks her head sideways, purses her lips, and gives me a doubtful look. Deciding to tease her a little, I continue, "In fact, I can do all of those things, and ..." I pause long enough to make sure she is looking at me, wondering what I will say next, "and I also can make a funny pucker-face, scratch my nose, and pull my ear all at the same time."

As I act this out for her, she giggles happily. Now, she says, "Do it again." So I do it all again – face-puckering, nose-scratching, and ear-pulling – and she rewards me with squeals of delight, before saying, "Once more." So I do, and she giggles happily again, just as if she had never seen it before. "Again!" she demands, laughing.

Realizing that she may never tire of seeing me make a pucker-face, I reply, with mock seriousness, "Oh, no. I better not. My face might stay puckered up this way, and then everyone will say 'Look, there goes a dried salmon. Let us eat her up for dinner.'"

I tickle her as I finish. Squirming and giggling, she breaks free and runs ahead up the beach. Immediately, she becomes intrigued with a large, beautiful seashell, and all thought of my funny face is gone. I catch up with her, and we walk along in silence for a while.

Each one of our steps on the fine wet sand makes a distinctive sound, and the rhythmic *chuk, chuk, chuk* of our footsteps matches the timing of the waves striking the shore. It reminds me of the chanting of my people around the lodge fires at night, and a sense of deep peace comes over me. I am glad to be alive, glad to be in harmony with this wonder-filled land. I gaze out beyond the surf – out beyond the playful sea lions – and I give thanks to the generous Great Spirit, who allows us to live here and who allows me to have a lovely daughter like Morning-Song.

Uplifted by the beauty of this place, we continue up the shore, picking our way through a group of head-high gray boulders. The sand is strewn with long strands of seaweed and rainbow kelp, thrown up by the waves. As we walk around one of the huge surf-rounded boulders, we almost stumble over a large female sea lion. When the sea lion bares her teeth in warning, both of us are startled and step backwards quickly. Morning-Song hides behind my legs, peeking around my skirt to look at the sea lion. I catch my breath for a moment, and wait for my heart to slow down. *[See inset.]*

Looking at the sea lion closely, I see that something is wrong. Her left eye is swollen shut, and she blinks the

> **Flash Forward**
>
> In my current life, as I walked along the beach in California one day, I came upon a sea lion that appeared to be sick. Observing it up close helped me to recall this past life incident.
>
> In this case, there were several triggers: sight, sound, smell, and the emotions I felt.

other eye slowly, as if in pain. Her breathing is labored and uneven. I make a hand sign for Morning-Song to keep silent. Out of reach of the sea lion's sharp teeth, I squat down on the beach to be closer to her head, and I look into her eyes. She stares directly back at me, and I sense her pain. Her eye is infected and badly swollen. On her back are three broad scars – orca teeth marks, most likely – but they are old scars and have fully healed. I look at them in wonder, for sea lions usually do not escape the jaws of a hungry killer whale.

I quietly murmur aloud to her, "You must be one very fast sea lion."

She flares her long whiskers and bares her teeth again. I speak gently, "Do not worry; I am no hungry orca. You are safe with me."

She grows quiet but still eyes me suspiciously, as I stare at the long nasty-looking scars on her back. "Very fast, indeed, to out-swim an orca." I pause for a moment, trying to envision her close encounter with those great gaping

Figure 1-37. "Swim-Fast bares her teeth in warning." *[Photo courtesy NOAA, Dept. of Commerce.]*

jaws. I shake my head in disbelief. Now I speak to her softly and soothingly, "What are you called, little one? You must have a name that the other sea lions call you."

I pause to look at her thoughtfully. "Hmm, but humans probably cannot speak it anyway. Therefore, you also should have a name that humans can speak. That way, we can know each other properly." I turn to my daughter, who is watching the sea lion intently, "What shall we call this brave one who out-swims an orca?"

"Let us call her 'Swimmer,'" she says very solemnly.

I nod; "That is a nice name, but she is not just any swimmer. She is a very, very good one."

"Yes, and she must be very fast, too," she adds.

"There. That is it. You have found her name. 'Swim-Fast.' Is that all right with you, daughter?" I ask with a smile.

She nods happily, and I turn back to the sea lion and say to her, "We shall call you 'Swim-Fast,' if that is all right with you. This is my daughter, Morning-Song. And I am called Meera, which is my short name. My long name is Reflection-on-Water. And so, now, you know us."

As I speak, the sea lion lowers her head to the sand and continues to look up at me with her one good eye. "Swim-Fast, the Great Spirit has granted me the gift of healing. Perhaps I can help your eye if you wish, even though I have never before healed a sea lion."

I begin to chant softly, my voice rising and falling in cadence with the wind and the waves. Morning-Song joins in a little for she knows most of the chant. I call out to the Great Spirit and to the Seal Spirit for permission to help Swim-Fast. I have learned always to ask for permission first, since sometimes it is not spiritually correct to heal a person or an animal. In some cases, their life span may be over, and it is time for them to move on into Spirit. Healing them would interfere with what is right for them. I sing the chant repeatedly, lifting my spirit up, trying to attune my consciousness with Swim-Fast, and searching for the right thing to do. As I enter a light trance, Swim-Fast slowly raises her head and looks deeply into my eyes. As she does, I see a misty glow of golden light form around her head. It is a sign from Spirit, and with that inward sign, I know that it is right for her to live.

"I will do my best, Swim-Fast, but only the Great Spirit can heal. I can only help to make that possible."

I look closely again at her swollen eye. It does not appear to be badly damaged. Beginning to chant softly again, I open my medicine bag. Digging around, I find a small bundle of thin, soft inner bark, wrapped up and tied with a leather thong. I motion to Morning-Song to unwrap it. As she does, the black oily ointment, made from whale oil, forest mold, and tree mushrooms, gives off a pungent, musty aroma. Swim-Fast wiggles her nose a little, as I place the ointment down in front of me.

Swim-Fast seems to accept me now, and she lowers her head gently to the sand, closing her one good eye. I reach out slowly with my left hand and place it lightly palm downward on her head. Her whiskers twitch a little, but other than that, she does not move. Her fur is cool and slick to the touch. She carries the faint aroma of seaweed and fish. Her nostrils open and close rhythmically as she breathes. I allow the healing energy from the Great Spirit to flow through my hand into Swim-Fast. My palm becomes warm as the healing energy flows. As she becomes visibly relaxed, her breathing slows down, too.

Without removing my left hand from her head, I pick up some of the ointment with two fingers from my right hand. I rub it gently first on her eyelid, next above her eye, and now below it. Swim-Fast accepts my touch without flinching, though I can feel her eye moving and trembling a little under the eyelid. After finishing with the ointment, I continue chanting softly. Her breathing has become very slow, and she appears to be sleeping now.

Motioning to Morning-Song to be very quiet, I stand up slowly so as not to awaken Swim-Fast. Moving in among the rocks, we gather some of the seaweed and kelp that has washed up on the shore. Each strand has small bulbs of air that help it float in the water. Occasionally, Morning-Song and I step on one, and the bulb makes a soft popping sound, but it is not loud enough to awaken Swim-Fast. When we have collected enough, we return to her and lightly pack the seaweed around her sleeping form to keep her warm. Only her nose is left exposed.

Next, we move higher up the shore to the base of the cliff. There, during storm surges, waves have exposed patches of well-rounded pebbles and stones. Showing Morning-Song what to do, I move through the bed, carefully selecting flat stones, some black and some red. Each one is about a hand-width across, forming a circular, flattened disk. I lift up my long dress to make a pouch, and we load them into it.

When we have enough, we return to Swim-Fast and carefully place the stones, one by one, about a foot apart, in a wide circle around her. These are for protection, so nothing will bother her.

When the circle of alternating black and red stones is closed, I squat down again, and look at Swim-Fast. Her nose and whiskers wiggle a little, so I know she swims in the Spirit World of Dreams. Her flippers jerk and twitch as if she were chasing fat salmon in the ocean. Morning-Song thinks this looks funny, so she clamps both hands over her mouth to keep from giggling aloud. I smile at her and make another "be quiet" sign to make sure she does not awaken the sea lion.

We watch Swim-Fast quietly for a few more moments. Her breathing is measured and even. Each in-breath is long and slow, making a soft "e-e-e-e-ah" sound – each out-breath is sharp and quick, making a louder "huh" sound. I watch and listen to her for a moment. "E-e-e-e-ah Huh"… "E-e-e-e-ah Huh"… "E-e-e-e-ah Huh." She sleeps well.

Satisfied that she is all right, I softly sing one last chant of protection and healing. Now, satisfied that I have done all I can, I stand and motion to my daughter. She takes my hand, and we quietly continue down the beach, searching again for healing herbs.

About a half Moon later, as I approach the same jumble of rocks on the beach, I wonder again about Swim-Fast. I had returned the next day to find her gone. I saw her flipper prints leading out to sea, so I thought she must have been doing better. I gaze out at the group of sea lions sunning and barking on the rocks in the water and try to recognize her, but they are too far away. Several of them splash around in the water, watching me warily and keeping a lookout for orcas.

Around one of the nearest rocks, I see a splash in the floating seaweed, and now, the head of a sea lion pops up. It stares at me and swims in towards the shore. My heart jumps as I see long scars on its back. *Swim-Fast!*

She splashes clumsily onto the shore about ten paces away. She stops and looks over at me cautiously. Satisfied that she recognizes me, she lumbers up to me, her fins making soft plopping sounds in the wet sand. She stops about an arm's length in front of me and stares up with large brown eyes. Both eyes are clear and fully healed. She raises her muzzle, sniffing the breeze to catch the scent of me again. Now, she wiggles her whiskers and pulls back the corners of her mouth in what surely must be a sea lion smile. It is her way of saying, "Thank you, Reflection-on-Water."

Smiling, I reach out to touch her gently on the head. "I am happy to have helped you, Swim-Fast. Swim well and swim fast, my friend," I say softly.

After I had my first vision of the Great Spirit, I have always tried to help any person, plant, or animal that needs help. I could not always do so – sometimes my faith was weak – but I have always tried.

Swim-Fast turns, flops back into the water, and swims off. So clumsy on land, she is sleek, fast, and graceful in the water, turning, rolling, and diving as she goes. I call out to her one last time, "Good-bye, Swim-Fast," raising my hand in farewell.

Fall, Eighteen Winters Later -- Meera is Forty

At Ease in Two Worlds
For many years, Meera worked to raise her children and train them in the ways of the tribe. By the time Meera reached forty, both children were married and had families of their own. When her son was old enough, she told him of his father and of the vision of him that she saw after his death. Her son accepted the story easily, asking Meera to help him learn from the mistakes he had made as Whale-Slayer. Meera was pleased with him.

Meera's daughter developed a strong interest in becoming a shaman after her mother. Meera was happy with this but did not push her daughter, allowing the desire to develop on its own.

In addition, Meera continued to increase her knowledge and understanding of the shaman's arts. She had learned to move easily and confidently both through the world of the living and through the world of spirit. Each world had become just as real to her as the other one, and Meera was satisfied with the lessons she had learned in both.

Walking back from the beach, I am very disturbed this morning. I was searching for some fresh fever-berries for the village leader's son, when I came across a dead orca, a huge female that had washed up on the beach. On her abdomen were great gaping holes where something had torn out massive chunks of flesh. Only a Great White Shark could have done that. It is a bad omen, for other animals almost never attack an orca, even the great sharks. As my totem animal, it is a very bad omen, indeed.

As I move away from the beach onto the path back to the village, suddenly I stop. There, lying in the path ahead of me is the twisted dead body of a Great-Horned Owl. This animal is also sacred to my clan. As a shaman, I see this as another bad omen. I step around the body and continue, but now, I am deeply worried.

Figure 1-38. At the age of forty, Meera looked a lot like this Makah woman. *[Photograph by E.S. Curtis, ca. 1915. Courtesy of the Library of Congress.]*

It is unusual to have two such omens on the same day. Is this some message from spirit? Perhaps about the village leader's son? He had come to me with what looked like a simple case of the winter cough, but he has not responded well. I have used all my chants and medicines, but he seems to get no better, and I am puzzled – and worried.

Approaching the village leader's lodge, I open the door and enter the dimly lit house. The village leader and his wife sit along the wall on the edge of their son's raised sleeping-bench. Mopping his brow, they chant softly to him. The firelight casts wavering shadows of them against the woven cattail mats that hang next to the bed.

As I approach, the village leader and his wife look up at me hopefully. Their son is still sleeping fitfully, sweating, and trembling with fever. Digging into my pouch, I sprinkle some more dried healing herbs and berries onto the smudge fire, watching clouds of smoke billow up to fill the lodge around us. Perhaps that will help him to breathe easier.

I do not show it, but I am deeply worried. He is no better, and I am almost at a loss for what to do next. However, there is one thing that I remember, one ancient remedy the old shaman described to me. It has been a long time, so I struggle to recall the formula, remembering that he said it was very powerful for the cough, when nothing else worked.

Reaching into my shaman's pouch, I take out several small deerskin bags. In a small wooden bowl, carved into the likeness of an orca, I mix ground herbs, mushrooms, and berries into a thick black granular paste. Forming it into a small ball half the size of a robin's egg, I move to the son's side. He turns to me, scarcely conscious and with his eyes barely open. Tilting his head forward, I gently open his mouth, place the ball far back in his throat, and put a cup of water to his lips so he can swallow it down.

After watching for a moment, I turn back to my pouch to prepare the fever-berries. After crushing the dried leaves and mixing the fever-tea, I am almost finished when the village leader's wife calls out in a worried voice, "Meera!"

As I turn around, the son makes a gurgling sound, and now his body lurches with a powerful convulsion. As I rush to hold him down, his eyes snap wide open with terror. Gasping for breath, he struggles to sit up. Frantically mopping his head to comfort him, I try to find what is wrong, ransacking my memories of illnesses and remedies. Still sitting upright, he slaps my hand away and clutches his neck and chest, clawing at his skin, still struggling to breathe. As I watch in horror, black foam spills out of his mouth and drools down his chin. His face turns red and now purple. His mother grabs him and shakes him wildly, screaming his name.

"What have you done to him?" his father cries, as he pushes me away from the bed onto the ground. Grabbing his son, he slaps him on the back to help him breathe. Sprawled on the floor in confusion, I stare at the black foam pouring from his mouth. Feelings of helplessness and terror flood through me, drowning me in fear.

With growing doubt and trembling hands, I pick up the pouches from the ground, frantically rechecking what I have just given him. Grabbing one bag, I look inside, and my heart almost stops. My hands shake, and growing panic comes over me.

Black mushrooms! I used the wrong bag. In small amounts, it is powerful medicine. In large amounts, it can kill a rogue bear. I have given the son a lethal dose of poison.

I slump to the ground in despair. I, who have sworn to heal, am about to take a life instead. I glance over at the son, who is now in constant convulsions. With my inner-vision, I see that his spirit has already gone. It only remains for his struggling body to die.

As I watch in shock, he convulses one last time and is still. Instantly, his mother begins weeping and calls out in her grief, "No! No! You have killed my only son. My son is dead." She sits rocking back and forth, sobbing uncontrollably, and cradling his lifeless body against hers.

As I sit slumped on the ground, the village leader stands slowly and turns to look down at me. His face is hard, and without a word, he simply points to the door. Heartbroken, with numb fingers, I gather my bags of medicine and rise to leave. As I do, I see Sings-on-the-Wind standing in the corner with her arms folded in front of her. Her face, too, is serious and hard. Slowly shaking her head, she turns and vanishes into spirit. She, too, has forsaken me. I saw the omens, but I did not understand. I was warned, but I did not listen. In deep despair, I stumble out of the lodge.

Three Days Later

A low-lying layer of swirling, gray mist drifts over the ocean and the land. It hides the tips of the great fir trees and the tops of the distant peaks, snow-capped during all four seasons. Visible beneath the hanging mist, the forested coastline stretches for miles in both directions. Through a few breaks in the clouds, long, luminous sunbeams make slowly shifting, silver-gold glowing streaks.

Small waves break restlessly over the smooth, rounded pebbles on the shore at my feet. The waves wash up onto the beach, pause briefly, and vanish down into the stones with a quick hissing sound. The fall air is damp and very cold. My soft woven dress falls down to cover my moccasins, but the cold air pushes its way relentlessly in through the seams and openings. I wrap up tighter in my long cloak, woven from twisted cedar-bark, and lined with duck-feathers. I shiver now – mostly from the cold, but also from the unknown. *What will they do with me?*

Far out beyond the bay, a pod of killer whales, my totem animal, glides and dives gracefully, their tall black fins slicing through the dark water. They move along the coast on some business known only to orcas. Out of respect, my hand moves instinctively to the ivory orca carving hanging on my necklace.

Behind me, gazing out towards the whale pod, a carving of the Orca Spirit looks out from the top of a cracked, weathered, lichen-covered totem tree, which is three times higher than my head. Does he long to swim free with them in the ocean, too? His carved face bears a permanent trickster's grin that seems to say "Yes-s-s-s." *[See inset.]*

My thoughts of the sea die away, and as I turn again to my own painful problems, a wave of sadness overwhelms me. I have not seen Sings-on-the-Wind since the day the village leader's son died. She has abandoned me.

"Great Spirit ...," I begin to pray inwardly, "you know ..." I hesitate, not knowing quite what to say next. My heart is heavy.

"You know that I am sorry, Great One. I have stumbled and let the tribe down. I await your judgment and theirs. Spare me or take me, I care not. I accept your decision."

> ### Flash Forward
> When I first saw old photos of the ancient totem poles in the Northwest, in a flash, a powerful sense of *déjà vu* awakened buried memories. The carved Orcas, Ravens, and Thunderbirds on them seemed very familiar, as if I had carved them with my own hands.
> This trigger was visual, and led to detailed memories of this lifetime among the Makah.

A cold, light, misty rain begins to fall. I look up and watch the tiny drops swirl down in slow motion, moving like miniature snowflakes and landing gently on my weathered brown face. I choke back my feelings so no one can hear, but tears begin to roll down my face. The fresh rain mixes with my salty tears and carries them down my cheeks, hiding them. I can taste the warm salt flavor on my lips.

"Meera," I hear Travels-Far, my son who was once my husband, softly calling me. "It is time." My daughter, Morning-Song, stands with him. With tears in her eyes, she says nothing.

As I turn silently to follow them, the village seems unnaturally quiet, like the bay before a storm. Quiet ... except for the crunch of beach pebbles at each uncertain step. Quiet ... except for the pounding of my heart.

My children lead me back into the village to the meetinghouse where the elders and all the tribe are gathered. I pull open the wood-and-deerskin door

Figure 1-39. "A pair of Orcas cruises past, heading out to sea." *[Photograph courtesy NOAA/ Dept. of Commerce.]*

Figure 1-40. "The carvings on the totem pole stare out to sea." *[Photograph by E.S. Curtis, ca. 1915. Courtesy of the Library of Congress.]*

and enter. In the center of the lodge, half a dozen great logs form a star-pattern, with a low fire crackling in the middle. A shadowy figure rises, slides one of the logs in towards the fire, and now stirs the fire with a stick to make the flames leap up brighter. Rising with the smoke, hundreds of tiny sparks suddenly flare and die out in less than two heartbeats. Several wide cedar smoke boards have been moved back on the roof, allowing the smoke to rise up and drift out of the lodge, but still the air is smoky with the aroma of cedar wood, pinesap, and fir needles.

Covered with intricate carvings, several thick round posts extend upward towards the roof, vanishing into the darkness. The roof is more than twice my height, and the firelight, shining through the smoke, casts eerie, flickering, light-and-dark shapes on the rough wood. The shapes appear alive, as if the tribe's shadow ancestors have gathered with us here in spirit.

The meetinghouse is longer than two great canoes, and there is a second fire farther away. I cannot see all the way to the other end, but I know it is filled with my people. Highlighted by the firelight, some of my tribes-people sit against the cedar-plank walls. I can see them only vaguely, the people I have loved and cared for all of my life. I was raised to be a shaman-woman, and I took a sacred oath to treat them as my own family, as my own children. I know all of them well.

I am not invited to sit, so I stand with my palms clasped respectfully in front of my dress. I lock my gaze downward at the woven cedar-bark mats covering the hard earthen floor. After an awkward period of silence, the village leader, overall head of all families, his hair silvered by age and wisdom, speaks softly, "Meera, for forty cycles of seasons you have been with us. Long ago, during the Great Wave, the Great Spirit and the Thunderbird sent you their blessings. You have healed our bodies, nourished our souls, and kept us in tune with the Great Spirit. For that, we are grateful.

"However, because of your actions, my son is gone, he who was to be village leader after me. Because of your actions, he has gone to be with our Ancestors. He came to you for relief of the winter cough that you have cured a hundred times before for our people. He came to you for healing …." The village leader's voice breaks, and he pauses to collect himself.

"Instead, you say … by mistake … you gave him too much of the black mushroom, and it robbed him of breath and stole the light from his eyes." He struggles to continue and looks down, choking back his grief.

Slowly looking up, he continues quietly, "How could this have happened? You say you do not know … and the tribe does not know either. Like the Ocean Wind, some things cannot be explained.

"And yet, the Great Spirit and the tribe hold that everyone must answer for their actions. Young or old, weak or strong, we all are judged for what we do ... especially when we take another life." His voice has gotten softer and softer, and he pauses again.

Barely audible now, he continues, "The tribe has met to decide what we shall do about this." He clears his throat. "I act not as a grieving father, but only as servant of the tribe when I speak these words. You will be sent to live alone on the Island of the Seals for one full cycle of seasons." *[See inset.]*

My breath catches for a moment and my heart aches, but my face is blank and unchanged. I hear soft muffled sobs and shuffling noises as others shift around in the dim light at the edge of the lodge. Others share my pain.

> **Exile as Punishment**
> At first, when I recalled this past life detail, I thought that the memory could not be correct. How could the tribe exile a healer who just was trying to do her job?
> However, McLaughlin (1970), on p. 87, verified that, among the coastal tribes of the Northwest, banishment sometimes was decreed for a shaman who made a mistake and injured a sick person. This would be similar to medical malpractice today.

He continues, "The tribe says you may not leave the island, and no one may visit you. The tribe will send someone back after one cycle of seasons has turned. If your breath is still in your body, we will welcome you back with great gladness and feasting. But if you have gone to join the Ancestors, we will gather your bones and return them to the village with respect. Here we will chant and sing of your good deeds around a great bonfire. Then we will bury your remains at a ceremony in honor of the Orca Spirit, your totem."

He pauses one last time and cannot bear to look me in the eyes. "Meera, my heart is sad to speak these words to you ... but through me, the tribe has spoken."

The Next Day

As the sun rises over the snow-capped mountains inland, Travels-Far, my son-who-was-my-husband, and my daughter, Morning-Song, come to my lodge one last time. Neither one can speak to me or touch me, nor can I speak to them, so I cannot tell them of the anguish in my heart. The entire village is quiet, and I will not hear another living voice any time soon.

I pick up my shaman bag. I can take no other supplies with me into exile. After I signal that I am ready, my son leads me to the great canoe pulled up on the shore, and I step in.

With tears in my eyes, I turn to look at my daughter, who stands on the shore softly chanting a farewell song. She will be shaman now. I touch my fingertips to my heart to tell her that I love her. As tears cloud my eyes, I quickly turn away.

Figure 1-41. Six men, including Meera's son, take her into exile. *[Photograph by E.S. Curtis, ca. 1912. Courtesy of Library of Congress.]*

Figure 1-42. "Into exile on the Island of the Seals." *[Photo courtesy NOAA/ Dept. of Commerce.]*

Six men of the tribe, including my son, help launch the canoe. *[See inset.]* They leap in, splashing light spray over my feet. No one speaks. Carved with fire and sharp stones from one great ancient cedar tree, the great canoe rides smoothly in the water. As the high prow points into the wind and waves, we move swiftly out towards Seal Island. The cold salt spray hits my eyes, and they burn a little, though whether more from salt or from tears, I do not know. Time passes like a dream vision, and I wonder if this is just a dream, after all. I think, maybe this will pass, and I will awaken tomorrow, safe in the village among the tribe. The crunch of the canoe on the rocky shore brings me out of my daydreaming. Soundlessly, I step out, and walk slowly into the tree line, too numb and too ashamed to look back at my people as they leave me.

Flash Forward
When I first saw one of these huge oceangoing cedar canoes, to my surprise, I felt a strong sense of grief. Seeing them had awakened this past life memory of riding sadly away from the village into exile. In the flashback, I almost could feel the grain of the creaking wood and smell the powerful aroma.

As a child, I often had played in my grandmother's cedar-lined closet. The intense aroma seemed eerily familiar.

A Half Moon Later

With sleep-blurred eyes, I stare out at the world. The island is mostly barren, with only a few trees. My body just fits into the fire-hollowed cavity of an old stump. The tree trunk, toppled from a lightning strike long ago, lies dead and gaunt now, broken on the rocks. The den is not large enough for me to lie down, so I sleep leaning against the inner trunk. I have stuffed the den with dry grass and moss, and pulled up long slabs of dead bark to seal the opening. The wind, bitter cold, whistles through every crack and crevice. Even though the cliffs shield this old tree from the unceasing wind, it is still very cold here.

I have not slept well, and I shiver uncontrollably. The barking of the seals on Rocky Point often awakens me, and I drift in and out of sleep. The cold has numbed my mind, so I cannot tell how long I have been here. I guess that one-half moon has passed. With each rising of the sun, I get weaker. I drink only a few handfuls of water each day, scooped from small pools of rainwater along the cliff. I was hungry for a while and ate herbs and grubs, but now, I eat no longer. My hunger has disappeared, and I grow more peaceful every day. Mother once said, "A starving person will not die hungry." She was right.

I begin to have almost constant visions now. One of them returns repeatedly: Mother stands in a great oceangoing canoe with a tall curved prow, larger than any other canoe I have ever seen. The sides are ornately decorated from bow to stern with intricate, colorfully painted carvings of the tribes' totem animals –

Figure 1-43. "From out of the mist of the spirit world, they come for Meera." *[Photograph by E.S. Curtis, ca. 1914. Courtesy of the Library of Congress.]*

Orca, Raven, Wolf, and Bear. I have never seen such beautiful work by human hands. The carvings seem almost to breathe and move with the rocking of the waves.

Mother calls out and signals for me to climb into the canoe. I am only slightly surprised when the Bear-carving speaks and tells me, "Come home with us to the Great Den, Meera. You will be warm there. You do not have to stay out in the cold anymore."

The Orca-carving says, "Yes-s-s-s, Meera, come with us. You will be free like an orca pod swimming in the open sea."

At the end of the vision, the sea mist closes in again around the great canoe. Except for a bluish glow in the mist, I can see them no longer, but I can hear them calling me still, as I wake up again to the harsh reality of a cold, aching body. I am sure now that I will not last one full turn of the seasons. I have no more fire in my heart to remain alive. This body is too old and worn out. It has given birth to a fine daughter and a son. I gave their spirits strength by teaching them the ways of our tribe and of the Great Spirit. Their lives are still ahead of them; mine is soon to be finished. Now this body is just an old wrinkled seed-husk, ready for the fire.

I drop into vision again, and Mother returns. With her is Sings-on-the-Wind! I am so happy to see her again at last. They float back to me through the mist, closer now than ever before.

"Are you finished here yet, Meera?" Sings-on-the-Wind asks softly, with her familiar smile.

"Why did you go away?" I ask her simply, without accusation. "I missed you."

"I never left you, Meera. In your confusion, you could not see me. But, now, it is over, and you have done very well," she says quietly.

"You have journeyed well and far," says the Wolf-carving on the canoe.

"You do not have to stay any longer," Sings-on-the-Wind declares.

The Raven-carving says, "You have passed a difficult test: you feel no sadness or bitterness. You can come home now, Meera. The Great Spirit is pleased with you." *[See inset.]*

The Orca-carving, also Mother's totem animal, says, "Come into the canoe, Meera. It is-s-s-s time. Come!"

And so I do.

With one last slow exhale, I step out of my seed-husk body and into the canoe. I feel a momentary twinge of regret at leaving it behind. I have lived in that body for forty winters, and it has served me well.

Off one side of the spirit canoe, a single great whale gracefully breaks the ocean surface. With a loud rushing sound, it blows a tall plume of misty breath high into the cool air. Its high-pitched call echoes out across the water, thrilling me deeply. Now, it arches over to dive back down into deep water, lifting its broad tail into the air as if to say "Good-bye."

> **Spiritual Test**
> If I had not passed this test and had held a grudge against my sentence of exile, I would have had to repeat this test in other lifetimes until I "got it right."
> Powerful negative emotions, such as despair, grief, fear, lust, anger, and pride, do not go away by themselves. Unless we resolve the feelings that come up in us, then in future lives, we will attract similar situations to the ones that caused them in the past. Under the law of karma, we will repeat them until we release them totally.

As the canoe moves further away, I turn back to watch my body for a moment, until the silver mist swirls around it, and we head out onto the Great Ocean. Satisfied, I give the body no more thought.

"Well done," smiles my Mother. Sings-on-the-Wind smiles, too, and nods.

The Orca smiles, "Yes-s-s-s, well done."

Relieved to be free, I nod slightly and smile, as we vanish into the mist.

Figure 1-44. "The great whale raises its tail as if in farewell." *[Photo courtesy of NOAA and the Department of Commerce.]*

Life Review & Analysis

GROUP-LINKS: In every lifetime, there are always many connections to other souls from our past lives. Becoming aware of those connections in each lifetime can help us to use our past life experiences to improve our present circumstances.

GROUP-LINK: "Save the Trees," The Environmentalist "Green" Connection

As I relived this lifetime, I became aware intuitively of a connection between the Makah tribe and some of those in the environmentalist movement. I realized that some of the people who try to save the old-growth forests in the Pacific Northwest are reincarnated Native Americans.

The coastal tribes existed for thousands of years along the Pacific with a strong tradition of preserving rather than destroying the abundant natural resources. Sadly, the current culture of the United States does not follow that path. Because of that, some of the Makah have come back to remind us that we would do better to cooperate with Nature rather than to exploit her.

Figure 1-45. The great coastal old-growth forests have stood for centuries. *[Photo courtesy of the Library of Congress.]*

Lessons Learned

Recalling a past lifetime is useful only if one uses the memories to become freer in the present lifetime. Reliving this lifetime as Meera brought up many powerful buried feelings:

- *Despair* over being "abandoned" by Sings-on-the-Wind, and despair over being banished to Seal Island.
- *Grief* over the death of Whale-Slayer, and grief over Meera's actions that led to the death of the village leader's son.
- *Fear* of earthquakes and tsunamis; fear of drowning; fear of starvation; and fear of being attacked by an orca or a shark.
- *Anger* at having to marry when Meera did not want to.

As I became aware of these feelings, I worked to undo them, using mostly the Sedona Method mentioned in "How to" Appendix A1. As I let go of all of these past highly charged memories, it was as if a heavy weight lifted from my mind. Even though those memories were far in the distant past, they still had been affecting me on a subconscious level. Undoing them has left me freer of unwanted emotions and freer to live in the present moment. Anyone can do the same thing with past life recall.

On the positive side, this lifetime brought more understanding into the present for the following:

- *Gender:* understanding the female point-of-view; giving birth and raising children; and understanding that spirit is more than being male or female.
- *Reverence for nature:* learning a deep respect for the natural world and for the cycles of the sun, moon, and seasons.
- *Healing:* gaining a deep knowledge of the gift of healing.
- *Intuition:* learning to listen to Spirit.
- *Transcending death:* experiencing a fully conscious death process, in which Meera crossed over consciously.

NOTE: Appendix A contains information about some simple yet very powerful spiritual techniques. They can free you from the undesirable effects of past lives and allow you to get the best out of your current life.

Alive 5 times

John Hogans: Fighting the Un-Civil War (1831 – 1865)

Background

Christened John Archibald Hogans, he was born in 1831 in Ware County, Georgia, west of Brunswick near the Okefenokee Swamp.

As one of the root problems that led to the Civil War, slavery was common in the South, but John's father, Archibald Hogans, refused to own slaves, although his neighbors did. He treated his colored workers with respect and paid them well for their work. Because of that, they respected him and felt a strong loyalty to his family. John's story begins on the family's farm when John was seven ...

Figure 2-1. Engraving of Confederate Gen. Robert E. Lee, the man who was Hogans' commander-in-chief. *[Reprinted from Jones (1875).]*

Summer 1838; Ware County, Georgia

Figure 2-2. At age seven, John Hogans would have looked something like this southern boy, photographed ca. 1860. *[Courtesy of the Library of Congress.]*

Daddy's sick and needs help getting in the cotton this year. I'm too young to help much – same with my brothers – so Daddy's hired a man named Mr. Tubbs to oversee the work. He's supervising our colored field hands.

Sitting on the porch swing, Clarice and I are snapping string beans for supper, watching the men work out in the field. Her calloused black hands move fast and sure, filling the bowl up with fresh green snap beans. I'm helping her. Well, actually, she's doing most of the snapping and I'm mostly snacking. When they're fresh-picked, snap beans are the best. They're real sweet and crunchy. Don't like 'em so much when they're cooked. *[See inset.]*

> **Flash Forward**
> Clarice was John's colored nanny in 1838. In meditation and as confirmed by Reflection (2002), I recognized that the same soul had incarnated as Clara in my present lifetime. She was again my nanny as I grew up in the rural South. Her strong common sense and warm worldly wisdom played a major role in shaping my early beliefs.
> Among other things, she taught me a ready acceptance of African-Americans who were still subjected to considerable discrimination in the South during the 1940s and 1950s.

"Johnny boy, you're gonna ruin your supper for sure. And then what's your Momma gonna say?" Clarice scolds me a little, though I don't pay no attention. She's good-natured, and we get along real well. I can ask or talk to her about most anything. Fact is, I spend more time with her than with Momma,

Figure 2-3. "Mr. Tubbs is helping Daddy out with the field work." *[Ca. 1860. Courtesy of the Library of Congress.]*

seeing as how she's always busy making and mending clothes for other people. She has to. With eight kids, she says she worries about having enough corn bread and clothes to go around.

Suddenly, we hear a ruckus from the fields. Mr. Tubbs is having a fit. Throwing his beat-up ol' felt hat on the ground, he screams at Jedediah, "You damned, useless, black S.O.B.! What the Hell's the matter with you? Ain't you got no sense?" Now he snaps a branch off a cotton plant and starts whipping Jed. The whip cuts long rips across the front of Jed's brown shirt, staining it red with blood.

Clarice stands up real fast, looking worried. Jed's her husband. I stand up, too, to see better. Jed don't wince or draw back or cower. He don't say nothing. He just takes it like a man. Mr. Tubbs cools off after a bit and stops, cursing Jed one more time, before walking off. With a pained look on her face, Clarice quietly sits back down.

Shocked and upset, I ask, "Why'd that man go and do that to Jed?" He's my friend, just like Clarice.

Without looking up, Clarice says softly, "Mr. Tubbs don't like dark people."

"You mean just *'cause* Jed's dark?"

She nods her head, and I have to think about that one for a minute. "Does he hate dark horses and whip 'em, too."

"No, he don't," is all she'll say.

Now, I'm *real* confused. "Clarice, I just don't get it. That don't make no sense at all. Not one bit."

Clarice stops shelling and looks at me real direct for a moment. Now, she says gently, "Johnny, the way I see it, the Good Lord likes color in this world. After all, He made horses, dogs, and birds in all kinds of colors. I believe the Good Lord did the same with people, making 'em in lotsa colors, too. The way I figure it, He just likes things that way."

She goes back to snapping more beans. I know she ain't finished, so I keep quiet. Looking up from the bowl of beans, she continues, "Now, the Good Book says the Lord made man in His image, but it don't say nothing about that meaning only the whites. The way I read it, the Lord made all men in His image – black people, too."

She stops snapping and looks me right in the eye, "Some men, like Mr. Tubbs, just can't see it. That's all." Now she starts snapping again, real fast.

I puzzle over that for a minute and say, "How come? 'Cause his eyes are bad like Grampa's?"

She gives out a long chuckle, "Now, wouldn't that be the berries, Johnny. Why, we could just go and get glasses for people like Mr. Tubbs."

I finally got it figured out, so I say to Clarice, "I'll be back in a minute." Jumping off the swing, I head off to find Daddy.

Opening the screen door, I head up to his bedroom. He's there lying on his bed with his clothes on, with a wet towel over his eyes. His shirt is drenched with sweat, and he's looking kinda pale. "Daddy, I'm real sorry to barge in. I know you ain't feeling good, but we gotta talk. There's a big problem."

Raising a corner of the towel, Daddy turns his head towards me. He's looking weak and shaky. "What's the deal, son?"

"It's Mr. Tubbs. We gotta get him to the doctor right away."

Laying the towel aside, Daddy sits up, looking real concerned. "What happened to Tubbs?"

"Well, he was out there just now beating on Jed, 'cause he needs glasses, and I don't think it's right. We ought to go to the doctor and get some glasses for him, before he starts beating on Jed again," I say indignantly.

Looking real puzzled, Daddy asks, "What in the world are you talking about, son?"

I figure Daddy must be a little addled today, what with being sick, so I take it real slow, one thing at a time, "Mr. Tubbs was beating on Jed out in the field...." I pause to make sure he's following. "He got Jed all bloody...." I stop again to make sure he gets this part, too. "And it's 'cause –"

Daddy holds up his hand to stop me. "Whoa! Hold it right there, son. That's all I need to know."

With that, he yanks on his boots and stomps down the stairs, yelling for Momma. Shoving open the screen door and almost knocking it off its hinges, Daddy heads straight for Tubbs. Now comes the loudest yelling, cursing, stomping, and shouting that I ever heard. And it's all coming from Daddy! Tubbs ain't saying nothing. He's staring at his boots, looking real sheepish. His big, floppy hat blocks his face so he don't have to look eye-to-eye with Daddy.

At the end, Daddy tells Tubbs, "I'll not tolerate you insulting Jedediah like that. You get off my farm, and if you ever come back, I'll kick your tail all the way to the next county!"

With that, Tubbs sets off down the road. I'm guessing that's the last we'll see of him. Daddy's a real big man, and he's not somebody to be trifled with. By now, Momma is out with Jed cleaning off the blood. Talking real soft, she takes his arm and walks him back to the house for some close attention to his cuts.

Daddy walks back up to Clarice and me on the porch. He's not mad no more, and he's got a faint smile on his face. "Maybe, Tubbs'll think twice before he does that again."

He kneels down in front of me and puts a big hand on my shoulder. Daddy's a good-hearted big bear of a man. He's got a big shock of white hair, a long curvy moustache, and bushy eyebrows. Makes him look real dignified. "Son, you did real good," he says. "Let this be something to remember the rest of your life. No matter what Tubbs and others like him may think, every man and every woman deserves respect 'til they prove unworthy – no matter what the color of their skin.

"Jed and Clarice and the other colored folks here on the farm are fine people and deserve to be treated that way. On the other hand, Tubbs deserves to be treated just like he was. If a man's full of poison and prejudice, he's not welcome at our house. You understand?"

I nod solemnly, and he pats me on the shoulder. As he walks back in the house, Clarice smiles at me and nods her head. I can tell she's proud of me. Though I'm not exactly sure why. I was just doing what was right by Jed.

"Why don't you come over here, Johnny, and have a few more of these snap beans?" she asks, so I do.

Figure 2-4. "There's lots to do this year, but me and my brothers ain't much help." *[Ca. 1860. Courtesy of the Library of Congress.]*

Plowshares into Swords

John grew up intending to become a Georgia farmer just like his father. With that in mind, he bought a small house and a farm in Ware County, Georgia, and began courting Rosetta Johns, a lovely, lively, local girl, who loved to dance. John, certain that she was the prettiest girl in Georgia, called her his "Georgia Rose." They were married in 1853, when John was 22.

Gradually, rumors of war reached rural Georgia. Slavery was not an issue for some of them, certainly not for John, who refused to practice it. The main issue for most Georgians was States' Rights versus Federal Rights. Inspired by loyalty to their state, most people were excited about showing those "rascals in Washington" that they couldn't push Georgia boys around. So, on April 22, 1861, when John was about 30 years old, after reassuring Rose that he would not be gone long, he joined many of his friends and relatives by enlisting in the Confederate Army's Georgia Infantry.

Our story continues nearly four years later with Lt. John Hogans and his unit engaged in rearguard skirmishing with the Union troops a few miles northwest of Farmville, Virginia ...

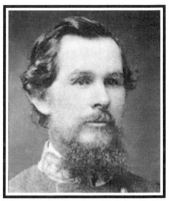

Figure 2-5. In 1861, John Hogans looked a lot like this. *[Courtesy US Army Center for Military History.]*

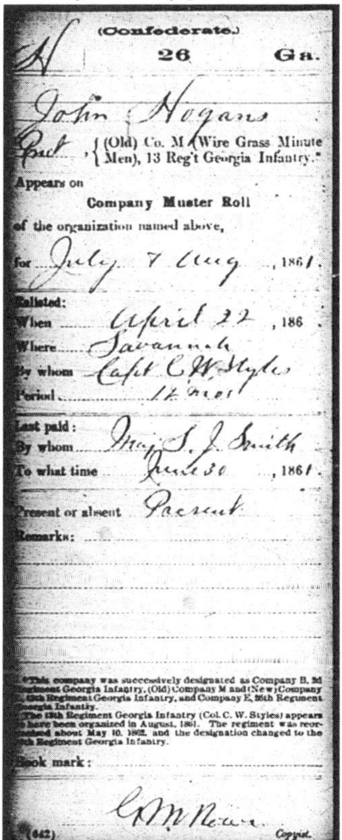

H (Confederate.)
26 Ga.

John Hogans
Pvt., (Old) Co. M (Wire Grass Minute Men), 13 Reg't Georgia Infantry.*

Appears on
Company Muster Roll
of the organization named above,
for July & Aug, 1861.

Enlisted:
When April 22, 186
Where Savannah
By whom Capt C. W. Styles
Period 12 mos

Last paid:
By whom Maj S. J. Smith
To what time June 30, 1861.

Present or absent Present

Remarks:

*This company was successively designated as Company B, 2d Regiment Georgia Infantry, (Old) Company M and (New) Company E, 13th Regiment Georgia Infantry, and Company E, 26th Regiment Georgia Infantry.
The 13th Regiment Georgia Infantry (Col. C. W. Styles) appears to have been organized in August, 1861. The regiment was reorganized about May 10, 1862, and the designation changed to the 26th Regiment Georgia Infantry.

Book mark:

G. W. Nean
(642) Copyist.

Figure 2-6. John Hogans' enlistment in the 26th Georgia Regiment. *[Courtesy of the National Archives.]*

April 7, 1865; Farmville

As the roaring of the cannons stops, the musket-fire quiets down a bit, too. It's only sporadic now. The blue-gray clouds of gunpowder smoke start to drift off the battlefield. I've grown to hate the smell of that damned stuff, since it only means that bad things are happening. We all breathe a sigh of relief now, 'cause it looks like the Yankees are giving up for awhile.

Across the field by the church, they're running back to their lines for the second time this afternoon. We fire a few more bullets after 'em – kind of a "going-away present." The Yanks've put up only a token fight, pestering and poking at us, and we held 'em – for now.

Our guys burned the bridges at Farmville and the railroad crossing three miles to the northeast at High Bridge, but they didn't manage to burn the wagon crossing. After putting up a good fight, Gen. Lee and our guys had to back off. That let the Yanks cross the Appomattox right behind us. Now, some of us're dug in on the high ground beyond Farmville, trying to slow the Yanks down some more, while the rest of the troops hightail it off to the west. The Yanks've been chasing us since Petersburg, and the going's been rough. They're hitting us hard again today, and we've been at it all afternoon.

A few bluecoats lay dead in the field by the church. Too bad a man has to get shot up so near a church. Just seems a shame somehow, not that there's ever any real good place to get shot up.

Gideon complains, "Them damn Yankees just never stop dogging us. Whatta they think, lieutenant, that a man can fight all day and march all night?" He looks real peeved about it all. "Don't they *never* need no sleep?"

Figures 2-7 & 2-8. War's end saw Gen. Grant and Gen. Lee leading opposing armies against each other in Virginia. *[Grant photo courtesy of the Library of Congress. Lee engraving reprinted from Jones (1875).]*

Having a Picnic at Bull Run

When the Civil War started, many people in both the North and South thought the war would be over after a few weeks or months at most. In the First Battle of Bull Run, civilians from Washington brought picnic baskets out to the battle to "watch the fun." All that "fun" would become the bloodiest war ever fought by Americans. The spiritual wounds have not healed even today, 150 years later.

After years of bloody battles, the final campaign of the war began in March 1865, when Gen. Robert E. Lee failed to break Gen. Ulysses S. Grant's stranglehold on Petersburg, Virginia. Forced to withdraw, Lee retreated west through the heartland of Virginia toward Appomattox along the stage-road to Lynchburg. Over the span of seven days, Gen. Lee and his haggard soldiers fought a nearly continuous series of running battles with the superior Union forces, including the Battle of Sailors Creek, Virginia, on April 6, 1865. During that battle alone, nearly one-quarter of the Confederate Army was killed or captured. [See map, Figure 2-9.]

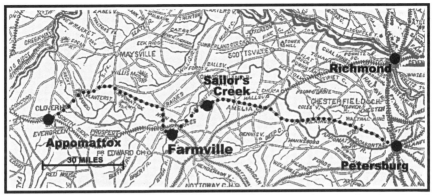

Figure 2-9. Adaptation of an 1862 map of Virginia, showing Lee's retreat from Petersburg to Appomattox. *[Courtesy of the Library of Congress.]*

Figure 2-10. "We send some 'going-away' presents after the Yanks." *[Courtesy of the Appomattox Court House National Historical Park.]*

Figure 2-11. High Bridge over the Appomattox; partially destroyed during the retreat. *[ca. 1863. Courtesy of the Library of Congress.]*

Shaking my head wearily, I respond, "Doesn't seem like it. They're tough." He doesn't say anything. Gideon isn't feeling real charitable towards the Yanks today.

"Speaking of needing sleep," I continue, "I'm gonna get me some. Now you or Ervin wake me up if any Yank 'visitors' drop by. And if none of 'em do, just leave me sleep 'til this old war's over, 'cause I'm real tired. Okay?"

"Oh, don't you worry none about that, lieutenant."

Seems like I haven't slept in a month, so with my rifle beside me, I bend down and crawl into a space under one of the fallen trees in the breastworks. Tipping my cap down over my face, I no more than shut my eyes good, when I hear a blood-boiling scream!

I sit bolt upright so hard I bang my head against the tree trunk overhead. "What the hell?" I sputter, rubbing my head. It suddenly dawns on me: "Spivey!"

Gritting my teeth and mad as a hornet, I squirm out from under the log looking for Spivey. He's staring over the logs at the Yanks. "Damnation, Spivey! Next time, you mind waking me the hell up before you give that damned yell of yours?" *[See inset.]*

"Real sorry, lieutenant," he says sheepishly. In spite of that yell of his, I always loved Ervin like another brother. With those big bushy mutton-chop whiskers and red cheeks, he looks like some kinda leprechaun. A real *big* leprechaun! Now if we could just swap that old Confederate cap for one of those flower-pot-style leprechaun hats,

> **The Boys from Georgia**
> Murray (1976) says that, in 1861, John Hogans enlisted as a private in Co. E of the 26th Georgia Infantry Regt. He was promoted to lieutenant in 1863.
> Pvt. Gideon Hays joined Co. E of the 26th Georgia on the same day that John did.
> Cpl. James Ervin Spivey enlisted as a private on the same day that Gideon and John did. He was appointed corporal in 1862. His fellow soldiers all called him 'Ervin' when he was behaving himself, or '*SPIVEY!*' along with other 'colorful' words, when he wasn't. He was a *real* one-of-a-kind character!

Figure 2-12. "The boys are taking it easy during a lull in the fighting." *[ca. 1863. Courtesy of the Library of Congress.]*

Figure 2-13. "The Yanks toss over a couple of cannonballs just to wake us up." *[ca. 1865. Courtesy of the Library of Congress.]*

then he'd be fit to fiddle. Looking real apologetic, he says, "I thought the Yanks was coming after us again."

Just as he finishes saying that, a Union cannon roars. Before we can duck behind the logs, the 6-pound shell whistles in over us. It smashes clean through the trunk of a small blackjack oak right behind us before the shell explodes, knocking us off our feet.

As a shower of dirt, bark, and splinters rains down around us, the tree tilts over in slow motion and falls towards us. Six of us scramble under cover of the log-breastworks, just as the crown of the tree crashes on top of us. Leaves, branches, bark, and dust fly everywhere.

After it all settles down, I stick my head up through a bunch of leaf-covered branches, spitting bits of leaves and dirt out of my mouth. Looking around for Spivey, I'm still feeling mad but beginning to see the lighter side of this, too. "Now, you see what you did, Spivey? You just had to go and yell, didn't you? The racket scared the piss out of those Yanks, and they fired that damn cannon out of sheer panic! Figured a whole herd of bulls and panthers was after 'em."

The other guys hoot and laugh, and I manage a smile, too. Spivey's rebel yell is famous on both sides of this old war. **[See inset.]**

"Take a look see, boys," I say, pointing towards the Union line. "Thanks to Ervin, those Yanks are really running now. They'll probably still be running by the time they hit the outskirts of Washington."

Ervin sports a real big grin: "That's what I was a-counting on, sir."

> **Ervin Spivey: "Gordon's Bull"**
> Pvt. G. W. Nichols, an "earwitness" said, "Ervin could yell the queerest that I ever heard. It was a kind of a scream … like a terrible bull, with a kind of neigh mixed along with it, and it was nearly as loud as a steam whistle…. The Yankees called him 'Gordon's Bull.' He would always halloo this way when we charged the enemy, and we were informed that the Yankees understood it as a signal for them to move back." *(From Nichols (1961).)*

Later that Night at Cumberland Church

The fighting's over for today. It's a balmy night, and the woods are dark and pretty quiet, though I can hear a little bit of the clanking and shuffling of camp activity all around us. With the moon nearly full, its strong light breaks through the trees here and there, making bright patches on the ground. I'm sitting down, leaning back on the log-works, and staring at the crackling fire, mostly 'cause there's nothing else to do. There's something soothing about hearing the wood crackle and snap as it burns – and it's real nice smelling the rich aroma of burning pine and oak logs. Sure beats the hell out of the smell of blood and gunpowder. There's no breeze to speak of, so the smoke's going straight up through the branches, carrying little dancing sparks with it. The fire's throwing long skinny shadows of Gideon, me, and Ervin far out into the woods.

Gideon's across the fire from me, cooking up a little supper. He's younger than me, but he's got a face that's thin and wrinkled like leather, so he looks about twice as old. This war hasn't been easy on any of us, especially the last year or so. Like all of us, he's tired of it, but just like all of us, too, he doesn't talk much about it. He's got a couple of small strips of some kinda meat stuck on his bayonet, roasting 'em over the fire. I'm not even gonna ask him what it is he's cooking. When he's finished charring the strips, he swings his bayonet over and offers me some. "Much obliged, Gideon, but you boys go ahead," I say, trying to act real charitable. I'm not telling him so, but looking at that charred meat, I'd rather go hungry tonight.

Munching on a piece of meat, Gideon tries some small talk: "Those Yanks still out there, lieutenant?"

I raise up a bit to look over the top log. I make out the Union campfires about a rifle shot away strung out through the woods, and I can see 'em moving around and sitting beside the fires. I bring up my old long-barreled rifle and put my eye to the sniper sight. I have a good view of one of the Yanks squatting by the fire, stirring a pot of something. Watching that Yank cooking makes my stomach flip-flop a little. Other than Gideon's mystery meat, it's been a while since we had any good, hot food.

I got that Yank right in my sights. I could squeeze off the trigger, drop him where he squats, and he'd never know what hit him … but I don't. Everybody's got a right to kick back a little, even the boys on the other side. But when they blow that bugle to sound the charge, well, then, all bets are off. I lower my rifle and flop back down. "Yep, too damn many," I say wearily.

The Yanks have been hot on our heels, and we've been fighting steady as we retreat west. The fighting wasn't too rough today, but it still takes a lot out of you. I take a stick and poke at the fire 'til the flames leap up again. "Well, boys, we slowed 'em down a bit today, but from the looks of things, it doesn't

Figure 2-14. Civil War black-powder musket. "I could drop him in his tracks if I had a mind to." *[ca. 1861. Courtesy of the Library of Congress.]*

seem to do much good. They just keep sending in a fresh wave of young 'uns to chase us harder."

"I was hoping we'd get to Lynchburg by tomorrow or day after," Ervin complains. "I'm ready for some more bacon and hot biscuits and gravy and maybe a pint or two to warm up the belly." Instead, we're bedded down in thick brush not far out of Farmville.

The rest of Gen. Lee's men are ahead of us off to the southwest, marching through the night. We'll be moving out and joining 'em soon, leaving the fires burning to fool the Yanks. By morning, all they'll find will be burned-out ashes. We'll be long gone, trying to make it to Lynchburg ahead of 'em.

I take out my pistol and start to clean it. Got no more gun oil, so I grab a rag and rub all the dust off, real careful-like. This old Navy Colt has seen me through a lot of tight spots, from the fields of Manassas to Fredericksburg, and Gettysburg to Petersburg. None of it's been easy. And my Colt's about as nicked up as I am. It's got six bullets in it, and by the end of this war, at the rate I'm going, the Yanks will have put at least the same number in me. *[See inset.]*

> **Flash Forward**
> As a teenager, my brother bought an old Navy Colt that had been found on a Civil War battlefield. As I held that pistol for the first time, I felt an eerie sense of déjà vu, though at the time, I didn't know why.
>
> Later, as I meditated, I recalled vivid memories of this lifetime and of using a pistol just like it.

These days I'm getting more and more sick of fighting. Been dreaming a lot about going home. I mean, I love these men like brothers, I do, but I'm tired of seeing 'em shot down one after another. And then there's the womenfolk. Even brothers like this don't make a man forget about the womenfolk. Fighting's just too damn hard. I'm ready to give it a rest.

Figure 2-15. "There's about as much lead in me as in my ol' pistol." *[ca. 1861. Courtesy of the Library of Congress.]*

As I slide my pistol back in the holster, I picture my pretty little Rose. I wonder if she's changed much; it's been two years now since I saw her last. I think a lot about her, and I try to write. Just seems like the fighting gets in the way most of the time. Besides, I'm not too handy with words. I hope she understands. It isn't that I don't care, 'cause I do, and I miss her more than I can say. Sometimes it just hurts too much to put what I feel down on paper.

Lately, as the fighting's gotten heavier, I think about her more often. Opening up my war-bag, I slip out a yellowed, wrinkled sheet of paper, and start to scribble:

My dearest Georgia Rose,

Never an hour goes by that I don't miss you more than I can say. In spite of my lack of fancy words, I decided to write to you. To tell it true, I would rather be back in Georgia by your side, but an unkind fate has got me bogged down here in the rolling hills of Virginia.

*These are sad days for the Grand Army of the Confederacy, and I fear that we shall not be able to hold out much longer. We are all tired and hungry, and I am distraught to see so many brave men sacrificed to the God of War. Around the campfires, the boys sing of the noble pursuit of war, but daily, I am painfully reminded that the truth is otherwise. We have both lost loved ones in battle, your family and mine. So where is the glory in a cold tombstone standing on an empty battlefield? [**See inset.**]*

> **Family Casualties**
>
> On Rosetta's side, Cpl. William F. Johns was killed in battle at Drewry's Bluff, VA, in 1864. He was in John's regiment in Co. G.
>
> On the Hogans side, Pvt. James Hogans enlisted in 1861, on the same day in the same company as William. He got sick and died in a Staunton, VA, hospital in 1862. According to MyTrees.com (2002), James was John's eldest brother. He was 35 years old when he died.
>
> Ironically, many more Civil War soldiers died from disease than from combat wounds *(Murray (1976))*.

I miss you terribly, my dearest, and constantly dream of being back with you soon. Until I once again enjoy your warm smile and gentle touch, I remain

Your devoted husband,

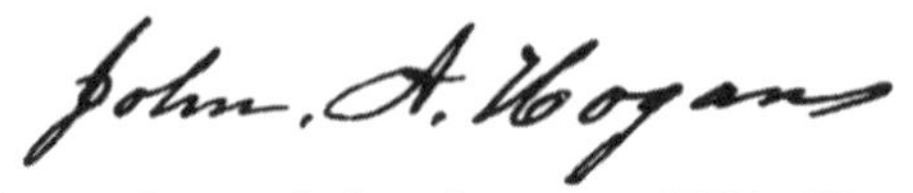

John. A. Hogans

Figure 2-16. Copy of John Hogans' actual signature, ca. 1864. *[Courtesy of the National Archives.]*

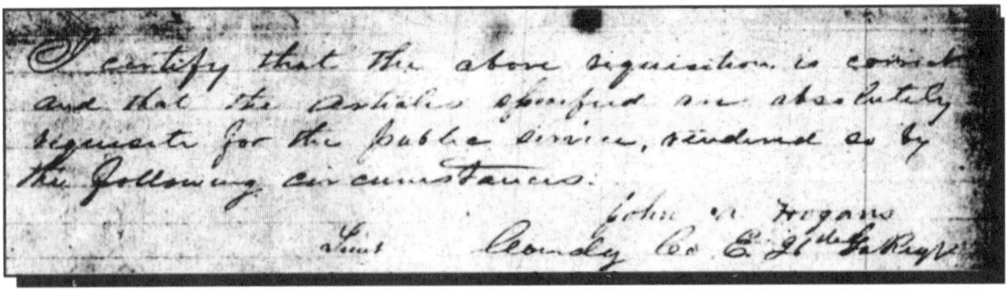

Figure 2-17. Copy of an actual 1864 army field report in John's handwriting. *[Courtesy of the National Archives.]*

With Rose in mind, I turn and look over at Ervin. He reminds me of Rose's kinfolk, William, who was killed last year. Ervin, like William, has got more guts and less sense than any ten men I ever knew. Keeping him in line has been a real "hat full." But when thing's get tough, I wouldn't want anybody else going in shoulder to shoulder with me. He's just plum fearless.

"Ervin," I call out. "How about warming up that harmonica of yours? We could all use a tune or two."

Figure 2-18 & 2-19. These photos remind me of the "boys." *[ca. 1862. Courtesy of the Library of Congress.]*

The firelight catches Ervin's tanned, red leprechaun face, and he flashes a big grin. Swinging around to grab his war-bag and rummaging a minute, he pulls out his harmonica. He's not Irish, but he knows just how to make a man feel glad: give him some music that'll make his feet start tapping. Putting it to his mouth, he begins with a good Irish round of "Bonnie Blue Flag:"

We are a band of brothers
  And native to the soil,
Fighting for the property
  We gained by honest toil;
And when our rights were threatened,
  The cry rose near and far
"Hurrah for the Bonnie Blue Flag
  That bears a single star!"

He does his best to lift our spirits, but nobody's joining in except me. So after one time through, Ervin switches over to "Johnny Comes Marching Home." *[See inset.]*

It was an old Irish melody, they say, but somebody went and wrote some new "marching" words for it, so I start out with 'em:

> **Flash Forward**
> In my current lifetime, as I sat with a construction crew, one of the men took out his harmonica and began to play "Johnny Comes Marching Home." Suddenly, I had a waking vision: superimposed over them, I saw the faint luminous images of my former Confederate comrades.

When Johnny Comes Marching Home Again, Hurrah! Hurrah!
We'll give him a hearty welcome then, Hurrah! Hurrah!
The men will cheer and the boys will shout
The ladies they will all turn out ...

I break off in the middle, seeing as how I'm the only one singing this one, too. That song just doesn't fit the mood tonight. I shift over to the old Irish words instead. The words are kinda sad, and they don't make war seem so proud. That seems to fit our mood better. After days of fighting and killing and struggling to stay alive, well Hell, sometimes, you just got to go and let yourself get sad. After a minute, a couple of men join in, too:

Where are your legs that used to run, hurroo, hurroo
Where are your legs that used to run, hurroo, hurroo
Where are your legs that used to run
When you went for to carry a gun
Indeed your dancing days are done
Oh Johnny, I hardly knew ye.

They're rolling out the guns again, hurroo, hurroo
They're rolling out the guns again, hurroo, hurroo

They're rolling out the guns again
But they never will take our sons again
No they never will take our sons again
Johnny I'm swearing to ye.

They continue on singing, but I fade off halfhearted, thinking again about Rose. My eyes start to mist up a little, what with me being out here and her being back home.

Now suddenly, we all hear a faint voice from the dark, "Hey, Rebs! Halloo! Can you be hearing me?" Whoever it is has an Irish lilt to his voice.

Startled, Ervin stops playing, and we grab our guns. The boys, crouching low and scuttling like crabs, join me along the log-works. Cautious, I poke my head up over the logs again and look over at the Union lines, raising my voice, "That you calling, Yank?"

"None other! Who you be expecting, Rebs, the Little People?" says the faint voice in the dark. Loosening our trigger fingers, me and Ervin trade relieved smiles with each other.

"Well now, Yank, shouldn't you be sleeping? Especially after that butt-whupping we gave you today," I call back. My guys let out a couple of chuckles.

"Naw, Reb, me ol' butt's just fine, it is, and I'm pulling picket duty, you see, or I would be a-sleeping. Glad I'm not, though, 'cause those lovely Irish tunes keep a-drifting me way. Name's Kelly, you see, and it sounds real sweet to these Irish ears of mine. Was wondering if you could be a-playing a wee bit louder, though. Having trouble hearing it over here."

We all laugh, and Ervin calls back to him, "What happened, Irish, you get lost? You've done wandered over to the wrong side of the war."

Kelly calls back, "Naw, I just looked around for the side that was warming the biggest kettle of bacon and beans."

Gideon jumps in, "On the other hand, maybe Kelly's eyesight's gone bad. You know – can't tell a blue uniform from a gray one no more. Well, don't you worry, Kelly boy; we got a spare gray one over here for you. Come on over; we'll help you put it on." We all laugh, and Kelly joins in, too. *[See inset.]*

Kelly calls back, "Truth be told, Rebs, right now I'm not too fond of any ol' uniform, beggin' me cap'n's pardon. Right now, I'd love just to be back in the ol' country with me ol' set of clothes."

> **Friendly Discussions**
> It was common for soldiers on both sides to exchange friendly conversations after battle.
> Sometimes, they would meet in the neutral zone between lines to play cards or to exchange tobacco, coffee, food, news, and other items *(Murray (1976))*.

"I know that feeling well, Irish, even though I was born here. How long you been over here?" I ask him.

"Oh, let's see now," he says. "You kinda lose track with bullets a-whizzin' over your head. Seems like I docked in grand ol' New York City a bit over two years ago."

"So how the heck you wind up lost in the woods of Virginia?" Gideon asks him.

"Well, Reb, let me think … Mmmm … Well, I steps off that big ol' ship, and a man with a big hat and a big badge comes up and says, 'Son, so you wanna be an American?'

"And I says, 'That I do.'

"And now he says, 'Well, all right, now you are one. And so, do you love your new country?'

"And I says, 'That I do.'

"So he steps closer and says, 'That's good. Here's your gun, so now go hunt some Rebs.' Took me a while to catch on though, 'cause, you see, I'd never heard that term 'Rebs' before – thought maybe they must be squirrels or something."

There's a hoot or two from the boys. "Biggest, meanest squirrels you ever seen, right, Irish?" Ervin shoots back. "These here 'squirrels' know how to crack some nuts." That brings even louder hoots.

Gideon adds, "Knowing what you know now, Irish, maybe you shoulda jumped ship and swum back to Ireland as fast as you could dog-paddle."

"Ay, woulda done it, Reb, 'ceptin' I can't swim."

"Well, Kelly boy," I say, "seeing as how you're a good Irish laddy, we'll try to give you a break tomorrow when the shooting starts. But you better be wearing an Irish-green neckerchief or something, so we'll know who you are."

"Otherwise," Gideon adds, "we might just accidentally shoot some holes in your Union butt."

"Naw, Reb, won't be a-needing no hankies. You'll know the sight of me just fine; I'll be the only Yank yelling like a true Irish banshee. But, Reb, I gotta ask you: Do you be any good at shooting? 'Cause, you see – and I'm not exactly a-bragging here – I've gotten real good at zigzagging. I could be a wee bit hard to hit."

"Well, Irish, as far as the shooting goes, let me tell it to you true," I say. "I know you don't have any of those fine Virginia smokes over there, but you likely got some of that gawd-awful Turkeyish tobaccy. Right?"

"Ay, that I do," he replies, "though I'm at a loss to see where this is a-going."

"Hold your horses, Irish. I'm getting there," I continue. "Why don't you just roll up a ciggyrette with some of that mule-dung tobaccy of yours. Then light it up and hold that old still-lit match out to your side. Then, I'll do you a favor and snuff it out … with just one bullet."

There's loud laughter and hoots all around. Kelly laughs and says, "Gonna be passing on that one, Reb. There's already been too many bullets a-whizzin' past me head for one day," he says. "But I gotta hand it to you, Reb. You can tell a tale as tall as me ol' gran'pappy could. It's a treat to hear a bit o' the blarney now and again. Tis a sad day when men like us gotta be on opposite sides of any ol' war. It just ain't proper."

I call back, "Right you be, Irish. A sad day, indeed."

He calls back, "Wish I coulda known you all better, but well, time to be going. Gotta get some rest – looking like I'll be doing some serious zigzagging tomorrow. So it's a 'Fare thee well' to all of you."

I call back one last time, "You too, Irish. Just like 'Johnny' in that old ditty – 'we hardly knew ye' – just a Yank voice out of the dark. But may the Good Lord be with you, and here's hoping you get back in one piece to wherever you call home."

I hear a couple of the boys add, "Amen."

After about half an hour, when most of the boys are already asleep, I decide to roll in, too. Closing my eyes for about a minute or two, I'm still thinking about old Irish, when all of a sudden, I'm standing about fifty paces in front of my home in Georgia, looking right up onto the porch! A soft golden light shows out through the windows from a couple of candles and lanterns. It's a full moon, and a chorus of crickets is singing in the woods. Dozens of fireflies are winking off and on around the house.

My heart goes to beating a little faster, and I'm thinking to myself, *Well, I'll be danged. This's gotta be a dream. I mean, it can't be real – but it's kinda spooky, 'cause it sure does look real.*

The moon is so bright that the house and the woods are lit up real well. In the clear bright light, I can just make out that familiar red Georgia clay. Growing up, we used to joke that when a Georgia man gets cut, you never see any blood. Instead, that old red clay just oozes out. I'd recognize the sight and smell of that stuff anywhere!

Off to the right side of the house, I see those two old pecan trees. One of 'em, I planted myself, and the other one was already here. Behind 'em, just beyond the clearing for the house, there's that stand of white pines and, here and there, an old gnarled oak or two.

The house is looking a little seedy, but I suppose that's only natural. Hasn't been a man around for a good while, making it hard for Rose to keep up with things like that. The whitewash is peeling off the boards, and a few of 'em are warped and pried up away from the others. Can't be too good for Rose when the wind gets to whipping through there. You'd have to really burrow

Figure 2-20. "Paint's kinda peeling off the house here and there, but it still feels like home." *[ca. 1862. Courtesy of the Library of Congress.]*

down under the quilts at night to keep warm. Easier to do when you got a man laying next to you, but when he's off fighting some damn-fool war, well, I guess a girl's just gotta make a few more quilts.

Off around the left corner, I see the garden, and boy, does it look good. Corn's about waist high. Got a few tomatoes coming in, and all the other stuff's growing green, too. Makes my mouth start to water. Can't tell you how long it's been since I ate anything in the Army that was green, leastways anything that was *supposed* to be green.

I got a ways to go to get up on the porch, so I decide to get moving. Now, all of a sudden, in a flash, I'm *on* the porch. Now, that sets me back a little, and kinda points out that what's going on here isn't quite normal. I just *thought* it, and like a flash, here I am, simple as that. Yep, *gotta* be a dream or something.

I start to move towards the door, when I hear a scratching noise come from under the left side of the porch. Before long, up pops the head of old Ben, my old flop-eared hunting hound. Ben hops up on the porch, looking around like somebody rang the dinner bell, and now he freezes, staring right at me with his ears on full alert. All of a sudden, tucking his tail and backing up real slow, he goes to growling and showing his teeth, and now, the hair on his back starts to stand up.

I call out real friendly, "Ben! Hey, Ben. It's me, John. Johnny-boy. Don't know how I got here, but I'm back home." I kneel down and start to pat the porch to call him over to me. Ben's reaction is like he just got struck by lightning. He lets out a big yelp and dives back under the porch so fast all I see is fur and four flying feet. Now, from under the porch I hear such a whimpering that I'm pretty sure he isn't coming out any time soon.

Figure 2-21. "Ol' Ben takes one look at me and thinks he's seen a ghost!" *[Courtesy of the Library of Congress.]*

Well, I gotta shrug my shoulders about old Ben, but I'm not waiting to figure this one out. I'm ready to go find Rose, so I go up to the screen door. I figure I don't want to surprise her too much like old Ben, so I decide to knock once or twice. "Rose!" I call out as I rap on the wood frame of the screen door, except the rapping doesn't work – my knuckles keep knocking but there's no sound. Dead quiet. *Damn!* I think, *Now, that's not normal either. Chalk one up for this being a dream.*

Dream or not, I'm real eager to see Rose, so I figure maybe I'll just do it the way I did getting over to the porch. Concentrating a little bit, I just 'think' about being inside the house, and 'bang,' in a flash here I am – inside! And there's Rose with her back to me!

"Rose! Rose, it's me, Johnny," I call out, but she doesn't seem to hear me. My heart jumps a little at seeing her, and my throat gets tighter. It's been a couple years since I saw her last, but see looks about the same, leastways from the back – trim and slender as ever.

Looking at our old black cast iron stove, she bends down to pop another split oak log into the oven's firebox. Balancing the log on one end, she unlatches the oven door with a poker and slides the log in, letting a few sparks drift up toward the ceiling. The fire highlights her features and my heart flip-flops. The firelight glistens a little off the sweat on her cheeks, and even working, she's just as pretty as ever. Shutting the fire door, she stands up and wipes her hands with her apron. She seems tired and worried, but I'm thinking that'll all be over here in a minute. Nothing like having your man come home from the war to lift your spirits a little.

I'm enjoying my moment here watching her doing her cooking-thing, when I walk over a little closer. I get up behind her to catch the smell of her hair. Yep, it's still got that familiar faint scent of roses, her favorite perfume. I always loved that about her. When I used to come in from work and give her a big hug, her hair always smelled like roses. It made me feel real good again, no matter how tough things had been that day. My Rose "by any other name would still smell just as sweet."

Suddenly, she turns around, and before I can get completely out of the way, her left shoulder passes right through me! *Well, damn!* It kinda tickles and tingles. I gotta admit, I never felt anything like that before. I rub my shoulder a little with my hand 'til the tingling stops. Just can't quite figure out what's going on here. *How'd she walk through me like that?* Maybe all those cannon shells going off has addled my brain a bit.

Rose continues past me about two paces, when suddenly she stops cold in her tracks, just like she heard a gunshot! She's noticed something, but she can't figure it out. Slowly, with a light frown on her face, she pivots around on one foot, scanning the room with her eyes. Outside, old Ben barks a couple of times and starts whining and scratching at the door.

"Somebody there?" she calls out softly, looking worried. Her voice sends a thrill of joy up my back. She keeps swinging around 'til she's looking right at me. After pausing a split-second, she spins right back to where she started. She looked right *at* me and didn't see me! Not even a flicker or a hint that I'm right in front of her! *Well, double damn!*

Now this has gotta be a dream, or maybe I've died and got sidetracked going to Heaven, or that other place. Maybe, I'm just a ghost now, kicking around the house. Real puzzled, I don't have a clue what's going on. All I know is it doesn't seem like either Rose or Ben can see me very well. *[See inset.]*

Rose doesn't act

> **Out-of-body Experiences**
> Sleeping and dreaming are just out-of-body experiences that everyone shares. When we leave the body during sleep, we usually go into the astral worlds, journeys that we remember as dreams.
> However, we can also visit 'real' places and people on earth. This is what John did on this occasion. Longing so much to see Rose again, he actually traveled back to Georgia in spirit. Animals, like old Ben, are often more sensitive to the spirit worlds than people are.

puzzled for long, though, and after a bit, she moves on over to our bed and, kneeling down, pulls out a small, shiny wooden box. I made it for her on her birthday out of cherry wood. Taking it over to the dining table, she opens it and lifts out a small stack of letters, tied with the blue ribbon from her wedding dress. I can tell from the handwriting that they're mine. It's not a real big stack, I'm sad to say. I wish I could have written more often, but well then, a war just went and got in the way.

Real gentle and loving-like, she picks up the top letter. I wrote it about a month ago before we had to make a run for it outta Petersburg. Opening it up, she starts to read, but before she gets very far, she starts to cry. At first, it's only a little, and now it gets to where she's sobbing pretty good. A few tears fall on the letter, mixing with the ink, making little round smeared spots on the paper. I want to go over, put an arm around her, and tell her that it's okay, that I'm here, and to hold her tight, but I know I can't. Don't know why, but I can't seem to touch her, to make that kinda physical connection. About all I can do is talk to her, even though she can't hear me. All I can do is talk, so I do.

Clearing my voice, I start in, "Rose, dearest Rose, I know you can't hear me with your ears, but maybe you can hear with your heart. So, mine's gonna talk to yours right now.

"Don't know any easy way to put this, Rose, but things're looking real bad now for Gen. Lee and all the rest of us. I mean, I can live with getting whipped by the Yanks, 'cause then I'd be coming home, and well, my pride'll heal after a spell. That's not the problem – there's something even harder to take than getting beat. See, lately, I been getting this sinking feeling that it's not gonna go okay for me. Don't know how I know it, but I do, and it's a feeling that just eats away at me. Rose, I don't think I'm gonna be coming home." Saying this to her chokes me right up, and I gotta stop for a while.

Wiping tears outta my eyes, I walk around behind her to stare out the window for a bit. It doesn't help much though, 'cause Rose is still crying away behind me. Makes it hard to talk, or even think clear, when both of us are doing it.

Once I get myself together, I turn and look at her sitting at the table. She's not more than an arm's length away, so I get this real strong desire to reach over and touch her silky smooth hair. I start to do it but stop in midair, knowing I won't be able to slide my fingers through it like I used to. My eyes mist up a little heavier, so I start speaking my heart again.

"You know, Rose, dying would be okay if I had never known you. I mean, I got over being afraid of dying a long time ago, right after that first day when the fighting got so heavy and the cannon shells were just blowing up all around. When I saw so many boys bleeding bright red, somehow, I just made peace with the Lord. I decided that if He was gonna take me, it would be according to *His* will and not some Union gunner's. That just put things in a different light. Having made it through so many battles and close scrapes, well, it seems a little strange, that now, when that the shooting's almost stopped, that the Lord would be calling me home. But that's just what I'm afraid's gonna happen.

"No matter what, Rose, the fact is that I *did* meet you, and everything got different. When I first laid eyes on you, Rose, you did me in and took my heart. At first, even as wild and exciting and as good as our loving feelings were, looking back, it was just puppy love. I mean, our loving each other just got better with every passing day, with every problem solved, with all the quiet happy times we spent, and with every crazy cockeyed jam we got into. No matter what happened, we were able to love and laugh our way through it. Our feelings for each other just got stronger and deeper and better all the time.

"I tell you true, Rose, I won't regret the dying itself, if that's what has to happen. I won't regret it, 'cause I don't know how I could pack any more love for you into my heart than I already got. It's plum full up already. But what I will regret is that I didn't get a chance to say one last 'Good-bye,' and to hold you tight one last time. That I didn't get to feel your lips on mine again, and to say I'm glad you picked me and glad I picked you, Georgia Rose. I'll be sad that I didn't get to say, one last time, 'Georgia Rose, I'll love you every breath I take, and then I'll love you some more after I'm gone.'"

I choke up and can't speak anymore. Tears cloud my eyes so bad I can hardly see Rose any more, but I can hear her sobbing quietly still. I reach out and try to touch her, to hug her. When I move my hands over to her shoulders, I feel that same tingle I felt before, and suddenly, with a startled look of surprise, she looks up from the letter. She's got a faint smile, and there's a hint of recognition in her eyes now. Under her breath, so faintly I can hardly hear, she says, "John?" She looks slowly around the room again. "John, is that you?"

Excited, I jump forward from the window to embrace her, thinking maybe she knows I'm here now. Maybe I can reach her after all. As I stretch out both hands, she starts to get up, when suddenly, there's a loud echoing boom, and now another, even louder.

Startled, I snap awake, throw off my blanket, and sit up. Ervin's still sitting by the fire softly playing his harmonica. At my sudden movement, he stops playing and looks over at me.

"Relax, lieutenant. Don't worry. Them cannons are a couple miles away to the rear. Go back to sleep. It's somebody else's turn to die tonight."

Groggy, I can only nod. I flop back down and pull my blanket over me, curling up, holding it tight and close, wishing it was Rose. I think I smell the faint aroma of roses … not sure, but maybe it wasn't a dream after all.

As John and the rest of Gen. Lee's troops retreated west, Gen. Grant, sensing that the end was near, sent his cavalry galloping across the Virginia countryside to outflank Lee's army. Union infantry continued to harass the Confederate rearguard troops with renewed energy. At the same time, Grant used captured Confederate trains to rush thousands of his infantrymen west, ahead of the fleeing Southern army.

April 8, 1865, Marching Past New Hope Church

Over the clink and clank of war-gear and the rattle of the wagons, it's hard to hear each other. But nobody's in the mood for talking anyway. We just march along in silence, caught up in our own thoughts and struggling with exhaustion. Hard to remember that last night I was happy to be thinking about Rose. Now, all I'm thinking about is keeping dry and staying alive. Heading west for Appomattox Court House, we're just coming up to the little village around New Hope Church. There're only just a few houses here.

The rain's over, but the Richmond-to-Lynchburg Stage Road is muddy and in real bad shape. Our weary boys march along single file, one wobbly line of men off on each side of the road, trying to stay out of the puddles that fill the deep ruts. Anyways, we gotta stay off the middle of the Stage Road to let all the wagons and artillery pass. As they go by, slipping and sliding in the ruts, the horses' hooves and the wagon wheels fling muddy water and lumps of mud all over us, adding to our misery. There's just no way to stay dry or warm.

Figure 2-22. "The Lynchburg Stage Road's in real bad shape." *[Ca. 1864. Courtesy of the Library of Congress.]*

Every mile seems harder than the last. The Yanks've been pushing us real hard ever since we left Farmville. We've been alternating between running and fighting hard to hold 'em back, but there's just too damn many of 'em. They just keep coming at us from all directions like a sack of mad hornets.

We're all dog-tired, running low on bullets, our boots are plum worn out, and our feet are, too. I got more blisters than I got toes, and some of the other boys are a lot worse off than me. Some of them're using their rifles like a crutch, making it real hard to keep up. Not that the rest of us are moving along real fast, even with the Yanks nipping at us.

Gen. Lee's been pressing us to move faster, and along the way, the roadside's littered with broken wagons, dead mules and horses, and lots of army bits and pieces. Cap'n Pearce, my commander, says we got to get rid of anything that slows us down. Some of the guys even been leaving behind real personal things that they wouldn't let go of normally. With no food and precious little ammunition, our situation's gotten downright desperate.

Once we came across a scene that made me just shake my head. A couple of squads of artillerymen were burying cannons and using axes to chop up the gun carriages and wagon wheels. Not enough mules left to pull 'em. But we couldn't just leave 'em and let the Yanks get 'em. Wouldn't do to have the Yanks shooting at us with our own guns.

Figure 2-23. "We been moving so fast, we had to leave some cannons behind. No mules to pull 'em." *[Ca. 1863. Courtesy of the Library of Congress.]*

We even came on some of our own men who just plain gave up, sitting by the side of the road, hungry and begging for food. But we weren't any better off than they were. Maybe it'll be a blessing for 'em to get taken by the Yanks. At least they'll be getting some hot food. It's sure been a sight to break a man down. Gen. Lee and the other officers try to put a good face on it, but it just doesn't look good for us, no matter how you cut it. Like my old Daddy used to say, "Things ain't all that rosy when a bear's chewing your shoe!"

Our company's just coming up on New Hope Church now, heading towards Lynchburg. Seeing the name, some of the guys go to joking that we're going through "No Hope" Church on the way to "Lynching-burg." We're in a bad way, to be sure. The Yanks got us on the run, and they ain't about to quit now. *[See inset.]*

Confederate Gen. Gordon described the ordeal of the retreat to Appomattox: "Fighting all day, marching all night, with exhaustion and hunger claiming their victims at every mile, with charges of infantry in the rear, and of cavalry on the flanks, it seemed the war god has turned loose all his furies." *(Murray (1976).)*

There's still a little bit of hope, though. The Cap'n says there's some train cars packed full of food, blankets, and bullets waiting for us at Appomattox Station. That's sweet music to my ears. We're all hungry and looking lean and bony. Everybody's uniform is a bit loose and floppy these days – kinda like we're all wearing hand-me-downs from our big brothers.

From the rear, I begin to hear a lot of noise like shouting. Damn! Don't tell me the Yanks are coming at us again. But I don't hear any shots, so I figure that can't be it. From around the turn behind us, the wagons start to pull over to the side of the road, and the men are looking back. The shouting grows louder 'til I can see group of officers coming up on us. In with 'em is a man on a gray horse. It's the General himself!

Figure 2-24. "Seeing Gen. Lee on Traveler was a sight for sore eyes!" *[Ca. 1865. Photo reprinted from Hamilton, Joseph (1917).]*

105

Now that's a sight for sore eyes – and sore feet, too! Gen. Lee is making his way through the ranks up the Stage Road, riding on Traveler, probably the most famous horse in the whole world. Everybody, on both sides of the war, would recognize 'em. He could have just as well ridden around us faster through the woods, but he's trying to lift the guys' spirits a little. I tell you, there isn't a dry eye near me – all of us just love that man so. As he rides towards us, a rolling cheer follows right along, with all the guys reaching out to try and touch him. From time to time, the General reaches out to lay a hand on a sleeve, an arm, or a shoulder, or to offer a kind word of encouragement.

As he rides up alongside me, I see he's got a few tears in his eyes, too. He knows it hasn't been easy, and he hurts for us, just like he would for his own family. I reach out and run my fingers across his tall leather boot as he passes, and my spirits soar, too. If somebody had never seen Gen. Lee, they wouldn't know what all the fuss was about. But for those of us who've seen the heart and soul of this man, why we'd march through Hell and take on the Devil himself blindfolded. He just has that kind of effect.

As the General passes out of sight around the next bend heading towards Appomattox, the cheering fades off with him. Looking around, I see more than a few smiles, and it seems like all of us are marching a little snappier now.

April 8, 1865: Camping at Appomattox

The Final Chapter of the War
The two armies reached Appomattox on the night of April 8, 1865. Both sides knew that there would be an important battle on the morning of April 9, which happened to be Palm Sunday, the same day that the Good Lord rode into Jerusalem for the crucifixion.

With things not looking too good on Palm Sunday for Gen. Lee either, he prayed that he could break through the Union lines, even though they had him nearly surrounded. On the opposite side, Gen. Grant prayed that he could force the retreating Confederates to surrender before they reached reinforcements at Lynchburg.

Finally getting a little sleep, I'm having some real bad dreams, when I hear a branch snap on the ground near my head. I jerk awake, and in one fluid motion, I roll sideways out of my blanket, grab my pistol, cock it, and point it at the intruder's head.

"Whoa, whoa, lieutenant! Cool your finger. It's just me, Ervin," he says, quickly throwing his hand up.

I slowly uncock my pistol and grab my head, too asleep to say anything after almost blowing a hole through one of my own men.

"Sorry about that, lieutenant. I was just bringing over some coffee," he says. "Just about time to be getting up anyway. It's our turn for picket duty tonight."

Figure 2-25. Troops outside Appomattox Courthouse, April 1865. *[Courtesy of the Library of Congress.]*

We're camped near a zigzag split-rail fence in a thick bunch of blackjack oaks. Nearly the whole Army, except for stragglers, has stopped between the river and Appomattox village. I pull out my Daddy's old gold pocket watch. It's nearly 10:00 at night. The moon is about full, and as far off in the distance as I can see, ghostly-white Army tents and campfires are sprinkled in among the trees and out across the fields.

The flash of cannon-fire briefly lights up the western sky, and now, a split second later, a faint boom echoes down the valley. It's coming from a few miles away out towards Appomattox Station. It's been going on for a while. Looks like the Yanks got here first.

I shake my head wearily. While we were marching in here today, we heard, far off to the south, the steady rattle and roar of trains heading west. The Yanks were outflanking us, moving troops out ahead of us all day. They're somewhere out there now. We're sure of that. We just don't know how many. There's probably gonna be lots of fireworks tomorrow around sunup.

Raising my voice a little, I call out, "Okay, boys, let's get going. Up and at 'em. We got picket duty. Wouldn't want 'em to finish the war without us, now, would you?" Faintly visible around the fire, a bunch of gray blankets covers man-lumps, some of 'em starting to stir.

Out comes Gideon's muffled, sleepy voice; "Oh, you go ahead and start without me, lieutenant. Won't hurt my feelings none. Just save a few Yanks for me ... along with some of that black-tar coffee." I don't answer him. He'll get up in a minute.

Figure 2-26. Union men after the capture of Appomattox Station, April 1865. *[Courtesy of the National Archives.]*

    I grab my faded gray Confederate jacket. It's a little rumpled, what with being used as a pillow, but then, nobody minds. After all, we're not going to some fancy dancing-ball out here. I slip it on and get a look at it in the firelight. I was sure proud of it when I first made the rank of lieutenant. It has all that fancy gold scrolly stuff all over the sleeve. It was the fanciest darn thing I ever owned. Now, it's a bit worn, torn, and frayed. Not that I'd be embarrassed to die in it. But I'd be real embarrassed to be captured in it.

    I go on over to the fire near Ervin and sit down on a log. Ervin hands me an old battered tin cup of thick, strong, black coffee and says, "Evening, lieutenant – again." I nod sleepily, as he tries to make small talk to help me clear my head: "When we get out of this – you know, when all the shooting and shouting stops – what you planning to do?"

    I take a couple long swigs of coffee. Ervin thinks maybe I wasn't listening, so he starts to ask again. "I heard, Ervin – just takes a little coffee to get my tongue wagging good again." I take another sip, enjoying the bitter taste. "Not real sure what I'll do. Assuming they don't send me home in a pine box, I'm thinking maybe I'll go round up the family and head out across the Mississippi. You know, like that newspaperman says, 'Go West, young man!' Think I'm gonna take him up on it – 'cept, in my case, it'd be, 'Go West, old man!'"

"Aw, you ain't *that* old, lieutenant," he says, trying to be charitable. "But I don't get it. Why you wanna go out West?"

"Oh, maybe see some cowboys and Injuns and all those buffaloes. Wouldn't even mind being a cowboy. You know, get me a horse and a big shiny six-shooter and a huge old cowboy hat, and then I'd just head out across the plains. Wouldn't mind that at all." *[See inset.]*

I cup both hands around the coffee cup to warm 'em up. "I'll tell you true, Ervin, I'm plum sick of walking. If I could sit me down on a horse, I'd be happy as a clam, never letting my walking feet touch the ground again. I'd just tie myself on that horse and sleep right up in that old saddle and never get down."

Ervin comes back with, "I'm with you there, lieutenant. Been on my feet about four years solid. So I figure, in order to get even, I'm gonna have to be plum off 'em for about the next four years. I'm not so sure about that horse idea, though. Think I'm just gonna go back to my sweet little woman and spend about four years tucked in bed with her." *[See inset.]*

> **Flash Forward**
> As a child, I put together many playtime costumes, including a replica Civil War outfit with a Confederate coat, hat, belt buckle, and gun. In addition, I had a complete cowboy outfit, as well as an Indian one. This imaginary playacting as a child helped reawaken real memories from this and other past lives.
> John Hogans' strong desire for a 'simpler' life out West led me to reincarnate on the Great Plains as a Lakota warrior (called "Sioux" by their enemies). I would soon get a very close look at "those cowboys and Injuns and all those buffaloes."
> For a while, life on the plains was simpler and more peaceful, but as you will see later, my new life did not stay that way.

> **Flash Forward**
> A few years before the war started, Ervin had married Emily Trowell. After the war, Ervin and Emily moved to Florida. Putting his unusual "vocal talents" to good use, he became – ironically enough – a preacher! *(MyTrees.com (2002).)*

Chuckling, I say, "I don't know, Ervin. That might be all right for about a week or so – you know – in bed with your wife. After that, seems to me, it's just gonna seem like work."

"Oh, you don't know my wife, sir," he says with a twinkle in his eye. I laugh, as he grabs the coffee pot and pours us both some more.

Taking another sip, I stare into the fire. "Looking back, if I'd have known that we were gonna be marching all over the whole danged country, I'd of enlisted in the cavalry. Now that's the life. You get to dress up in those fancy dandy uniforms with a feather in your hat and just go out for a nice old horsey ride. Now those guys got it made. Everybody looks up to 'em. *[See inset.]*

"Well, yeah, lieutenant, 'cepting for the fact that on that nice old horsey ride, there's guys in blue trying to shoot your fool head off."

"Yeah, I know. I like to skip over that part."

"Kinda hard to skip over the bullets these days, lieutenant," complains Ervin.

Flash Forward

This admiration for the brave and daring cavalrymen of the war and my strong desire to be a horse-soldier carried directly into my next lifetime, as well. The Cheyenne and Lakota Plains warriors ranked among the most highly skilled horsemen who ever lived.

This is a good example of how a strong desire for something in one lifetime may cause it to appear in a future one. It is proof of the old saying, "What you hold in mind is what you get."

We stay quiet for a while, lost in our own thoughts. I grab a twig and stir my coffee a bit, even though it doesn't need it. "You know, when we lost ol' Jeb *[Cavalry Gen. Jeb Stuart]*, I think the war plum turned against us. Now there was as fine a horseman as I ever saw. We just got nobody to take his place. Been looking kinda shaky ever since."

Ervin says, "Yep, and not just him. Lately, we been losing a whole bunch of good generals." He takes a long sip of coffee. "On the other side of it, the Yanks got that damn Custer. He's been giving us fits, just popping out of nowhere, causing all kinds of trouble. Now there's a man who *needs* to get shot!"

"You know, I saw that damn guy up at Gettysburg," I respond. "Looks like some strutting rooster to me. And they say he doesn't mind getting the glory while his men do the bleeding."

Someone's coming through the bush, so just to be on the safe side, we put a hand on our guns. The cap'n walks into the firelight and sits down. "I caught the tail end of that, boys. Sad to say, but that damn Custer popped up again tonight."

"How's that, cap'n?" Ervin asks, pouring him a tin of coffee.

Cap'n looks up. "All that firing to the west – that's Custer. Those blue devils got the damn supply trains!"

"Holy hell," I mumble, my shoulders slumping down.

"Got 'em this afternoon. Along with a bunch of our cannons. And they're blocking the road to Lynchburg. Took our boys by surprise. Then Custer's boys had the nerve to drive one of those trains up and down the tracks, tooting the horn like they were having some kinda party. Just taunting us!"

For some reason, Custer just brings out my ornery side. "You know, that Custer's got a thing for that kinda pony-piss. It's bad enough those damn

Figure 2-27. Maj. Gen. George Armstrong Custer. *[Ca. 1863. Courtesy of the Library of Congress.]*

Figure 2-28. At the Battle of Appomattox Station, Custer's cavalrymen captured supply trains just like these. *[Ca. 1865. Courtesy of the Library of Congress.]*

Yanks been nipping our damn butts all the damn way out of Petersburg; now that damn horse's ass wants to rub it in besides!" *[See inset.]*

My voice keeps rising, just like my temper. "Why, I'd like to get that gosh-darned son-of-a-buck alone in the back of a barn for about ten minutes. I'd show him what Southern pride's all about!"

Ervin jumps in, "And I want him five minutes when you get through."

Calming down a little, I sigh and ask, "What're we gonna do without those trains, cap'n?"

He looks real worried. "Doesn't look good. Not good at all. Those train cars were full of beef, bullets, and biscuits. Now we've got next to nothing left. Even the best knock-em-down soldiers can't fight with empty stomachs and guns."

"So what we gonna do next, cap'n?" I ask, a little softer now.

He doesn't say anything for a while, only stares at his boots and hands. His face is pale. "Boys, this is just between you and me. It's not going any farther. Got it?" We both nod.

"Give me a fill-up," he says, holding out his cup to Ervin, who pours it and now kicks up the fire a little bit. Me and Ervin are looking worried here.

> **The Custer Connection**
> John's intense dislike for the general was partly because of Custer's seeming carelessness with the lives of his own men. Partly, it was because of his successful campaigns against the South. Custer's daring tactics led to many battle defeats for the Confederate army. His last feat, capturing the vital supply trains at Appomattox, was one of the decisive turning points that led to the final surrender.
>
> My dislike for Custer was so intense that I was drawn to him again in my next life.

Cap'n is looking real bad. His eyes are red and sunken, and I can smell whiskey on his breath. He's been taking it hard these past few weeks – he's a proud man, and getting whipped like this doesn't set well with him. Pulling a banged-up silver flask out of his jacket, he pours a slug of "courage" into his coffee and gulps down a mouthful. Lowering his voice, he says, "Word's going round that Grant sent over a letter last night asking General Lee to throw it in."

Ervin and me give each other surprised looks, as the cap'n continues, "Word is that some of our generals want to do it and some don't. Some of 'em can't take it any more, seeing their men go down. General Lee, along with Longstreet, asked 'em to make one more try to break out for Lynchburg. They feel we got to give it one more go. So today's the day, boys – at sunrise. After that ...." He trails off and doesn't finish.

We all stare at the fire, kinda lost in our thoughts about "what if." We stay that way a while, and me, I'm tired of thinking about killing. I start thinking again about heading out West. Anything 'cept being a damn marching man. I think I've done more than enough walking for a long while.

In my head, I'm sort of ambling out across the prairie on my horse, when all of a sudden, we hear gunfire real close by. "Let's go, boys," the cap'n yells, jumping up. "Looks like some damn Yanks dropped by for supper!"

We race off towards the firing at the east edge of town. Bright muzzle flashes fill the night and men are yelling. Horses are whinnying over the sound of hoof beats. Union cavalry! *[See inset.]*

As I run headlong into the fighting, I hear a bunch of hoof beats off to the left. In the bright moonlight, I see shapes of several soldiers galloping through town. There's just enough light to see that the riders are wearing dark coats. Yanks!

I skid to a stop, snap my rifle to my shoulder, and fire. There's a powerful blast and a bright flash that blinds me momentarily. I can't tell if I hit anything, and I struggle to reload by feel alone.

Cavalry Charge

Late in the evening of April 8, after capturing the trains, about a dozen troopers from Custer's 15th New York Cavalry charged from the west through the village of Appomattox. They were met with fire from Confederate skirmishers on the east side of town. They were driven back and their leader, Col. Root, was killed *(Calkins (1987))*. John fought with one of Custer's cavalry troopers.

Because of my intense dislike for Custer and his troopers and because I didn't get over these feelings, this same karmic pattern would be repeated in the very near future – in my next life as a Lakota warrior!

Out of the dark, I hear one of the Yanks galloping straight towards me, whooping and hollering! I still can't see clear, but I can hear right where he is.

As he gets closer, I give up on reloading. Crouching down, I grab the warm barrel of my rifle. As he comes right up to me, I give a roundhouse swing with all my might. With a loud "whack" my rifle hits something, shattering the wooden stock, and stinging my hands. There's a shrill whinny from the Yank's horse.

The trooper yells, "Damn your sorry hide, Reb! You nearly killed my horse!"

With that, the Yank fires his pistol square into my face. His horse must have jerked as he shot, 'cause the bullet grazes my temple and doesn't hit me. But the blast burns the right side of my face real bad. Intense pain buckles my knees. Grabbing my right eye, I spin around and fall face down on the ground.

I struggle to get up, shaking my head to clear my eyes. Still holding my hand over my right eye, my vision's starting to come back a little. Staggering around, I just can make out the blurred shape of the Yank still in front of me, struggling to control his horse.

Dimly, I see him raise his pistol again. Diving sideways by instinct, I crash into the bushes just as he fires again. A sharp burning pain sears into my right thigh. I'm hit!

Figure 2-29. "With me on my back, Custer's man curses and races back through town." *[Detail of engraving reprinted from Jones (1875).]*

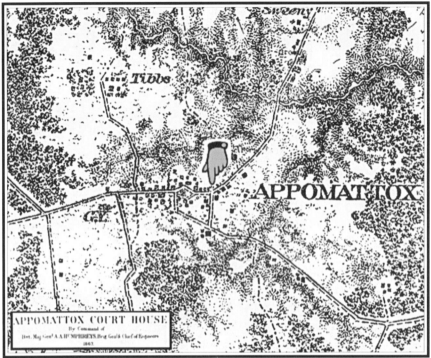

Figure 2-30. Map of Appomattox from 1867, adapted to show where Hogans was wounded – on the east side of town near "Surrender Triangle." *[Courtesy of the Library of Congress.]*

Grabbing my leg, I crawl sideways and flip over on my back. The Yank fires again but misses. Now cursing me one last time, he gallops off, retreating through town the way he came.

It's too dark to see, so I slide my hand cautiously down my thigh. It's wet with blood. The bone is shattered, and I can't move my leg. Weak and dizzy, I try to yell out for help to Ervin and the others, but all I can manage is a few weak croaks.

My head's aching real bad, and I'm getting weak and dizzy. My eyes won't focus right. The bushes are spinning all

Figure 2-31. This is the Kelley house in Appomattox. Hogans was wounded about 150 feet straight out from the front door on the left. *[Courtesy Library of Congress.]*

around, and bright colored sparks are dancing in front of me. I grab my head with both hands to try to make 'em stop. But they don't.

I'm queasy like I'm falling down a well or something … a deep well … real dark … spinning … falling … down….

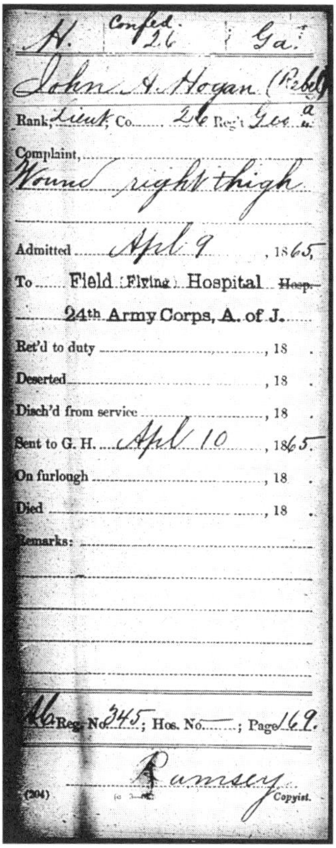

April 10, 1865, at the Hospital near Appomattox

Somebody screams out next to me, and I wake up with a start. As I move a little bit, sharp pain shoots down my right side. "Oh, God!" I moan. Every danged bone and muscle in my body aches like they've never ached before – and my head feels like a horse sat on it.

There's a bandage over my right eye, and I can see only out of the left one. My mouth is dry as a stale biscuit. I'm lying in a big hospital building on a cot, with a bunch of other guys on beds nearby. Some of 'em are moaning, tossing, and turning. All of 'em have lots of white bandages stained with blood. All kinds of smells are in the air: whiskey and liniments for the pain; strong lye

Into the Hospital

After being wounded on April 8, John was treated first in a Confederate hospital tent. Then, on April 9, 1865, he was taken to the Army Field Hospital for further treatment.

H. Confed. 26 Ga.

John A. Hogan (Rebel)

Rank, Lieut; Co. 26 Reg't Geo. a

Complaint, Wound right thigh

Admitted April 9, 1865

To Field (Flying) Hospital ~~Hosp.~~

24th Army Corps, A. of J.

Ret'd to duty ...., 18

Deserted ...., 18

Disch'd from service ...., 18

Sent to G. H. Apl 10, 1865

On furlough ...., 18

Died ...., 18

Remarks:

Reg. No. 345; Hos. No. ......; Page 169.

(204) Ramsey, Copyist.

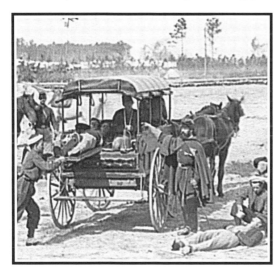

Figure 2-33. Copy of Army Hospital records showing that John was admitted on April 9, 1865, with a wound in his right thigh. *[Courtesy of the National Archives.]*

Figure 2-32. John was loaded onto an ambulance like this and taken first to the field tent hospital. *[Ca. 1865. Courtesy of the Library of Congress.]*

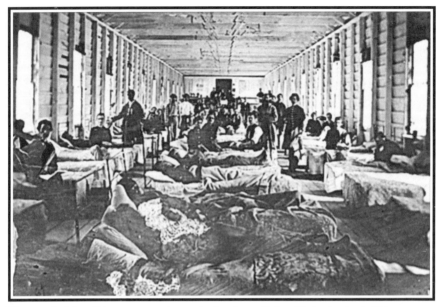

Figure 2-34. "Never cared much for hospitals. Only bad stuff happens when you're in one." *[Ca. 1865. Courtesy of the National Archives.]*

to clean up all the gore; and that unmistakable smell of death and disease. Not a one of 'em is a good smell, including even the whiskey. I'd sure rather be somewhere else.

I hear a rattling noise off at the end of the room and raise my head a little. A hospital orderly, a steward, is rummaging through a trunk over past the end of my bed. Tall, thin, and bony, he's got a beard almost down to his chest. His tattered gray coat is unbuttoned and flaps around as he digs through the trunk. He pops up holding a couple of small bottles of yellowish-white pills. As he does, he sees I'm awake and asks, "How you doing, lieutenant?"

Mumbling, I reply, "Truth is, I can't tell. Everything hurts. Why don't you tell me? How *am* I doing?"

As he walks over beside the bed, he takes the top off the bottle and shakes out a couple of pills. "Here. These'll help the pain."

"What are they?" I ask weakly.

"Opium," he says. "These'll numb it right down."

Tilting my head up, he pops the pills in my mouth and gives me a little water. After I choke 'em down, he pops a couple of 'em into his own mouth and swallows 'em down, too.

"You get shot up, too?" I ask, looking up at him, puzzled.

He shakes his head and says, "Sometimes, I think I'd feel a lot better if I had been shot up. I tell you, lieutenant, hard as it is for you to believe, it's not easy watching all you boys coming in here, all full of bullet lead. It hurts me real bad, too, just in a different way. These pills just make it a little easier to do what I gotta do for you boys. That's all." *[See inset.]*

I nod my head; "So what's the damage?" I ask him again.

"Well, it was touch and go there for a while." He stands up and looks down at me real serious, "and the surgeon says you're still not out of the woods."

"Okay, but what's the damage?"

"Sure you want to know, lieutenant?" he asks with a pained look on his face.

> **Anesthetics**
> The most commonly used painkillers were morphine and opium. Union surgeons alone handed out nearly *10 million* opium pills to the soldiers. Because surgeons did not know the dangers of these drugs, as many as 500,000 men may have gone home seriously addicted to morphine and opium *(Adams (1999))*.
>
> Incidentally, the hospital orderly was reborn as my uncle in my current lifetime, during which he became a doctor. He also had some trouble with prescription drugs in his latest incarnation. This tendency to abuse drugs had carried over from the Civil War.

After I nod, he takes a deep breath and continues; "You had gangrene – in the right leg. It's gone – the leg, I mean. The surgeon had to amputate it above the knee. And the right eye's burned real bad. We're not sure you'll ever see out of it again. Sorry, lieutenant. I'm real sorry …," he trails off.

"Well, that sure explains this splitting headache." I turn away and look down the row of beds at the other guys. Now I say, as much for me as for him, trying to make light of a bad deal, "Well, I guess there's a good side to it, huh? At least I won't have to worry about having a sore right foot any more."

Still looking real serious, he says softly, "No, I suppose you won't, sir. Guess that's one way to look at it."

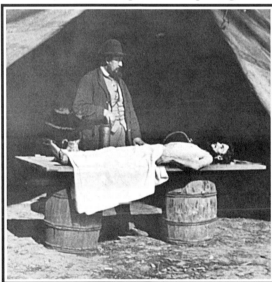

Figure 2-35. Surgical procedures were primitive by modern standards. *[Ca. 1864. Courtesy of the Library of Congress.]*

"As far as the eye goes …," I answer, pausing because I'm hesitant to say what I'm thinking. But I decide I gotta make light of all this, even if the steward doesn't understand. "As far as the eye goes, can you get me a patch or something to wear?" I pause to watch his face closely. "And why don't you bring me a peg-leg and a big old parrot, if you can find one. Always wanted to be a pirate. Now's me chance, matey," I say in a raspy pirate's voice. I try to smile to show him I'm joking, but my face is too swollen.

Humoring me, he says, "I'll see what I can do, sir." He bends down to check the bandages on my leg. He acts more upset by all this than I am. I've always believed that if you can't change something, you might as well just go on and get used to it as fast as you can.

Out of the corner of my one good eye, I see somebody coming in. It's a damned Yankee officer! Struggling to sit up, I grab instinctively for my pistol but it's not there.

The steward grabs me. "Easy, sir! Easy. It's okay."

"What the hell's he doing here?" I demand, glaring at the Yank.

He speaks soothingly, almost in a whisper, "Guess you didn't know, sir, since you've been knocked out since Saturday. General Grant had us surrounded, and General Lee didn't want any more boys dying, so he called a truce. We surrendered. You're in a Union hospital now. I'm here helping the Union surgeons take care of you and the rest of our boys."

Shocked and feeling low, I can't say anything. He goes on, "We'll all be going home soon, sir. If you'd of been lucky for only a couple more hours, then …" He chokes a little and continues, "Sorry, sir. I know an 'if only' won't change anything."

I stare at the ceiling for a moment or so, and he starts to turn away. "Wait a minute," I call after him. I start digging away in my shirt pocket, but it's empty. Grabbing him by the arm, I ask, "They find a letter in my pocket?"

"Right here, sir," he says pulling it out of the trunk at the foot of the bed.

Relieved, I hold it, and look closely at it for a few seconds, checking the address for Mrs. Rosetta Hogans. It's got a few small bloodstains on it, but I hand it back to him. "Will you see that my wife gets this? Please? That'll let her know I'm okay. But don't let 'em tell her anything about me getting shot up. Okay?"

He nods and starts to turn away again. I touch him on the arm again, and whisper, "Thanks."

He smiles, nods, and walks towards the door.

The pain is disappearing as the opium starts to take effect. I lay my head back down on the pillow. Now, as I drift off into the deadening haze, everything seems better.

April 12, 1865: Union Army General Hospital

I wake up later with a nagging thirst. My mouth is dryer than ever, though thankfully, the headache's gone. I raise my head to look for the steward, but the room's empty except for me and the other boys. I decide to get up and get some water, telling myself, "Well, boy, you're not gonna be a helpless burden to anybody, so you might as well get used to doing things for yourself."

Figure 2-36. Union surgeons and hospital stewards in front of their tent. [Ca. 1865. Courtesy of the Library of Congress.]

I struggle out of bed and kinda flop onto the floor. Though it's tough, I manage to drag myself over towards the door where the water is. After a minute or two, I reach the open doorway. Grabbing the edge of the door and the jamb, I pull myself up to a half-sitting, half-kneeling position. I rest here for a minute to catch my breath and let my spinning head slow down. Looking outside, I can see full moonlight scattering through the trees. Now that the fighting's done, it seems real quiet and peaceful.

After a minute or two, I see the steward coming with a lantern, holding some papers that he's trying to read by the lantern light. He's walking fast and doesn't know I'm there, so I call out, "Halloo. I could use some water."

He doesn't look up and just keeps right on coming.

"Hey," I yell out, but he's still coming. "Hey! Whoa! Damn it, hold on!"

Before I can crawl out of the way, he hits into me, walking plum through me like I was thin air. There's just a little tingling sensation as he passes clean through. Stunned and confused, I say, "Tarnation! What the hell's going on?"

A voice comes out of the dark from under a big oak tree nearby. "He couldn't see you, son ... or hear you either."

The voice sounds real familiar and I squint to make out the dark figure standing in the shadows. "Daddy? That you?"

The figure starts ambling over towards me. It is! It's Daddy! Stunned, confused, and surprised to see him, I can't speak – I can only stammer.

Daddy looks the same. He's still got that shock of white hair, curved moustache, and those bushy eyebrows. It's so good to see him again. Only problem is – Daddy's dead! Died in 1846! I should know – I helped bury him when I was fifteen.

"How you doing, son?" he asks quietly. I'm still staring at him.

Finally I recover my voice, "Not so good, Daddy. But what the hell are you doing here? You shouldn't be standing in front of me. You're dead!"

"Aw, don't you believe it, son. Do I look dead? Sure don't feel dead," he says with a smile. "Here, take my hand," he says, sticking his big paw out towards me. I reach out and touch it reluctantly. "See. It's real enough. Right?"

"Daddy, I'm chock-full of opium, so please don't be fooling around with my head any. This has got to be some kinda opium dream."

"I'm not fooling, son, and it's no dream. As you can plainly see, I'm alive. That is, the real 'ME' is still alive. True, my old body is sleeping in the cold hard earth ... but the real 'me' lives on. In spirit, of course ... just like you."

"Daddy, now just what do you mean by that crack about, 'just like you'?"

"Son, I don't know any easy way to break it to you. Your body's dead ... just like mine."

"Aw, you're crazy, Daddy. I'm not dead ... *yet*. Sure, I'm pretty beat up. I'm missing a leg, and my right eye's bad, but I'm still here. I'm a mess, really a mess, but I'm still kicking!"

Shaking his head back and forth, he just points down at my legs and counters with, "Son, you might just as well stand up, 'cause, since you last looked, that old 'still kicking' leg of yours grew back."

Glancing down at my legs folded under me, I'm stunned. My missing leg's not missing anymore! I get up off the floor, carefully putting weight on both legs, shifting back and forth. Standing there in the doorway, I start dancing around and slapping my legs with my hands to make sure they're real.

Daddy continues, "And what's more, son, soon as you stop dancing around, you can throw that head bandage away, 'cause there's nothing wrong with your eye anymore either."

I put my hand up and gingerly lift up the bandage. I can see out of that eye perfectly. "I ... I ... I don't get it, Daddy. Is this a dream or what?"

Daddy says, "Now, boy, we already covered this 'dream' theory of yours. By the way, you better get out of the doorway, son, or that steward's gonna walk right through you again."

I step back just as the steward rushes out through the doorway. Daddy turns around and walks over to my cot and motions for me with his hand. "Over here, son."

While he points down at the cot, I walk over hesitantly: "Oh – my – God!" I'm staring down at ME. Only the 'me' on the cot has bandages in place of one leg and is white, pale, and not breathing. My jaw drops in amazement and I panic. "Get the steward, Daddy!" I yell. "We got to get some help! I'm dying!"

"Relax, son, you're already dead – that is, I mean, the earth part of you. It's gone – deceased and dead – soon to be pushing up daisies."

I'm listening, but it's not really sinking in yet. I just keep shaking my head back and forth.

"Son, now you listen to me. In case you hadn't noticed … YOU," he says, thumping a big knuckle on my chest, "YOU are still here." Jabbing a finger at the body on the bed, he says, "THAT is *not* you. That's just the earth part of you. That is, it *used* to be. Right at the moment, it's not doing too good."

He pauses to let it sink in a little more, but I'm still too dazed to say anything, so he continues, "Well, son, I see you're gonna need a little more time on this. There's nothing more to be done, so let's get out of here. Always hated hospitals. Come on. I'll show you something."

Stepping behind me, he grabs me gently by the shoulders with his two big hands and starts steering me straight towards the wall. I figure out what's coming and dig in my heels a little.

"Daddy … Daddy!" I yell. "No! DADDY!" Now he pushes me right through the damned wall. I stare down at my chest in shock, watching the wood planks as they pass clean through my body without a sound, tingling and tickling as they go through. I stagger a little after getting outside. "Ah … Ah … Damn it, Daddy! I wish you hadn'ta done that."

He chuckles good-naturedly. "Just trying to make a point. When's the last time you walked through a wall?"

"Never!" I shoot back.

"Now, you see. That's just my point. Earth bodies don't walk through walls, son. Meaning this isn't your earth body. Yours is back in there, dead as a stump." He puts an arm around my shoulder. "Personally, I like it better this way. I never go through doors anymore. It's just so much easier walking through the walls."

I shake my head. "I'll stick to the doors, thank you very much."

For the first time, I look around outside. The bright moonlight reveals wagons, tents, and horses, all scattered among the trees and buildings. Mixed in through all of the clutter of war, dozens of men lean against trees and fences or lie on the ground, trying to sleep. A few are talking quietly, and some are playing cards – all of 'em taking it easy, just trying to forget about war. Some nurses and surgeons hurry by, looking frazzled and *un*-relaxed. They definitely aren't able to take it easy.

"This way, son," Daddy says, motioning me to follow him down one of the wagon paths between the rows of tents. As we pass one group of men, I hear a voice call out, "John! Hey, Johnny boy! … and Daddy, is that really you?" It sounds like my brother James. It is! He's sitting on the ground, leaning against a split-rail fence, along with a bunch of other guys.

Figure 2-37. "There's James! Sitting by the fence." *[Photo of a hospital yard, ca. 1865. Courtesy of the Library of Congress.]*

"Daddy, there's James!" I exclaim. With a big smile, I hurry over to him, and Daddy follows right behind. When I get close, I'm shocked. James doesn't look good at all – he's real thin and pale. His skin looks bluish, his eyes are sunken, and he's too weak to stand.

"James. James. Damn, it's so good to see you." I grab him happily by the shoulders.

Daddy says, "Hello, son, you doing okay?"

James smiles weakly and shrugs. Now my excitement goes cold. "James … are you sure you can see me?"

"Johnny boy, I haven't gone blind. You're as plain as my nose. Why wouldn't I see you?" He looks puzzled.

"James, 'cause I'm dead."

He turns serious, "Now, don't joke like that, Johnny boy. That's bad luck and you know it. Daddy, don't let him talk like that. I don't want to hear none of it. Not one bit."

I look back at Daddy, who just shakes his head back and forth. Turning back to James, I say real easy, "It's okay, James. Take it easy. What I meant to say is 'I'm dead-tired' is all."

He looks relieved, "Aw, yeah, me, too, Johnny boy. And I'm real cold and shivering. I keep asking for help, but nobody listens. I guess they're all too upset with the surrender and stuff, and kinda got lost in their own problems. There for a while, I thought maybe I was going crazy. I mean, I kept talking and calling out, but nobody paid me no mind. You and Daddy are the first ones that ever answered back." *[See inset.]*

> **Ghosts**
> About two years earlier, while in the Army, James had gotten sick and died. Since then, still confused about being dead, he'd been following along behind the Army as a spirit.
> This happens often when a soul passes over under violent circumstances. On many of the world's battlefields, lost souls still wander around, confused about the fact that their bodies have been killed. It can take centuries for some of them to "wake up" and move on.

Daddy walks up, squats down in front of him, and tells him, "James, son, I think I can help." He puts his big hand on the crown of James's head and, right away, James's face starts to soften and relax, and now he closes his eyes. "Son, now you stop worrying, you hear? You're gonna be just fine. Now, you just stay put here, and take it easy. I'll make sure you get some help real soon. All right?"

Without opening his eyes, James nods sleepily. Daddy gets up, puts a finger to his lips to keep me quiet, and motions me to move on down the path. After we're away from James, I ask, "Daddy, I think I already know the answer, but ... is James gonna make it all right?"

He nods. "He's coming around real slow. But don't you worry; he'll make it through okay. Some of the others won't be so lucky. For them, getting killed on a battlefield is just too hard to take. They're gonna be here for a lot of years, confused and alone, 'til they finally wake up. But they'll all make it by and by, and we won't give up on 'em 'til they do."

I stop and glance back one more time at James, who seems to be at peace, still leaning against the fence. In the end, I couldn't watch out for either James or myself. Now, we're both gone.

I think about Rose again. She always liked James a lot ... just like he was her own brother. My heart hurts, and I begin to feel real bad. She's losing a husband and a brother-in-law both in the same war. And we're losing her. I'd have liked to say a proper good-bye to her, but well, some things just don't get finished the right way. I picture Rose in my mind and my heart starts to ache even worse. Suddenly, the air begins to shimmer a little, and I think maybe that

Alive 5 times

I can just make out the shape of our little house in Georgia. I'm straining to see it better, when Daddy gives me a call. My little house shimmers and disappears.

With Daddy waiting up ahead, I turn around and hurry after him, thinking to ask him about Rose. As I do, something catches my eye off in the woods out beyond the edge of camp. I gotta squint a bit to make it out. Some kinda bright light's flickering and shimmering out there. It's kinda bluish-white, and it casts long shadows of the trees. It doesn't look like fire or anything like that and it doesn't make any noise. I can't quite make out what it is, though it feels real nice and inviting. Kinda cozy-like. A sweet peaceful feeling comes over me. Now, I got to admit, it's been a real long time since I felt anything that peaceful, not since seeing Rose the last time. I point it out to Daddy; "What in blue blazes is that?"

"Well, why don't we just go over and find out," he suggests.

"Now, you just said 'we,' but I'm guessing that you already know what it is. Am I right?"

He says, "You are, son, but it's better just to show you. Come on. Let's go take a look-see."

Taking me by the arm, he starts guiding me towards the light. We gradually leave behind the hospital, the broken bodies, and the wrecked war-gear. We keep moving out slowly through the scrub brush and oaks towards that shimmering light. It feels as if it's pulling me in, and I want to hurry up and get there. That thing feels REAL nice!

We're about halfway over to it – kinda moving along real dreamy – when I get to noticing something seems different. A lot different. So I look down.

"Holy Moses!" I shout, grabbing Daddy's arm. "Our feet aren't touching the ground!" Daddy and I are about three foot up in the air and climbing.

"Take it easy, son." He looks over and says real smooth-like, the way you talk to a kid, "Don't worry. That's normal."

"Flying's *not* NORMAL, Daddy! What the hell are you talking about?"

"All right, so it's not normal – for you, anyway – but you'll get used to it."

"I'm not so sure about that!" Holding tight to his arm, I sneak a close look down at the ground again. It doesn't look like we're about to fall or anything, so I calm down a bit, but I keep an eye on the ground just in case. I'm not letting go of his arm just yet.

"What the devil's going on here? Just what else am I gonna have to 'get used to' – besides FLYING? Why don't you just up and tell me?"

"Well," he says, tugging at his moustache a little. "It's kinda hard to explain."

"Well, you just try me, Daddy. Nothing could be more surprising than flying. Believe me. So you just lay the cards out."

"All right, here goes. You know that light up there we're heading for?" I nod, and he continues without looking over at me. "Well, it's kinda like a doorway – an entrance – going from a little room to a big one."

As we float along, he pauses to let that sink in … but it doesn't. "Daddy, what's all this about 'little rooms – big rooms'? You lost me there," I complain, still looking down. "The last time I looked away from these 'flying' feet, we weren't near any *rooms*. We're in the middle of the gosh-darned woods."

"Well, yes and no, son. But don't you worry; it'll get clearer. When we get over to that light," he says, pointing his finger straight at it, "you'll be able to step through that 'doorway' and go somewhere else – and that 'somewhere else' is a mighty nice place."

I stop. "Hold on, Daddy. Now you're not talking about heaven, are you? 'Cause if you are – and I hope you're not – I don't think I'm gonna quite measure up, you know. Fact is, I'm downright positive I'm not gonna measure up. I've broken at least half those commandments, maybe more, some of 'em more than once, and besides that –"

"Whoa. Whoa. Slow down, son. You got to pause now and again." Daddy lays his arm on my arm, trying to calm me down. "Trust me – they're gonna let you in no matter how you measure up."

We keep drifting along, and he continues, "You know, it's not really 'heaven' – at least, not the way the preachers talk. It's a lot different – a whole lot different. I know, it was for me. I mean, it's not like you get to sit around on fancy cloud-pillows all the time and play a harp. You got to do things – not work-type things, mind you. I mean it's not like you're gonna have to work for a living anymore, but there're lots of interesting things to learn and do, and everybody wants to be doing 'em. It's a real nice fun place, and everybody gets along real well. Besides, if you want to, you get to fly everywhere."

"Sounded okay up 'til that flying part," I say, teasing him a little. "Anyway, Daddy, it sure sounds like it beats Army life. From what you say, I think maybe I could get used to it – even the flying part. Long as I don't have to *walk* anywhere, I'm for it."

"Oh, you'll like it. You will. It'll seem real familiar in just a short while. It just takes a bit to remember it all. You know, it's kinda like getting hit on the head. You forget some things, and then after a while, you get to remembering 'em again."

"Daddy, I *did* get hit in the head – and the leg, too – by gosh-darned Yankee bullets!"

"Okay, son, never mind. I just meant that as a 'what if.' Most everybody who comes up here has trouble remembering at first, whether or not they've been looking down a loaded gun barrel."

We continue drifting on for a bit, with me mulling over what Daddy just said, getting more curious by the minute. Finally, I ask, "Give me a hint. What kind of other things am I supposed to be remembering?"

He looks over at me for a moment or two as we continue. "Well, you're pretty much over the worst of it by now, but let's come at it from another way. Let's go back at what most people have the hardest time with – I know, I sure did."

I wait for him to continue. "Most people are real surprised when it first hits 'em that they're dead. And they find out they're not their physical bodies. That they're spirits … you know, souls."

"Yeah. I'm still wrestling with that one," I complain.

"Okay, well, let's take a closer look at it. Think back to when you were in that hospital. You were looking *at* your body. Right?"

I nod, and he continues, "So you weren't actually *in* your body. You were *outside* it, looking *at* it. Right?"

"I guess so," I mumble.

"Well, either you were in it or you weren't. Which one?"

"Okay. Okay. I was *outside* it!"

Tucking his hand inside his jacket just like a big-city lawyer talking to the jury, Daddy announces in a loud voice, "Therefore, gentle trees of the jury, I rest my case: the accused admits he is *not* the body. Case closed." With a hearty laugh, he claps me on the back.

"Very funny," I mumble sarcastically.

"Aw, don't worry about it, son. It'll get clearer over time," he says cheerfully.

I look over at him doubtfully, "Got any more surprises?"

"Well, let's see," he says, tugging on his moustache again – he always does that when he thinks – "Well, here's one you'll like."

"Probably not," I mumble under my breath. If he heard me, he doesn't show it and just keeps on talking good-naturedly.

"This is just a baby step past the last one: *If* you can accept that your spirit's been born into an earthly body once, *then* it makes perfect sense that your spirit could get born into a new earthly body *again*. How does that sound? Make sense?" he asks.

Shaking my head, I say, "I'm not even gonna touch that one, Daddy. A bullet just tossed me out of my old body – and now you're talking like I'm supposed to slip right back into a new one. Not a chance. Count – me – OUT!"

He says, "Well, you might change your mind. You see, you've always been kind of a 'quick study' as a spirit – you know, pushing to learn new things as fast as you can. It's maybe a little like being, say, in school and your teacher says, 'Well, son, you can learn even faster if you move up with the older kids.'"

126

I start laughing so much I almost choke; "You can't be talking about me, Daddy." I'm shaking my head and laughing still. "My teacher offered to move me somewhere, all right – out to the woodshed to meet her 'Board of Education.' That deal doesn't sound like me."

Daddy looks like he's trying real hard to be patient. "Son, that was just another 'what if.'"

> **Flash Forward**
> As it turned out, in 1865, John's resistance to being born again was misplaced. My soul had already incarnated in 1863 as Sorrel Horse, a Lakota boy. (More about this concept in a later story.) John's powerful desire for a simpler life on horseback out West was already being fulfilled. Sorrel Horse was two years old in 1865.
> In addition, as Sorrel Horse, my soul would meet Custer and his troopers again ... but more about that in the next story.

"Sorry, Daddy. I know I'm not making this easy for you. It's just that I'm a little touchy about schooling. As you might recall, it took me a good while just to make it out of school the regular way." *[See inset.]*

"Never you mind, son. You can't take book-learning with you anyway. Now, common sense and understanding – that's a different matter."

He looks away, and we keep floating on over towards the light. "Everything'll get clearer. You'll see. Anyway, I was just trying to make the point that, in the past, you asked for a special deal. Each time, after each life was over, you kept wanting to get reborn fast – real fast. But, in any event, nobody forced you into it. You asked for it, and you can change your mind. It's your call."

I try reasoning with him, "Now, Daddy, I just got through watching sizeable chunks of me get blown off. I'm in no big hurry to come back and let 'em 'chunk' me up again. You sure you got the right guy?"

He leans over, purses his lips, furrows his brow, tilts his head back and forth, and pretends to check out my face. "Yep. You're the one," he says with a big wide grin.

"Well now, Daddy, if that's what I decided, then maybe I'll just go and change my mind."

"You can," he says.

"Well, maybe I'll just do that."

"That's good. Whatever," he says, and we leave it at that. Keeping silent, we continue to walk or hover or fly or whatever it is we're doing.

Now, kinda nonchalant-like, he throws out, "But you won't."

"Now, darn it, Daddy, how do you know what I'm gonna do?" I'm getting a little peeved.

Stopping, he turns towards me, "I just do. See, we're not just father and son. We've been friends a long time ... a real LONG time. A lot more than just this time around. And I know you. I mean, I *really* know you. I'm betting that after you've been up here a short time – after you've gotten your memory back – well, then, you'll be raring to go get born again."

"Says YOU!" I shoot back.

"Well, okay. You can change your mind," he says agreeably.

"And I just might." I'm still a little huffy.

"You can," he says.

"That's right. I can. Now, we got that straight."

"Uh-huh," he nods.

We both go silent again, floating over to the light. Just as I'm beginning to think he got the picture, he says real quiet, under his breath, "But you won't."

I whirl around, or whatever you gotta do when you're floating in the air, and just glare at him. He walks on past a few steps, now turns, and looks back. With a faint smile, he says, "What?" real innocent-like, and shrugs his shoulders with a "What-did-I-do?" gesture. Looking right into my eyes, still with a faint smile, he waits for me to say something.

With a big sigh, I say, "Okay, Daddy. I give up. Have it your way. Why don't we just change the subject?"

He walks back and puts one of his big arms around me; "Aw, son, your old daddy's just teasing you a bit. Truth is, you get to have it your way. Always have. Always will. Everybody does."

I'm not sure I follow him exactly, but I just nod and don't say anything. We walk on towards the light in silence for a while. Now I think I better ask, "Anything more I ought to know?"

He thinks for a moment, tugging that moustache. "Well," he says, "here's an easy one: you hear me talking to you? Right?"

"Of course. What kinda question is that?"

"You see my lips moving?" he asks.

Stunned, I say, "Well … no." Now that I think about it, mine aren't moving either. "How're you doing that?"

"Well, in spirit, see, we 'talk' to each other with thoughts instead of voices. Sure, you can wiggle your lips if you want to, but most people don't."

"Daddy, you're just full of surprises," I say, shaking my head back and forth. I walk on in silence for a short spell, trying to take in his latest surprise. "But, to tell the truth, Daddy, that one wasn't too much of a shock – not like walking through walls or flying. Actually, I guess I've already gotten used to that one already, even without knowing it. And I like it, too. It means people gotta tell you exactly what's on their minds. They can't lie. Yep, I like that a lot. People *gotta* tell you the truth. Daddy, I *really* like that one." He just looks at me and gives me one of his big warm smiles.

We continue on, and I'm getting all dreamy again, looking at the light. We're almost there now. I start straining my eyes a little to see what's up there.

Looks like I can make out some silhouettes or something. I point 'em out to Daddy. "Looks like there're some people up ahead. Anybody you know?"

"Yep, and you do to. It's your Momma, a couple of cousins, and some real special friends. Come to welcome you back. You'll see 'em clearer when we get closer."

"All of 'em dead, too?" I ask.

"Well, no, they're all really quite alive, actually more so than before ... but I know what you mean. For some of 'em, their earthly bodies are *quite* dead. Most of 'em went through the 'door' some time ago. It seems like Home to 'em now. Soon, it'll seem like that to you, too."

He waves to 'em, and they wave back. I wave, too, and I can start to make out Momma. Doggone, it'll be good to see her again.

Daddy says, "You got one more surprise in store for you, son. Right there next to your Momma. It's Rose. She's waiting to see you, too."

Stunned, I start to say, "Daddy, don't tell me she's ...."

"Naw, she hasn't crossed over yet," he interrupts. "Won't cross for quite a while. But she can visit, you know – at night, I mean, when she's sleeping. Won't be like having her around all the time, but then you've been off to that dumb ol' war anyways. This'll be a lot better than that!" *[See inset.]*

Feeling a surge of happiness at seeing both Mama and Rose again, I start hustling on, but Daddy stops. Looking back at him, I say, "Well, what's doing, Daddy? Let's get moving. The womenfolk are waiting."

> ### Dream World
> When a loved one crosses over, you can still visit with them in your dreams or in meditation.
> Just visualize the person you want to visit. Create a mental image of meeting and talking with them just as you once did.
> Then after you go to sleep or when you meditate, it is likely that you will meet in the astral worlds. When you are finished, try to recall all the details.
> Often, it is possible to resolve unfinished issues with a loved one this way.

"Son, this is where I gotta leave you ... for a little while anyway. I can't cross over just yet. Got to go back, 'cause I promised I'd finish this job. There're lots of boys, including James, who need help back down there. They're a little confused, just like you were, and I promised I'd help out." He puts his hand on my shoulder again. "Don't worry, son. They'll take good care of you," he says, pointing to Rose, Momma and my friends. "You'll be okay."

"I know. I'm feeling better all the time." I'm getting eager to cross that doorway.

"That's the spirit," he says, giving me a big wink.

I hesitate for a moment, struggling to find a way to thank him for all he's doing – for me and for the others, too. Our eyes meet, and we just look at each other for a minute or two. Just two old soul-friends drinking deep of each other. He says softly, "You're welcome, old friend, but you don't need to thank me. You'd have done it for me, too. In fact, you've done it for me a bunch of times. That's just what you do when you care about someone. Right?"

I just nod to him, so full to overflowing with good feelings that I can't talk. He gives me a big, long bear hug.

Finally, I work up my courage: "Daddy, there's something important I gotta ask." I look down, a little afraid to hear his answer. "It's about the boys. I know some of 'em back down there. Now, I don't know if I'd be any good at it – not like you – but some of 'em would recognize me, and I think maybe I could help – if you think I could. I mean, I'd really like to give it a try."

"Son, I was hoping you'd ask. And don't you worry; you'll be just fine at it. Lord knows, there're plenty of boys to go around, and it'll take a good while to bring 'em all back."

He puts a hand on my shoulder again. "But that can wait a little while. For now, you need to go on up with the others. Take a little time to sort things out. Then when you're ready, I'll come get you. Okay?"

I nod my head and give him a big smile, real happy that he wants me to help.

"All right, son. Now, you get going." He smiles and gives me a friendly slap on the back. "You can't keep the women waiting any longer. And I'll see you later. You and I have some more boys to be bringing back."

With that, he turns and heads back down towards James and the other boys, raising a big hand and waving it back and forth real friendly-like. "See you soon, Daddy," I whisper, my eyes misting up a little.

"John?" Rose's faint, sweet voice shakes me out of my thoughts. Turning, I rush on up towards the group, waving to 'em and giving silent thanks to the Lord for a second chance to see 'em again. I felt real bad about not giving Rose a proper good-bye. I thought I'd lost her, but now, I'll get to hold her close again. How lucky can a man get? Don't know exactly how it works up here, but, if I'm *real* lucky, maybe Rose'll be wearing that perfume of hers again! Always loved the smell of roses when I came back in from having a really rough day.

Figure 2-38. John Hogans' body was buried on the Appomattox battlefield on April 13, 1865. *[Courtesy of P. Schroeder, Appomattox Court House National Historical Park.]*

> **Final Resting Place**
> Later, John's body was moved to the Confederate Cemetery at the Appomattox Court House National Historic Park. He is there along with nineteen other boys who gave up the ghost that day. Only eight of them are known by name.
> When they made the new tombstone, they misspelled John's name, accidentally leaving off the "s," but by then, John didn't mind. The body of John Hogans is still at Appomattox today – though, happily, I've moved on!

Life Review & Analysis

GROUP-LINKS: In every lifetime, there are many connections to other souls in other past lives. Becoming aware of those connections in each lifetime is very useful if you wish to use your past life experiences to improve your present circumstances. These connections are one of the reasons we say "history repeats itself." Often, the same souls are the ones doing the repeating.

GROUP-LINK: "Johnson & Johnson for President," The Lincoln-Kennedy Connection

While working on the details of John Hogans' life in a hypnosis session, some surprising information came up concerning the assassination of Abraham Lincoln. On Good Friday, April 14, 1865, just two days after John Hogans'

Figure 2-39. Engraving of the assassination of Pres. Abraham Lincoln. *[Courtesy of the Library of Congress.]*

death and the war's end, John Wilkes Booth assassinated President Lincoln at Ford's Theater in Washington. It appears that the Confederate Secret Service originally conceived the plot as a means to kidnap Pres. Lincoln, but not to kill him. The intention was to paralyze the North while allowing time for the beleaguered Southern armies to recover.

When the plot was discovered by the Union War Department under Edwin Stanton, a group of Northerners decided to co-opt the plot for their own purposes and to help the kidnapping succeed. Some Union politicians felt that the soon-to-be-defeated South should be viewed as a conquered country, whose assets should be regarded as the "spoils of war" and divided up among the victorious states. Millions of dollars were at stake, and these men wanted to profit from the defeat of the South. However, Pres. Lincoln strongly opposed this, insisting that it was time to heal the wounds caused by the war. Because of Lincoln's adamant position, members of his own party decided to allow the South to kidnap him to keep him from interfering with their plans.

John Wilkes Booth, chosen by the Confederate Secret Service to organize the mission, gathered other conspirators around him. A group of wealthy Maryland Confederate sympathizers, including Dr. Samuel Mudd, Dr. William Bowman, Col. Samuel Cox, and Thomas Jones, assisted Booth with money and plans.

At first, Booth followed orders to arrange the kidnapping, but then, unexpectedly, Gen. Lee surrendered at Appomattox on April 9, 1865. With this change of events, Booth became more desperate and more resentful of Lincoln, whom he likened to "the tyrant, Caesar."

Figure 2-40. Wanted poster from 1865 for Booth and two other conspirators. Because the dollar was worth more back then, the $100,000 reward would be worth millions today. *[Courtesy of the Lib. of Congress.]*

During the week after the surrender, unknown to most of the other conspirators, Booth changed his objective from kidnapping to assassination. On April 15, 1865, after Booth shot the president, the authorities quickly moved against the supposed ringleaders. Within a short period of time, most of the alleged conspirators were either dead or in prison, seemingly putting an end to this dark chapter of United States history. But did it?

In an unexpected twist, my own meditation, along with information from Reflection (2002), indicates that nearly all of those Lincoln conspirators were involved in some way with the assassination of President Kennedy nearly 100 years later. Some reincarnated as Kennedy conspirators; others came back as policemen, reporters, or just simple bystanders for this historic event, so similar to the one that occurred during the last days of the Civil War.

Figure 2-41. Dealey Plaza, Dallas, 1963: In an odd twist of karma, about two dozen souls who were involved with the Lincoln assassination would be involved here in Dallas nearly 100 years later. *[Courtesy City of Dallas.]*

SOUL-BALANCE, or karma, arranged for the various players to be present at both assassinations. Group connections can be powerful, and the influence of karma can extend over hundreds or thousands of years.

Some of the more unusual Lincoln-Kennedy connections are as follows:

Figure 2-42. *Abraham Lincoln and Charles Lindbergh photographs courtesy of the Library of Congress.*

#1. ABRAHAM LINCOLN to CHARLES LINDBERGH

In 1865, unlike today, many people strongly disliked **Pres. Abraham Lincoln**. Some newspapers caricatured him as being ugly and ungainly. Tired of the constant criticism and bickering, the soul who was Lincoln dreamed of a less contentious future ... and he got one. Reincarnating as the boyishly handsome **Charles Lindbergh**, he achieved lifelong fame and the love of millions of people. As such, he received a well-deserved reward for a very difficult lifetime as Lincoln.

While not a direct participant in the JFK assassination, Lindbergh was undoubtedly distressed by the event. Perhaps this soul could empathize with President Kennedy, since he went through the same experience himself 100 years earlier.

Figure 2-43. *Artistic representation of Samuel Cox, adapted by the author from a painting. Photo of JFK courtesy of the Library of Congress.*

#2. COL. SAMUEL COX to JOHN F. KENNEDY

Most people remember **Pres. Kennedy's** civil rights record as one of supporting African-Americans. Such was not the case in his previous incarnation. As **Col. Samuel Cox**, a wealthy Maryland plantation owner, he supported secession and slavery, and along with Thomas Jones, a close relative, Cox acted as a secret agent for the South.

Very upset with Lincoln's policies on slavery, Col. Cox became one of the leaders who supported the plot to kidnap Lincoln but was not aware of the plans to assassinate him. Col. Cox was accused of helping Booth escape into Virginia and was briefly jailed.

In order to balance the karmic events that he had set into motion, Col. Cox reincarnated as John F. Kennedy to experience assassination firsthand. Oddly enough, Thomas Jones, Col. Cox's relative, reincarnated as H.L. Hunt, Kennedy's adversary, in order to play out a revised version of their old karmic drama of "How to Kill a President." They held "starring roles" in both of those dramas.

Figure 2-44. *Mary Lincoln photograph courtesy of the Library of Congress. Jacqueline Kennedy photograph courtesy of the JFK Library.*

#3. MARY LINCOLN to JACQUELINE KENNEDY.

In 1865, **Mary Todd Lincoln**, sitting an arm's length away when Lincoln was shot at Ford's Theater, cradled the dying president in her arms. In an odd repeat of history, during her next lifetime as **Jacqueline Kennedy**, she also cradled President Kennedy, dying after he was shot in Dealey Plaza.

In addition, as Mary Lincoln, she was considered homely and socially ill at ease. Because of the criticism of others, she developed the desire to be beautiful, well-bred, and well-thought-of. Her desire was fulfilled as the gracious Jacqueline Kennedy.

Mary Todd Lincoln became very distraught after Lincoln's death. Never recovering from the incident, she was hospitalized in an asylum near the end of her life. On the other hand, the same soul, as Jackie, became a role model for others who looked up to her for her handling of the difficult and traumatic events in her life.

Figure 2-45. *Andrew Johnson engraving courtesy of the Library of Congress. Lyndon Johnson photograph courtesy of the LBJ Library.*

#4. ANDREW JOHNSON to LYNDON JOHNSON.

The soul who was **Andrew Johnson** reincarnated later as **Lyndon Johnson**. As we review history, we find some striking similarities between the lives of the two men. Contemporaries accused both men of having been a part of each respective assassination and of organizing the cover-ups that followed. Both were tactless and impatient, and both were one-term presidents. Because Andrew Johnson was not accepted or effective as president, he was driven from office. Deeply resentful, he wanted another try at it. As Lyndon Johnson, he was effective but, as before, was not well liked or fully accepted. He was driven from office by his Vietnam policies.

Reflection (2002) indicated that both men had advance knowledge of the impending plot and "looked the other way" in order to further their own self-interests in becoming president. Choosing to undertake some very unusual and difficult lessons, this soul experienced becoming president *twice* through assassination.

Figure 2-47. *Pinkerton photograph courtesy of the Library of Congress. Hoover photograph courtesy of the LBJ Library.*

#5. ALLAN PINKERTON to J. EDGAR HOOVER.

Pres. Lincoln chose **Allan Pinkerton** to establish the first Secret Service for the Union Army, in order to spy on the Confederates. After the war, Pinkerton resumed work at his Pinkerton Detective Agency, the first such agency ever founded. The company logo was a huge black and white eye, which gave rise to the popular term "private eye." The agency played a major role in ending the crime careers of men such as Jesse James, Butch Cassidy, and the Sundance Kid.

Having developed an attraction to spy work and for apprehending the "bad guys," this soul reincarnated as the famous FBI boss, **J. Edgar Hoover**. In a repeat of history, this soul was involved in the investigations of the assassinations of two presidents.

Figure 2-48. *Grant photograph courtesy of the Library of Congress. Colby photograph courtesy of the National Archives (NARA).*

#6. GEN. U.S. GRANT to WILLIAM COLBY.

Warned in advance of the covert Lincoln kidnapping plans (but not the assassination plans), **Gen. Grant** declined at the last minute to attend Ford's Theater on the night of the assassination. Because of his war efforts and his support for the plot, Grant was rewarded with his party's nomination for president a few years later, and he succeeded Andrew Johnson as president.

The same soul returned as **William Colby**, who would become head of the CIA. Colby gained notoriety for running assassination squads in Vietnam, and it is alleged that he used those same talents to organize the assassination of JFK, believing he did so in the national interest.

Grant was president when most of the Indian Wars took place in the western US, and he did little to change the Federal policy of extermination. Some of those exterminated Indians were reborn as Vietcong soldiers, most notably Crazy Horse, as well as Geronimo as Ho Chi Minh. The same soul that had been Pres. Grant had to fight them again as Colby, except that this time he lost.

Figure 2-49. *Artistic representations of Thomas Jones and H.L. Hunt, by the author, based on existing photographs of both men.*

#7. THOMAS JONES to H.L. HUNT.

Thomas A. Jones was a Maryland planter, slave owner, and Southern sympathizer who hated Lincoln and his policies toward the South. He was also the chief Confederate Secret Service agent in Maryland. Reflection (2002) indicated that he reincarnated as **H.L. Hunt**, a man with similar hatreds for the Kennedy clan. This same soul was an alleged mastermind of both the Lincoln kidnapping and the Kennedy assassination, planning and financing both.

It would appear that he had many reasons to act against Kennedy. Hunt was strongly anticommunist and felt that Kennedy had "gone soft" on Russia. In addition, as an oil billionaire businessman, he stood to profit richly from the war in Vietnam. He and other industrialists feared that Kennedy was planning to back down from the communists in Southeast Asia.

Others have alleged that Hunt was directly involved in the assassinations of Robert Kennedy and Martin Luther King. In an odd twist of karma, Jones (H.L. Hunt) conspired to kidnap Pres. Lincoln with Col. Cox, who later would become president himself as JFK!

Figure 2-50. *Booth photograph courtesy of the National Archives (NARA). Author's representation of the shadowy "CIA man," who is still living.*

#8. BOOTH to CIA OFFICER.

Reflection (2002) revealed that the soul who was **John Wilkes Booth** incarnated to play a major role in the JFK assassination. He came back as the **"CIA Man,"** who assisted the Mafia killer on the grassy knoll by providing crowd control. Several eyewitnesses who tried to reach the grassy knoll testified to having seen and talked to the man, who was wearing a disguise. The man is still alive today.

In another surprising karmic twist to the story, Reflection indicated that this same soul was formerly a Roman senator who stood by as his fellow senators assassinated Julius Caesar. As a hint of that past connection, Booth was often heard to refer to Lincoln as "that tyrant, Caesar."

This soul seems to have a powerful compulsion to assassinate leaders, although he is not alone. There were many others involved with both assassinations.

CHART: OTHER PLAYERS IN THE ASSASSINATIONS.

Fifteen other soul-connections are shown in the chart that follows. In these events surrounding the deaths of Lincoln, JFK, RFK, and Martin Luther King, history has repeated itself with great power, offering a stunning example of reincarnation and karma in action.

Description of the Individual's Life in Lincoln's time:	Description of the Individual's Life in Kennedy's time:
Audience member: for the "American Cousin" play at Ford's Theater (photo); not part of the plot. (1)	**Lucien Sarti:** Corsican Mafia; #1 shooter, fired from the grassy knoll; wore official uniform. (2)
Confederate assassin and saboteur: part Indian; spent most of the war behind Union lines.	**"B.D. Fortis,"** alias for #2 killer; CIA assassin; fired from lower floor of Dal-Tex Bldg. (photo). (3)
Edward Sothern: lead actor in the play at Ford's Theater; knew Booth but not about kidnap plot. (1)	**Paul Mondoloni:** #3 killer; Mafia drug runner; CIA informer; fired from in front of Depository (photo).(3)
Confederate soldier: served under Gen. Robert E. Lee; not part of assassination or kidnap plot.	**Lee Harvey Oswald:** patsy for the plot; did not kill Kennedy; did not know anything about the plot. (3)
George Atzerodt: tried to kill Vice-Pres. Andrew Johnson; was hanged as one of the main conspirators. (1)	**G. DeMohrenschildt:** CIA contact man for Oswald; shot himself rather than testify on JFK to the Senate. (2)
Dr. Samuel Mudd: jailed as a conspirator; involved in the kidnap plot but not in the assassination plans. (2)	One of the **Dallas doctors** at Kennedy's autopsy; not involved in assassination plot or the cover-up. (2)
Samuel Arnold: jailed as a conspirator; was involved in plans for the kidnapping but not assassination. (1)	**Earlene Roberts:** Oswald's landlady; was not aware of plot or of Oswald's covert connections. (2)

Identification Keys for the photo are: **(1)** these photos are courtesy of the Library of Congress; **(2)** author's drawings based on existing photographs; and **(3)** these photos courtesy of the JFK Archives, City of Dallas.

	Mrs. Mary Surratt: proclaimed that she was innocent, but she knew Booth's plans and was hanged. (2)	**Dallas Police officer:** rode behind JFK in the motorcycle escort; not part of or aware of Kennedy plot. (3)	
	Lewis (Payne) Powell: tried to kill Sec. of State Wm. Seward; hanged as a conspirator. (1)	**Spectator** in Dealey Plaza that day; was not involved in the assassination plot this time at all.	No Photo
	David Herold: helped Booth escape from Washington; for that, he was hanged as a conspirator. (1)	**Spectator (female),** who took photographs of Kennedy motorcade; was not part of the plot. (3)	
No Photo	**Dr. Wm. Bowman:** Maryland landowner; supported the plot to kidnap Lincoln but not to kill him.	**Robert F. Kennedy:** was killed later by the very same group of conspirators who had killed his brother. (1)	
	Charles Forbes: Lincoln's footman and messenger; was involved in Booth's plot to kill Lincoln. (2)	**One of Kennedy's bodyguards:** near limousine that day; had been on alert for threats to JFK. (2)	
No Photo	**John Parker:** police bodyguard; key player; deeply involved in helping Booth to kill Lincoln.	**Dallas Police officer:** rode behind JFK in motorcycle escort; was not involved in assassination plot. (3)	
	Dr. Charles Leale: first surgeon to reach Lincoln and to treat his wounds that night at Ford's Theater. (2)	**Abraham Zapruder,** who filmed a famous movie clip of JFK as the motorcade went through Dallas. (2)	
	Laura Keene: lead actress in "American Cousin," the play that was showing at Ford's Theatre that night. (2)	**Spectator (female),** who filmed another movie clip of the event that day at Dealey Plaza.	No Photo

Figure 2-51. *Lee photograph courtesy of the Library of Congress. Martin Luther King photograph courtesy of the National Archives (NARA).*

GROUP-LINK #2: "The General is King," The Robert E. Lee - Martin Luther King Connection.

On April 4, 1968, about one hundred years after John Hogans' death, James Earl Ray was alleged to have assassinated **Martin Luther King** in Memphis. In hypnotic trance, Reflection (2002) revealed that the high-level planners of King's assassination were incarnations of the same souls that had planned Lincoln's assassination. They same group already had killed John Kennedy a few years earlier and would kill his brother Robert on June 5, 1968. Their group karma has deep roots.

As one of the most surprising footnotes to this story, Reflection (2002) stated that the soul of **Gen. Robert E. Lee**, Virginia's favorite son, who died in 1870, reincarnated as Martin Luther King. He did so in order to balance some of the personal karma incurred by his role in the Confederate Army. Having adversely affected the lives of so many African-Americans as Robert E. Lee, he came back as Martin Luther King to balance things out and help African-Americans move ahead in a society that, in some ways, still has not progressed very far beyond the days of slavery.

Lessons Learned

Recalling a past lifetime is useful only if one uses the memories to become freer in the present lifetime. Reliving this lifetime as John Hogans brought up many powerful buried feelings:

- *Despair* over being wounded and being unable to return home to Rose.
- *Grief* over having to leave Rose; grief over seeing our Southern way of life destroyed; and grief over seeing so many men killed so needlessly.
- *Fear* of the overwhelming chaos of warfare; fear of dying.
- *Anger* at Custer, who played a major role in the defeat of the South; anger at Custer's cavalryman for mortally wounding me.
- *Physical Pain* caused by the bullet wound to my leg and by the amputation; pain caused by the other Yankee bullet, which left me nearly deaf and partially blind.

As I became aware of these feelings, I worked to undo them, primarily using the Sedona Method mentioned in Appendix A1. As I let go of these past painful memories, it was as if a heavy weight lifted from my mind. Even though these memories were far in the distant past, they still affected me on a subconscious level. Undoing them has left me freer of unwanted emotions and freer to live in the present moment. Anyone can do the same thing with past life recall.

During and after the times that I am experiencing a past life scene, I always ask myself, "What lessons did I learn from this experience?" Then, I try to apply those lessons to my present life. Some of the positive experiences of that lifetime were:

- *Devotion to family:* I experienced the camaraderie of a large family – a pair of loving parents, five brothers, and four sisters; and a close relationship with my wife, Rose.
- *Development of conscience:* I explored the conflict of fighting for the cause of slavery, a cause that I did not accept.

NOTE: Appendix A contains information about some simple yet very powerful spiritual techniques. They can free you from the undesirable effects of past lives and allow you to get the best out of your current life.

Sorrel Horse: Battle of the Little Bighorn (1863-1876)

Figure 3-1. Battle of the Little Bighorn, 1876. *[Detail from drawing by Schreyvogel. Reprinted from Brady (1904).]*

Historical Background on Custer's Last Stand

After my previous Makah and Civil War lifetimes, my soul incarnated on the Great Plains as a Cheyenne boy named Sorrel Horse who was adopted into the Lakota tribe. They also were called the "Sioux" by the whites and by some hostile tribes, but the Lakota never used that term to describe themselves.

In this lifetime, among other experiences, Sorrel Horse was at the Battle of the Little Bighorn. His name, translated as: "He who owns a Sorrel Horse," is mentioned many times in the historical records of interviews with some of the Indian survivors. [See the books by Hardorff in the bibliography.]

What Really Happened that Day?

Some of Maj. Reno's soldiers survived the battle, but because they were pinned down elsewhere, they did not witness Custer's Last Stand. There were no white survivors from that part of the battle. Because of that, the Battle of the Little Bighorn has become one of the most enduring and hotly debated mysteries of American History. But what *really* happened that day? Now it can be told through the eyes of Sorrel Horse, since I was there. The story that follows describes the battle in high detail, some of which is sure to be controversial and some of which has never before been revealed.

The Lakota felt a bond to the land and to *Wakan Tanka*, the Lakota name for the Great Spirit, in what was both their culture and their religion. The encroaching white man could not, and would not, understand such a deep faith, and by the summer of 1876, the white men had become such a problem that the Native Americans had to find a solution. In the largest enclave of tribes ever assembled, seven tribes met on the banks of the Little Bighorn River to decide what to do.

On June 25, 1876, a small group of Crow and Arikara scouts, who had allied themselves with the army, rode with the 7th Cavalry under George Armstrong Custer. Though he was a Lieutenant Colonel, he preferred the title of General, his rank during the Civil War. The soldiers approached the village on the Little Bighorn intending either to force the Indians onto reservations or to kill many of them. They would accomplish neither that day.

Reasons for Custer's Defeat

Custer's profound defeat had its roots in political infighting far from the plains of Montana. Earlier in the year, Custer had incurred President Grant's wrath by filing a complaint that alleged massive corruption in the U.S. Indian Service. His complaint became headline news, and Congress summoned him to testify. Those politicians who opposed Grant used the hearings to embarrass the president. A furious Grant punished Custer by removing him from command in the Indian Wars.

Although Custer's apologies and his political support caused Grant to relent, Custer was given only a secondary role in the Indian Wars. Custer, now worried that his military career was in serious jeopardy, became determined to redeem himself in battle with a glorious personal victory.

Because he was so desperate for a win, Custer overlooked several serious problems. First, he ignored the warnings of his scouts about the enormous size of the camp; he was outnumbered 20 to 1 (over 11,000 Indians to only 600 troops). Second, he ignored the fact that his highly touted 7th Cavalry consisted mostly of poorly-trained raw recruits, many of them immigrants who spoke only limited English, who had never fought in close combat with Indians, and who had never even fired their rifles from horseback.

However, Custer's major problem was more serious than the others, as you will see as our story unfolds. What follows is the story of that day, as I experienced it in the body of Sorrel Horse, a 13-year-old Lakota warrior ...

The Day of the Battle of the Little Bighorn

Hunched over and creeping quietly through the tall, wild grass near the edge of the river, my best friend Whirlwind stops abruptly. He remains motionless, silent. I do the same. He has spotted the "enemy" moving through the shallow water along the riverbank. Slowly, he gives a hand sign for me to be very still. Intently and gradually, he lifts his bow. Rising slightly on his toes, an arrow already strung, he pulls the arrow back to the hilt of the iron arrowhead. When the owl feathers of the shaft touch his cheek, he lets the arrow fly, and the taut string resounds with a twang. In the blink of an eye, the arrow plunges deep into the flesh of the "enemy."

"Ho, brother!" Whirlwind shouts. "Surely, the Council will have to give me my first feather now."

Figure 3-2. Whirlwind, the closest friend of Sorrel Horse, looked a lot like this young Native American. *[Photograph by E.S. Curtis, ca. 1910. Courtesy of the Library of Congress.]*

Excited with the triumph, Whirlwind wades headlong into the river to count coup. A few leaps ahead of Whirlwind, Straw Dog, his favorite hound, splashes into the stream, taking the arrow in his teeth, tugging at the "enemy" vigorously, and plunging his head underwater to grab his head. After a moment, Straw Dog raises his head, barks loudly several times, and plunges his head underwater again. I am several steps behind as Whirlwind rushes into the water, hastily pushing the dog aside. He plunges his arm into the water, up to his elbow, grabbing the "enemy" by the head and pulling him to the surface.

"Surely this one is a great "chief." Maybe they will give me two feathers," he crows, proudly displaying his kill – a small, still wiggling trout. *[See inset.]*

Laughing, I shake my head and reply, "If that is the chief, it must be a tribe of very small warriors."

> **Counting Coup**
> Warriors won a feather by counting coup, that is, by touching an enemy warrior, usually with what was known as a coup stick. A warrior showed the greatest bravery by counting coup on an opposing warrior who was still alive.
> At this time in the story, neither Whirlwind nor Sorrel Horse had yet earned a first feather.

Figure 3-3. The camp along the Little Bighorn River. *[Photograph by E.S. Curtis, ca. 1908. Courtesy of the Library of Congress.]*

Whirlwind tosses the fish in his bag and announces as if serious, "Little brother, many more "warriors" of this chief's tribe are out there. I must do my duty. I return to the war path to engage the "enemies" of my People."

I nod, playing along with him as he returns to the river. Eventually I lose interest and my worries return. We, the Lakota and our allies, know the soldiers are out there somewhere. Scanning the hills to the east and north, I notice only a few warriors along the high bluffs guarding the camp. Other than that, I see nothing but tall grass, sagebrush, and brown earth. The elders tell us that there are only a few soldiers and that there are many of us. They say that they have never seen so many of our People come together before – but still I worry.

To the south, I see many teepees with lazy blue ribbons of smoke rising from the campfires. Seven tribes of Lakota and Cheyenne are gathered here today on the prairie. Most are near the banks of the river where the ash, elder, and cottonwood trees provide the comfort of some concealment. The tribes have set up buffalo-skin lodges with seven great circles of teepees shining white in the sun – one for each tribe. Warriors, women, and little ones, are milling around, working, laughing, and playing. *[See inset.]*

> **Seven Tribes**
> These were the **Uncpapas** under Sitting Bull, the overall spiritual leader of this gathering of tribes; the **Oglalas** under Crazy Horse, one of the most widely respected war-chiefs; the **Sans Arc**; the **Minneconjou**; the **Brules**; the **Blackfoot** Sioux; and the **Cheyenne** under Ice Bear.

Figure 3-4. Cheyenne warrior-guards riding the bluffs above the river. *[Photograph by E.S. Curtis, ca. 1910. Courtesy of the Library of Congress.]*

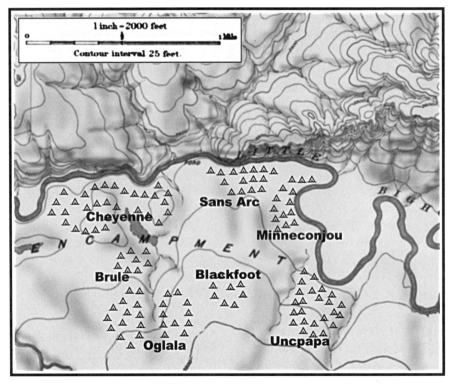

Figure 3-5. Shaded contour map, showing the encampment about as it appeared in 1876. Based on information from Lt. Godfrey, one of the survivors. *[Notations added. Adapted from a map courtesy of the USGS.]*

Shading my eyes with my hands, I gaze up at the sky. It is a hot, summer day, with the sun not yet directly overhead. Other than a few high wisps of clouds, the sky is clear and bright blue. I sit at the northern end of our camp near the Cheyenne circle, on an old, smooth log along the creek, with my bare feet dangling in the cool water.

Picking up my rifle, I begin cleaning it carefully. A giant cottonwood tree spreads its wide branches out over the stream, giving shade from the heat. As the prairie wind moves gently through the leaves, they rustle slightly, sending flickering patches of light dancing around me.

Figure 3-6. The "Gun that Won the West." *[Photograph courtesy of the Library of Congress.]*

From the river, Whirlwind shouts again and I look up. Proudly, he holds up another fish, even smaller than the last. Stuffing the fish into his bag, he splashes over and sits down on the log beside me.

As I rub the dust off the brass body of my rifle, Whirlwind, who is like a brother to me, watches intently in silence. He moves in closer to look at the gun, fidgeting around, as if he wants to reach out, grab it, and finish cleaning it himself. I am very proud of my fine gun, which the traders call a Winchester. It is a special gun, and only a very few warriors have one like it. I am happy to show it off to others who do not have one, like Whirlwind. Pretending not to notice his attention, I work the lever several times quickly to cock the rifle and eject cartridges onto the ground. Whirlwind's eyes grow big. He is amazed. He has seen me do this at least a dozen times, but he never fails to be surprised. That is why I like him as a friend.

In normal times, I would be dreaming of hunting buffalo with my new rifle, but these are not normal times. Many of our People have abandoned the reservations, and this has not pleased the *wasichus [Lakota word for "white men"]*. Our People were tired of the rotten food, bad treatment, and broken promises. Now, war brings us together – a war that we did not seek – a war that we do not truly understand.

"I hear Sitting Bull talk, along with Crazy Horse and the others," Whirlwind breaks the silence. "Some argue that we must fight the *wasichus*. Others say we must find out what they want and seek a way to live in peace with them. For me, I prefer to fight – that is what they want – that is what I want. On this matter, we agree." He thumps his closed fist on his chest as he finishes.

"I am not yet a full warrior, so the elders do not ask my opinion," I offer, "but it seems the only thing the *wasichus* want is to see us dead, so that they may step over our cold bodies and take our land without argument."

Whirlwind nods in agreement. "They come to us with broad smiles, carrying trinkets in their hands. Behind our backs, they sneak into the Black Hills to dig up our sacred lands. They look for the shiny yellow rocks, and then they fight among themselves to see who can grab the most." In disgust, Whirlwind kicks at a small rock buried in the ground. When it comes loose, he grabs it and tosses it angrily into the river.

"They are crazy for these rocks," he says with a crooked smile. "Like the buffalo eating crazyweed. Their eyes become wild – their tongues hang out – they stagger around and cannot walk straight." Jumping up, he sticks two fingers from his forehead like horns and wobbles around like a drunken buffalo. We both laugh.

Whirlwind sits down again. "I have no use for the yellow rocks, brother, but I would go find them, and trade them to the *wasichus* for things I want, such as a fine gun like yours." He reaches over and slides his fingers with envy along the rifle barrel.

"Better to take one from the enemy, like I did," I caution. "The white traders cannot be trusted to sell you a gun that works right. And then there are the bullets that come from the traders. Just yesterday, I went out to hunt rabbits. I pulled the trigger, *click*. Nothing happened! I had to try three bullets before one would fire. I should have walked over and clubbed the rabbit with the rifle. It would have been easier."

I do not tell Whirlwind that my bullet missed the rabbit, which promptly ran away in panic. I have too few bullets for practice with my new Winchester, so hitting anything is mostly a matter of luck. I worry that after shooting at an angry *wasichu*, he will not run away like a frightened rabbit.

As I go on about traders and bullets, Whirlwind gets more and more annoyed; "Oh, be quiet!" he finally says. "You just do not want me to have a fine gun like yours. But I do not care what you say; I will get one! With a gun like that, I will become a great warrior, someday maybe even a chief." He looks at me defiantly.

I was truly just trying to be helpful, but now, I can hardly hold back my grin, "Yes, brother, you will be a mighty chief, a great leader – always trying to lead the pretty young women to your teepee."

He pushes me playfully, "Hah, like you are some expert on chiefs – or on young women, for that matter."

I shove him right back. We both laugh and, now, become silent for a while. I know from hearing the elders talk that they are worried. Our People have honor, and most *wasichus* have none. But they have powerful weapons, and their bullets never run out.

Several moons ago, Sitting Bull had a dream vision. He saw the sun rising over the eastern prairie. Far, far away at the horizon, the grass began to turn black, as creatures, like ants, swarmed towards him across the prairie. In the vision, Sitting Bull squinted hard trying to see those creatures clearly. What were they? Were they buffaloes? As they came closer, he could see that they were herds of *wasichus*, never-ending, stretching to the horizon. Sitting Bull awoke, and remembering his dream vision, he became more worried for our People.

I, too, am worried. We have proven to them that we are great pony-warriors. The *wasichus* are good fighters, too, though not as brave as we are. But when one of them falls, two ride out to take his place. Now, more and more, after one of our warriors has fallen, only children and old men are left to take his place. In the old days, neither Whirlwind nor I would be fighting. We would be tending horses, dreaming of being great warriors, and fighting for the attention of the young women – but not fighting *wasichus*.

In our tribe, a child usually does not become a man until fourteen summers have passed, but I am big for my age, and I have seen and done things that have aged me quickly.

Figure 3-7. Sitting Bull photo, taken circa 1878, only a few years after the Battle of the Little Bighorn. *[Reprinted from Brady (1904).]*

I learned that the *wasichu's* gun made him into a powerful warrior. Not long ago, after the fierce battle with Three Stars *[Gen. George Crook]*, I found this rifle under the body of a dead *wasichu* scout. The barrel was blue-black, but the body was bright yellow-gold and warm. It was heavy, and as I held it, a sense of great power flowed through me. I have not yet counted my first coup or won my first warrior's feather, but at that moment, with this Winchester in my hands, I grew up and became a man.

As I sit recalling that day, I idly run my fingers along the rifle stock, tracing the small cuts in the wood. They were there when I took it from the enemy scout — small V-shaped notches — cut with a knife and smoothed out with use. Another warrior told me the *wasichus* make these marks to count their "kills." I shake my head, thinking a notch is such a small mark to stand for a man's life-blood.

Suddenly, a dark shadow moves in front of me. Looking up, I see the silhouette of a man. With his head blocking the sun, I cannot make out his features, but I recognize his moccasins and leggings as Arapaho.

As I shade my eyes with my hand, he begins to speak in sign language. "Children - not - play - with - gun. Not - safe. Give - me - gun. I - keep - until - you - are - warrior."

He holds out his hand to take the gun. Defensively, I slide it back on my lap, and now I sign back to him, "No! You - not - safe. Not - know - which - end - bullet - goes. You - pull - trigger. Blow - hole - in - head." **[See inset.]**

Sign Language
Many tribes used this in order to communicate with each other, since often they could not speak each other's language. Since sign language is a simple abbreviated form of speaking, few words are used, and when written, it tends to sound childlike.

Figure 3-8. "I can see only his legs, but I recognize his leggings and moccasins as Arapaho." *[Denver Public Library, Western History Coll.; Rinehart, X-32131.]*

When Whirlwind laughs, the Arapaho leans forward menacingly, narrowing his eyes and tightening his face. His fingers flicker rapidly, making signs, "Watch - out - baby - boy. Some - night - no - moon. Wild - wolf - find - your - teepee. Kill - while - you - sleep. Take - gun."

While he is signing, I slowly swing the rifle around, pointing the barrel at his knees. As he finishes, I sign back, "Wolf - not - get - gun. Only - get - mouthful - bullets."

Suddenly, he tries to grab the barrel with his hand. I jerk it away from him. Whirlwind and I jump up, confronting him nose-to-nose, glaring angrily. Never breaking my gaze with his eyes, he turns his head slightly to the side and spits on the ground. We stand with eyes locked for five long heartbeats. Finally, he walks away slowly, still holding my gaze. As he leaves, he signs, "You - me - not - finished!"

He makes the Lakota hand gesture for a strong insult. Whirlwind steps towards him, making the same sign twice in return. *[See inset.]*

As we watch him leave, Whirlwind says, "I have seen him before. He is a renegade that is crazy to kill *wasichus*. I do not know his name, but I shall call him 'Spitting Wolf.'" He glares in his direction.

With a sigh, I say, "Brother, I have almost no memories of times without war. Though Crazy Horse and the others love to fight, I am tired of it. Having seen too much death, I long for peace. I would gladly give up this rifle to see Mother and Father again. I am no longer eager for battle. Instead, I have my eye on several girls ... and maybe ..." My thoughts trail off, and I do not want to speak of them, even to Whirlwind.

A young Cheyenne girl, about our age, walks down to the river to fill bladder bags with water. *[See inset.]*

I know she sees us, and I have tried to talk to her before, but since I am not a warrior, she will not look or at speak to me. Even our women are caught up in the madness of war. A woman will

---

Hand Gesture

This serious insult was delivered with a quick hand motion somewhat like throwing dirt in someone's face. According to legend, the gesture originated with the Oglalas, whose name can be translated roughly as "The Dirt Throwers."

Flash Forward

In my current lifetime, a part-Indian friend taught me a few dozen Oglala words, which I used on my sixth-grade classmates. However, not only did they have no idea what I was talking about, they also thought I was crazy.

This was especially true of one young girl, who had grown up in Indian country in South Dakota and for whom I developed a serious though futile attraction. She looked remarkably like the young 14-year-old girl in the photo on the next page.

Years later during meditation, I recognized her as one of the young girls who, in a repeat of karma, had haughtily spurned my interest as Sorrel Horse.

Figure 3-9. This 1903 photo of a young girl looks remarkably like my classmate who showed no interest in me or in the Lakota language. *[Photograph by E.S. Curtis, ca. 1903. Courtesy of the Library of Congress.]*

not accept the attention of a man who has not killed an enemy warrior and won a feather. In the old times, the greatest honor was won by touching the enemy in battle and letting the enemy live. Now, the *wasichus* have taught us to kill without honor. This war is poison to our People.

After looking around to make sure no one is nearby, Whirlwind leans over and speaks in a low voice, "I know Crazy Horse is a great man, but he is too crazy for me. His eyes look too far beyond this world. It is right for People to call him The-One-Who-is-Different. I do not feel at ease around him. If you have not counted coup, he does not even see you. He looks right through you. He makes my skin feel funny."

I nod my head, "I know. That is why I feel closest to Sitting Bull. He is the same as Father was, wise about the spirit world, yet able to live in our world, too. I can talk to him whenever I need some wise words. He does not look down on anyone." *[See inset.]*

> **Sitting Bull**
> When Sorrel Horse's family was killed by Custer's men, Sitting Bull adopted him and his Grandmother into his band of Lakota, even though they were Cheyenne. He became like a grandfather to the young man.

Whirlwind says, "True, Sitting Bull is wisest, but without a doubt, Crazy Horse is fiercest. Maybe the *wasichus* will think he is too crazy and leave us alone. That is my prayer. I, for one, do not wish to return to the reservation."

"There is no 'wishing' for me. I will not go there!" I declare with sudden fierceness. "The whites demand that we go, but I will not!"

My anger grows, and I jump up, "Why would I be so foolish? Out here, I can ride my pony as fast as the eagle, feeling the wind in my face and the prairie sun on my skin. I can let my hair fly free with no … no …" I practically spit it out, "with no *wasichu* telling me what to do!"

Whirlwind is not surprised at my strong feelings. He says, "Crazy Horse beat Three Stars less than a moon ago, and now there are so many more of us. Even now, our People arrive daily from all over the plains. Surely, the troopers will be afraid to attack us here along the river. Sitting Bull and Crazy Horse believe we are safe … for now."

He looks up to see if I am okay, "Tell me again of the vision Sitting Bull had last night."

Calming down a little, I sit down again. I repeat the vision to him, just as if I were seeing it myself, "From out of the blue sky, dead soldiers come falling upside down into our camp. *Wakan Tanka* speaks and says, 'I will deliver them to you, even greater than with Three Stars.' At the end, Yellow-Hair *[Gen. Custer]* tumbles into camp with the other troopers. He wears a sad face. *Wakan Tanka* says, 'Here is a great warrior who is ready to die. I give him to you.'"

I stop to look at Whirlwind, "Sitting Bull thinks that soon we will have a great victory over the Yellow-Haired Chief."

Whirlwind has never seen the white chief, and most others here have not seen him either. Only the Southern Cheyenne know what he looks like. I first saw him when I was very young. Even though our chief flew the flag of truce, he attacked our camp at Washita, killing my father, mother, and sister, along with many other women and children. I was young, but I will never forget his face. I have seen him several times since then, when he has ridden into our camp to parley with our chiefs. It is a mystery to me that some of the Cheyenne leaders speak highly of him, even though he has killed many of our families. *[See inset.]*

Even though I respect the fighting abilities of my enemies, I will be glad to see Yellow-Hair die. To me, as one of the greatest *wasichu* chiefs, he represents all

> **Flash Forward**
> The Lakota called Gen. Custer "Yellow-Hair," or "Long Hair," because he often wore his blond hair very long. However, just before this battle, he had cut his hair short so that it would be easier to care for in the field.
> When I first saw a photo of Custer in my current lifetime, I felt an instant, intense dislike for him. Puzzled and curious, I explored those feelings, uncovering vivid memories of this lifetime and of my previous life as John Hogans, in which another one of Custer's cavalrymen had fatally wounded me at Appomattox just 11 years earlier.
> It also reawakened memories as a Roman soldier in hand-to-hand combat with the soul who became Custer. But more about that story a little later ...

Figure 3-10. "Custer's troopers attacked the camp at Washita, even though it was under a flag of truce." *[Frederic Remington drawing of the "Attack on Dull Knife." Reprinted from Brady (1904).]*

Figure 3-11. Sorrel Horse's sister was killed by troopers at Washita, but she reincarnated soon after as a Lakota girl named Lucille. This is the 1907 photo of her. After Lucille died, the same soul reincarnated again as a spiritual friend in my current lifetime. *[Photograph by E.S. Curtis, ca. 1903. Courtesy of the Library of Congress.]*

that is bad with them. To me, he is the chief of the liars and thieves. He stands for the death of my sister and parents, for the loss of freedom of my People. I look forward to meeting him again on the battlefield.

Whirlwind comments, "If Yellow-Hair is coming here to die, I will gladly help him. I will be the first to strike him with my coup stick." He stands up, raising both arms to the sky. Turning slowly from east to west, raising his voice, he boasts loudly to me, to the dragonflies, and to the grasshoppers, "Let it be known to all, I, Whirlwind, shall count coup on the white chief's head of yellow hair."

I try not to laugh at this thought. With a gleam in my eye, I look at Whirlwind. He is several winters older than I am, but he is a full head shorter. "Hah, you are not tall enough to count coup on Yellow-Hair's head. Better you should count coup on his kneecaps instead," I say.

As Whirlwind shoves me roughly, I fall off the log backwards, laughing. With a big grin, he jumps on me, straddles my chest, and holds my shoulders down; "I will count coup on you this day, brother, and win my first feather."

Choking with laughter, I struggle weakly against him, and we both have a good laugh. Still wrestling, we hear shouting from the south end of the village. Quickly, both of us sit up. Several Uncpapa warriors, some of the camp sentries, are galloping towards us. One of them is shouting, "Bluecoats! The *wasichus* are here!"

Many of our People are running in our direction. Some women and children are heading for cover in the thickets. Now we hear rifle shots – soldier

Figure 3-12. "Custer leads the troops and wagons towards the village." *[Photo of Custer with his troops, ca. 1874. Courtesy of the National Archives.]*

Figure 3-13. "The sentries race back to alert the village. The *wasichus* are coming!" *[Frederic Remington drawing of the "Pony War-Dance." Reprinted from Remington (1897).]*

rifles! Both of us jump up. Glancing at each other in excitement and surprise, we turn to race for our lodges. Over the crowd noise, with a big grin, Whirlwind yells, "I will count coup before you do, brother." I grin as I run off.

As I run, I wonder where the soldiers have come from. Why do they attack now? The troopers never attack at full sun.

I rush as fast as I can south to Grandmother's teepee in the Uncpapa circle. It is total chaos. Women are searching for their children. One woman clutches a young child and shrieks frantically for her other ones. Dogs are barking and running, unsure if the noise is fun or trouble. Some women and children are on foot, hurrying away as fast as they can, carrying buffalo-skin rolls of their possessions; others have already mounted horses and are racing away from the fighting to safety. With all the pounding feet and hooves, dust clouds rise throughout the village.

The Battle Starts

Late on the morning of June 25, 1876, Gen. Custer and the 7th Cavalry approached the huge Indian village camped along the Little Bighorn River. Custer commanded 595 men in 12 companies; he was about to attack what he believed to be a village containing no more than 3,000 warriors. Prior to reaching the camp, the soldiers had sighted several groups of hostile Indians. Certain that the element of surprise was gone, Custer decided to attack immediately, rather than wait for sunrise the next day.

Custer divided his troops into four battalions: (1) one company, containing about 130 men, stayed with the pack train carrying the ammunition and supplies; (2) Capt. Frederick Benteen, with three companies of about 125 men, was ordered south of the camp to block possible escape routes; (3) Gen. Custer commanded five companies of about 210 men. He continued north along the bluffs east of the river and the village; (4) Maj. Marcus Reno, leading three companies of about 130 men, was ordered to cross the Little Bighorn River and lead the first attack against the village from the south. Shots fired by Reno and his troopers began the battle.

Note: The battle scene descriptions that follow summarize many sources, including archaeological research and eyewitness accounts from some of the warriors and from some of Maj. Reno's troopers who survived. My own past life memories as Sorrel Horse are interwoven with the rest.

Figure 3-14. "The troopers attack the lower end of the village." *[Frederic Remington drawing of "The Charge." Reprinted from Remington (1897).]*

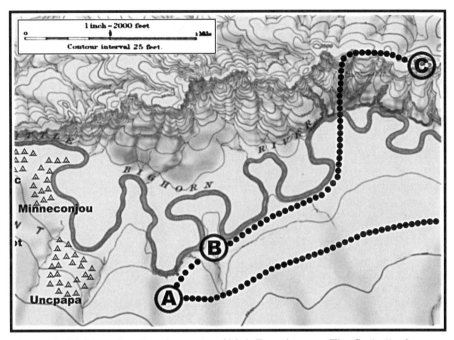

Figure 3-15. Map showing the route of Maj. Reno's men. The first attack came at **(A)**. Next, under heavy fire, Reno retreated to **(B)**. Finally, in a panic, he and his men scrambled across the river onto the bluffs at **(C)**. All of this took only about half an hour. Based on information from Lt. Godfrey, one of the survivors from Reno's command. *[Notations added. Adapted from a map from the USGS.]*

All around me, warriors race towards their teepees, making loud trilling war cries and searching for their horses. I have to dodge in and out of the frenzied rush of people to keep from being trampled. Weaving in and out among the teepees, I seek out the fastest route with the least obstacles.

As I approach the Uncpapa circle, I dimly see soldiers on foot and on horseback off to the south down along the river. I see puffs of smoke followed by the rapid *crack, crack, crack* of rifle fire. Bullets fly over my head, making buzzing sounds like angry bees. Several bullets kick up puffs of dirt as they crash into the ground around me. Dodging the bullets, I turn and run between two teepees.

Suddenly, an Oglala warrior on a buckskin pony gallops through at full speed from the other direction. With a bone-jarring thud, the pony's shoulder smashes into me, roughly tossing me on my back against the teepee cover. The first warrior gallops past; now a second one follows him. They do not pause to look back. Shaken but not hurt, I dust myself off, grab my rifle, and hurry onward.

Reaching Grandmother's lodge, I jerk back the flap and rush inside. Grandmother already has spread out my war gear on my buffalo robe. First, I pull on my elk-skin leggings and now my breechcloth. My pulse races with the rush of

Figure 3-16. "Custer's Crow scouts watch from the bluffs." *[Photograph by E.S. Curtis, ca. 1905. Courtesy of the Library of Congress.]*

war, and my hands move like flickering fire, but in my mind, all is slow motion, never fast enough.

Next, I grab Father's beaded war moccasins with the thunderbolt battle design. Inside, on the soles, spirit designs have been painted for protection. If I should die in battle, these moccasins will carry me to my ancestors in the land of *Wakan Tanka*. With them on, I am connected to all my family line. *[See inset.]*

Next, above each bicep, I fasten narrow buckskin straps, decorated with copper, turquoise beads, and hawk feathers. Grandmother pulls back my long hair and loops a braided buckskin thong around my head. Reaching up to touch my head-thong, I say a silent prayer. Perhaps by the end

> **Flash Forward**
> As a teenager in my current life, I was given an authentic pair of very old, beautifully beaded Lakota moccasins. As I touched them for the first time, I triggered powerful feelings and memories of this past lifetime.
>
> The soles were made of buffalo-hide, cut from an old cover from a tribal teepee. Inside, on the soles, faint medicine designs were still visible that had been painted on the teepee long ago.

Figure 3-17. "One of the chiefs points towards the attacking soldiers." *[Photograph by E.S. Curtis, ca. 1903. Courtesy of the Library of Congress.]*

of this day, if I am blessed by *Wakan Tanka*, I will have counted coup. Then, this thong can hold my first golden eagle feather, the sign to all men that I am a warrior.

"Hurry!" Grandmother urges, sensing my thoughts. "Hurry or there will be no more coup to count."

I do not answer; I only move faster. Grabbing a small, round, *wasichu* mirror, I spread war paint on my cheeks, using two fingers to make yellow and red vertical bars. Briefly, grudgingly, I admire the mirror, this example of *wasichu* ingenuity. They have great skills – making mirrors and guns. "Great skills, but why will they not leave us alone?" I mumble aloud as the anger wells up. "I do not admire that quality in them."

Figure 3-18. Sorrel Horse's moccasins might have looked like this pair. *[Denver Public Library, Western History Coll.; Poley, P-413]*

167

"What did you say?" asks Grandmother.

"Nothing," I say. "It is nothing."

We hear a loud *pop* and now another one. Instinctively, we both drop down to the ground. Bullets! Narrow shafts of bright sunlight stream in through two round bullet holes in the teepee. The bullets have passed right through the teepee over our heads. Now, we hear a loud *crack*. A shower of splinters rains down over us, and the south side of the teepee bows in sharply. A bullet has shattered a teepee pole, which leans in towards us like a dog's broken leg.

Keeping low, I frantically pull on my breastplate to cover my chest. It is made of long, narrow ocean shells along with owl and hawk bones. It belonged to Father and to his father before him. The pieces of bone can stop arrowheads, but they cannot stop bullets. Even so, I always wear it in battle against the bluecoats.

Hurrying, I strap my medicine pouch around my waist and grab my coup stick; they were given to me by Sitting Bull, so that I will be brave in battle and not fear death. Finished now, I am ready to fight. I glance one last time at Grandmother, who smiles, touches me on the forearm, and says, "Go now. Get going." I smile back.

Grabbing my rifle and bullets, I duck out of the tent into a scene of pandemonium. Hundreds of people are running in all directions. Dogs bark excitedly, chasing after the people and horses or cowering in fear. Clouds of fine dust fill the air. Gunfire and shouting still echo up the valley from the south. All around me, groups of warriors are racing frantically south to protect the village.

My first thought is to find my pony. Looking toward the western hills, I see herd-boys bringing our war-ponies back to camp. Some warriors have found their ponies already and are galloping off toward the fighting to the southeast. I look around anxiously, but I do not see my own pony. Finally, off in the distance, I recognize one of our herd-boys, driving a bunch of horses. The ponies are skittish and afraid of the gunfire, and the boy has trouble

Figure 3-19. Sorrel Horse's breastplate would have looked like this one worn by a Lakota named Crow King, ca. the 1880s. *[Reprinted from Brady (1904).]*

moving them to the camp. I cannot tell if my pony is among them, but I do not wait. I take a chance and race off across the flat bottomland to meet them.

Strong feelings well up inside me as I run: anger that we were surprised by the attack; excitement that I might win a feather today; fear that I could be injured; and irritation at having to run across these fields for my horse.

My breastplate bounces around wildly with each step, hitting my arms, neck, and face. At full speed, I race around prickly pears and through prairie dog villages. I must be very alert so as not to catch my foot in a burrow and break my leg. I imagine the tribe around the campfires telling the story after the fact, "Oh, yes, Sorrel Horse showed great courage in the battle. He was injured in a fierce struggle with the prairie dogs ... and they won."

Sweat streams down my face, and my arm aches from carrying the heavy rifle. Though it seems like it is taking forever, I am getting closer. Through the sweat and dust, I strain to see if my sorrel pony is with the herd. Finally, I see him. I put my palm to my lips and make the trilling call that is my special signal to him. He whinnies, tosses his head, and trots over with an excited look; he knows we are about to fight. Almost out of breath, I stop to give him a loving rub on his nose. Other than Whirlwind, he is my best friend.

He still has his rope-bridle on, and I flip the reins over his head. In one fluid motion, I grab his mane with my left hand and swing my right leg over to land on his back, keeping a tight grip on the rifle. I tap my pony's sides with my toes, and he lunges off towards the creek. As we approach camp again, I see many warriors – alone and in small groups – rushing south to the fighting.

One group, made up of about twenty young Santee boys and old men, trots by heading north along the river. Most are on foot, although a few have their horses already. The Santee leader, Walks-under-the-Ground, calls out to me, "Join us, brother. Ride with us to guard the buffalo ford."

I consider this for a moment, looking wistfully in the direction of the fighting. I can still hear rifle fire to the south, but I nod to him and swing my pony around to join the group. I am disappointed to be riding away from the fight, but it is the duty of young men to protect the women, children, and the old ones. Even though I am young, I have the right to decline a leader's request, and ride off to fight as I wish. Out of respect for Walks under the Ground, I do not. Perhaps there still will be time for battle honors later today.

We move off along the river towards the ford near the Cheyenne camp circle. Those of us on horses have to move at a slower pace, as the other men trot along on foot. All around us, women and children stream off to safety in the north. Many have left already, but many more are still in camp, and they raise dense dust clouds as they move away.

Figure 3-20. "An Oglala war party gallops towards the fighting." *[Photograph by E.S. Curtis, ca. 1907. Courtesy of the Library of Congress.]*

Major Reno's Retreat; The Fight at Medicine Tail Ford

The Warriors are like Bees after a Bear

Thousands of angry Lakota and Cheyenne warriors charged out to face Reno's three companies of 130 men. **[See Figure 3-15, (A).]** After fighting for about 15 – 20 minutes, Reno and his men, outnumbered about 20 to 1, retreated into the thick trees lining the river. **[See Figure 3-15, (B).]** There, Bloody Knife, the chief Arikara scout, was shot in the head and died while fighting alongside Reno. When the scout's blood splattered across Reno's head and face, the major panicked and retreated east across the river, with his frightened men following closely behind. The warriors killed about 30 more of the 130 troopers as they ran. The survivors finally reached a defensible position high on the sandy bluffs on the east side of the Little Bighorn River. **[See Figure 3-15, (C).]** Shortly after Reno's retreating men reached the bluffs, Custer and three companies moved towards the buffalo ford at the river. For the first time, Custer and his men saw the full extent of the massive Indian village stretched out before them. One of Custer's scouts told him that it was the biggest village he had ever seen during 30 years of living on the plains.

Benteen Rides to Help Reno

Not long after Reno reached the cliffs, Capt. Benteen's battalion of 125 men arrived, with the pack train arriving shortly after that. Pinned down on the cliff tops, the troopers returned sporadic fire against the attacking warriors.

Figure 3-21. "While Reno attacks, a Crow scout points Custer's men towards the buffalo ford." *[Frederic Remington drawing of the "Borderland." Reprinted from Remington (1897).]*

Urgent Request for Reinforcements

Custer ordered his aide to send an urgent message to Benteen that read: "Come on. Big Village. Be quick. Bring packs." Worried that his own position would be overrun, Maj. Reno, Benteen's superior officer, convinced Benteen to ignore the order and keep their troops together.

Custer's intention was to cross the river and attack the north end of the village. He planned for Reno and Benteen to draw most of the warriors off to the southeast, so that he could enter the village with little opposition. Custer expected that Reno's attack would also prompt the women and children to flee to the north and west of the village, and he planned to capture as many of them as possible. It was standard military procedure for the cavalry to capture the Indian families and hold them for ransom. If he could have done so, Custer would have forced the warriors to surrender in order to save the lives of their families.

Figure 3-22. W.W. Cooke, Custer's Adjutant *[Denver Public Library, Western History Coll.; Barry, B-205]*. Artist's drawing of Cooke's note to Capt. Benteen. *[By author, based on photo of the actual 1876 note.]*

Suddenly, on the bluffs above the east side of the river, one of our scouts appears, frantically waving a red blanket – the signal for an enemy attack. Walks-under-the-Ground shouts, "Come on. We must hurry! Hokahey!" *[Lakota battle word meaning, roughly, "Let's go!"]*

As he urges his pony off towards the ford, my pony and I set off after him. We race along the edge of the cottonwoods and ash trees that line the creek, leaving behind the warriors who are on foot. My excited pony's mouth is open, with flecks of foam blowing back along his jaw, as he strains to run as fast as he can.

Now, we hear it – *crack! crack! crack!* – rifle fire! The Long-knives are attacking at the ford. In panic, women and children are fleeing off to the west away from the ford. Just over the ridge ahead of us, we can see tips of many flags moving towards the buffalo crossing. Fluttering in the breeze and bobbing up and down, the soldier flags are visible all the way up Medicine Tail Coulee. There must be hundreds of Long-knives. We urge our ponies on even faster. *[See inset.]*

As we round a finger of dense trees, we come out into the open with a clear view of the ford. On the far side of the river, blue-jacketed soldiers pour out of the mouth of the coulee in columns of four horses abreast. Many dismounted soldiers already fill the approach to the ford, with their gray horses held in groups behind them. Facing the ford with their rifles raised, they fire sporadically into the dense trees and bushes along the river.

On both sides of the river, several dozen warriors lie well hidden in the dense brush; all are shooting at the soldiers. Quickly, we dismount at a safe distance,

> **"Long-Knives"**
> This name is derived from the swords of the troopers, who are usually portrayed riding into battle with sabers drawn. However, according to Lt. Edward Godfrey, a soldier who fought under Reno in the battle, most of the troopers did not carry sabers because they made rattling noises that might alert the warriors. Only a few of the officers actually carried sabers into this battle.

Sorrel Horse: The Battle of the Little Bighorn

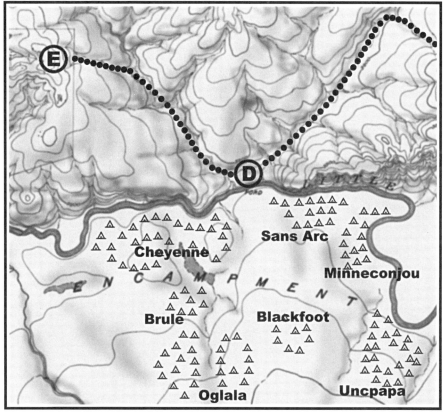

Figure 3-23. Map showing Custer's movements around the ford. First, Custer rode down Medicine Tail Coulee to the ford at (D). Then, he and the troopers retreated towards Calhoun Hill at (E). *[Notations added. Adapted from a map courtesy of the USGS.]*

tie our ponies to bushes, and move ahead to join our brothers. We are careful to stay out of direct view of the soldiers; their guns can shoot more accurately and further than ours can. *[See inset.]*

As we creep forward, I recognize several Northern Cheyenne warriors. Bobtail Horse raises up over the brush just enough to fire and flips onto his back to reload his old flintlock rifle while lying down. White Shield, Buffalo Calf, and Roan Bear are all lofting arrows over the river into the soldiers. They do this lying down, so as not to expose themselves to the rifle fire. Mad Wolf is too

> **Springfield Model 1873**
> The cavalrymen carried new carbines with a range of over 400 yards, which was greater than that of the warrior's lever action Winchesters and other older weapons. While the Springfield carbine was more accurate than the repeater, it was much slower to reload, a major disadvantage for close combat.

173

Figure 3-24. "Custer charges toward the buffalo ford." *[Kelly drawing, ca. 1886. Courtesy of Denver Public Library, Western History Coll.; X-33659.]*

old to fight well, but he keeps busy, shouting insults at the *wasichus*. White Cow Bull, an Oglala, is off to their left shooting rapidly at the enemy with a repeater just like mine. Most of the other warriors are shooting arrows. We are badly outnumbered by the soldiers, so we are very careful. We spend most of our time staying low behind cover so that we do not get shot. When we do shoot at them, we pop up just enough to get off a shot and then quickly duck down under cover.

Sounds of sporadic rifle fire echo down the coulee. Some of our warriors must be attacking the soldiers who are still riding down towards the river. We hear the noise of the *wasichu* horns sounding up and down the coulee as they send messages to each other. All of this noise can be heard throughout the village.

From all directions now, warriors come running to join the fight. Most are on foot, not having had time yet to get their horses. Along the tree line, far off towards the fighting to the south, I see groups of warriors turning their horses and racing back towards us. Now that they have heard the shooting, we must stop the soldiers at the ford until they arrive.

Without exposing myself, I cautiously spread apart the sagebrush in front of me to look at the soldiers. A group of soldiers watches the action from horseback about forty paces back from the river. These *wasichus* are not dressed in blue coats. One of them is a small dark man on a dark horse, who does not look at all like a *wasichu*. *[He was Custer's favorite scout, Mitch Boyer.]* By his side, a tall *wasichu* stares across the river through a pair of black field glasses and shouts directions to the other soldiers. This man wears buckskin pants, a blue shirt, and

Figure 3-25. Gen. Custer wore his hair both long and short at times. At the time of this battle, he wore his hair short. *[Courtesy of the National Archives.]*

a wide-brimmed hat. It is Yellow-Hair! He rides a large, spirited sorrel horse with white stockings and a blazed face. He shouts most of the orders, sometimes riding back and forth near the other soldiers. He has short golden hair and a big moustache. My heart pounds with excitement at seeing this old enemy of my People. I would know him anywhere.

Yellow-Hair shouts more orders. Now the man with a shiny horn blows more loud noises. Some bluecoats on gray horses and some on bay horses begin to form into a group near the mouth of the coulee. With a shout from Yellow-Hair and a long blast from Horn-Man, the men spur their horses towards the ford, led by a man with a colored flag on a pole. They ride fast towards the river, yelling, lashing their horses, and shooting pistols at us. With the dismounted soldiers firing at the same time with long rifles, we mostly keep down under cover.

After holding our fire until they get close to the river, now we shoot as fast as we can to make them think there are lots of us. The leading soldiers charge into the river with their horses, splashing water in all directions. Bobtail Horse shoots his musket, killing the lead soldier, who falls into the river, dropping his flag. Another trooper scoops it up on the run.

Aiming at one of the charging soldiers who has yellow stripes on his sleeve, I squeeze the trigger. The bullet misses him but hits his horse in the back, killing it instantly. The horse stumbles and flips over, collapsing into shallow water near the bank. As the soldier struggles to get his legs clear of his dead horse, a warrior rises from the tall grass and sinks an arrow into his chest. He slumps over backwards into the water and does not move. No feather for me.

Behind the fallen man, more and more soldiers charge towards the river. Panic grips my heart. We are about to be overrun! A flood of yelling soldiers is pouring out of the coulee; there are just too few of us to stop them.

Walks-under-the-Ground, who also has a repeater like mine, calls out to me from the nearby bushes: "Shoot the Big Chief. Quick, try to hit him."

Raising my Winchester to get Yellow-Hair in my sights, I squeeze the trigger. *Crack!* Missed! I curse silently. If only I had practiced more!

Walks-under-the-Ground fires his rifle a second later. *Crack!* Yellow-Hair rocks violently backwards – he is hit! Dropping his field glasses to the ground, he grabs the saddle horn of his horse, struggling to stay in the saddle. I see dark red blood flowing down his blue shirt onto his buckskin pants. He is badly hurt but not dead. *[See inset.]*

> **Wounding Custer**
>
> This was the turning point in the battle. During and after the Civil War, eleven horses had been shot from under Custer, yet he had been wounded only once. He promoted the idea of "Custer's Luck," the myth that he could not be injured in battle.
>
> After the warriors had seriously wounded the previously "invincible" Custer, the other soldiers began to fear that their luck, too, had run out.

Walks-under-the-Ground yells out a great victory whoop. Expecting another feather, he has a big grin on his face. My own feather must wait. My heart pounds so much it hurts, and I feel dizzy with the excitement of almost shooting Yellow-Hair.

Immediately, there is chaos among the soldiers. The dark man and another soldier in buckskins hurry over on their horses to help Yellow-Hair *[Boyer and Tom Custer]*. Supporting him on each side, they ride off up Deep Coulee to the north. Yellow-Hair moves his arms in a jerky fashion, and his heads bobs around as they ride off. He is pale and losing a lot of blood. *[See inset.]*

Buckskin-Man shouts to Horn-Man, who makes a loud sound with his horn. The soldiers, who had stopped in midstream in confusion, wheel around and hurry back to the far bank, shooting at us over their shoulders. The standing soldiers with the gray horses fire at us, too. We mostly keep our heads down, but some warriors are starting to cross the river in pursuit. When the soldiers quickly shoot several of them, they all hastily retreat to cover.

The bay horse troops follow Yellow-Hair up Deep Coulee, passing between two bunches of gray-horse soldiers. At the same time, behind

Custer's Wound

Lt. Godfrey, who was on the burial detail from Reno's command, described this particular wound. He said that Gen. Custer had been shot in the left chest, with the bullet entering his lung but without passing all the way through his body (Welch (1994)).

According to Reflection (2002), this wound was not fatal, but it was very serious, requiring medical attention by Dr. Lord. To ease his pain, the doctor treated Custer with powerful narcotics, which further impaired Custer's decision-making ability.

Figure 3-26. First time ever revealed: this is a photo of Walks-under-the-Ground, the first warrior to wound Custer. Having survived the battle, he went on to star in Buffalo Bill Cody's Wild West Show. In an odd twist of karma, he traveled to Paris in 1889 to perform in front of me in my next incarnation – but more about that later. *[Photo from Cody's Wild West Show, ca. the 1880s. Denver Public Library, Western History Coll.; Salsbury, NS-141]*

Figure 3-27. Mitch Boyer, Custer's favorite half-breed scout, with Capt. Tom Custer, the General's brother. *[Denver Public Library, Western History Coll.; Nast, X-31214; Barry, B-53.]*

them, the other soldiers who were still up in the wash wheel their horses around and retreat up Medicine Tail Coulee. *[See inset.]*

The chief of the gray-horse soldiers rides back and forth behind the standing soldiers. Shouting to them, he quickly forms them into two lines. As he shouts again, they raise their long rifles. Several of our war-leaders motion frantically for us to keep very low. I squirm backwards to find a lower spot behind my bush.

> **First Time Revealed**
> Historians have speculated for more than 100 years about why Custer and his troops suddenly retreated from the buffalo ford.
> Many people have offered different theories, but this is the first time that anyone has presented intricate details about the serious wounds suffered by Gen. Custer. This scenario about a fatally wounded Custer effectively explains all of the puzzling events of that day.

When Gray-horse Chief yells again, all his men fire at once with a deafening blast of gunfire. Bullets whiz and hum overhead. As I cover my head with my hands, a few small branches and leaves, clipped by the flying bullets, drift down over me. With my head pressed to the ground, I smell the sweet aroma of crushed buffalo grass and the sharp aroma of black powder. Still with my head down, I hear Gray-horse Chief yell again. There is another deafening volley of bullets. After another blast from Horn-Man, the battle grows quiet.

Cautiously, I peer over the sagebrush. Forming two lines, one on each side of the wash, the gray soldiers are retreating in an orderly fashion up Deep Coulee, protecting Yellow-Hair from rear attack. The last few men are walking backwards, keeping their rifles pointed at us. All around, warriors whoop and yell out war cries at the retreating soldiers. Old Crazy Wolf gets up, yells some final insults at the soldiers, and struts around as if he had just defeated them with his bow and arrow alone.

With every passing moment, more warriors arrive from the fighting to the south. Riding towards the gunfire, hundreds and hundreds of mounted warriors gallop to the ford and splash across the river to chase the soldiers. Brave Wolf and Two Moons, war-leaders for the Cheyenne, have just arrived. Gall, war-chief of the Uncpapa tribe under Sitting Bull, has just ridden up with many warriors. Hollow Horn Bear has arrived, leading a group of Brule warriors. A few Oglala warriors are here, shouting that Crazy Horse is right behind them. Iron Tail arrives with word from Sitting Bull to the warriors. Shouting to some of the Uncpapas, he rides off after the soldiers.

Several bands of warriors follow the gray-horse soldiers, being careful to stay hidden from their deadly rifle fire. Other bands ride up Medicine Tail after the other retreating soldiers. More warriors gallop along the river to the north, heading for the ford by the beaver dam at Deep Ravine, planning to circle around Yellow-Hair's group and cut them off.

Figures 3-28 (above). Hollow Horn Bear *[Courtesy of the Library of Congress.]*

Figure 3-29 (right). The Lakota war-chief Gall *[Courtesy of the National Archives.]*

I raise my rifle, shaking it in the air and yelling out a war cry, too, though mostly from relief. We came very close to losing the battle. If the *wasichus* had managed to get by us at the river and capture many women, it would have been bad for us. If Yellow-Hair had not been wounded, the soldiers would not have turned back. They would have taken the entire village. Today, we have been blessed by *Wakan Tanka*.

Figure 3-30. Iron Tail, the Uncpapa aide to Sitting Bull. *[Reprinted from Winch (1911).]*

Retreating up Deep Coulee to Calhoun Hill; The Attack at North Ford

The men of Custer's battalion were badly demoralized after Custer was wounded. Facing Indian fire from the west and from the south, some soldiers retreated east back up Medicine Tail Coulee. The rest, including Custer, retreated northeast up Deep Coulee. The companies soon joined up on Nye-Cartwright Ridge and then moved on to a defensible position located on Calhoun Hill. **[See Figure 3-31, (E).]**

During their retreat, Custer drifted in and out of consciousness. On Calhoun Hill, his chest wound was treated by Dr. Lord, one of the company surgeons. The treatment allowed him to remain conscious, and he resumed command, helping to direct the strategy for the rest of the battle.

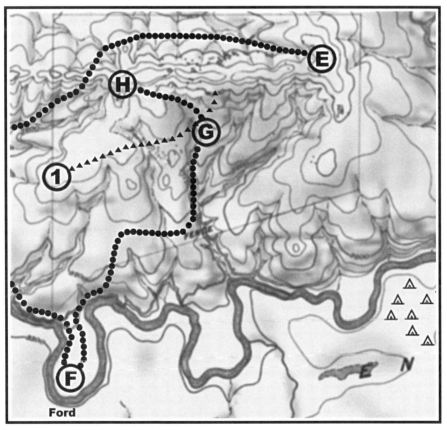

Figure 3-31. Map showing Custer's movements at the end of the battle. Calhoun Hill is at **(E)**; the North Ford is at **(F)**; the Basin is at **(G)**; and Last Stand Hill is at **(H)**. The 'Coup Boys' gathered at **(1)**. *[Notations added. Adapted from a map courtesy of the USGS.]*

Revising the Battle Plan

Realizing that their situation was difficult but not hopeless, Custer decided to continue trying to capture the women and children. He felt that this was their only real chance for success. To give him time, he sent three companies under Capt. Keogh to counter the growing threat of the incoming warriors. Two of the three companies, commanded by Capt. Calhoun, deployed on Calhoun Hill itself, while the third company, under Capt. Keogh, waited in reserve.

Meanwhile, the warrior chiefs left a small group of men to keep Reno's soldiers pinned down on the top of the cliffs, while the other warriors raced towards the new threat posed by Custer. At this point, there was only very light fighting around Custer's troops and around Reno's men. At this point in the battle, only a few of Custer's men had been killed or injured.

Unlike the classic Custer myth, there was no headlong retreat by the soldiers, pursued by thousands of howling Indians. Archaeological evidence, such as bullets and cartridges, shows that most of the Indians slowly infiltrated around the positions of the soldiers, engaging in long-distance sniper fire. The soldiers, far from retreating in disarray, organized in conventional skirmish lines, returned fire, and kept the warriors at bay.

During this time, Chief Gall said that they would creep up on the soldiers, jump up to fire, and then hide again. Also, they would raise sticks, blankets, and dummies to trick the troopers into wasting ammunition. Overall, there was only sporadic firing, as the warriors crept steadily closer to the soldiers.

Custer Moves to North Ford

Custer and the other two companies of about 100 men headed north towards Cemetery Ridge (today, the site of the monument). With Custer conscious all the time now, he and his soldiers were searching for another way to cross the river. From their vantage point on the hills, they clearly could see thousands of women and children still fleeing north from the village along the west side of the Little Bighorn. If his men could capture them, Custer felt they could win the battle.

About two miles north of Medicine Tail Coulee, Custer and his men rode down onto the river floodplain attempting to cross at a place now called North Ford, also known as Ford D. **[See Figure 3-31, (F).]** Archaeological evidence indicates that, as they approached the ford, they were ambushed and driven back by hostile fire from about 100 mostly Cheyenne warriors. Several men were killed near the river, including the civilian reporter, Mark Kellogg, whose body was found there after the battle.

Custer retreated hastily to the Flats just below Cemetery Ridge. Realizing now that his men were almost surrounded and in very serious trouble, Custer deployed his two companies near Cemetery Ridge. Company E, the grayhorse troop that was commanded by Lt. Smith, moved up near the crest of the ridge. Looked after by Dr. Lord and Tom and Boston, his two brothers, Custer remained in the Basin below Cemetery Ridge protected by Company F, led by Capt. Yates. **[See Figure 3-31, (G).]**

The Charge of the "Suicide Boys"

Infiltration continued as thousands of warriors crossed the river and crept into position surrounding Custer's troops. At first, the warriors fought a guerilla war, sniping at the soldiers from cover. Gradually, however, enough warriors had assembled to allow direct frontal attacks on the soldiers. One such group, led by Crazy Horse, prepared to attack the troops to the south near Calhoun Hill.

Another group, led by the Cheyenne war-chief, Two Moons, prepared to attack Custer's group of men to the north. This warrior group gathered below Cemetery Hill near the present-day museum. **[See Figure 3-31, (1).]** Although there were some experienced warriors in this group, it was made up mostly of young boys who were incorrectly called the "Suicide Boys." A more correct name would be the "Coup Boys," since their goal was to count coup, remain alive, and win a feather, not to commit suicide. They were given a special honor to charge first into battle.

About 20 of these boys, both Cheyenne and Lakota, gathered near the Flats to begin the charge against the soldiers. They had all taken a sacred vow in their warrior societies to show bravery in battle and to try to win a feather. They came to be called "Suicide Boys" probably because, by the end of the battle, nearly all of them were either dead or wounded.

Both Whirlwind and Sorrel Horse had taken this vow, too, though Whirlwind was down at the Reno Fight and did not take part in the charge against Custer's men.

Ahead of us on the high ground east of the creek, we are watching two groups of bluecoats. We are almost ready to go after them, like angry crows after hawks.

Two Moons yells, "It is a good day to die, my brothers. Let no one sing around the campfires that you were not brave today. Hokahey!" He kicks his pony and rushes off towards the *wasichus*, followed by dozens of screaming warriors, including me. My heart beats wildly with excitement. Wide-eyed, I gallop off to earn my feather!

Charging towards the high ground, we separate into groups. My group does not go directly at the soldiers; instead, we circle around to one side, riding fast and dodging to make it harder to hit us. On the other side, another group circles to catch the soldiers in cross fire.

A third group of warriors races towards the soldiers who are holding the horses. Yelling, banging war shields, and waving blankets, they try to stampede the soldiers' horses and it works! The gray horses are terrified. They jerk away from their handlers, knocking some of the soldiers to the ground, and gallop away. Without horses, the soldiers will die here today.

Our charge is the signal for the other warriors to attack down to the south, and Crazy Horse and his warriors move against the soldiers on Calhoun Hill.

Figure 3-32. Two Moons, war-chief of the Northern Cheyenne, led the Coup Boys against Custer. *[Ca. 1910, courtesy of the National Archives.]*

They have been waiting for this moment. On foot and on horseback, they swarm out of hiding to attack.

There are thousands of us – so many that not all warriors can even get into the battle. There are only a few of the soldiers. Sitting Bull's vision is right; *Wakan Tanka* has given them to us. Our horses are so many that their hooves stir up clouds of dust. We ride very fast, and it is hard for the soldiers to pick targets through the thick clouds of dust.

As I race in close to the soldiers who are nearest the river, through the dust, I see a soldier with buckskin pants. It is Yellow-Hair again! He is in the middle kneeling on the ground surrounded by a few soldiers. He has a bloody white bandage around his chest. He looks weak, but he shoots his pistol at any warrior who comes near.

Figure 3-33. "Terrified, the soldiers' horses race away as their handlers struggle to control them." *[Frederic Remington drawing of the "Horse Handlers." Reprinted from Brady (1904).]*

Yellow-Hair looks oddly peaceful, with a faint smile on his face. *[See inset.]* I can see in his eyes that he knows death is near, and that this is his final moment. Sitting Bull's vision is true – the white chief is ready to die – he welcomes it. *Wakan Tanka* has given him to us.

Trying for a great coup, I urge my pony towards the white chief. As I do, another warrior moves in next to me, riding a powerful pinto pony. It is Stands First, from Crazy Horse's Oglala band. Because of the noise

> **Custer's Body**
> Lt. Bradley, who helped bury Custer, said that he looked like he had just died of natural causes. His expression was that of a man who had fallen asleep and enjoyed peaceful dreams.
> Pvt. Coleman, who also saw Custer, said that he lay with a "faint smile on his face" *(from Marques (1976))*.

of battle, he gives me hand signs, "Come – charge – *wasichus*. Win – feather – today!" Already wearing several feathers, he has proven himself a skilled warrior. Giving me a wide grin, he whips his pony and gallops towards the soldiers.

Guiding my pony in behind Stands First, I follow him in among the soldiers. Raising my rifle, I try to get Yellow-Hair in my sights. It is not easy. My pony jostles my hands with each footstep. Taking a deep breath to steady my hands, I squeeze the trigger – *crack!* Did I hit Yellow-Hair? I squint through the dust and smoke. No, missed again! I curse my rifle. I am beginning to think that this rifle does not shoot straight! *[See inset.]*

Hearing my rifle shot, the white chief turns towards me, raising his pistol. Quickly, I cock my rifle for a second shot, when suddenly Stands First rushes in on Yellow-Hair's left side, striking him violently in the head with his wooden coup stick, knocking off Yellow-Hair's wide-brimmed hat. The white chief slumps to the ground. With blood running from the corner of his mouth, he struggles to get up again.

Wrestling to control his excited and skittish pony, Stands First fires his pistol down at Yellow-Hair from close range. The bullet strikes the white chief in the left temple. He collapses and does not move. Stands First yells in triumph. Now, before the other soldiers can shoot at him, Stands First whips his pony and races away from the soldiers. As he rides out, he rips out the colored flag that was stuck into the ground near Yellow-Hair. Waving the flag over his head triumphantly, Stands First gallops off towards the river.

A great satisfaction wells up inside me. The Yellow-Haired Chief is dead. He killed my parents and would have killed every one of my People today if he could have done so. He looked upon my People with hatred and arrogance. Now, Stands First, one of my People, has killed him, and we look down upon him in defeat. Now he can kill no more. *[See inset.]*

My satisfaction is short-lived. Shaking my head in despair, I feel a great sadness for my

> **Flash Forward**
> While meditating one day, in a flash, I saw an image of the back of a warrior riding a pinto pony into the middle of a group of blue-coated soldiers. As I explored that image, more details of the charge of the Coup Boys came back to me.
> Scenes from past lives, like this one, have always come to me at random. Sometimes, it takes years before I am able to piece them together into a complete story.

> **Custer's Death**
> In a hypnotic trance-regression session, Reflection (2002) revealed that at this point, Custer was brain-dead, although he was not clinically dead; his heart was still beating and he was still breathing. Never regaining consciousness, he died before the end of the battle, before his famous "Last Stand" ever occurred.
> Therefore, far from being the last man to fall, Custer actually was one of the first.

Figure 3-34. "Stands First races his pony in among the soldiers." *[Frederic Remington drawing of the "Way of the Indian." Reprinted from Remington (1906).]*

Figure 3-35. First time ever revealed: this is a photo of Stands First, the Oglala warrior who killed Custer. *[Photo ca. 1907. Courtesy of the Library of Congress.]*

People. I know the *wasichus* will not let things end here. There will be many more Long-knives to replace their fallen chief.

A pistol explodes nearby, and the bullet buzzes past my head. I am startled back to reality. Seeing the trooper who shot at me near his fallen horse, I nudge my pony ahead, raising my rifle to fire. *Crack!* He slumps to the ground. Spurring my pony, I strike him with my coup-stick.

At last, I have done it! I yell out a coup-cry in triumph – I have my first feather! I yell the coup-cry again. Thinking of Whirlwind, I hope he has gotten a feather as well, but if he has not, I will have fun teasing him about it. Eager for more feathers, I turn my pony and urge him back into the battle.

> **Stands First**
>
> For over a century there has been continual speculation about which warrior killed Custer. To our knowledge, Reflection is the first to identify Stands First as the one who did it. At the time, most of the warriors did not even know Custer was at the battle; they learned about it weeks later.
>
> Such was the case with Stands First. Over the years, he came to suspect that Yellow-Hair was the man he had shot, but fearing retribution from the whites, he never said so, taking the secret to his grave – until now.

Figure 3-36. "The trooper's bullet buzzes past my head." *[Frederic Remington drawing, ca. 1892. Courtesy of Denver Public Library, Western History Coll.; X-33634.]*

The Final Battle around Custer Hill

The Young Soldiers were Unprepared

The soldiers were mostly very young. Some of them were newly arrived immigrants who spoke only a little English. Nearly all of them were poorly trained. The Army issued the soldiers only a few cartridges every year for firing practice, and many of them had never fired a single bullet from horseback. For most of them, according to one of the Reno's cavalry survivors, it was their "first real battle at close range with real Indians." When they first encountered fierce-looking, screaming, heavily armed warriors charging at them, they were unprepared ... and terrified.

Sorrel Horse and the other boys charged in among Custer's soldiers on the north end of the battlefield. **[See Figure 3-31, arrow from (1).]** Simultaneously, other warriors attacked the troopers on Calhoun Hill. Under the onslaught, the skirmish lines collapsed. In the heat of battle, many of the soldiers panicked and fled. Indian eyewitness said that, at the end, they ran like frightened buffalo. Later, Capt. Benteen (from Fox (1993) p. 229) said, "It was a rout, a panic, until the last man was killed." Lt. Hare, who helped bury the bodies afterward, said, "The men were struck with panic and did not fight well."

Fleeing the warriors, the soldiers from Calhoun ran on foot or on horseback towards perceived safety on Custer Hill a mile away to the north. Mounted warriors raced in among them, killing them at will with axes and spears, not needing to waste bullets on them. Of 120 men, only about 20 soldiers made it to Custer Hill. They thought they were running towards safety, but none of them would live beyond the final fight.

Until they arrived on Custer Hill, none of the men from Calhoun Hill knew about Custer's second and fatal wound. They all believed in the famous "Custer Luck," but now his luck had run out ... and theirs, too. Hoping for a miracle and determined not to leave Custer behind to be captured, his brothers and fellow officers carried his brain-dead body from near the Basin up to Last Stand Hill. **[See Figure 3-31, (H).]** It was a lifeless shell; for all practical purposes, Custer had died before his body ever arrived for his famous "Last Stand."

At the end, on Custer Hill, there were about 100 soldiers left out of 210 who started the battle. Some tried to run for the river, where they were cut down. Some of them just quit fighting and waited in a daze to die; only a few put up much of a fight. Within the span of only a few minutes, all of them were dead.

In all, from the first shots in Medicine Tail Coulee to the last shots on Custer Hill, the entire Custer battle episode lasted less than an hour. It was over quickly.

As more soldiers fall and as our rifle fire begins to cut away at their ranks, some of the *wasichus* turn to run, but it is too late. They take heavy fire from all sides. The soldiers leave a trail of bluecoat bodies and dying horses as they fight their way back to the high ground.

Figure 3-37. "The soldiers bunch together on the Hill." *[Frederic Remington drawing of "The Last Stand." Reprinted from Remington (1897).]*

Overpowering battle sounds come from all directions: rifles cracking; soldiers shouting; horns blowing; horses whinnying; warriors blowing shrill eagle-bone whistles; wounded men screaming in pain or crying for water. Strong smells, too: the nose-tingling odor of black powder; the sweet aroma of newly crushed sagebrush; the pungent iron-like smell of fresh blood; and the unmistakable, indescribable odor of death.

In the wild confusion of war, our galloping ponies race past the *wasichus* on all sides. I drop the reins in front of me; I do not need them in the heat of battle. Guiding my pony with toes and knees, I hold my rifle with both hands, picking targets carefully to not waste bullets. Snap the lever to reload, pick a target, squeeze the trigger – *crack!* War cries all around. Snap, aim, squeeze – *crack!* The thrill of battle. Squeeze. *Crack! Crack! Crack!* **[See inset on next page.]**

Our rifle fire is devastating as our repeaters rain bullets down on them. Firing wildly in all directions, some of the *wasichus* huddle together in small groups. Many bluecoats are wounded, and our warriors dart among them, at first striking them with coup sticks, and now killing them with clubs, axes, knives, spears, or pistols. Some of our warriors have only bows and arrows, but even their fire is deadly. Thousands of arrows fall from the sky into the groups of soldiers. Intent on the warriors around them, the soldiers do not see the falling arrows until they pierce their heads, shoulders, and arms. Some arrows plunge

Sorrel Horse: The Battle of the Little Bighorn

Figure 3-38. "The soldiers kill their horses for cover." *[Frederic Remington drawing. Reprinted from Remington (1897).]*

into the horses, which go crazy with fear, charging around, knocking over soldiers and trampling them. For the soldiers, there is nowhere to hide from this deadly storm.

In panic, some bluecoats try to run away, while others fight bravely and fiercely even though they know they are trapped and will die on this

Firepower

Recent excavations have found evidence indicating that the warriors had more than 200 repeating rifles like that of Sorrel Horco, while the troopers, who carried single-shot carbines, had none *(Fox (1993) p. 250).*

Bullets and cartridges recovered on-site suggest that the warriors had 350 – 400 guns, meaning that the 210 cavalrymen were outgunned nearly 2-to-1. Overall, the warriors were better armed than the soldiers were *(Scott (1989) p. 118).*

Figure 3-39. "The warriors race in among the soldiers, killing them at will." *[Frederic Remington drawing. Reprinted from Remington (1906).]*

day. Not one of them wants to be captured; they fear our vengeance for trying to kill our mothers and sisters. There is no order to the battle now, only chaos. Each warrior competes to count coup on a soldier; each soldier struggles to survive. Dust clouds rise over the battlefield, and seeing clearly is difficult. The soldiers try to hide from the barrage but it is no use. One by one, they go down.

Chasing one of the soldiers fleeing on foot, I race in to count coup on him. As I get closer, he throws away his rifle so that he can run faster. Grabbing his pistol, he shoots wildly over his shoulder in terror, trying to hit me, but he does not even come close. I am almost on top of him, raising my arm to strike him with my coup-stick, when suddenly, an arrow thumps deep into my right chest under my upraised arm. With sharp pain shooting through my right lung and down my arm, I almost fall from my pony. Losing the grip on my rifle, I drop it. My pony adjusts instantly to keep me on and now slows to a walk. The trooper races off ahead of me on foot, his life spared for a few more moments.

Dazed, confused, and in shock, I think, *I must get my rifle.* I start to jump down for it, but the arrow is in the way. Having entered my chest from the side, it angles downward and sticks out below my rifle arm, jutting out from my chest just beyond the edge of my breastplate. With both hands shaking, I reach up to grip the arrow, snapping the arrow shaft close to my chest wall. The splintered end sticks out about two fingers width. I feel no more pain than a bee-sting now. There is only a little blood on the outside, but inside I feel a warm flow trickling down into my right lung.

I look at the broken shaft in disgust. One of my own People has wounded me! Did some warrior shoot me in anger, I wonder. Have I made an enemy? Tossing the arrow away, I can think of no one, except "Spitting Wolf." This is a great humiliation. The tribe will laugh and claim I have had coup counted on me – by one of my own! Whirlwind will tease me forever.

As I sit here on my pony, my addled brain does not clearly recognize the serious danger; my pony and I are walking slowly across the middle of a battle-field as bullets kick up small puffs of dirt and grass all around me. Dazed by my wounds, I idly wonder, *What could be causing that?* My pony twitches nervously with each puff and now begins to trot off down towards the river.

Suddenly, my leg jerks forward violently as a bullet rips through my right thigh from behind, almost pitching me off my pony. Instinctively, I grab the mane of my startled pony, which now races away from the danger. I slide one hand down to feel my leg, touching sharp, protruding bone splinters. Raising my hand, I see warm red blood covering my fingers. *[See inset.]*

Suddenly dizzy, I lean forward onto my pony's neck and hold on firmly. Sensing my trouble, he hurries off the battlefield and crosses the creek towards Grandmother's lodge. My mind becomes dim, but my hands never loosen their grip on my pony's neck. I think idly for a moment that we should go back for my rifle, but now my pony is in control. His eyes are guiding us now. My own eyes go black.

> **Sorrel Horse**
> Wooden Leg, an eyewitness of the battle, said that Sorrel Horse was hit by a soldier's bullet while galloping across the level area near where the stone house of the Cemetery now stands *(Marquis (1931))*.
> The bullet wounded him in the right thigh, fracturing the bone. In a repeat of history, the wound was almost identical to the Civil War wound that had killed John Hogans 11 years previously. In a surprising replay of karma, Custer's men did that, too.

Quiet after the Battle

Suddenly the sky is darker, and the sun has grown dim. Standing alone on the prairie, I look around in confusion. *Is this a dream? Where is everyone? Where is my pony?* Feeling dizzy, I cannot remember clearly, except vaguely recalling something about fighting *wasichus* and dropping my rifle. My thinking is fuzzy. Rubbing my head, I feel very confused.

Around me in the faint light, the buffalo grass grows as high as my chest. It is parched, brittle, and so thick that it is difficult to move through it. As the wind blows, the dry blades bend and sway, making a rustling, crackling sound. In front of me, a lone sagebrush grows high above the level of the grass.

Hearing a familiar high-pitched screech, I look over my shoulder to see a large eagle gliding soundlessly towards me over the buffalo grass. My heart leaps as it passes right over me to land on top of the sagebrush. Balancing precariously, it sits there staring intently at me, bobbing its head up and down. I stay very still so as not to frighten it away. Seeing such a magnificent bird is a very good omen indeed!

Figure 3-40. "The eagle glides in soundlessly over my head." *[Courtesy of the National Archives.]*

Overhead, rapidly moving storm clouds block out the sun. A bolt of lightning flashes and, almost instantly, the booming crack of thunder rolls across the prairie. The eagle flares its wings briefly in surprise but does not fly away. That was close! I look around nervously.

Suddenly without warning, a blinding, blue-white lightning streak explodes the sagebrush right in front of me. Like a rabbit tossed by a wolf, I am thrown backwards, landing heavily on the ground and knocking the wind out of me. Instantly, the powerful booming shock wave pounds into me, making my muscles ache. Gasping for breath, ears throbbing with pain, I clamp my hands over my ears. Warm blood trickles from my nose.

Almost in slow motion, a dozen flaming clumps of sagebrush arc slowly out of the sky, landing in the grass around me. Everywhere the clumps land, the tinder dry grass explodes into fierce, bright-hot flames. Sizzling and crackling, the flames spread in widening circles, devouring the surrounding grass. Chunks of charred eagle flesh land around me while a few feathers float down in narrow spirals. A feeling of deep fear comes over me. This is not good at all!

Trembling, I struggle to stand. Thick trails of smoke drift over the prairie. As each moment passes, the smoke grows thicker. With the sharp, pungent aroma stinging my nose and burning my eyes, I stumble backwards away from the fire and move away at a trot.

Glancing over my shoulder, I see a terrifying sight. The deadly wildfire is following me, moving faster than the wind! Breaking into a fast run, I turn to sprint parallel to the fire front, hoping to get around the edge of the fire line.

Just ahead of me, three buffalo break through the grass, running from the fire in panic. A wild thought enters my head. Maybe I can jump on the back of one of them; maybe a buffalo can carry me to safety. Running as swiftly as I can, I strain to keep pace with the buffalo, but they are too fast. They outdistance me,

Figure 3-41. "Ahead of me, the sagebrush explodes into flame." *[Courtesy of National Interagency Fire Center, BLM.]*

and the sound of their hooves grows fainter. Panting and out of breath, I lean over to rest with my hands on my knees.

What is that noise? It sounds like Grandmother's voice, calling out to me. How can that be? I look around for her, when suddenly, the sound of hoofbeats grows louder behind me. Another buffalo is coming right towards me! Excited, I crouch in the grass ready to leap as it passes. With a great bellow, the shaggy animal crashes through the grass near me. I am stunned. The animal is WHITE!

Forcing aside my surprise, I leap into action. Dodging its deadly horns, I grab the buffalo's thick coat as it plunges past. Locking my fingers into its coarse hair, I swing up onto its huge back as it lumbers past. Now, gripping the huge beast with my legs, I lean forward as it thunders across the prairie.

Safe now, I look down at this wondrous animal. The back and hump of the beast are a pure creamy white! Its head, legs, and belly are much darker but still lighter than most. The White Buffalo is holy, sacred to *Wakan Tanka*. I am blessed, indeed, to be saved by such a rare creature. Only one person that I know, Sitting Bull himself, has ever seen the White Buffalo. It is good medicine for me and for the tribe.

Alive 5 times

My fear begins to lessen now that I am headed for safety. The White Buffalo, plunging powerfully through the grass, seems unaffected by having me on its back. It continues onward as if nothing had happened.

Just as I begin to ease into the rocking rhythm of the running buffalo, I see in my side vision a bright flare of orange and red. Jerking my head around to the right, I am horrified! Not far off to the side, racing along faster than we are moving, huge tongues of flame writhe and reach forward to ignite the dry grass. On the left, it is the same. On each side of me, the deadly flames are leaping ahead faster than the White Buffalo can gallop. We are caught in the center of a broad crescent-shaped wall of flame. Like the encircling jaws of a wolf clamping down on a rabbit, the raging wildfire is closing in around us.

Determined not to give up, I kick the buffalo furiously with my heels to get it to gallop faster. My heels thump into its furry sides repeatedly, but they have no effect. The buffalo already runs as fast as it can.

Without warning, the animal slows to a trot, stops, and turns to face the fire. Its jowls are flecked with foam, and its great red tongue hangs out of its mouth. It is exhausted. Panting from exertion, its great chest heaving in and out, it just stands there, staring vacantly at the oncoming flames.

Figure 3-42. "Dazed, the exhausted buffalo stands facing the fire." *[Frederic Remington drawing. Reprinted from Remington (1895).]*

196

Panicking, I kick the great beast repeatedly, but it will not move. Leaping off its back, I start to run away. Struggling through the tall, thick grass, I go only a short distance before I, too, am exhausted. It is no use. I am trapped. In dejection, I turn slowly towards the raging fire. The firelight is so bright that it hurts my eyes. The heat scorches my face. Using my arms, I shield myself from the intense light and heat and resign myself to death.

Enormous sheets of flame, ten times my own height, rise furiously above the dry grass. In front of me, a huge sinuous whirlwind of fire bends and dances on the leading edge of the inferno. The heat is so intense that it creates its own wind. The flickering flames, swirling smoke, and glowing embers spin and twist as they are sucked into the funnel, riding the powerful updraft currents and rising far up into the clouds. Sunlight flickers dimly through the swirling smoke and flames. Hungry to consume all things, the wildfire draws the smoke back into itself with such power that the wind bends the tall grass over and rips off the seed heads. They fly into me like tiny arrows, lodging in my hair, and stinging my exposed skin. The howl of the screaming winds is deafening. My long, black hair streams out ahead of me in the roaring wind, obscuring my sight. Like everything around me, I am being pulled relentlessly into the consuming flames.

There can be no escape now. Looking back at the White Buffalo still standing behind me, I vow to meet the fire bravely. Beads of perspiration roll down my face, only to be blown away by the wind. The salt of my sweat burns my eyes. Breathing is painful and difficult as the superheated air scorches my lungs.

Over the noise of the firestorm, someone calls faintly to me. It is Grandmother again, but I cannot hear her very well. I do not answer. It is too late anyway. It is my time to die and I am ready. I close my eyes in resignation.

Figure 3-43. "The sun is almost obscured by the swirling smoke." *[Courtesy of the US Department of Agriculture.]*

"You have come back!" Grandmother says softly. Cool water trickles down my forehead. Surprised at her voice, I struggle to open my eyes, but my vision is blurred. Feeling around with my left hand, I recognize the familiar feel of my buffalo skin blanket and the rough wood rail of my raised sleeping platform.

Finally, my eyes focus a little. Dimly visible, Grandmother is beside me. Rocking back and forth slowly, chanting, she mops my face with cool water.

"I thought I had lost you," she continues. "Your pony brought you back, but you had already slipped into a fever-dream, twitching and moaning." As I shift position, my right leg throbs painfully. I stifle a moan.

Continuing to mop my forehead, she says, "You called out to *Wakan Tanka*, but I had to hold you down. You shouted something about an eagle and a White Buffalo and pointed with your finger. I tried to comfort you, but you shook and trembled, and sweat streamed off your body. I tried to call you back from the Spirit World, but you could not hear me. Now you have come back on your own." She shakes her head gently, "I did not think you would return!"

My vision of the spirit fire is a fading memory. Searing pain fills my mind instead. I attempt to hold very still, trying not to move my rib cage, moving only my stomach to breathe. This helps a little, but the wounds still hurt badly, though I do not show any pain; doing so would be a disgrace. *[See inset.]*

My mouth is dry and my tongue is swollen. Unable to speak clearly, I signal Grandmother to come closer. I rasp out the words, "What has happened? Is the battle over?" She does not answer, only nods her head once.

"Whirlwind?" I ask.

She shakes her head slowly back and forth. "He fought fiercely and died bravely. He shot an arrow into the Chief of the Arikara and became a warrior today. Now he can wear his eagle feather in the Land of *Wakan Tanka*." I turn my face away to the tee-pee wall, choking back feelings of loss for my friend.

"Whirlwind," I speak inwardly to him, "perhaps I will join you soon enough. Then, we both will have died with honor defending our People." In my mind, I form a picture of him, smiling as I last saw him, eagerly running off to battle. I make an inward promise to him, "Brother, I will find you wherever you are in *Wakan Tanka*'s endless meadows."

Flash Forward

Years ago, I was lying down in a class, learning a yoga technique called "stomach breathing." This procedure involves breathing by moving the diaphragm rather than by moving the chest muscles.

The goal is to hold the ribs expanded but to keep them as still as possible, using the diaphragm to fill the lungs. This results in fresh oxygen moving deep into the lungs.

As I practiced this technique, I triggered vivid memories of this event in which I struggled to control the pain.

Sorrel Horse: The Battle of the Little Bighorn

Figure 3-44. "I will search for you among the endless meadows, Whirlwind." *[Ansel Adams photo of Yellowstone, ca. 1942. Courtesy of the National Archives.]*

My thoughts drift off to a time before the soldiers ever came, when Father told me the story of a hunting trip he once took deep into the Valley-of-Steam. Such wonders! Huge spouts of hot water and steam. Great mountain meadows of lush green grass. Deer so tame that he could feed them grass by hand. Elk herds so large that he could close his eyes, shoot an arrow, and bring down one. Vast flights of ducks and geese; a single arrow could bring down two of them. And ice-cold streams filled with fat fish. Laughing and splashing like children, Father and his friends caught fish by hand. Surely, I think, the land of *Wakan Tanka* must be like this. What a fine time Whirlwind and I will have there.

A harsh shaft of bright light shines through the flap of the lodge and brings me back from

Flash Forward
Today, this place is called Yellowstone National Park. When I was a young boy, my uncle and aunt visited Yellowstone and returned to show us fine movies and photos of this great, wonderful park. Entranced with the Park's beauty, I vowed to go there someday.

Nearly a dozen times, I have made plans to visit Yellowstone, but the plans always fell apart. As of this writing, I have not gone yet. This pattern of wanting to go but not being able to do so is a holdover from that lifetime. Sorrel Horse did not make it to Yellowstone either.

199

Figure 3-45. "My father saw many great wonders in the Valley-of-Steam." *[Ansel Adams photo of Yellowstone, ca. 1942. Courtesy of the Natl. Archives.]*

dreamtime. The medicine woman comes inside. Looking first at my leg and next at my chest, she declares, "We must try to remove the arrow." I nod silently.

The broken shaft sticks out between two ribs and I can feel it wedged in. The arrowhead must be down inside my lung. I know from hunting buffalo that removing it will not be easy. She asks if I am ready; I nod stiffly and clench my teeth. Using a piece of leather, she grips the shaft firmly and pulls the shaft straight up and out with a smooth quick snap of her wrist. She holds the shaft up for us to see. This is not good. The arrowhead is gone; it remains inside me.

The head is most likely made of *wasichu* iron, filed to knifelike sharpness. It was tied onto the shaft in such a way that it would remain on as long as the shaft moved forward. However, blood loosens the leather bindings, and when the shaft is pulled backwards, it slides free, leaving the arrowhead inside. This method is good for killing buffalo ... and men. Now, with every muscle movement, every breath, the sharp arrowhead slices deeper into vital flesh. Death comes faster.

As I breathe in and out, air whistles and gurgles quietly through the hole in my chest. I feel detached and weak, but oddly peaceful. The medicine woman packs my wounds with a handful of crushed herbs, leaves, and berries; the mix smells sweet and pungent. Now she wraps my chest and leg with a soft cloth and gently tells me, "I must go now. Many others are wounded, too." I nod and close my eyes, drifting off again. *[See inset.]*

Sunlight coming through the lodge flap awakens me. As my eyes adjust, I see that Sitting Bull has entered the lodge. As he walks over to me, two other members of our council enter behind him and sit down quietly along the teepee wall.

I struggle to sit up, but he motions me to stay down and now nods to me in respect, one warrior to another. I am proud for one moment and now embarrassed to have him see me wounded like this. My medicine was not strong today.

> **Flash Forward**
> Some time ago, I had a severe case of the flu with a lot of chest pain and coughing. Most of the symptoms went away, but a sharp chronic pain continued in my right lung and chest.
> As I meditated to find out why, I asked, "Have I ever had a pain like this before?" Suddenly, I saw the image of a Lakota arrow sticking out of my chest. As I relived being shot with an arrow as Sorrel Horse, the pain in my chest lessened, then disappeared, and never returned.

He has been like a grandfather to me, and with pride in his eyes, he looks down at me for a moment. Opening his medicine-bag, he takes out a deerskin bundle. "The council has met," he says softly, "and we have decided not to wait for a ceremony." Gently, he picks up something and holds it out towards me. "Here is your first eagle feather, my son."

Stunned and overjoyed, I reach out with a shaking hand to take the feather. I am too weak to reach all the way, so Sitting Bull puts it into my hand and curls my fingers around it.

Softly, he says, "You showed great bravery today, charging in among the *wasichus*. Other warriors have said that the camp was saved because of the actions of you and the others who fought the soldiers at the ford today. The People thank you."

I am so choked up that I cannot speak. Tears start to come to my eyes, but I force them down. It would not be very brave to cry while receiving a feather for bravery!

"That feather," he continues, "is very old. I took it from my own war-bonnet, which I will wear no more in battle. No one knows how old it is. It was worn by my father and by his father before him. They were all brave men who served their People well. Follow in their footsteps. All brave men are merely great followers who discover that others choose to follow them as well. Let it be so with you, my son."

I can only nod to him, and he smiles at me in return. He takes Grandmother aside and they talk quietly for a moment. He comes back over and looks down at me. His shoulders are slumped a little. Now that my excitement over the feather has waned a little, I notice his weariness.

Figure 3-46. "The council members sit down quietly along the wall of Grandmother's lodge." *[Inside of a Cheyenne teepee. Photograph by E.S. Curtis, ca. 1900. Courtesy of the Library of Congress.]*

"Tomorrow we must leave. More *wasichus* are coming," he speaks quietly. "We will break into small bands to travel faster. You will go with the band that heads for the Wolf Mountains. We must look for a place where the soldiers will leave us alone."

I think longingly of the Valley-of-Steam, but it is in a different direction. He continues, "We seek only a place where we may live in peace. Perhaps we must go to the Land-of-the-Red-Coats, beyond the reach of the Great Chief of the Long-knives. We must be guided by *Wakan Tanka* and go where He leads us."

I have not been to the Land-of-the-Red-Coats, but I have heard it is very cold. I would prefer the Valley-of-Steam, but it is not for me to say.

Sitting Bull turns to Grandmother to ask, "Can he ride?"

She shakes her head. He looks at me again, "Then we will make a pony-drag to carry you."

With the rashness of youth, I announce, "No! I will ride like a warrior or I will not ride at all. I will only slow you down. Leave without me."

Sitting Bull looks down at me for a moment, with that same tolerant look that Father had. "We must leave in the morning, and we will not leave you behind, or

Figure 3-47. Sorrel Horse's warrior feather came from Sitting Bull's own war-bonnet. *[Ca. 1880s. Courtesy of the National Archives.]*

any of the wounded. More soldiers will be coming soon, and they would surely kill you. I will have someone prepare a pony-drag for you."

I stay quiet, knowing not to argue with him any more. He nods to us and leaves. Grandmother fills a buffalo horn with the tea-that-numbs-pain. I drink it and close my eyes, still holding the golden eagle feather.

My sleep is fevered and restless. I have a dream vision of Mother and Father walking towards me from out of the glowing mist of sunrise. They both wear shining white deerskin clothing with long fringes and turquoise beadwork. We stand along a clear rippling stream in a beautiful mountain meadow, filled with wildflowers in full bloom. Great, towering, snow-capped mountains rise behind them. They smile at me.

Blue light shimmers around them. I have never seen them like this. Entranced and surprised, I have trouble speaking; "I am ashamed that you must see your son like this."

"Like what?" they ask.

"Wounded by a bullet and an arrow," I say, pointing down to my leg and chest. Amazed, I feel around for the wounds, but they are gone. I am dumbfounded.

They smile at me, "You are in the Spirit World now, my son. When Whirlwind crossed over, he said you needed us, but we already knew. And so we have come to meet you."

Suddenly, the scene begins to spin. I feel dizzy and disoriented, as if I am falling off a very tall cliff. Mother and Father fade from view, and I wake up in the teepee again. Blood has filled my lung. I cough and cough, until I can cough no more. Grandmother comes over to stroke my forehead and chant softly to me. Exhausted, I drift off into dreamless sleep.

In the afternoon of the second day after the battle, my buffalo skin blanket is tied onto two wooden poles that are attached to my pony. Two warriors lift me onto the pony-drag. Grandmother uses deerskin strips to tie me on so I will not fall off. As I look around, I see many other wounded warriors already on pony-drags.

Figures 3-48 (above). "We stand in a great, magnificent, mountain meadow." *[Ansel Adams photograph of Yellowstone, taken in about 1942.]*

Figure 3-49 (below). *[Photo of Yellowstone, taken in about 1872 while Sorrel Horse was still alive. Courtesy of the National Archives.]*

The women have stripped the buffalo-skin covers from many of the lodges, and only the poles stick up into the sky, like skeleton ribs of giant buffalo carcasses. Many possessions and other supplies are scattered around the camp. All of them will be left behind. We must travel light and fast, and Sitting Bull has had to make room for the wounded. From one end of camp to the other, funeral teepees or burial scaffolds have been hastily built. Each holds the body, dressed in the finest clothes, of a warrior who will fight no more.

> **Crossing Over**
> When someone's body is severely injured or killed, the soul leaves the body and passes into the astral or Spirit World. There, loved ones and friends who have passed over already meet the soul to make the transition easier.
> As with the parents of Sorrel Horse, these loved ones always know in advance that we are coming. They are there to welcome us and to reassure us, no matter whether the soul's astral visit is temporary or long-term.

I see smoke and smell it on the wind. Recalling my dream vision of the prairie wildfire, I feel uneasy. Rolling my head to face Grandmother, I ask, "What is that?"

"The warriors burn the prairie grass to make smoke to cover our passing. Up there," she answers, pointing to the hills, "there are still some soldiers with guns." *[The remaining troops of Maj. Reno and Capt. Benteen.]*

Before long, we join the line of passing People and ponies. Tied to the drag, I cannot look ahead, only backward; the line extends back as far as I can see. People are leaving quietly, their gazes turned downward. We have won a great victory, yet the People do not look happy. They know many more soldiers are coming. There will always be more and more soldiers.

The People are disappearing, along with the great herds of buffalo. In spite of this victory today, I fear our People will be beaten down by the

Figure 3-50. Using pony-drags to move camp. *[Photograph by E.S. Curtis, ca. 1900. Courtesy of the Library of Congress.]*

Figure 3-51. "A burial scaffold is built for one of our fallen warriors." [Photograph by E.S. Curtis, ca. 1900. Courtesy of the Library of Congress.]

relentless Long-knives, trampled like the prairie grass under the great hooves of buffalo. The *wasichus* have ridden from the sunrise into our lives, and now my People disappear into the sunset. Why has this happened? Why must we feel this pain? *Wakan Tanka* is full of such mystery.

After a while, we move away from the river onto the bluffs. I take one long, last look at the turquoise-blue river, at the golden sun sparkling on the water, at the green crowns of the cottonwood trees. One last smile at Grandmother walking nearby, and now I slowly close my eyes. My body shudders a little.

In an eye blink, I stand beside the trail, watching Grandmother and my battered body passing by. Whirlwind is to my left, Father and Mother on the right. Other warriors, who have passed on into spirit, stand nearby. My People, those who are still living, continue before us in a great line that snakes out of view over the hills. None of my People can see us, except for a few medicine men and medicine women, who nod to us in respect and continue on their way.

Without shifting my gaze from the moving line of People, I speak to Whirlwind, Father, and Mother, "I am ready to die. And if I must die, then I am glad to die free. Life on the reservation was not for me – to be kept tied like a wild pony in a corral. I am glad to die before I had to see my People caged by the *wasichus*. I am glad to leave my body out here under this great blue sky, to leave it in this vast expanse of land that I love so deeply." I fall silent, sad, but glad my life is over.

Mother touches my arm lightly. "Son, you cannot stay with us."

In disbelief, I whirl to face her. I am too stunned to speak.

"It is not time yet. You must go back," she continues.

"It is true," says Father.

Whirlwind speaks, "Brother, unlike me, you have not reached the end of your life's journey."

Figure 3-52. "The last of our people disappear over the hills." *[Photograph by E.S. Curtis, ca. 1905. Courtesy of the Library of Congress.]*

Mother looks at me with great love, "*Wakan Tanka* tests all of us. He will give you the test of pain and despair, but it will not be more than you can bear, and you will gain great strength from it. When you join us again soon, you can stay. The next time, you will not have to return to that broken body."

Father says, "We will stand beside you again when the time comes."

We turn again to gaze out over the long slow-moving line of our People. I am silent, but my heart aches. Now, with a shudder, I am back in my pain-wracked body, looking up at the brilliant blue sky. Faint clouds of grass smoke drift slowly over us. My eyes are burning, though I do not know whether it is from the smoke or from the pain of having to return. I long to stay with Whirlwind and my parents.

Sixteen Days Later

Despite what Mother said, it *has* been almost more than I can bear. For most of the last moon, we have been on the move, trying to keep ahead of the soldiers. We know the *wasichus* will be very angry, and they will shoot us all if they find us. My heart is heavy and my body weak. I am weary and ready for death. I have asked the medicine men to remove the arrowhead, but they will not. "It is too close to your heart," they claim. "We cannot risk taking it out. You will surely die."

"Take it out," I said to them. "Let me die." But they would not.

My badly shattered leg has become red and swollen, and the veins in my leg have turned greenish-black. I can no longer feel anything below the wound. I have come to tolerate the constant pain, accepting it only because I hope death soon will take me away. I pray to die before the soldiers capture us and take us to the reservation. I do not wish to be some captive hawk living under the gaze of the *wasichus*.

At dawn, as we are camped along the Powder River, some of my friends visit my sleeping platform in Grandmother's lodge. They know how much I am suffering. One of them says, "We have heard of a great medicine woman living in a cave high in the Bighorn Mountains. It is said she can help heal a sick body and a sick spirit. She has strong medicine and powerful chants that can remove the arrowhead and make you strong to fight the *wasichus* again. It is said that she can sing a chant so powerful that no bullet can ever touch you again. If you want, we will take you to her."

Another friend speaks, "The Elders say that a great storm will be here soon. If we leave tonight, the snow in the mountains will hide our tracks from the soldiers."

I glance over at Grandmother, who nods. Ready for a chance to be healed, I turn back to my friends and nod my head.

Later, in Early Evening

My friends tie me to my pony, lashing my wrists together around his neck and securing my ankles together under his belly. They bind my buffalo robe around my body with the fur side turned in for warmth. They fasten leather pads to our ponies' hooves, so they will be harder to track. Mounting their ponies, they lead me silently out of camp.

Traveling across the river basin, we head directly for the shelter of the foothills. As we enter the mountains, cold rain begins to fall. It is growing steadily colder. First, the rain turns to sleet, and now, as we ride higher into the mountains, the sleet turns to snow.

In spite of the snow, I am elated with the taste of the mountain air and a chance to heal this pain, but as we ride on, I grow weaker. The further we go, the more I learn the true meaning of pain. Every one of my pony's footsteps is like a knife into my heart. Each bounce sends shivers of pain shooting through my right arm and leg.

Just when I think I can bear no more, just when I think I will scream out in pain, I hear the words, "*Wakan Tanka* will give you no more than you can bear."

"Mother!" I exclaim aloud. My friends quickly signal for me to keep silent.

The sight of her soothes me like a cool mountain pool. Her spirit hand reaches out and touches my forehead, and the torment lifts from my mind. For the first time in many days, a great sense of peace floods through me. Since that day on the Little Bighorn, I have hardened my heart against the pain of my injury. Inwardly, I have complained about being unable to ride, hunt, and move freely as I wished. Now all of those feelings melt away. Instead of fearing pain, instead of struggling against it, I accept it as a brother.

Sorrel Horse: The Battle of the Little Bighorn

Figure 3-53. "The snow will hide our tracks from the soldiers."
[Photograph by E.S. Curtis, ca. 1908. Courtesy of the Library of Congress.]

With Mother's healing touch, I make peace with the iron arrowhead that pains my heart, and at last, I make peace with the *wasichus* who have pained my heart in a different way. I see clearly that the ways of *Wakan Tanka* are beyond the grasp of my mind. It is useless to struggle against Spirit's ways. Better just to accept the life I have been given, as painful as it is.

The Elders say that all things seek balance: dawn follows night; clear skies come after a prairie storm. That is the nature of things. Each person, as well as each race of People, whether white or brown or other color, is given a trail to follow, and each is in the hands of the Great Spirit, whether we can see it or not.

I know now – at last – that I have arrived at the end of my own journey. With a slight shake and shiver, I slip out of my fevered, broken body and stand beside the trail. The snow is falling heavily now, and the world is white and quiet. Mother, Father, and Whirlwind stand quietly nearby smiling, as they promised. Mother touches me gently on the arm. We all watch the small group of my friends move away up the trail. We watch my pony picking his way carefully along the rocky path, with my body slumped over his back.

Mother whispers softly, "It is done now, my son."

I nod and am silent, watching my lifeless body vanish into the curtain of falling snow. The whirling flakes fill in the hoof prints, and before long, the scene shows no sign of my passing.

A World of Endless Springtime

Relieved that the pain is over, I turn towards Mother. As I do, I notice a faint glow coming from the snow near my feet. Following the depression of the trail, a thread of radiant pulsing blue light runs under the snow. Fascinated, I bend down to look closer, scraping away the top crust of snow. Beneath it, a small pulsing rivulet of water, only a hand-width across, flows downhill towards the Powder River.

Figure 3-54 (left). "Relieved that it is over, I watch them disappear into the snow." *[Photograph by E.S. Curtis, ca. 1903. Courtesy of the Library of Congress.]*

Figure 3-55 (below). "The snow begins to melt away before my eyes!" *[Ansel Adams photo of the Snake River, ca. 1942. Courtesy of the National Archives.]*

Puzzled, I bend closer to look at the glowing, luminous water and to scoop up a handful. The water is warm. Suspended in the water in my cupped hand are countless flecks and dots of pulsing light, smaller than grains of sand. They roll and swirl around as if they are living creatures. Entranced by the sight, I study them for many heartbeats. When I look up, Father, Mother, and Whirlwind are gone. Standing up again, I search around, wondering what happened to them. Gradually, I hear the faint trickling sound of flowing water. Looking down again, I see that the tiny, glowing stream has widened. Spellbound, I watch as it grows several paces wider right before my eyes. As it laps onto my moccasins, I step back, only to see it expand again. Wherever the sparkling water touches the snow, it melts instantly and disappears.

Astonished, I watch as the water touches a withered clump of prairie grass, and the grass blades suddenly straighten up, changing from dead to alive, from dry brown to vibrant living green. I cannot believe what I am seeing. It is truly miraculous!

The stream spreads wider and wider, awakening life and restoring vibrant life and rich color to everything it touches. As the luminous water laps against the roots of a winter-bare tree, the tree trunk trembles slightly. Within a few heartbeats, leaf buds form, and with a gentle rustling sound, they unfold into a canopy of bright green leaves. Wild cherries and raspberries bloom and ripen within the space of ten heartbeats. Birds flock in to pull off the ripe, luscious berries. As quickly as a bird eats one berry, another grows back in its place! I am overwhelmed by the stunning beauty all around me. Springtime is happening right before my eyes.

Figure 3-56. "With stunning speed, springtime unfolds around me." *[Photos of Yellowstone, ca. 1871. Courtesy of the National Archives.]*

In and around the roots of a nearby tree, the luminous water laps up against the cold skeleton of a jackrabbit. With its bones pulled apart, it has been dead for many seasons. I watch in stunned disbelief as the bones slide slowly back together across the ground. Rabbit fur begins to appear on them, and within seconds, the skin has plumped up with muscles and flesh. Stretching its legs as if awakening from a restful sleep, the rabbit turns to a nearby clump of lush grass and begins to nibble away. As it nips off a stalk of grass and chews it, the broken stalk grows slowly back to its original full length. The rabbit reaches down to nip off another stalk, and that stalk grows back, too. I gaze on in wonderment. I never would have believed this if I had not seen it.

Nearby is a wild plum tree, its branches sagging with a heavy load of ripe, luscious fruit. Now this will be a delicious test! Reaching up, I pluck off a large purple plum. Before I can even start to eat it, a bloom appears at the same spot and grows into an even larger plum – fully ripe. Shaking my head in wonderment, I bite into the plum. It is like no other I have ever tried – juicy, sweet, and so alive that it makes my mouth tingle. I laugh happily like a child. There is so much to discover here.

Animals, too, are everywhere. The sky is filled with flocks of ducks and geese. Throughout the canopy of trees are songbirds. I can see foxes, wolves, and bears. Herds of elk, deer, and buffalo roam all around, but they do not seem to fear the hunting animals or me. Here there is no death, so no animal is burdened with fear. They know that they cannot die. If anything happens, soon they will be restored to life. All around me is the wonderful, peaceful, bountiful creation of *Wakan Tanka*.

Figure 3-57. "None of the many animals fear me at all."
[Courtesy of the National Archives.]

Figure 3-58. "What a glorious land this is!" *[Ansel Adams photo of Glacier National Park, ca. 1942. Courtesy of the National Archives.]*

I laugh aloud and call out to the entire world, "Such wonders! Is there no end to them?" My voice echoes off the nearby hills.

I hear a musical laugh from the edge of the woods. It is Mother! Smiling, she walks out into view and says, "No, there is no end."

Father and Whirlwind are behind her, too. Their pure-white deerskin clothing and intricate turquoise and gold beadwork sparkles and glows in the bright sunlight.

Father smiles and says, "We stepped aside for a moment so you could explore it for yourself ... with all the wonderment of a child."

"We all felt the same when we first came here," says Whirlwind, grinning. Putting an arm on my shoulder, he continues, "As you lay wounded on your buffalo skin robe, I heard you say that you would meet me in *Wakan Tanka's* endless meadows. So you have, my brother. Welcome!"

I am so full of joy that I can barely speak. I put one arm around Mother and rest the other one on Whirlwind's shoulder, gazing into their eyes with happiness. I manage only to say, "And what a welcome it is, my family."

With a big smile, Father joins the group, linking arms to complete the circle. Indeed, what a welcome it is!

Epilogue

Under orders from the President and his generals, contemporary U.S. Army accounts told a very different story from what actually happened that day at the Little Bighorn. The Custer Myth of the noble buckskin-clad hero fighting to his last bullet captivated the country. On the other hand, the "massacre" of Custer and his men so outraged the nation that it produced a terrible backlash against the Indians. Within 15 years, the Army had crushed all Indian resistance, and many of the greatest Plains warriors were either dead or in captivity. The end of the fighting signaled the end of a way of life as the Native American Great Plains culture vanished into history.

During our research, one of the mediums contacted the spirit of Custer to ask if he wanted to add to the story. He told us, "I would like others to know that I was neither a fool nor a hero. I was just a man caught up in an extraordinary event. My men were poorly trained, but that was not their fault. True, we were outnumbered and outgunned, but that didn't cause the defeat. After all, Maj. Reno and nearly all of his men survived – and they faced the same number of Indians.

"Everything changed when I got wounded. Fear is a powerful emotion, and all men feel it in battle. However, for the troops, seeing me get shot was just too much to take. Fear got the best of them. People can argue about who might be to blame. Looking back, I say, 'No one.' That day was just meant to turn out that way."

The life of Sorrel Horse was one of harmony and oneness with the natural world and Great Spirit. He lived at a truly historic moment in the struggle between the white man's greed to *own* land versus the Native Americans' *stewardship* of the world as a gift from the Great Spirit … a gift that could belong to no man.

It was also a life of great courage. My soul was able to explore and embrace bravery at a time when the Old Ways were disappearing.

Life Review & Analysis

GROUP-LINKS: In every lifetime, there are many links, or connections, to groups of souls from the present back to other past lives. Becoming aware of those connections in each lifetime can help us to use our past life experiences to clarify our present circumstances. These connections are one of the reasons we say "history repeats itself." Often, the same souls are the ones doing the repeating. Here are some from the Lakota lifetime:

Figure 3-59. Some Vietnam era antiwar protestors were reincarnated Native Americans. *[Courtesy of the National Archives.]*

GROUP-LINK: "From Geronimo to Ho," the Vietnam Connection

It can be said that a country, like an individual, has a soul of sorts and it, too, has Group-Link connections or karma. Because the annihilation of the Indians by the U.S. Government was based on greed, eventually the scales of karma had to be balanced. One of these opportunities came about in the 1960s with the advent of the "Hippie" movement and the Vietnam War.

My intuition showed me that some of the Vietnam War protesters were former Native Americans who were still struggling with their views of the unjust actions of the U.S. Military. Carrying over their attitudes from that previous era, some of them still showed a preference for Indian-style clothing, and some chose teepees over conventional housing. Many also displayed an attraction to peyote, mescaline, and marijuana, all sacred plants and herbs for Native Americans.

In addition, some of the Vietcong were former Indians, most notably Ho Chi Minh, who had a karmic soul connection to Geronimo, the wily Apache war-leader.

Figure 3-60. Geronimo and Ho Chi Minh. *[Photo courtesy of Denver Public Library, Western History Coll.; Addison, X-32892. Drawing is author's interpretation of Ho Chi Minh, using existing photographs.]*

Both had no love for the U.S. Army. Crazy Horse also reincarnated as a Vietnamese general in order to complete his own soul issues with the United States.

In addition, there was a Group-Link with Lyndon Johnson. Reflection (2002) indicated that, during a previous lifetime, Lyndon Johnson had been Vice-President Andrew Johnson, who helped craft the government plans to exterminate the Plains Indians. As part of that soul's karmic balance, he returned as President Johnson, who supported a lot of fine legislation that helped Native American tribes. On the other hand, the Vietcong, some of whom were former Indians, soundly defeated President Johnson in Vietnam, even though they appeared to have no chance to win against a more powerful adversary.

Furthermore, Johnson was "defeated" in this country by antiwar protestors, some of whom had been Indians, as well. His past karma cost him reelection and tainted the good things he accomplished as president.

Because of our nation's treatment of the Native Americans, we lost the Vietnam War, in spite of superior weapons, technology, and funding. It seems clear that karma is far more powerful than battle plans and bombs.

Figure 3-61. D-Day casualties in 1944, and college students in the 1960s. *[Courtesy of the National Archives.]*

GROUP-LINK: "D-Day to Peace March," the WWII Connection

My intuition also tells me that some Vietnam peace protesters had died in World War II and reincarnated right away. I know this to be true in my case, as well. Because WWII happened about 20 years before Vietnam, many of these reincarnated souls were draft-eligible college students at the time that the Vietnam War draft started. Having just had their previous bodies blown apart, often as soldiers, they were none too happy about having it happen again.

During that time in the 1960s, unknown to me at the time, I reawakened my own past life resistance to the U.S. Army. These feelings led me to oppose the war, actions that almost got me imprisoned in Fort Leavenworth.

Only later did I come to accept, understand, and release those powerful feelings that had their roots in two recent past lives that were connected with the U.S. Army. The first life was this one as Sorrel Horse, 100 years in the past on the open plains of Montana; the second was as a young German women killed in an Allied air raid on the Peenemunde V-2 rocket works in Germany during World War II. Neither life made me a fan of the "glories of war."

Figure 3-62. A Roman centurion and Gen. Custer. *[Courtesy of the Library of Congress and the National Archives.]*

GROUP-LINK: "Custer crosses the Rubicon," Roman Connection

Meditating on my connection with Gen. Custer, I asked, "Why is it that I was shot and killed by Custer's troopers in *two* successive lifetimes?" It was clear to me that I had done something to Custer in the past that needed to be balanced out.

When I explored this during a hypnotic regression session, Reflection revealed that my Group-Link with Custer has spanned more than 2,000 years! I had first encountered Custer in a lifetime when I was a Roman legionnaire. At that time, Rome was embroiled in a bitter civil war between Octavian and Marc Antony, famously allied with Cleopatra.

According to Reflection, I was fighting as part of Antony's army against the army of one of Octavian's generals. This same soul would later become Custer. In fierce hand-to-hand fighting, I wounded the general seriously in the *right leg (!)* with a powerful slash of my sword, knocking him to the ground. Honor was still important to warriors in Rome at that time, and he asked for mercy with honor, not out of weakness, since he was willing to die, but as one warrior to another. Ignoring the warrior code and cursing him with disdain, I killed him like an animal.

Because of my lack of compassion for him, I had to endure two lifetimes of being killed by his cavalrymen in order to balance the scales of higher justice. Even then, the balance was not complete. The final balancing comes by revealing in this book the true story of Custer at the Little Bighorn; it comes by telling his story without any animosity for that soul; it comes by accepting him completely just as he is. After more than 2,000 years, this final balancing will heal things between us at last.

This Group-Link has been a powerful lesson for me. The actions we take and the attitudes we hold can have an extremely long-lasting impact on us, either negative or positive. My connection with Custer has spanned more than 2,000 years. Looking back, if I had showed compassion and let the General live, I could have been spared all of these problems. I should have followed just one simple rule, "Do unto others ...."

Lessons Learned

Recalling a past lifetime is useful only if one uses the memories to become freer in the present lifetime. Reliving this lifetime as Sorrel Horse brought up:

- *Despair* over the loss of the Lakota way of life.
- *Grief* over the death of my parents and Whirlwind.
- *Fear* of being wounded or killed in battle.
- *Revenge* against Custer for what he did to the Lakota people and me.
- *Physical pain* caused by the wound in my chest and my leg.

As I became aware of these feelings, I worked to undo them, mostly using the Sedona Method mentioned in Appendix A1. As I let go of all of these past painful memories, I felt instantly better, and my mind was more at peace. Undoing these memories has left me freer of unwanted emotions and freer to live in the present moment, rather than to be stuck in the past. Anyone can do the same thing by using the technique of past life recall.

Some of the positive lessons my soul learned from the life of Sorrel Horse included the following:

- *Family Bonds:* That life is far better for having experienced the bonds and love of family, friends, and tribe. Today, doctors and scientists know that people who are socially active and have a strong circle of friends and family are far less likely to become ill or die prematurely.
- *Harmony with Nature:* To live a life more in tune with nature and in harmony with the spirit world, something many of us do not give enough thought and respect to in today's harried world.
- *Forgiveness:* The power of forgiveness for Custer, for the *wasichus*, as well as for members of my own tribe.
- *Physical Pain:* How to deal with and accept a lot of pain.
- *Belief System:* To fight for what I believe in. That does not mean that I fight all of life's daily battles. As the famous credo advocates, I learned "to accept the things I cannot change ... and to change the things I can."

NOTE: Appendix A contains information about some simple yet very powerful spiritual techniques. They can free you from the undesirable effects of past lives and allow you to get the best out of your current life.

Louis St. Jacques: Drinking with Vincent van Gogh (1870-1914)

Figure 4-1. Rare photos of Vincent van Gogh at the ages of 13 and 19. *[Photographs reprinted from Tralbaut (1959).]*

Background

The life of Louis St. Jacques (pronounced as 'Loo-EE Sin-Zhak') overlapped the final six years of the life of Sorrel Horse. Such an overlap is possible for several reasons. First, because children sleep a lot, their lives are often less eventful and require less attention for the soul. Overlapping two lives that way is less demanding.

Second, we grossly underestimate our abilities as souls, choosing to think of ourselves as extremely limited bodies. The soul is not subject to the same constricting limitations as the body. At the soul level, all of us have many more abilities than we currently are utilizing.

In our story, Louis met and formed a friendship in 1886 with Vincent van Gogh, the Dutch artist, who had moved to Paris in early March. Vincent's brother, Theo, who was already living in Paris, sold paintings by various artists through a small gallery in the city. Theo, who supported Vincent financially, agreed to let his brother stay in his Paris apartment.

> **The Artists in Montmartre**
> Louis also met some other contemporary painters, such as Henri de Toulouse-Lautrec and Paul Gauguin. At the time of the story, none of these artists had a popular style, and the art establishment of the day dismissed them as "bohemians." Of course, these painters are world-famous today, but they were not famous at the time Louis knew them. In fact, Vincent, creator of some of the world's most beloved and valuable paintings today, sold only one known painting during his lifetime. Some of his paintings were thrown away after his death because no one wanted them.
>
> Where possible, our story will be told using contemporary photos and paintings by the artists themselves. We begin in Paris, when Louis was 16 years old ...

Figure 4-2. View of Paris and the Seine from the Louvre Gallery. *[Ca. 1909, courtesy of the Library of Congress.]*

Paris (1886)

Racing across the bridge, dodging among the people and carriages, I feel a rising panic. *Papa will kill me*, I worry.

Abruptly darting in front of a buggy and horse with blinders on, I frighten the poor animal. It rears suddenly, and the buggy driver yells at me while struggling to control the horse. With heart pounding, I run even faster without looking back.

Figure 4-3. "Running headlong across Alma Bridge, I am almost trampled by a horse!" *[Ca. 1890. Courtesy of the Library of Congress.]*

Papa is scrupulously punctual, but I am not. Usually this is not a problem, because Papa mostly ignores me, but today is different. He left word with the butler for me to be home by noon for a "talk." It sounds serious, and I am late, late, *late!*

Matching my fast-moving feet, my mind races imagining what Papa could want with me. I ransack my memory for all the things I have done wrong that he does not know about. Maybe I can make up an alibi in advance .... No, too many. I will just have to improvise.

Taking a shortcut home, I turn up the market street. Not too far now. I will not be *too* late. Papa can be positively fierce when he is angry. With that image powerfully filling my mind, I fail to pay attention to where I am going. Appearing suddenly, a vendor pushes a tomato cart out of a side alley. Before I can veer away, I collide with him with a great crash that tips over the cart and sends us both sprawling.

As I land with a thud on the paving stones, a sharp pain shoots through my knee. Moaning, I roll over to inspect the damage. My trousers are torn, and

Figure 4-4. "Racing down the street, I have to dodge in and out among the vendors." *[French street, ca. 1890. Courtesy of the Library of Congress.]*

blood is oozing from my knee. *Oh, God, what have I done?* Gingerly poking my bloody knee, I am suddenly relieved. *Tomato juice!* I laugh aloud.

The vendor, thinking I am laughing at him, stands up and begins shouting at me and cursing. Ruefully, I think, *Is there anyone who is not mad at me today?* He starts moving towards me ominously, waving his arms wildly. Not waiting a moment longer, I jump up and run off towards home. Just as I think I have escaped, I hear a loud splat as a fast-flying tomato lands squarely on my coat back. I think, *Times like this make me hate vegetables!*

Without looking back, I sprint the rest of the way home. Reaching our front door, overcome with exhaustion, I bend over panting with hands on knees. Brushing the street dust off, I try to compose myself as best I can – at least, for someone who smells like a bag of tomatoes.

Hoping no one will notice me before I can change, I quietly open our ornately carved, gold-leaf-trimmed Baroque entrance door (in other words, "ugly"). Tiptoeing inside, I turn around to close the door silently behind me.

"Good afternoon, sir," the butler says from behind, startling me.

"Is it?" I ask sullenly, turning to face him.

Figure 4-5. The butler says, "Sir, your father awaits you." *[Reminds me of the butler; from Vincent's "Portrait of a Man," Dec. 1888. Reprinted from Faille (1939).]*

"Your coat, sir," he says, holding out his hand. When I give it to him, he turns up his nose and holds it far out in front of him with two fingers.

Scrambling to make up a story about the coat, I start out with, "You see, as I was ...."

He interrupts, "Sir, I require no further details. I shall take care of the coat for you. Your father awaits you in the study." With that, he turns and leaves still holding the coat out in front of him.

I swallow nervously and turn to face the study door, which is closed. Cautiously knocking once, I enter when I hear Papa say, "Come!"

He sits at his desk, writing with a quill pen. Without looking up, he says evenly, "Late as usual, Louis." It is not a question, so I stand silently.

"Where have you been?" he asks.

"Out," I say.

Uh-oh, wrong answer! Papa jumps up from his desk, glaring at me. "'Out,' you say. 'OUT!' And just where is 'out'?" he shouts, not really expecting an answer. Meanwhile, I just stare at my shoes.

"Why do you insist on befriending those bohemian bums and whores? You will never amount to anything!" Papa, his face purple, begins shouting. I have learned just to agree with him when he gets this way. Like a summer storm, it will pass.

Figure 4-6. "Papa is usually annoyed with me, and he can be truly fierce when he is angry." *[A look-alike for Papa. Detail of Manet's "Painting of a Man," ca. 1859. Reprinted from Meier-Graefe (1912).]*

"Of course, Papa, I am truly sorry. I shall do as you wish," I say, intending to do no such thing. Even though I am afraid of him, I have learned just to suffer through his tirades. I know that he never does more than just shout at me. He will forget about this soon enough. His only real interest is money and business.

I keep my gaze down, not looking at his eyes – that only makes him angrier. I am about half a head shorter than he is, so I just stare at his high collar and tie. Blocking out the noise of his voice, I notice the bulging veins in his neck. That is odd, I think, suddenly curious. They just pop out right above his collar. Perhaps Nana is using too much starch.

"Louis, you never show any inclination for business. I am at a loss to know what to do with you!"

As he says my name, I pay attention again, losing interest in his veins. Turning away from me, he begins talking aloud about me in the third person, as though I were no longer there.

"I should have been stricter with him in his younger days. Now I pay the price. I have been far too lenient with him."

"That is a matter of opinion," I mutter quietly under my breath.

He whirls to face me, shouting, "What did you say?"

Shocked that he heard me, my mind races and I stammer lamely, "Papa ... I, uh ... I simply said, 'In this *matter*, I accept your *opinion*.'"

He glares at me intently, trying to decide if I am lying. I feign my best look of innocence.

"Harrumph," he snorts, adding, "I have a meeting now, Louis, but I have not finished with you yet over this." With that, he stomps out of the room.

My shoulders slump in relief. I have just gotten a reprieve from the guillotine – at least temporarily.

Leaving the study, I walk across the hall to the drawing room and sit on the chaise lounge to regain my composure. I stare at the ornately carved mahogany woodwork and flowery silk-covered walls, adorned with paintings from many artists. Nothing is really to my taste – nymphs dancing, Pan and his flute, coy goddesses, and muscle-bound gods. All of it is so contrived and fake, nothing from the real world. I shake my head in disbelief. Everything in this room is spotless, polished, meticulously neat, and so phony. Everything is exactly in its proper place – except me! I wonder miserably, *How was I ever born here?*

I am truly disgusted with Papa's attitude. As an art dealer, he puts himself out as a great patron of the arts. He routinely tours the Louvre with friends and clients with the same reverence most people reserve for a cathedral. Attending the finest exhibits around the city, Papa and Ma-Maa buy many paintings and sculptures, whatever catches their fancy with no thought of cost.

However, I am convinced that Papa truly does not appreciate art – does not understand it. It is strictly a business for him. He buys art only because his peers expect it of him, because it is part of his "image," and because he intends to make a profit. In truth, he can barely conceal his distaste for artists. He looks down on them the same way he looks down on our cook or the butler. Expecting them to do their jobs well, he pays them well – he is not cheap – but frankly, he does not like any of them.

That is not my way. I cannot stand his stuffy, boring friends and business associates, all with too much starch in their collars. I chuckle quietly as I recall his purple, distended veins. Perhaps someday, I shall annoy him so much that his veins will bulge uncontrollably.

I imagine myself calling, "Ma-Maa. Oh, Ma-Maa. Papa's head has finally exploded." I laugh aloud, catch myself, and choke it off in mid-laugh, fearful that he might hear me. No, I like real people, like Vincent and Paul *[Gauguin]* and Henri *[Toulouse-Lautrec]*, people who have genuine feelings and who know something about the world, at least something worth knowing.

Ma-Maa glides in gracefully, dressed in a frilly emerald-green chiffon dress with a matching gold-lace sun-hat. I groan silently; Ma-Maa's entire life revolves around fashion. Stopping in front of the full-length mirror and fussing with her hair, she asks me, "Do I look all right, dear?" Still depressed about Papa, I sit up a little but do not answer.

Glancing over at me, she tries to console me, "Do not pay too much attention to Papa. You know how he is." Not really expecting a response by now, she chatters on lightly, "I am off to a splendid lecture at the Louvre with the Ladies Club."

"That is certain to be dull," I mumble under my breath.

"Pardon me, dear? What did you say?"

"That should be wonderful," I reply lamely, speaking louder.

"Indeed! Perhaps you would like to go, too," she says, brightly. "Though I will be with all the ladies, I am sure you would love to hear the professor's talk on the classical painters."

Mulling over that prospect briefly, I mumble, "I would rather shoot myself."

"What was that, dear?" she asks, looking at me suspiciously.

"Ma-Maa, I think your hearing is going bad. You should have the doctor check it." She looks at me doubtfully, so I continue, "I said that 'I will have to *excuse* myself.'"

"Oh. And what will you be doing today, my dear?"

Knowing she is not truly interested, I start mumbling again, "Smoking and drinking with Vincent."

Half hearing me, she pauses for a fleeting moment, puzzled. Questioning her hearing now, she decides not to ask again and responds cheerfully,

Figure 4-7. Detail from a photo of the Louvre, my mother's destination, ca. 1890. *[Courtesy of the Library of Congress.]*

"That is nice, dear. Do be home for supper." With that, she turns and breezes out the door.

Miserable, I slump down further on the chaise lounge. At least, Vincent and Paul will talk to me like a human being. Even though I am young, they treat me like one of them. Sometimes though, since I often buy the drinks, I suspect that it is because I have money. I know that times are hard, so I do not mind. After all, it is not my money, it is Papa's, and money is the one thing Papa has that I do like.

With satisfaction, I think of all the artists that I see in the cafes, cabarets, and dancehalls. Unlike my dreary life, their lives are wild and unpredictable, especially so for Vincent. Of all of them, I like him the most; he has a great fiery intensity, a fierceness of purpose about him. After putting up with Papa today, it will be good to see him again.

Later that Day at the Café

My chair grates noisily across the hard floor as I slide up to the table with Vincent, Paul, Henri, and one of Henri's several girlfriends. Vincent's brother, Theo, is at the table, also. Most of the others have already ordered cheap wine or absinthe. Not caring much for either, I call for a glass of Pernod.

Figure 4-8. "I am eager to get away from Papa and get back to the Café." *[Vincent's "Cafe Terrace, Arles, at Night," Sep. 1888. Reprinted from Tralbaut (1969).]*

Even though it is midday, this corner of the cafe is very dark. Vincent probably picked the table; sometimes he prefers to avoid the light and to avoid people, as well. We are well away from the floor show at the other end of the café. Since the songs and dance numbers can be quite noisy sometimes, it is easier to talk in our secluded corner. We have come not for common entertainment, but rather for the uncommon pleasure of each other's company.

Figure 4-9. Vincent's "Self-portrait," 1887. *[Reprinted from Meier-Graefe (1922).]* Paul Gauguin's "Self-portrait," 1888. *[Reprinted from Morice (1919).]*

Figure 4-10. Henri Toulouse-Lautrec, ca. 1890. *[Reprinted from Esswein (1912).]* Theo van Gogh, ca. 1890. *[Reprinted from Tralbaut (1959).]*

As usual, they are having a passionate discussion, and as usual, I am content to remain quiet and revel in their friendship, like some sun-seeking flower drawn to the light. I can think of no better life than to be around such artists.

Attendance at these get-togethers is ever changing, though Henri and Vincent tend to be regulars. Usually Emile *[Bernard, the painter]* is around but not today. Greatly satisfied to be among them again, I glance around the table, listening to their heated discussion. They are not discussing art, as is usual for them, but clothing, of all things. Now, that is something worth arguing about – their clothes. Mother of God! I just do not understand their love of dark-colored, dreary clothes, which are so unlike their vivid, vibrant palettes.

Paul says, "If there must be a choice between paints for canvas or canvas pants, then indeed, the choice is clear – clothing can wait. No self-respecting poverty-stricken artist, of whom we are magnificent examples, my friends, would choose otherwise. Is that not correct, Vincent? I think you are our foremost expert on this," he says with a mischievous smile. "What do you say?"

Seeing where Paul is going with this, Vincent holds up his hands in mock protest and shakes his head. In this clothing matter, I agree with Paul, Vincent is

Figure 4-11. "The music and dancing sometimes makes the cafe extremely noisy." *[Toulouse-Lautrec's "Moulin Rouge," 1890. Reprinted from Jewell (1944).]*

Figure 4-12. Toulouse-Lautrec's "Jane Avril" Poster, 1893. *[Reprinted from Hiatt (1896).]*

the worst. As an artist, he often overlooks his appearance, since for him, spending every franc for paint and canvas is of utmost importance. Mind you, Vincent is capable of dressing very fashionably and does so on occasion. However, when he is engrossed in his painting – which is most of the time – he prefers to wear the same clothes until they fall almost to tatters.

With a wry smile, Paul jokes to the rest of us, "If he does not spend more on clothes, Vincent will be the only artist in Paris to hire nude models and then be forced to paint them in the nude himself." We all laugh.

Smiling, Vincent finally joins in the fun, "My friends, sometimes I must count my coins so carefully that there is only one way to afford to paint a nude model and that is to do a nude self-portrait."

There is good-natured laughter all around. As it subsides, Paul places his hand on Vincent's arm and says with deep seriousness, "If you do so, my good friend, and *if* you value our friendship, please do *not* show it to us!"

Everyone roars with laughter, including Vincent. We order another round of drinks, and this warmhearted council of kindred spirits continues.

After a while, Theo, looking worried and withdrawn today, gets up and takes his leave. "If you starving artists will excuse me, it is time to try to sell some of your paintings."

As Theo leaves, the talk shifts to a well-known group of artists in the city, who pander to the taste *du jour* of the Parisian art trade. Papa represents many of them, but "real" artists disparage them.

"They are like trained apes!" storms Vincent, acidly referring to this group. "No, I take that back, for I choose not to disparage apes, who could certainly paint better than those leeches!" The others join in, raising their voices in agreement.

Henri jokes, "Vincent, be careful. Now you disparage leeches." More laughter.

"They are nothing more than paltry wallpaper peddlers," Paul says, emphasizing the *p* in every word, "putting pretty paint on paper to be pasted on the paneled partitions of the petty bourgeoisie." He pauses, and now, with a roguish smile, continues, "But you know, their art serves a purpose, it gives the idle rich something to do. Think of it. They can sit around in their proper groups with their proper friends having proper debates about the proper 'meaning' of a painter's work."

Now he mimics the stilted accent and stuffy demeanor of an aristocrat, holding an imaginary monocle, "*Au contraire*, begging your pardon, monsieur, I believe that, in this magnificent work, the esteemed artist was philosophizing about the dire difficulties suffered by those poor, eternally misunderstood creatures, the wood nymphs." Henri laughs the loudest at Paul's antics, perhaps because he comes from an aristocratic background.

Vincent joins in again, "And poor 'wallpaper' it is, for being so costly. They insist on painting fantasy pictures of brutish gods and fleshy goddesses prancing naked along the Seine. I ask you, my friends, when is the last time you encountered a naked goddess strolling along the river walk?"

Henri speaks up, putting on a serious face, "Why, last night, as a matter of fact ..." He glances at his lover, as she elbows him in mock protest, "... though perhaps it was just hallucinations from the absinthe." Lifting his glass up to eye level, he suspiciously inspects the emerald-green liquid. *[See inset.]*

We all laugh – except Vincent, of course. We have grown to accept his seriousness. He is often that way, except when a woman is with him and he softens up somewhat. Vincent is not without humor, mind you; it is just that art is his "religion," and most people do not joke well about holy things.

Absinthe

This is an alcoholic drink made from an extract of wormwood. Emerald green and very bitter, it once was popular among artists and writers, who believed that it stimulated creativity. It was the drink of choice for Edouard Manet, Edgar Degas, Oscar Wilde, Edgar Allen Poe, and Pablo Picasso, among others.

However, chronic use led to addiction, hyperexcitability, delirium, convulsions, and vivid hallucinations. Many countries banned the consumption of absinthe early in the 20th century.

Vincent continues, "The main problem is that they have no feeling for their work. They are out of touch with reality."

With a crooked finger, he tamps his old worn pipe, packing down the mixture of tobacco and opium. "A great artist – first, foremost, and last – must have a great capacity to feel. If he has that ...," he pauses to light his pipe, "then talent and technique will take care of itself. Great passion will always find its way out of the soul." Taking a deep draw on his pipe, he closes his eyes. As he leans back in his chair, the smoking mixture begins to have an effect, and his face mirrors his mild euphoria.

Though usually silent, I speak up impulsively, "I will be a great artist someday."

Figure 4-13. "Last night, I saw a goddess bathing in the Seine! Or was it perhaps the absinthe?" *[Detail of Renoir's "The Bathers." Reprinted from Jewell (1944).]*

Suddenly, all eyes turn to me. My cheeks turn red, and I slouch down a little lower in my chair, shocked by my own brashness. No one laughs, but there are friendly smiles all around, even from Vincent, who stares thoughtfully at me for a moment.

"You cannot be a great artist," he says matter-of-factly, still with a faint smile on his face.

"Why not?" I protest.

"The world is too easy for you, young sir," he says without harshness. "Your father is rich, and his wealth protects you from the world, so you do not feel its blows. You know pleasure but not much pain. You know abundance but not lack and poverty. A great artist must be able to embrace pain deep within his soul. He must know the heights of heaven and the deepest reaches of hell."

"Go easy on the boy, Vincent," says Paul amiably. "After all, the rest of us have the opposite problem. We wake up each day in hell and try to paint our way to heaven. We know pain and poverty much too well."

Vincent looks contrite, admitting, "Paul, you are right. Please do not be offended, Louis. Sometimes I feel tired and old, and I resent the struggle far too much." Vincent puts down his pipe, "One moment, my mind is ecstatic with new ideas; then the next, it is shackled by the same old frustrations, without the means to move forward, except for the generosity of my brother, Theo." *[See inset.]*

He turns to me again, saying, "I look at you, Louis, who aspire to be an artist, and I wish that a new generation of artists should be more fortunate than we are. For 'old' artists like us, life

---

Theo van Gogh

Vincent's brother supported him financially for nearly all of his life, allowing him to paint freely. Even though Vincent produced nearly 900 known paintings and over 1,000 drawings, he and Theo managed to sell or barter only a few of them during his lifetime.

Soon after Vincent's death, most people considered his paintings to be worthless. Hundreds were thrown out or given away. However, in 1990, exactly 100 years after his death, Vincent's "Portrait of Dr. Gachet" sold for more than $82 million.

has given us more than enough pain. That knowledge alone, young sir, should dissuade you from becoming an artist."

Paul, having sent the conversation in this serious direction, tries to lighten it up by proposing a toast. "Well said, Vincent. Here is to 'painless art' from this day forward."

It does not work, and there are only polite smiles. Vincent continues, "Perhaps, among all of us here, Henri is closest to a balanced outlook." He smiles at his handicapped friend, who lowers his eyes and stares into his glass. "Henri's family is rich, too, so he does not feel the pangs of lack. Yet fate has given Henri the chance to feel the pain of humanity and to know despair and rejection. Because of that, I predict that Henri long will be known as a great painter." *[See inset.]*

Henri Toulouse-Lautrec
He was already physically frail when, at the age of 14, he broke both legs. This accident caused his legs to cease to grow, so that as an adult, he was only about 4'6" tall.

Because of his poor health and his abnormal appearance, Henri drank increasingly more as he got older, seeking out the company of others on the fringes of Parisian society.

Henri looks very humble and serious, "Thank you, Vincent, my dear friend. In truth, all of you know that art is in my blood. Yet, my foremost passion has become …" He pauses to raise his glass in toast, "… to get more alcohol in my blood!"

With laughter all around, we cheerfully raise our glasses in toast, assuring Henri that, in this regard, he is well on his way to success.

In spite of my laughter, I worry about Henri and Vincent, less so about Paul. The opium, tobacco, and absinthe affect them more and more as time goes on. I know that these things certainly affect me, and the results are not always to my liking. I know that Papa would not like those effects either, and so far, I have hidden them from him. Vincent and Henri claim that smoking and drinking help release the "muse of creativity," but on occasion, I have seen it bring out dark demons in them as well. Perhaps, this is the cost for their brilliant bursts of creativity, but I am not so sure. I am not so sure at all.

Becoming serious once again, Henri turns to me, "My dear Louis, do not let my well-intentioned, grumpy friend dissuade you. If you truly want to be a painter, you should try it. To do so, you must be observant, not only of nature, but also of other painters. But most important: you must study and work at it with strong desire."

"Here is my suggestion for you." He takes out of his pocket a crumpled scrap of brown paper and scribbles on it. When the front side is full, he continues on the back.

He hands me the paper. "This is a brief introduction from me, along with the name and address of a personal friend who is an art teacher. He is very

Figure 4-14. Blowing smoke rings: "Oh, Yes! I need more alcohol in my blood!" [Manet's "Absinthe Drinker," 1858. Reprinted from Meier-Graefe (1912).]

Figure 4-15. Absinthe, the "Green Fairy." [Vincent's "Still Life with Absinthe," Sep. 1887. Reprinted from Faille (1939).]

good. Tell him I sent you. Tell him you are interested in being an artist, and you want to start as a model. Tell him you will work for free."

"A *model!*" I protest. "I do not want to *be* a model – I want to *paint* models!"

"As you wish," Henri smiles and shrugs politely, "but this would be a good way to begin by observing other artists at work and by seeing how they paint you. Then, you will see if you have it in you to become an artist."

I do not say anything. The conversation shifts and moves on, but I do not hear it. After recovering from the initial shock of Henri's suggestion, I resolve to try it – reluctantly.

Later that Month in Montmartre

With growing trepidation, I walk slowly down the avenue. Turning this adventure over in my mind, I have serious doubts about my own body – at least, about baring it in front of strangers. Am I good enough to be a model? I do not know. I think my proportions are good, perhaps better than most, even though I am on the thin side.

At the beach, not long ago, the wife of a family friend remarked that I look like Michelangelo's David, only thinner. I did not know whether to feel flattered or not. At any rate, the way she gazed at my swimming trunks made me think that she really did not have "art" on her mind. I decided not to have any "art" discussions alone with her.

Turning into a side alley, instantly I come to a halt. The alley is filled with about a dozen Parisians. Fearing for my safety, I worry that I am dressed too expensively for such a place. Swiveling my head around, I consider turning back but finally decide against it. Taking a deep breath and resigning myself not to risk the ridicule of my friends, I continue into the alley.

Figure 4-16. "I am having second thoughts as I head down the avenue to the studio." *[Photo of Ave. de la Gare, ca. 1890. Courtesy of the Library of Congress.]*

With the alley people watching in silence, I raise Henri's paper scrap periodically comparing it to the faint addresses on the weather-streaked walls. Finally, it matches the one on this old, dirty brick building in front of me. The structure is in a state of remarkable disrepair – brick chips, dust, and broken wood lie all along the walls. Filthy fetid water slowly drains along both sides of the street. Drawing in a deep breath, I open the door. Inside is a dilapidated warehouse with nearly the entire southern wall framed with square panes of yellowed, dirty glass. Light shines through the glass, but I cannot see details of anything beyond. Below the glass, near the far wall, mismatched badly worn easels and chairs face a raised wooden stage. A single tall stool stands alone on the platform. The dirty wood-plank floor is worn and bare. Small splintered chunks are missing from a plank here and there, and the light fades to darkness down below the floor.

About six or seven students stand near a large stern-looking man who certainly must be the teacher. He wears a white smock – well, that is, it is not exactly white – it is covered with multicolored streaks and splatters of paint, which, by

Figure 4-17. "I fear I am dressed too well for this part of town." *[French photo, ca. 1890. Courtesy of the Library of Congress.]*

the way, perfectly match those on the floor. Thinking wistfully of my spotless home, I furtively turn to leave.

The teacher calls out in a booming voice, "Model. Model! Are you Henri's model?"

I freeze, roll my eyes up, and turn back to greet him with a forced smile. "Yes, sir," I admit meekly.

"Come. Come, we are ready for you," he shouts enthusiastically. "You can change in there. Use the robe," he says pointing to one of several small rooms off to the side.

Changing into the dirty robe, I reluctantly return to the studio. The teacher is busy with a student, so I mount the platform to sit on the stool.

"No!" he shouts. Startled, I jump off the stool. "You must stand," he insists, motioning with his hand as if to shoo me away from the stool.

At that point, the door from another dressing room opens, and a dark-blonde woman in a similar dirty robe walks towards me. I recognize her as Claudette, one of Henri's prostitute friends. I do not know her very well, but I have seen her a few times in the dancehalls. We trade polite hellos. *[See inset.]*

"The robes," the teacher calls out, impatiently waving his hand back and forth at us. "Get ready, class. We will do charcoal studies today."

Slipping out of her robe in one fluid motion, she gracefully sits lightly on the tall

> **Flash Forward**
>
> The same soul who was Claudette also played a role in my current lifetime. As one of my earliest lovers, now called Claudia, she was a lovely free-spirited person who had a major influence on my young sexuality. Her attraction to promiscuity and a bohemian lifestyle was present in both lives.

Figure 4-18. "Seeing the teacher standing by the windows, I try to leave before he sees me." *[This old photo from the 1890s reminds me of the studio. It was taken of an art-printing studio that Vincent once used. Reprinted from Tralbaut (1959).]*

Figure 4-19. "Claudette gets ready for our modeling session." *[Reminds me of Claudette; from Manet's "La Femme," 1880. Reprinted from Meier-Graefe (1912).]*

stool. I try not to look at her nude body as I remove my robe, but from the corner of my eye, I can see her lovely figure. She is exquisitely proportioned. I tremble just a little.

"No, no!" the teacher shouts at me. "No undergarments." I am still wearing my shorts. Shyly, I remove them. This is the part that I have been dreading. I cover my privates discreetly with both hands. I am self-conscious that ... well, that ... hmmmm ... that my "manhood" is still in its childhood, if you understand what I mean. I look furtively around to see if anyone is laughing, but no one is paying any attention to my inadequacies, real or imagined.

The teacher walks over briskly. He grabs both of my hands, jerks me over towards Claudette, places one of my hands on my own hip, and arranges the other one loosely around Claudette's neck and shoulder. He steps back for a moment to view the pose, and now he steps in to move one of her arms around my waist.

Being this close to the nude and beautiful Claudette causes me to tremble even more. "Oh, my God!" I moan inwardly. I have never seen a woman nude before – not even Ma-Maa – God knows, especially not even Ma-Maa. I mean, I have seen statutes and paintings and girls at the dancehalls, from a distance, but that is not the same. Shifting just my eyes, I glance down at her perfectly rounded breasts, gently moving up and down as she breathes. I moan softly again. "Oh, my God, she is beautiful!" I thought I knew something about women, but this is not the same.

Sweat breaks out on my forehead. "God help me!" I fear that I am starting to blush. My gaze drifts along the graceful curve of her arm; I can see the tiny golden hairs standing up. Now my gaze moves down past her rose-colored nipples to the lovely curve of her belly, and now on to the dark-blond triangle of hair around her womanhood.

"Oh, God. My God. DEAR GOD!" I whisper aloud in agony, over the noise of my pounding heart. Hearing me, Claudette turns her eyes up to meet mine. She smiles sweetly, and now glances down at my groin, lingering for a moment. Her gaze is like a jolt of electricity! She moves again to meet my eyes, purses her lips a little in a faint kiss, and now, still smiling, looks away.

I panic. That familiar tingle in my groin begins to grow, and I panic even more.

"Mother of Moses!" I swear to myself. "I cannot let this happen in front of Claudette and the entire class."

Quickly, I take several rapid, shallow breaths, and now I gaze slightly above Claudette's head and stare intently at the wall, summoning all my youthful concentration. I visualize Papa with his distended neck veins. That helps. Trying to escape notice, I slowly move my hand from my hip to hide my privates again.

"Stop moving! Be still!" the teacher shouts. That helps even more. I count the bricks in the wall, hoping to calm down. "One brick – two large bricks – three large red bricks – four large hard red bricks. Saints of Heaven! What have I gotten into?" I moan again silently, struggling to concentrate.

Gradually, breath by breath, wrestling with my imagination, I begin to get my powerful feelings under control. I take a deep breath and let out a very quiet sigh. At last, I am regaining composure. The feelings are subsiding, and it is not a moment too soon.

"Thank you! Thank you!" With a sense of relief washing over me, I send some charitable thoughts heavenward. Relaxing more, I shift my right leg forward a little.

"Be still! Please, be still," the teacher shouts again, sounding distinctly annoyed.

I am okay for about five minutes. Involuntarily, I jerk my left foot sideways – something is tickling my instep. First, I glance at the teacher, whose back is turned, bending over to help a student. Now, looking down quickly, I kick the bug away. Hearing me, the teacher turns to glare but says nothing. He turns back again to his student.

I am okay for about three minutes, until my right foot begins to tingle. The teacher still has his back turned, so I wiggle my foot.

"Still, PLEASE!" he snaps, without turning around.

What is it with this man? I think. He has the ears of a guard dog.

I am okay for about one minute, until my nose begins to itch. I wiggle it a little – it does not help. I wiggle it a little more – no good. I wiggle it violently – still nothing. Finally, desperate, I move my hand up in slow motion to scratch my nose, and I get my hand about midway up.

He whirls around and shouts, "What are you *doing*? Be *still!* These poor students are trying to draw two people *at rest*. They are not drawing a *foot race*. If you keep this up, they will create nice drawings of a nude woman and a *blur*, which will be *you!*"

I cannot see him well, but his veins must be bulging by now, just as Papa's did. Summoning all the concentration I can muster, I manage to remain unmoving, at least acceptably so, until lunch break. I am careful not to look directly at Claudette again.

"Time for lunch. Back in thirty minutes. On time, please." Welcome words from the teacher.

Putting on my clothes, I slip silently out the door, following some of the students to lunch. As I move back up the street, out in the Paris sunlight, I take several long deep breaths of freedom.

"That is the end of my modeling career," I decide, relieved at last. "This is one 'blur' that is out of the picture – forever." I hurry faster up the street, feeling happy to retreat from my defeat. I do not look back.

About One Week Later

Entering my favorite café a few days after my birthday, I look around for my usual group of artist-friends. Vincent, Henri and a few others I know sit at a side table, so I join them.

Henri sees me coming and greets me with a wide smile; "So, here is that budding artist's model." The others smile and laugh.

Oh, no! I think. They know! I had hoped to leave my modeling adventure quietly behind me. I just smile in return, and add emphatically, "Ex-model!"

"Ah, such a short career," says Vincent with a mischievous smile. "And you held such promise. It is a pity that you retired at such a young age."

I keep quiet, knowing that if I comment, it will only make the conversation more embarrassing. I shoot my hand into the air to order a glass of absinthe.

Not ready to let me off so easily, Henri continues, "Well, obviously modeling is not for you, and perhaps I gave you wrong advice, my young friend. You clearly told me that you wished to be a painter, rather than a model. To correct my mistake, we have all pooled our meager funds to buy you a painting lesson. Are you interested?"

Surprised and excited by this new revelation, I respond eagerly, "Yes. Why, yes, of course!"

Just now, my glass of absinthe arrives. I take several long swallows, and within a few moments, I feel the familiar warm glow fill my body and mind.

"Good," Henri continues. "We have arranged for a lesson with a 'master.' If you want to paint, you must know your subject matter intimately – you know, with your eyes, hands, and all the senses. When an artist paints a rose, for instance, he should touch it gently, savor its aroma, and feel its sharp thorns, letting them draw blood, if necessary, so that he may know the full essence of that rose before he paints. With that in mind, Vincent and I have arranged a lesson for you, my young painter-to-be, to explore the nature of such a 'rose.'"

Figure 4-20. "It is good to join my friends again!" *[Reminds me of the café life. Detail of Renoir's "Boating Party," 1881. Reprinted from Jewell (1944).]*

Without hesitating, he turns to the back of the café and signals with his upraised hand. Much to my surprise and dismay, Claudette walks over, smiling and waving to all of us.

"We have bought you a lesson with Claudette," Vincent announces.

Now I am truly stunned. "But ... but ..." I stammer. "I do not understand. I really know nothing about even the simplest techniques of painting. What use do I have for a model when I cannot paint?"

With the air of conspirators, Vincent and Henri exchange amused looks. I sense that there is more to this than there appears, but I am still puzzled.

Henri looks at me with a sweet, impish smile, "She will be your canvas, my boy, for your first 'masterpiece.' Your 'brush' contains 'paint' if you catch my meaning," he says with a wink, "although you may run out of 'paint' before Claudette is through with you." They laugh uproariously as my face turns bright red.

Oh, my God! I think to myself, too stunned to speak. *They have hired a prostitute for me!*

Vincent, ignoring my discomfort, says, "She is a very skilled 'artist' in her own right, one of the best. We understand that you are not experienced in such matters of the heart and body, so you will learn much from her. This is our gift to you, for a boy to become a man. Enjoy!" They raise a toast to me. Feeling a rising panic, I forget to toast them back, downing the last of my absinthe in one gulp and calling out nervously for more.

Ignoring my unease, Claudette takes my hand, asking demurely, "Are you ready for your 'art' lesson?" As my head races with a thousand excuses, none of them believable, she takes my hand and pulls me gently out of my chair, leading me to the stairs at the back of the café. Feeling stunned, intrigued, fearful, and excited, all of them at the same time, I am too confused to resist, so I follow along after her up the stairs to the temporary room that she uses when she is working.

Inside the room, I stand in the middle of the floor, not knowing whether to sit, stand, or run. Still holding my hand, she asks sweetly, "Have you ever undressed a woman?"

Terror races through my brain, and without answering, I blurt out, "Can I have a drink?" My voice is too high-pitched, like a young choirboy, so I deliberately lower it to a masculine pitch, saying brusquely, "I want a drink – more absinthe – now!" Cursing under my breath for acting like a caveman, I quickly add, "Please." Smiling, she pours me a glass, and I down it in one gulp.

"Here, this will make it easier," she says, offering me an opium pipe. She lights it for me, and I take several deep inhales. Within seconds, I feel the drug begin to take effect, enhancing the sensuality of the moment, making every one of my feelings more intense, though that seems scarcely possible. I pass the pipe to her, and she draws deeply before putting it down on the old battered chest-of-drawers.

After I finish, she moves closer and places my hand on the top button of her blouse. My fingers grasp it with the paralysis of rigor mortis until, smiling, she asks sweetly, "Have you forgotten how buttons work?"

I shake my head weakly and unfasten the first button and the next. With the last one, she slips gracefully out of her blouse. She wears no undergarment, so I stare at those incredibly lovely breasts once again. They mesmerize me completely.

She is breathing a little faster now, feeling the excitement of the moment, and I begin to get aroused as well, finally overcoming my fear. Her dark eyes sparkle in the dim light, and I sense that she likes me, that this is not just a job. I like her, too. A lot.

Standing on her toes, she leans forward, kisses me lightly on the neck, and leans back again. Taking my right hand, she cups it gently under her left breast. The touch of her bare skin is like an electric shock but at the same time like stroking velvet. My hand trembles as beads of perspiration form on my forehead.

Figure 4-21. "So, Louis, have you ever undressed a woman?" *[Reminds me of this event; detail from Manet's "Nana," 1877. Reprinted from Meier-Graefe (1912).]*

I begin to feel dizzy, almost drunk, though I know that this feeling is not from the absinthe or the opium. It comes from touching this woman.

She reaches out, unbuttons my shirt, and deftly slips it off. Next, she reaches down to unbutton my trousers. I tense a little with apprehension, but she does not appear to notice, and for me, there is no resisting or refusing her now. She has hypnotized me with her sensuality. Her soft, flowing hair brushes my thighs and loins as she slips my trousers and undergarments down to my ankles. Eagerly, I step out of them.

With motions like a graceful ballerina, gently turning and swaying, she removes her skirt, standing there in front of me now with both of us completely nude. She steps slowly forward and touches her lips to mine in a light, gentle kiss, and now she embraces me.

As I feel her soft breasts press against my chest, she whispers in my ear, "Relax, my dear Louis. I will be gentle and show you how to find pleasure with a woman."

I nod weakly, as she moves her lips down to kiss my neck, while at the same time slipping her hand down to lightly caress my stomach. My muscles tremble involuntarily, but she does not stay there for long, moving down instead to stroke my loins lightly. As she touches me down there for the first time, the first woman ever to do so since my childhood, I am afraid that I will pass out!

"Oh, God," I moan under my breath.

As her nimble fingers gently explore my manhood, looking me directly in the eyes, she says approvingly, "Ooh! Very nice!" Continuing, she smiles seductively, "When we modeled together, I thought you would 'fill out' nicely."

I can no longer control my tongue to speak, so I just stand mute, overwhelmed by her knowing touch and by powerful sensual feelings for this woman.

Leaning away from me, she looks up with a compelling smile, and now, without breaking our gaze and while still holding my hand, she backs over towards the bed. Gracefully, first sitting and now reclining sinuously across the bed, she pulls me down gently on top of her. Our lips join passionately as I revel in the incredible feeling her warm silky body touching mine. Words are no longer necessary, or indeed possible for me, as her experienced hands take control of my body, teaching me all that is necessary. Submitting myself to her, we join our heated bodies with indescribable feelings and in incredible ways that I would never have thought possible. Time and space vanish; Claudette is my universe now.

I awaken, staring up at the dim ceiling. As I roll my head to the right on my pillow, I see Claudette curled up sleeping peacefully next to me. She has turned her head to the wall, and her long hair cascades all around her face, hiding it from me. She breathes rhythmically and evenly. A few long stray hairs drift around lightly, moving back and forth with her shallow breathing.

Sliding back the sheets and quietly swinging my feet out of bed, I rest them on the worn wood-plank floor, making certain to move slowly so as not to awaken her. As I sit upright, my head explodes with dizziness, like a rough hangover, and my loins ache as well. The air is cool, and I shiver a little. I rest my head in my hands to ease the dizziness and stop the pounding, but it does not help. Maybe it was the absinthe or the opium, but I feel tired and drained, and I groan silently.

As I think back over the intimate moments of the past few hours, all I can recall is the pleasant blur of flesh. Our time together was both more and less than I expected, and it was confusing, to say the least. While it was enjoyable, it was disappointing as well. I like Claudette, but my heart was not truly involved, just my loins. I know she likes me, but I know her heart was not fully in it either. In spite of her profession, she has a steady boyfriend, so in the end, it was just a work assignment, compliments of Vincent and Henri.

I try to stand, but a wave of nausea sweeps over me. I need a drink to settle my head. Wobbling over to the chest-of-drawers, I pour another glass of absinthe, gulp it down, and pour another, trying to be quiet so as not to disturb her. Feeling confused, I would rather not talk to her anyway.

The nausea begins to subside. More and more, I feel the need for alcohol to make my day right. I just feel too bad, too depressed, without it. For good measure, I light the opium pipe and take a few long puffs. That helps even more. It just makes it easier to face myself. I cannot say that my life is a happy one, but a least absinthe and opium make it bearable.

Searching for my scattered clothing, I struggle to get dressed in the dim light. With mixed feelings, I take one last look at Claudette. As if dreaming, she moves fitfully and murmurs something in her sleep. She is no longer the alluring goddess of the last few hours; now she is rather like a lost child, curled up in bed alone. Sadly, I turn and leave the room, alone as well, staggering a little as the alcohol and opium take greater effect.

Sliding into Addiction

This incident was a major turning point in Louis' life as he began the downward slide into addiction to drugs, sex, and alcohol. Drugs were legal and readily available throughout Paris at that time, and his mentors, Vincent, Paul, and Henri, used drugs freely and frequently. Furthermore, as Vincent became increasingly unhappy with city life and his failure to find success as an artist, he hid his frustration by using ever more drugs and alcohol.

Since arriving in Paris in March of 1886, Vincent had been living with his brother, Theo, where Louis visited him as often as he could. Vincent had become one of the pivotal mentors in his life; Vincent was much more important to him than even his own father was. Idolizing Vincent, Louis developed the same addictions. Unhappy with his own life, like Vincent, he sought escape in the company of his artist-friends and in the drug-induced visions of the inner worlds of his mind.

One Year Later (Winter 1887)

It is early evening when Vincent and I begin walking from the apartment he shares with Theo on Rue Lepic. We are heading to Emile's house for the evening.

Vincent needs to get out of the house. Even though he genuinely likes people, that trait is not always apparent. Because of his volatile and opinionated nature, Vincent often offends those around him, including his very tolerant brother. He has been arguing with Theo all afternoon and has decided to get away before he says something he will deeply regret.

The whole day has been cold, overcast, and dreary, in other words, a typical winter day in Paris. However, the night sky is now somewhat clearer, though much colder, with the stars shining through here and there among the fast-moving clouds. We wear heavy coats, scarves, and hats to shield us from the cold.

Vincent is usually depressed and miserable during the cloudy winter days and nights, and tonight is no exception. Turning to me as we walk, he says, "I long for sunnier days and am ready to move to the South, Louis. Without sun, I am like the flowers of the field; I fold up into myself and become dormant. I have to get away from this gray, lifeless city. It is slowly strangling the life out of me. Both my inspiration and my pallet have turned gray to match these God-forsaken skies." He pulls out a flask, and we share a drink as we walk.

"I know. I have noticed it in your paintings," I respond. Having known him for nearly two years, I am on easy terms with him now, less in awe of him. I treat him more as a beloved older brother with whom I am free to speak my opinions. We may not agree, but we are free to tell each other so.

He continues, "It has been months now, and I have finished only nine or ten dreary, uninspired paintings for Theo. Is it any wonder no one will buy them? They are as devoid of life as a gravestone. Who would want them?"

Figure 4-22. "Gradually, the absinthe and opium are taking control." *[Manet's "Absinthe Drinker," 1859. Reprinted from Meier-Graefe (1912).]*

Figure 4-23. Photo of the apartment building where the van Goghs lived. In the 1880s, Vincent and Louis would have walked out this door onto Rue Lepic on their way to the cafes and restaurants of Montmartre.

Figure 4-24. Vincent's painting, completed in 1887, showing his view of Paris from the apartment window. A version of this painting sold for more than $20 million in Nov. 2000. *[Both figures reprinted from Tralbaut (1959).]*

I nod as we continue walking, "You do need a rest from the city, my friend, though I would hate to see you go. Perhaps it would be only for a short while." I am silent for a few paces, choosing my next words carefully. "In any event, I agree that you must do something to reinvigorate your work, because to be honest, your recent choice of subjects has been dreadful. Of the ten you mention, only one is full of color and liveliness, the one with the Italian woman.

"The others, dear friend, leave much to be desired. You have done two paintings of the statue of a headless Venus. In addition, you have done four self-portraits of yourself looking just as energetic as a headless statue."

He does not appear to be getting defensive, so I continue, "But the worst, my friend, and only a true friend would tell you this, are the two paintings of the skulls. Skulls, Vincent? Can you truly expect Theo to sell those to a collector? My friend you *must* leave the city, if only for a while, in order to save your sanity and your art."

Vincent stares ahead and now answers despondently, "Louis, I am painfully aware of what you say; my inspiration is at a low point. Of all that I am or have attempted to be, I do painting the best. All the other things – human relationships, a pleasing appearance, or an attractive personality – I have no talent for any of them. Even when I am painting well, I am not fully satisfied that my work is good enough; but when I am painting poorly, I am *truly* lost!"

I try to cheer him up by saying, "You are being too hard on yourself. When I think of your summer paintings, Vincent, such as the garden scene and the field with the lark, well then, only fools would fail to find the inspiration and life in them, Vincent. They are wonderful!"

Figure 4-25. Vincent's "Plaster Statuette of a Female Torso," Winter 1887. *[Reprinted from Faille (1939).]*

He responds, "You have given the answer yourself, Louis: summer paintings. My winter paintings have been killed by the frost," he answers ruefully.

As we continue to walk, he puffs on his pipe. After a few moments, he says, "Lately, I have been thinking a lot about Arles and the lifestyle in the South of France. As you know, I have come to love the art of Japan, and I feel that Arles may very well be as close as I can come to that country in my lifetime."

I add, "During springtime in Arles, I hear that the trees in full blossom may remind one of Japan. You know, cherry blossoms and all that. Very lovely!"

He nods without comment about that, but continues on, "In addition, I have been envisioning something excitingly different, Louis; something more Japanese than Western; something that I cannot do here in a city full of distractions." He is silent for about five paces.

"Which is?" I finally ask, impatient with his long silence.

"An artists' colony," he responds, "one in which artists may live and work surrounded by others of like mind and temperament." He puffs a few more times before adding, "A community in which we might pool our resources to find a better standard of living. One in which we would no longer be slaves to the art dealers and could negotiate better prices and arrange our own shows."

Surprised by this wonderful new idea, my mind is spinning with the possibilities, so I am unable to say anything right away.

He continues, "It is just an idea, and I do not have a full vision of it yet. What do you think?"

Overcome with excitement, I finally recover my voice, "That is wonderful, Vincent. Revolutionary! I have never heard of such a thing, but it makes so much sense. I would love to be a part of such a community – to be around creative people all the time. Why, the possibility makes me giddy! What an incredible idea. Simply brilliant!"

Vincent looks over at me in surprise, "Louis, I am afraid you misunderstand me. I did not ... I ... Louis, you are not an artist, as you have said so yourself. The colony would be only for artists."

Figure 4-26 (above). Vincent's "Gardens of Montmartre," Summer 1887. *[Reprinted from Faille (1939).]* **Figure 4-27 (below).** Vincent's "Wheatfield with a Lark," Summer 1887. *[Reprinted from Faille (1939).]*

Figure 4-28. Vincent's "Japonaiserie: Flowering Plum Tree," Sep-Oct 1887. *[Reprinted from Jewell (1946).]*

Stopping under one of the gas streetlights, I protest, "But surely, there is something I could do. I would reconsider being a model – or maybe I could clean brushes – or make canvasses. Surely, there is *something* I could do!"

He puffs a few times on his pipe, considering this, while I wait with growing eagerness. His face, bathed in the glow of the gaslight, seems softer than it does in the daylight. "We shall see," he says finally. "It is a new idea, and I have not worked it out fully yet. There is a possibility."

Reluctantly satisfied, I continue in silence for a while, until he mumbles, "I know, I know. I must go to Arles."

I quickly glance over at him. Vincent has been talking to himself more lately, responding to unheard comments, and sometimes arguing forcefully with some inner voice. I do not say anything, though I am worried for his health.

He walks along silently for a while, looking now and again at the occasional stars that appear above us. He passes me the flask again, and I take a full swallow and hand it back. He empties the flask and slips it back into the side pocket of his wool coat. After tapping his pipe on a wrought-iron fence post to empty the ashes, he refills it with his favorite "creativity" mix and lights it. With every few steps that we walk, he puffs on the pipe, and the tobacco flares slightly, bathing his face in a faint glow.

Walking west, we have come to the intersection of the Boulevard de Clichy and Avenue Rachel. Off to our right, down the avenue, is the Montmartre Cemetery. The darkened graveyard makes me feel colder, so I motion silently to Vincent, and we cross to the other side of the street.

Vincent speaks again, quietly and gently, "As for the skull paintings, I have been thinking more about death these days, Louis. Along the lines that – and mind you, I am only speculating – along the lines that life is only one side of a coin, one side of an equation, with death the line that separates them. We are on one side, but what lies on the other side? That is the true question, the real mystery for us to solve."

I do not respond, but he knows that I am listening, so he continues, pointing to the sky with a bony finger, "You and I look up at those stars as mere pinpoints of light, but what if each star was a complete group of worlds just like our own solar system?" Vincent stops to face me on the sidewalk, puts his hand on my sleeve, and asks, "We cannot go there now, but what if at death, Louis, we could travel to one of those distant stars to begin a new life?" I remain silent, listening intently.

After studying the sky again for a moment, he continues, "If that were so, then I would select one." He extends his arm again, picks the brightest star, and points a finger at it. "'There,' I would say, 'there it is! That is the one. I am going there.' And then, Louis, as this current lump of flesh begins to turn to dust, I would set out to begin a new life, hoping for it to be substantially better than my old one."

Vincent puts an arm around my shoulder, and we start walking again slowly down the street. "What do you think of that crazy idea, my friend?" he asks with an inquiring look.

I think for a minute, gazing up at the stars as we walk, our shoes clicking softly on the sidewalk. "Well," I answer, "that looks like a good enough star for me. I'll try it if you do."

Figure 4-29. Photo of Boulevard de Clichy, a few blocks from Vincent's apartment. The famous Moulin Rouge is at the right in this photo, but it was not built until 1889, a few years after this night in 1887.

Figure 4-30. Vincent's painting, completed in 1887, is an earlier view of the same boulevard shown in Figure 4-29. *[This figure and the one above are both reprinted from Tralbaut (1959).]*

He chuckles aloud, "Well, you know, if death is the way to get there, then there are several ways to do it. Let us suppose that living in a body is a little like renting a place, such as Theo's apartment. Well then getting old and dying is somewhat like being evicted from the apartment. The landlord comes along and just throws you out, like it or not. On the other hand, leaving sooner is more like saying 'I am not paying the rent anymore; I am leaving.' Then, it is off to a new place – or a new star, as the case may be."

As what he is suggesting dawns on me, I get a little worried. I know he has been deeply depressed lately. Holding my voice very even, I ask him, "Are you thinking of 'leaving' early, my friend?"

He responds somewhat evasively, "Oh, I think about lots of things, Louis."

"Vincent, that is not an answer." I chide him a little.

He is silent for about five paces. When I glance at him again, expecting an answer, he puffs on his pipe once and says reluctantly, "No, I am not really planning to leave, Louis. However, I am certain that I will not die of old age. I do not have any details or plans, really – this is just a sense that I have."

I counter with, "Please do a favor to all your friends who love you, dear Vincent. Do not 'leave' soon. Please promise me that."

With a quiet voice, he answers, "Do not worry." That is all he will say, though it is not exactly a comforting answer.

Soon we arrive and knock on Emile's door. He is having a get-together with a few friends who are artists, writers, and poets, and he welcomes us loudly and heartily. I know some of the people, but Vincent knows the rest and introduces me. Thick smoke from tobacco, opium, and hashish wafts through the air. The party has been going for a while, and now, a few people are already lounging around on pillows and couches with eyes closed, content with their journey to the dream worlds. A few couples are kissing and embracing languidly in the dark corners of the room.

Emile's girlfriend hands me a large glass of wine and offers me a silver platter with various "appetizers." I recognize the irregular brown lumps of hashish and the opium pipes, but there is something new on the plate.

"What is that?" I ask, pointing to a large chocolate-colored ball on the plate.

"I call it a Dreamball," she answers. "It is something new, and I ...." After waiting expectantly for her to continue, now I realize that her mind has wandered off. She stares at me with a vacant smile. She has already been using the opium pipe, apparently, and she has totally forgotten my question. Gently, I touch her arm to call her mind back for a moment.

"And?" I ask, pointing again to the ball.

"Oh, that is a Dreamball," she answers with a cheerful smile, "with hashish, opium, and foxglove *[this natural herb contains digitalis, a powerful heart rhythm regulator]*. You will like it. It is the newest rage. Energizes your heart and fills you with a delightful energy. Adds to the euphoria of the other stuff. It is marvelous. Try one."

I pick up one and look at it closely. It looks just like some kind of chocolate candy.

"Just swallow it," she says lightly. "It tastes too bad to chew." At this, she puckers her face and shivers a little.

We both laugh as I swallow it down in one big gulp, followed by a half a glass of wine. As she puts down the tray and moves off to join Emile, I reach down to pick up another Dreamball. Popping it into my mouth, I swallow it. If one is good, then two should be even better. I down the rest of the wine and now pick up another full glass of absinthe.

After a few minutes, the accustomed euphoria starts to build, and I look for a comfortable spot to sit. A powerful urge to close my eyes sweeps over me, all the better to easily slip into the dream worlds. As I search for an out-of-the-way place, I begin to feel very dizzy. The room rocks and sways, and the walls appear to get shorter, now longer, shimmering like a mirage. Maybe two Dreamballs are not so good after all.

Vincent is nearby, and seeing the odd look on my face, he rushes over, grabbing my shoulder to steady me. "Louis, are you all right?" he asks with a worried look.

First, I nod my head up and down, but now, thinking better of it, I feebly shake my head back and forth.

With panic flooding in my brain, I struggle to remain standing. The room spins out of control, and I crash forward, tearing away from Vincent's grasp and collapsing headfirst onto the floor. That is the last thing I remember clearly.

The Hangover
Many hours later, Louis regained consciousness, managing to stagger home before dawn, drunk with wine and still hallucinating from the Dreamballs. When he tried to open his front door, it was locked, and he collapsed on the front steps. The butler found him there at first light, unconscious.

After his drunken episode, Louis' movements were severely restricted, so he was not able to see Vincent again for the next few months. On February 20, 1888, before Louis was free to move around again, Vincent finally left Paris and moved to Arles in the South.

After his move, Vincent continued to plan for his artists' colony, where people of like mind could live and work together, collaborating to produce more inspired works of art than they could produce on their own. Both Theo and Paul showed mild interest, until at Vincent's insistence, Theo arranged for Paul to join Vincent in Arles on October 23, 1888. Excited by his new community and freed from the demands and temptations of city life, Vincent created some of his most beloved paintings while in Arles.

Near Arles, North of Marseilles (Dec. 1888)

Are we not there yet? So impatient I can no longer stand it, I slightly lift the corner of the leather window cover of the coach to look out. *Damn!* Still nothing but farms – not a town in sight.

The road has gotten rougher, and suddenly, the coach lurches violently. One of the two women lets out a muffled chirp, and instinctively, everyone grabs a coach strap for support. Quickly, I glance around at the women and the man in the opposite seat. I look away just as swiftly. The man is staring intently at me again. Wearing a black coat and black hat, the man has a thick, drooping black mustache that gives him an ominous look. With rising panic, I fear that Papa has sent an agent to trail me. I grip the strap tighter and slouch down in the coach seat.

Anger and indignation rise in me. The worst thing that could happen is for them to take me back. I could not stand that again – having to live in Papa's house pretending to be something that I am not. I would rather be dead!

In one sense, running away from home was not easy because the future is much more uncertain. On the other hand, I had no choice. I had to do it. Living a lie was slowly draining the life from me. I felt like a prisoner in a castle among strangers who claimed to be my family.

Figure 4-31. Vincent's "Farmhouse in Provence," Aug. 1888. *[Reprinted from Faille (1939).]*

The last straw was when I heard that Paul was moving to Arles to join Vincent in his artists' community. I was so excited that I could not sleep for a few nights. To be a part of that community became my sole goal in life. It was then that I made the decision.

Carefully, I laid out the details of my escape. I have been cautious to hide my plans, so that they will not know where I am. Perhaps, in a few months, they will stop looking for me and leave me alone. In any event, Papa will disown me for this, so it will be finished between us no matter what.

I glance again at the man in the black hat. To my relief, he is no longer looking at me. Anxious to reach Arles, I unfasten and raise the leather flap that covers the coach window. My heart jumps as I see cottages along the coach road and buildings in the distance. We must be near!

"Close the flap, you imbecile!" the man shouts at me, as dust rolls in through the window to swirl inside the coach. The woman nearest to me coughs modestly and covers her mouth and nose with a handkerchief.

"Pardon," I offer to them contritely. "I did not realize about the dust." The man, looking very irritated, brushes dust off his coat and removes his hat to do the same.

Figure 4-32. Vincent's "Harvest at La Crau" near Arles, Aug. 1888. *[Reprinted from Jewell (1944).]*

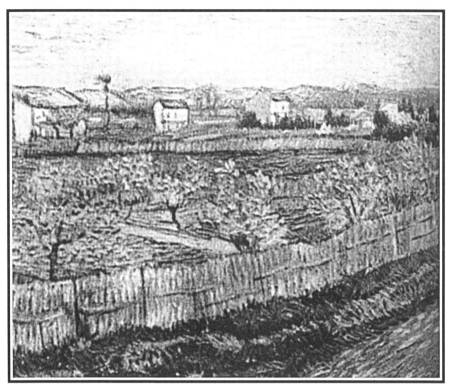

Figure 4-33. Vincent's "Le Crau with Peach Trees in Blossom," painted near Arles in August of 1888. *[Reprinted from Faille (1939).]*

The coach gives one more powerful lurch and suddenly moves along smoother than before. Judging by the clopping of the horses' hooves, we have moved from the dirt country road onto the cobbled streets of the city. At last, we must be entering Arles.

I lean forward anxiously in my seat. Overcome with enthusiasm, I reach for the leather curtain again before catching myself. With my hand paused midway to the window, I glance over at the man, who is glaring at me sternly. Without a word, I withdraw my hand sheepishly.

Suddenly, the driver calls out, "Whoa! Whoa!" and the stage begins to slow down. When it stops, he hops down, opens the coach door, and says, "Arles Station. Twenty-minute rest stop. For those going on to Marseilles, please be on board promptly."

Darting out the door before the ladies can get off, I grab my canvas valise from the rack on the rear of the stage and hurry into the station house. Inside, I approach the white-haired, wrinkle-faced old man at the ticket counter, who is slowly scribbling on a yellowed sheet of ledger paper. In his faded dark blue

Figure 4-34. Vincent's "The Tarascon Stage," Oct. 1888. *[Reprinted from Faille (1939).]*

uniform with a flat-topped hat, he looks as if he has been sitting in the same spot for the last twenty years.

Excitedly, I say, "I am looking for Vincent van Gogh."

Without looking up, he shakes his head and responds in a slightly raspy voice, "Never heard of him."

"But he lives here!" I protest.

Without moving his head, he looks over his wire frame glasses at me and says, "So do I. Never heard of him."

Confused, I stammer, "He ... uh ... Vincent came ... he ...."

Finally looking up, he says, "Vincent van Gogh, huh. Cannot be French. Not with a name like that. Sure you got the right country, boy? Sounds Dutch to me. Maybe you should try one of those countries up in Scandinavia. It's north. That way," he offers helpfully, poking his thumb north back up the stage road. Only a slight twinkle in his eye shows that he enjoys teasing a city boy. He looks back down and continues writing.

Finally, I recover my composure and insist, "He *is* here. I know it! Red-haired fellow. About this tall." I hold my hand up about four inches over my head. "Moved here in February. A painter from Paris."

Suddenly, he looks up with a slight frown, "Ah, the mad painter! Why didn't you say so?" With a thick bony finger, he points south up main street into town, "Look for the 'Yellow House.' Can't miss it, sonny. It's the ugliest one around. He painted it that way, you know." He looks at me over his glasses again, saying, "He should give up on house painting, if you ask me. Stick to the artworks. Though I don't like them much either." With that, he gives me instructions to Vincent's House, as if it were the only yellow one in town – and from his comments, it might be.

Excited to see Vincent again, I rush off down the street, swinging my heavy bag by my side. Before long, out of breath, I am standing in front of the Yellow House, which is *very* yellow indeed.

It will be so good to see him again – and Paul. They probably will be surprised, but then ... well, they will just have to get used to me. I am here to stay!

Figure 4-35. Vincent's "Yellow House" in Arles, Sep. 1888. *[Reprinted from Tralbaut (1959).]*

Taking a deep breath, ready for the unknown, I reach out to knock on the door. Before I can, I hear loud shouting from inside. First, I hear Vincent's voice and now Paul's. They are having an intense argument.

Through the door, I hear Vincent yell, "You are an *ingrate*, taking advantage of my brother and taking his money. You do not think like an artist. You still think like the *stockbroker* you used to be – with only an interest in taking money!"

Paul shouts back, though his voice is not as loud and is more controlled, "Excuse me! *You* are the expert in taking your brother's money. You have done so all your life!"

Ignoring this remark, Vincent responds with an even louder voice, "No, not like a stockbroker. Like a prostitute! Flashing your beguiling smile, while scheming to 'perform' for your 'clients' at an ever higher fee! You, sir, are not an artist. You are a *whore!*" Vincent almost spits out the last word.

Paul becomes quieter now, but his words take on an ominous tone, "At least I make *some* money from my work, unlike you, Vincent. No one wants your wild-looking paintings. You complain only because you are jealous of my meager success. I can no longer tolerate your ravings, Vincent; it is time to for me to do something about them."

Clearly stung by Paul's words, Vincent, without responding, jerks open the front door to leave. I wish I were not standing there, but I am.

Vincent, his face red with anger, stares at me in surprise. "What are you doing here, Louis?" he asks me with a harsh edge to his voice.

"I … uh," I stammer, "I have come to join your artists' colony." At the end, I try to smile.

He answers sharply and sadly, "There is not one, Louis, as you can hear. Go home." With that, he walks past me abruptly.

I call out after him hopefully, "Then, I am here to help you form one, Vincent. I am here to stay."

Still angry, he whirls around to face me. Softening a little, he says, "Louis, how can you be a part of an artists' colony? In the first place, there is no colony. It has failed. In the second place, you are not an artist." He stares intently at me for a moment and continues, trying to reason with me, "What skills do you have, Louis? How would you make a living? Where would you live? You cannot stay here."

Stumped, I say, "Well ... I ... uh ...."

Before I can clear my head, Vincent says in a more friendly tone, "Louis, walk down to the Hotel Carrel. It is just down the street. Stay there tonight. In the morning, I will meet you at the hotel restaurant for breakfast. We can talk when things are calmer, and then you can return home." Without waiting for a response, he turns and hurries off – probably to the brothel – especially after arguing with Paul.

Softly but firmly, I say to him and to the world at large, "I am here to stay."

Vincent's Studio (December 23, 1888)

Vincent's Health Dooms the Colony
Vincent's increasing health problems doomed the collaboration with Paul. Vincent began to become delirious. In addition, he continued to abuse alcohol and drugs, which caused him to have frequent hallucinations. All of these things began seriously to affect his physical and mental stability.

Figure 4-36. Vincent's "Interior of the Restaurant Carrel in Arles," Aug. 1888. *[Reprinted from Faille (1939).]*

> **Frequent Arguments**
> Vincent and Paul began to argue more frequently about everything from art theory to food choices. About a week after Louis arrived, the arguments became violent. Later, Paul wrote that while in the Night Café on December 14, Vincent threw a glass of absinthe at him, narrowly missing his head. Vincent apologized the next morning, but the damage was done. Paul announced that he planned to return to Paris. Over the next two weeks, Vincent's behavior became more erratic, as he obsessed about the failure of his community, his abandonment by Paul, and his personal artistic failures.
>
> Many have wondered: *what actually was wrong with Vincent?* Reflection (2003) indicated that by today's medical standards, Vincent would be diagnosed as suffering from manic depression. Reflection stated that his illness was not truly mental, as is commonly supposed. Instead, Vincent suffered from a severe chemical imbalance in his body that was the root cause of the disease. Furthermore, the imbalance led him to abuse tobacco, caffeine, alcohol, and drugs, all of which further aggravated the problem.

For the last hour, I have been fantasizing constantly about a tall glass of cool absinthe. I am tired of sitting. Fidgeting around, I slide my hand slowly and quietly into my pocket to glance at my watch.

Figure 4-37. At the café shown here, Vincent hurled a glass of absinthe at Paul. Referring to this painting, Vincent wrote, "I have tried to suggest that the Night Café is a place where you can be ruined, go mad, and commit crimes." *[Vincent's "Night Café" in Arles, Sep. 1888. Reprinted from Elgar (1958).]*

"Will you sit still?" Vincent says firmly, studying me from behind his easel. He is painting my portrait – against my better judgment, I might add. He is on a tight budget, so he can ill afford to hire models. To help him out, I have agreed to pose for him, albeit reluctantly, considering my last such experience.

"I am *very* thirsty," I protest.

Exasperated, he stands up to glare at me and, without a word, storms off towards his bedroom. Surprised at his sudden reaction, I think, *What is his problem? All I want is a drink!* I lean forward to look through the doorway, but I cannot see anything. He makes loud noises as he digs around in his closet, sending boxes skidding roughly across the floor.

When he returns, I pretend that I was not paying attention. "Here," he says, handing me a half-empty bottle of wine, which I gladly take from him, mumbling my thanks.

He is still grumpy but seems to be returning to normal. "Paul says I should paint from memory. It will be easier, he says. In your case, which memory should I use? I have forty of them – each with you in a *different position!*" Turning around, he begins vigorously cleaning his brush. Muttering to himself, he says, "This is why I prefer landscapes. Trees and mountains do not run off to the café for a drink!"

Turning around to face me again, he announces firmly, "That is it, Louis. I am finished. There were a few minor touches that I wanted to add, but for the sake of your peace-of-mind and mine, I have cancelled them. The painting is done. Come take a look."

I am eager to see the portrait. Vincent has concealed the work-in-progress from me, thinking that I am too much of an art critic. This will be the first time I have seen it.

Walking briskly around the easel, I study it for a minute and pronounce, "Well, I very much like your choice of colors. The one you used for the background is exceptionally rich, though all of the colors are magnificent,

Figure 4-38. Vincent's painting of his bedroom in Arles, Sep. 1889. *[Reprinted from Meier-Graefe (1922).]*

Figure 4-39. Vincent's portrait of Louis, "Young Man with a Cap," Dec. 1888. *[Reprinted from Meier-Graefe (1922).]*

Vincent. So wonderfully like the natural colors here in the South." I pause, as a slight frown forms.

Vincent, studying my face, asks, "What?" He likes for people to comment on his paintings, and he listens carefully. He does not always agree with criticism, but when he does, he incorporates it in his work. He is not overly sensitive the way some other artists are.

Hesitantly, I say, "Well ... mmm .... I do not know ...."

Impatient, he demands, "Well, what is it, Louis?"

"The eyes," I say reluctantly. "The eyes are ... well ... tilted. See," I explain, holding my palm up to the head and moving it back and forth horizontally, "both eyes are not level."

With an innocent shrug, he says, "True. But then, I paint what I see. The fact of the matter is that *your* eyes are tilted. I just painted them as they are."

"They are not!" I respond defiantly, whirling to face him.

Art Mystery Revealed

Known as "*Jeune Homme a la Casquette* (Young Man in a Cap)," Vincent's painting of Louis was painted between December the 13th and the 23rd, 1888, according to art scholars. There is one puzzling feature about it though: while Vincent often wrote about his paintings in letters to Theo, he did not mention this one. There has been no clue as to the identity of the model – until now. When I asked Reflection (2003) the reason, they indicated that it was because Vincent did not intend to have Theo sell it. Since it was a gift to Louis, Vincent was silent about it.

Because of the events that were soon to unfold, Louis was not able to retain the painting, so it passed into the hands of others. Vincent's belief that eventually the painting would be valuable was true – it was sold at auction in New York in 1995 for more than $13,000,000. When Vincent died 105 years earlier, it was judged nearly worthless. Indeed, as Vincent thought would happen, a jaded world finally caught up to his work.

Seeing that I am so serious, he struggles to suppress a smile. Finally, when I realize that he is joking, he breaks into loud laughter, saying, "Louis, for a moment I thought you would be demanding a mirror to check the tilt of your eyes." He laughs heartily again, and I join in reluctantly.

Shrugging his shoulders, he continues, "Louis, I am an artist – not a photographer. I *interpret* what I see. If your eyes are not *actually* tilted, well then, I shall make the case that they *should* be. In my view, everything has a tilt or wobble to it, even if we cannot see it with our eyes. I merely tried to paint the tilt that is evident in your nature, dear Louis – a likeable tilt at that, I might add."

Relieved, I offer, "In that case, Vincent, I shall treasure your lopsided view of my tilted nature." We both chuckle again.

Vincent says, "Louis, I have a surprise for you." I look at him expectantly as he continues, "This picture is my gift to you. Though it has only sentimental value now, perhaps someday it will be worth something. Keep it until then, and you may sell if for a good price, if you wish, assuming the art tastes of this jaded world ever catch up to my work. Or just keep it, Louis, as a token of my friendship."

Overwhelmed, I can only murmur, "I will *never* sell it, Vincent!"

He holds me at arm's length and looks directly into my eyes. Continuing softly, he says, "Louis, it is time for you to go home. Take the painting with you after it dries. You came following a dream that was not meant to be. There will be no artists' colony. I fear that relations are permanently broken between Paul and me. The colony is dead."

I protest, "Vincent, you and I can do it. Do not give up!"

He shakes his head sadly, "No one will come, Louis. They are all like Paul – addicted to life in Paris. They do not like the country … and now after my arguments with Paul, they will all think I am just a madman. No one will come."

Tears come to my eyes. I cannot give up on my dream to live and work among creative, inspired people. I cannot admit defeat and return to Papa and to a life among the hollow-eyed walking dead in Paris.

Vincent says softly again, "Louis, you must go home. It is almost Christmas, a time to forgive and be thankful. Your family cares about you. It is over for you here, so go back. If you return home in time for the holidays, your homecoming will be your gift to your family. In spite of what you may think, they love your dearly."

Speechless with defiance, with eyes full of tears, shaking my head in denial, I turn and run out of Vincent's studio.

December 24, 1888, the Day before Christmas

The morning sun shines into my eyes through the brothel window, awakening me. Groggy and groaning with pain from a roaring hangover, I roll over in bed, pulling the pillow over my head. With great effort, I try to collect my thoughts. The last thing I remember was being drunk in bed with three "working girls." Here in a house such as this, you never lack company as long as you have money. However, I am not a fool. The "love and affection" of these girls is only as wide as my wallet, which is rapidly becoming thinner.

Figure 4-40. Vincent's "The Brothel," a legal house of prostitution in Arles, Oct. 1888. *[Reprinted from Faille (1939).]*

Unable to sleep any longer, I swing my stiff legs over the edge of the bed and lever myself slowly into a sitting position. After struggling to get up, I stumble over to the chest of drawers, steadying myself on the wall as I go. Staring vacantly into the mirror, I idly think that Vincent is right. My eyes are *definitely* tilted. And my ears – and my nose. *Everything* about me is tilted this morning. I splash some icy water from the washbowl onto my face and dry it with my rumpled shirttails.

Looking into the mirror again, I run my hands through my tousled hair. I do not like what I see. Staring back at me is "Louis, the Great King of Failures." Vincent does not want me – I am not an artist. Papa does not want me – I am not a businessman. No one wants me who matters. I am nothing, and there is nowhere to go. I moan aloud as despair floods through me.

Suddenly, I hear loud noises from the drawing room of the brothel. A few of the girls are shouting. Now, my room door slams open. It is Francoise, one of my "entertainers" from last night.

"Quick! It is the police!" she whispers loudly. "They are asking for you."

"Damn!" I mutter under my breath. "Papa has found me!" In a fit of panic, I try to slide open the window to escape, but it is jammed. As I tug on the window frantically, I hear a voice behind me.

"Trying to get some fresh air, monsieur?" It is the local gendarme. Turning around slowly, I offer the police sergeant a weak but charming smile. My mind races with alibis and stories. In my head, I practice saying evenly and nonchalantly, *Why, no, I am not Louis St. Jacques. Never heard of him.*

"We are looking for Monsieur Gauguin," the officer says, much to my relief. "Have you seen him?"

"He has not seen him," offers Francoise.

The policeman glares at her briefly in annoyance. Then, looking back at me, he says, "Well?"

Composing myself, since it appears he is not after me, I respond innocently, "Monsieur who? Never heard of him."

Sternly, the sergeant says, "Do not play dumb with me, monsieur. I have seen you with this Gauguin. He is the painter from Paris."

Sheepishly, I say, "Oh, *that* Gauguin. Well, let me think. Hmm ... I have not seen him since two days ago."

"See. He has not seen him," offers Francoise again.

Ignoring her comment, he says to me, "Well, please inform us if you see him, and I advise you to be careful. We consider him to be quite dangerous."

Totally surprised, I laugh aloud, "*Paul?* Surely we are not talking about the same Gauguin!"

Speaking firmly and seriously, the policeman says, "We have solid information that this Gauguin had a hand in the violent attack on Monsieur van Gogh, who is now in extremely serious condition. The doctor does not think he will survive. I suggest, monsieur, that you consider this Gauguin to be a dangerous man."

Shocked beyond words at this information, my knees become weak, and I collapse into a chair.

The man continues; "We found Monsieur van Gogh this morning in a pool of blood at his home. There was a razor nearby. We have been told by witnesses that the two men argued violently last night."

Francoise offers, "Vincent was here at midnight. Came in very quietly. Had his head wrapped in a bloody bandage and asked

Figure 4-41. Vincent's "Self-Portrait with Bandaged ear and Pipe," Jan. 1889. *[Reprinted from Jewell (1946).]*

for Rachel. When she saw him, she promptly fainted." She grimaces and shivers, adding, "Ughh! It was dreadful!"

Still ignoring her, the man questions me, "Did you see anything of this?"

Before I can open my mouth to respond, Francoise replies, "He passed out and could not see anything at all."

Obviously annoyed with Francoise, the man asks me again, "Monsieur, did *you* see anything?"

Finding my voice, I speak softly, "She is correct. Since I was drunk, I do not remember any of this."

Gloating, Francoise mutters, "See, I told you."

Losing his patience, the policeman turns to her, "Madame, I am not interrogating you. Since the gentleman is not a deaf-mute, let him answer, if you please."

"Well, you are wasting your time," she responds in a huff. "I am the only one who knows what he knows. He was too drunk to remember his own name."

Increasingly irritated, the police officer starts to argue with her again. Before he does, I cut in, "Where is Vincent now?"

The sergeant answers curtly, "At his house."

Suddenly determining to be by Vincent's side, I shove my way past Francoise and the officer and rush recklessly out the door. Following me, he calls out, "Monsieur, wait! You cannot go there. We are still investigating."

Racing down the street as fast as my unsteady legs can carry me, I dodge through townspeople until I arrive at the Yellow House. A large crowd has gathered outside, attracted by word of the tragedy involving the "crazy painter." Policemen hold the crowd back, but I manage to push my way to the front just as they carry Vincent out on a litter. In despair and shock, I see that he is deathly pale, with a blood-soaked bandage over his head. As I watch, two men load him into the horse-drawn ambulance from St. Paul's Hospital. Dr. Rey, the local physician, follows and climbs into the ambulance behind him.

Figure 4-42. Vincent's "Portrait of Dr. Rey," Jan. 1889. *[Reprinted from Faille (1939).]*

Overcome with grief, I attempt to push through the crowd towards the ambulance. A burly policeman grabs me, insisting, "Stay back!"

After struggling feebly for a moment, I ask, "Is he alive?"

Still holding me by the arms, he replies, "It does not look good. He has lost a lot of blood." Looking closely at my face, he asks, "Are you family?" I do not answer.

Across from me, two policemen are gripping Paul tightly by each arm and interrogating him. Showing no fear or emotion, he appears to be talking evenly with them.

Near me, an elderly lady says to a friend, "I told you nothing good would come of this. Even if the mad painter recovers, we should not allow him to stay. He has been nothing but trouble, bringing his Parisian ways to our town, drinking and carousing. He is not respectable!"

After the men close the doors of the ambulance, the driver clucks to the horse and snaps the reins. The ambulance slowly pulls away, carrying an almost-dead Vincent towards the hospital. Overwhelmed by despair, I push my way back through the crowd. My world has come crashing down around my ears. Paul is in custody, accused of attacking my only true friend, while Vincent, the only good thing in my life, is dying on the way to the hospital. I am in shock beyond belief.

I stumble down the street back to the brothel, overcome with emotion, feeling numb and confused. Most of the girls are gone, out in the street watching and chattering about the incident. The few who are still inside are talking excitedly about Paul and Vincent. They ignore me. Picking up a full bottle of absinthe, I stick it under my arm. Opening the drug chest, I grab a handful of Dreamballs and stumble back to my room.

Feeling more miserable than at any time in my life, I sit down on the edge of the bed. Staring at the Dreamballs in my open hand – there are about six of them – I pop them solemnly into my mouth one by one, washing them down with absinthe. I finish nearly the entire bottle.

Nothing matters anymore. Today, something has died within me. I no longer wish to live in a world such as this.

Quickly, the drugs and alcohol begin to take effect, and that familiar euphoria begins to ease my pain. Relieved at last, I am glad that this will be over soon. If Vincent is to die today, then I shall join him.

Suddenly, I begin to feel nauseous, and my chest feels as if a vise seizes it. It is difficult to breathe. In a panic, I tumble forward off the bed and fall to my knees. I did not expect this! I claw at my chest with both hands, trying to scream for help. My shirt buttons pop off and fly across the room.

Frantically, I clutch my chest. My lips move, but I cannot make a sound. My chest is constricting, and I cannot get enough air to form words. Now, with searing pain, my heart starts beating so rapidly that I cannot count the beats. Suddenly it stops! I fall forward headfirst onto the floor, banging my head sharply on the bare wood boards.

As I slip into unconsciousness, the room fades from view. The pain is gone now, but I do not know where I am. At first, there is only total darkness. Now slowly, I begin to see details. In all directions, the deep black begins to change into many shades of gray. Far off in the distance, there is some sort of horizon where the sky is the lightest shade; directly overhead, the sky is dark but not quite black. As I look down, I see nothing but blackness below me.

I can barely make out the outlines of my chest and legs, but I sense that I am not standing on anything. I wiggle my feet and move my legs. Nothing, they touch nothing. I hang suspended in space. A wave of fear creeps over me. *Where am I?*

"Hello," I call out tentatively, but my voice is muffled as if in a thick fog. The smell of acrid smoke fills the air.

"HELLO!" I call out again louder, but there is no answer and no echo.

Now, I hear a faint sighing like the wind. "S-h-o-o-o E-e-e-e. S-h-o-o-o E-e-e-e." It sounds almost like someone – or some *thing* – is breathing. "S-h-o-o-o E-e-e-e." It comes from far below me.

A rising sense of panic grips me, and I feel cold. "Hello. Help me!" I call out. No one answers.

"S-h-o-o-o E-e-e-e." It is louder now, and I am certain that it is coming from below me. As I look down, straining my eyes, I see that the darkness is getting somewhat lighter. It looks as if the ground is coming up to meet me – or that I am falling. Panic grips me tighter as I fear that I will crash into the ground, or that the ground will rise up to crush me!

As I stare at the ground approaching from below, the sound grows even louder, and I can hear it better. Stunned, I realize that something is calling to me, "L-o-o-o E-e-e-e. L-o-o-o E-e-e-e."

I try to run, to get away, and my legs move frantically, but I do not go anywhere. There is nothing under my feet. My feet just flail away over emptiness.

The white ground that is rising to meet me is getting clearer now. A vast bed of boulders appears to be rushing up towards me. Right under me, the whiteness begins to form into a cone or a point reaching up towards me like the sharp tip of a mountain peak. Though the light is dim, I can see detail better now. To my horror, I see that the white boulders are skulls, thousands of skulls, tens of thousands of them, as far down as I can see, all with hollow eye sockets staring up at me. Terrified, I want to flee, but it is futile. The pile of skulls rises up under me with a constant clattering noise, slowing as it gets closer. The sighing sound grows louder. White jawbones move in unison, chanting out the constant call: "L-o-o-o E-e-e-e."

The skulls are just below my feet now, a huge mountainous cone stretching far down into the darkness below. As they tumble up around my feet and now my calves, I pump my legs to try to stay on top, but inexorably, the skulls pin my legs and fill up around me. I am terrified that they will engulf me, but when they reach the level of my chest, they suddenly stop rising. One skull is just in front of my chin, gazing at me with hollow lifeless eyes. I shiver uncontrollably with fear.

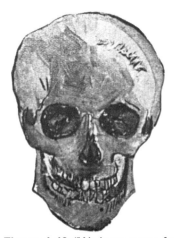 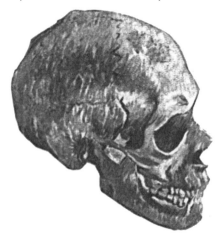

Figure 4-43. "We have come for you!" *[Vincent's "The Skull," Winter, 1887. Reprinted from Faille (1939).]*

Figure 4-44. "You are between worlds now." *[Another version of Vincent's painting of "The Skull," Winter, 1887. Reprinted from Faille (1939).]*

There is no motion anywhere. Finally, it is silent. The skulls have surrounded me, so I cannot move. They are motionless now, and all is deathly quiet, except for my rapid, labored breathing.

Now suddenly, with a rattling sound, the skull in front of me moves a little. The jaw pivots open, and the skull speaks with a dry, hissing whisper, "Loo-ee, we have come for you."

Struggling with fear, I protest, "Get away from me! Let me go! I do not belong here."

The skull says, "Where can you go? You do not belong anywhere, Loo-ee."

"How do you know my name? What am I doing here?" I demand.

"You are between worlds," Skull says simply.

"Well, let me out of here," I shout, "and who the devil are you anyway?"

"You," Skull says flatly.

"What the hell are you talking about?" I demand, irritated.

"I am you. It is as simple as that," Skull answers.

Another nearby skull joins in, "True. Me, too. I am you, also."

Another one says, with a dry laugh, "And me, too."

Easy, Louis, I try to reassure myself, *this is just an opium dream. None of this is real.* The first Skull cackles and counters with, "We are just as real as you are, Loo-ee. We are just earlier versions of you. You have lived before — and we are the bodies that you discarded after you wore us out. As you can see, there are many, many skulls. You are only the last one, the top of the pile. There will be more in the future. They will be piled on top of you." The Skull lets out a raspy laugh.

"Leave me alone," I demand indignantly.

"Can't do that," the first Skull says with another laugh. "Just not possible! We will always be with you!"

"Drop dead!" I spit out.

There are chuckles all around me, as the pile shakes with laughter. "You must not be paying attention, Loo-ee. We all dropped dead long ago." More laughter.

I am not going to put up with this, I mutter to myself, struggling to get free. *This is not real!*

As I squirm around, I cause one of the skulls to roll down the hill, leaving a skull-sized hole in the pile. I twist and shift around, until I become frustrated and finally give up. In the hole where the skull once was, I see a flicker of movement. Looking closer, I see two large, yellow-green, luminous eyes coldly staring at me from the dark hole. Now a scaly head appears.

"*Snake!*" I scream, breaking into a cold sweat. "A snake! I hate snakes. I hate them, hate them, *hate* them!" I shout again. Squirming, I try to escape, but I just get more exhausted. As a huge cobra squirms out of the pile, it flares its hood and locks its unwavering, unblinking gaze on me. Shivering with fear, I close my eyes so as not to look at it, but that is even more terrifying, so I open them a tiny bit again. The cobra's head is level with mine, eye to eye, and its tongue flickers in and out, almost touching my face. Frantically, I struggle again, futilely trying to get away.

A deep voice comes from the snake. It has a singsong lilt and cadence to it:

"There is nowhere to run and nowhere to hide
You decide.
Now it is time to live or die."

The luminous yellow eyes stare at me without wavering.

"What are you talking about?" I ask.

"You must decide to live or die. Choose your side," the Voice demands.

The words cut through me like a knife, and I am suddenly overwhelmed with despair. "I don't know," I moan. "Don't ask me to choose," I whisper.

"You must. Now, you are neither alive nor dead. You are in-between, so you are nothing. You cannot stay this way. *Choose!*" the Voice demands.

As the Voice finishes speaking, scenes from my life form in a shimmering panorama before my eyes. All of the bad, along with the good, flashes across my vision. Full of regret, I view countless images of hurting others, of failing in my responsibilities, of rejecting chances to help, and of refusing to do what was right and good. Sadly, there are very few good deeds to review. I have been selfish, and I have missed many opportunities. Most of my life, I have chosen to run away and hide from my problems, and I yearn to do that now, too, to make myself disappear. It is too painful, much too painful, to accept my life as it is.

"I am afraid to die and afraid to live," I whimper, sobbing quietly. "I cannot choose."

"You are mostly dead. You might as well finish it," says the Voice. I begin to feel that maybe I should.

"No, live," says the first Skull.

"Die if you wish. It is for you to choose," says the Voice again. I am confused. I just cannot make up my mind.

"No. No. Choose to live," says another skull.

"By all means, live. Face your fears. Live, Loo-ee. Live!" adds another.

One by one, the skulls all add their voices to the chorus with a rising crescendo, "Live, Loo-ee! Live! Live! You can do it!" The chant grows louder and more insistent. As it does, I am aware that my heart is beating louder and louder in rhythm with the cadence, and now my chest, not just my heart, but my chest begins to thump loudly in rhythm, too.

Reluctantly making my decision, I say, weakly, "Maybe I *could* do better if I go back. I can try. I would like to try again."

"Yes, Loo-ee! Yes!" answer all the skulls.

The Voice says, "So be it."

With a mighty heave, I cough violently, and my head snaps sideways. The room is suddenly visible. Dr. Rey is crouching over me pounding my chest with one hand and shouting, "Live! Damn you, boy, live!" With the other hand, he slaps me across the cheek again to revive me.

"Look, he has come back!" shouts Francoise. "He is breathing!"

Dr. Rey demands impatiently, "See if that ambulance is here yet!"

Through blurred vision, I see faces around me, but as I watch them, they ripple and distort wildly. The doctor mops my face and brow with a damp, cool cloth. I smile feebly and now, exhausted, fall into a deep sleep. *[See inset.]*

> **Flash Forward**
> Dr. Rey gave Vincent and Louis a crucial second chance at life. In an unusual bit of karma, the soul who was Dr. Rey would play a crucial role in my current lifetime as well. According to Reflection (2002), this time he provided me with my crucial first chance at life – as my father.

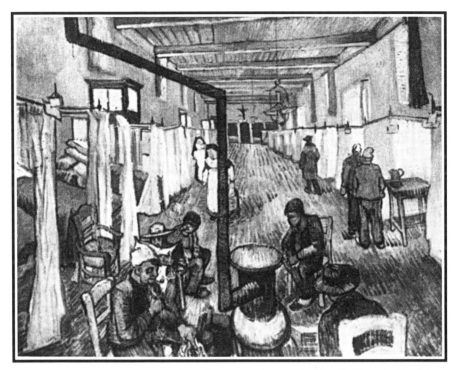

Figure 4-45. Both Vincent and Louis were taken to St. Paul's Hospital in Arles. *[Vincent's painting of the hospital, Apr. 1889. Reprinted from Faille (1939).]*

The Final Argument

The night before, on December 23, Vincent and Paul got into one final violent argument. Later, Paul wrote a letter describing the event. In it, he recounted that Vincent, apparently despondent about Paul's threatened departure, confronted him on the street in Arles. Paul gave two different accounts, one in which Vincent appeared to be holding a razor. Fearing for his safety, Paul spent the night in the local hotel.

When he returned home in the morning, Paul found Vincent near death with blood splattered everywhere. At first, the police detained Paul as a suspect, but they released him when it became clear that Vincent had cut himself with the razor. Suffering a mental breakdown, Vincent had become delirious and slashed off the lower third of his left ear. Then, the local newspaper reported that, at about 11:30 PM, wearing a bandage and a large beret to hide the wound, he staggered off to the brothel to present the severed ear as a gift to one of his favorite girls.

Paul immediately cabled Theo who rushed to Arles on Christmas Day. Vincent, locked in his hospital room for his own safety, was still delusional and in serious condition, though he showed some signs of progress.

Theo and Paul Leave on Christmas Day

Shocked at Vincent's erratic behavior, Paul refused to visit Vincent in the hospital, even though Vincent kept asking for him. Paul left Arles later on Christmas day with Theo on the night train. Convinced that Vincent was unbalanced and dangerous, Paul never saw Vincent again, though they eventually corresponded again by letter.

Beginning in May 1889, Vincent was hospitalized several times over the next few years for his mental condition. He alternated between making some improvements in his health and then getting worse. Even so, he continued his remarkable and inspired output of paintings.

Louis and the Man-in-Black

When the ambulance arrived, Dr. Rey took Louis to the hospital, where he recovered quickly. His father's private detective, the mysterious man-in-black on the stage, telegraphed Louis' family about the situation and, after removing Louis from the hospital, escorted him back to Paris.

Louis' brush with death caused him to rethink the direction of his life. Powerfully affected by what he had seen in his vision, he was relieved that he had "returned from the dead." Others, however, especially his father, were not so pleased that he had gone there in the first place. Louis had gravely underestimated his father's interest in his welfare.

After he had recovered fully, Louis had a long serious talk with his father; that is, his father talked at length and Louis listened. His father did not shout and did not accuse, but he would not be denied. Things would be different now.

Having gained valuable insights during his near-death experience, Louis apologized to his family for his past actions and activities. Louis had accepted, as Vincent had pointed out, that he would never be an artist, and now he determined to make something of his life. Humbly, he asked his father to teach him about art trading. Stunned, his father agreed, even though he was still skeptical of Louis' long-term commitment.

Moreover, whether Louis liked it or not, his "career" at the cafes ended with this overdose. Until his father died several years later, Louis never again went out without supervision. His father assigned chaperons to look after him, and he was not able to bribe the chaperons to look the other way.

Because of the chaperons, Louis was unable to visit Vincent, Henri, or Paul until after his father died. Louis would not be able to see his friend Vincent again for another seven years.

On the Road to Auvers, France (1895)

The road has many potholes, and the carriage rocks roughly back and forth. Brown clouds of dust, stirred up by the horse's hooves, roll in around the leather curtains that only poorly seal the windows. It settles on the black-lacquered wood, the leather seats, and on my pressed black suit and hat. Raising my silver-topped cane, I rap loudly against the carriage roof for the driver to

Figure 4-46. Vincent's "Green Wheatfield with Cypresses" outside Auvers, June 1889. *[Reprinted from Faille (1939).]*

slow down, but he does not hear me – apparently. Sometimes these country people delight in "torturing" unsuspecting Parisians. Bracing myself, I sigh in resignation and pull on my gray calfskin gloves. After dabbing a little fragrant oil on my handkerchief, I clamp it firmly over my nose and mouth, determining to make the best of this miserable ride.

It has been seven years since I last saw Vincent, not since that day when Dr. Rey took both of us to the hospital. The doctor gave both of us a second chance, though Vincent's chance turned out differently than mine.

After they carried me back to Paris, it was not easy living under the watchful eyes of Papa and my chaperons, but I did it. As he promised, Papa taught me to be an art dealer, and even though we have different tastes in art, we developed a solid love and respect for one another. I learned much from him, and I believe, in the end, he learned some useful things from me.

Ah, me, but now Papa has gone, God rest his soul, and the servants are no longer under such threats, so it will be good to meet Vincent again. I speak to him silently, *So I have come to see you again, mon ami.*

As the carriage lurches to a halt, I push aside the window shade to look out. We have arrived outside the little town of Auvers, about twenty miles north of Paris.

The coachman opens the door, and I step down into an early summer scene right out of one of Vincent's paintings. Here, before my eyes, are all the rich colors that I recall from his palette: brilliant blues, vibrant greens, and glowing gold, the astounding colors of an exuberant, fertile earth.

Ahead of me, a low hill rises, crowned by well-tended shrubbery. A warm, humid breeze rustles through their leaves and branches. Off to each side are expansive fields of wheat and corn, alternating blocks of green and gold, some with head-high stalks, and some recently mowed and dotted with haystacks. The aroma of freshly cut hay carries on the breeze. Small flocks of field birds flutter through the wheat looking for quick meals. Farther away, several birds, ravens perhaps, call raucously to each other and flap away lazily towards the horizon.

Vincent is around here somewhere. With a few cut flowers in hand, I set off alone up the small stone path that leads to the top of the hill. I walk up slowly, savoring the sights, sounds, and smells, which are so unlike those of a cultured, manicured Paris that is, at the same time, often dirty and noisy. The only sounds are the breeze, the chattering birds, and the tapping of my cane on the flagstone path.

Figure 4-47. Detail from Vincent's "Thatched Cottages" outside Auvers, 1889. *[Reprinted from Meier-Graefe (1922).]*

Figure 4-48. Detail from Vincent's "Wheatfield with Crows," painted in Auvers, July 1890. The location is close to the cemetery. *[Reprinted from Elgar (1958).]*

As I walk, I search around for Vincent, finally spotting him in front of a low rock wall that is overgrown with grass.

With a lump in my throat, I quicken my steps in excitement – it has been far too long since I last saw him. At last, I stop, staring wordlessly at Vincent. Behind him stands a large, upright, chiseled gray stone, with the words: "Here Rests Vincent van Gogh, 1853-1890." The letters look as if the stonecarver had chiseled them only yesterday. *[See inset.]*

> **At Peace at Last**
> With his sanity on shaky ground, Vincent moved to Auvers in 1890, where he began to receive treatment from Dr. Paul Gachet. Vincent enjoyed the lack of pressure at Auvers, but his illness continued to worsen. In despair over his condition, Vincent shot himself on June 27, 1890, and died two days later.
>
> Ill and overcome by his brother's suicide, Theo died six months later in the Netherlands. In 1914, his family moved his body to Auvers to a grave beside his brother. Almost inseparable in life, they remained so in death.

Tears cloud my eyes, and rubbing them away with my gloves, I murmur, "Hello, again, mon ami. Hello, brother-of-my-heart." I pause to remember him as I saw him that last afternoon in Arles, with his rumpled clothes and ever-

Figure 4-49. The headstones of Vincent and Theo in Auvers. *[Reprinted from Tralbaut (1959).]*

present pipe. I had planned to say so much, to explain, to apologize, to rationalize, but now the words escape me.

Pausing to clear my eyes, I gaze out at the great rolling fields around us and now turn to his grave again. I speak aloud as if he could hear me. Somewhere, somehow, I believe that he truly is listening. "When I returned to Paris, I missed you terribly, old friend. Nevertheless, you were right not to return to Paris and to come out here to the country around Auvers instead. You were never a city-dweller, Vincent, to grow pallid in dark cafes. You were always a man of the fields, the earth, and the countryside. You drew your inspiration from the lightning storms over these fields and from the golden sun that ripens the grain when the rain is done. Sadly, that same fiery inspiration that filled you sometimes "scorched" your friends."

I pause a moment to recall the many faces from my days in the Paris cafes. "I hear that neither Paul nor Henri visited you before or after your death, when you ended your pain, old friend, with a single bullet into your too-sensitive heart. I know that they still loved you, even if they could no longer bear to be around you. The fire of passion that burned in your soul, Vincent, could warm your friends as well as sear them. I am not sure that flesh can contain such a fire. Perhaps that was your undoing – no mortal can embrace such power for long. No heart can contain such passion without breaking."

I kneel to place a few purple irises at his feet. "You were right, mon ami, when you said that I cannot be a great artist. My path is different from yours, longer and less painful, I suspect; and my path is different from my father's, as well. I see the mistakes he made: of living distant from the vagaries of fortune, of placing himself above the rank-and-file, of being color-blind to the bright hues of life. His choices were his own, but because of you, I shall not follow him. I have listened to you well, and each day, in some small manner, I endeavor to 'measure the heights of Heaven and plumb the depths of Hell.' Somehow, Vincent, I will always find a way to live my life so as to include them both – as you tried to do, my brother."

I choke up, unable to say more – only unspoken feelings remain in my heart. Once more, I gaze out over the ripening fields, watching the broad, rippling, slow-moving wind-waves sculpted by the breeze. In the distance, at the far horizon, great billowing white clouds span from earth to sky. The ravens are gone now and all is peaceful.

"I wish it were not so, my friend, but *au revoir*, until we meet again, perhaps on that bright star you pointed to that night in Paris. Good-bye, my friend. Good-bye for now."

The tears return, and with an aching heart, I turn and walk down the hill.

Figure 4-50. Vincent's "Wheatfield with Cypresses" painted outside Auvers, Sep. 1889. *[Reprinted from Faille (1939).]*

> ### Louis' Closest Friends are Gone
> Many of Vincent's painter friends joined him before long. Toulouse-Lautrec's chronic alcoholism eventually caused a complete breakdown, forcing him into a sanatorium in 1899. Though he recovered temporarily to resume his hectic life, he died two years later in 1901. Having vowed to "burn himself out" by the age of 40, he was only 36 when he died.
>
> In 1891, Paul Gauguin abandoned France to live in Tahiti, took a native girl as his wife, and fathered a son with her. Poor and suffering from syphilis and poor, he returned to France in August 1893 to sell some paintings.
>
> In my current lifetime, I have had a strong romantic notion of an idyllic life in the South Seas. I longed to visit Tahiti, and almost did on several occasions. Suspecting a past Group-Link, I meditated to try to find the source of these strong feelings. As I did, the old memories emerged of Louis seeing and talking to Paul about Tahiti when he returned to Paris in 1893.
>
> Finding little success, Paul returned to Tahiti in 1895. Suffering from syphilis and recurring strokes, his health grew steadily worse. He died of a stroke in the Marquesas Islands on May 8, 1903.
>
> Within the span of a little more than a decade, all three of them were gone, all three of these passion-filled men whose dazzling works inspired Louis and so many others after him.

One Year Later in Paris (1896)

With only a few minutes to spare, I check my hat and coat and follow the usher to our family box in the balcony. Tonight, I am depressed and need some diversion. There have been many times when I regret my decision to learn the art trade, and tonight is one of them. Why is it that most people with money, the ones who can afford to collect art, are the ones with the least ability to appreciate it? I have spent all day fielding asinine questions from such people. One couple stands out particularly.

Peering closely at the painting, the woman asked, "Why do you suppose the artist chose chartreuse rather than crimson?"

I was tempted to tell her, "Perhaps, it is because he has never seen red-colored grass!" Apparently, she does not know crimson from cabbage.

Before I could think of a polite answer, her husband asked, "I consider that the cathedral in the painting is, well, a little too crooked."

I imagine saying to him, "Very well. If you like, I can have the artist paint in some flying buttresses to keep it from falling over."

Ah, me, I have just spent an entire day finding out why the "boor" is in "bourgeoisie." On top of such torture, they walked out without buying a single painting. Frankly, however, I was somewhat relieved. I hate sending good paintings to bad homes!

Figure 4-51. She complains, "Oh my goodness, I'm afraid chartreuse will *never* do!" *[Reminds me of the two boors; from Lautrec's "Alfred la Guigne," 1894. Reprinted from Jewell (1944).]*

In any event, to clear my mind, I am attending a performance tonight at the Opera Garnier. I have heard many good things about the current performance and wish to see it for myself.

As the curtain goes up and the performance begins, I relax and lose myself in the entertainment, forgetting about crimson and cathedrals.

Figure 4-52. The Opera Garnier in Paris is located about one mile from Vincent's old apartment. *[Ca. 1890s. Courtesy of the Library of Congress.]*

Figure 4-53. Photo of the inside of the Opera, taken during its inauguration in 1875. *[Courtesy of the Library of Congress.]*

One of the performers attracts my attention. She is not the lead, having only a secondary role, but her voice is marvelous, and she outshines the lead singer in all respects. The lighting is dim, but even so, her golden hair sparkles and shines, though no more so than her smile. There is some quality about her, something special, some indefinable something that mesmerizes me. I sense that I have seen her before; she seems so familiar. I struggle to recall where, though I know that it is not so. If it were, I would have remembered her vividly. I cannot take my eyes off her. She is as luminous as any angel is, though I am no expert in angels, unless they are the fallen kind. As the performance progresses, I grow more enchanted. Leaning forward in my seat, I hang on each note, on each change of melody, on every word, and on her every movement.

Figure 4-54. "The third act is particularly moving!" *[Reminds me of the opera; from Degas painting, 1878. Reprinted from Jewell (1944).]*

Near the end of the third act, as she finishes a particularly moving solo, I can no longer contain myself. I jump up enthusiastically and applaud vigorously to show my appreciation. I continue until she glances directly up at me. Only now, to my embarrassment, do I realize that I am the only one clapping. The scene is not yet finished, and the audience and a few performers are looking up at me sternly. Sheepishly, but with undiminished appreciation, I quickly sit down again.

When the opera is finally over, excitedly I jump up again to add my applause. I continue to clap without stopping entirely through the second curtain call, until I am the last one applauding. Only now, reluctantly, do I stop.

The finely dressed woman next to me, perhaps sympathetic to my embarrassing scene, says to me with a polite smile, "She certainly does have a lovely voice!"

"She is angelic!" I enthuse. Now before I can stop my tongue, I blurt out, "Did you know that she is my wife?" I am stunned at what I have just said. My mind races trying to think of a graceful way to take it back.

The woman looks surprised, "I did not know that Margot had a husband. Why, that is wonderful! When were you married?"

Margot. What a lovely name, I think to myself.

"Well, not yet, actually," I say to her, trying to act nonchalant, "but it will be soon."

Figure 4-55. "The lady next to me says, 'She does have a lovely voice!'" *[Reminds me of the opera; from Mary Cassatt painting, "At the Opera," 1880. Reprinted from Jewell (1944).]*

She smiles again, "Well, that is nice. Have you set a date?"

"Well, not yet, actually," I say, a little sheepishly, "but I intend to ask her soon."

Puzzled, she nods her head slowly, saying, "Well, that is …" She pauses to measure her words carefully. "That is, uh … unusual. Do you mean that you haven't actually asked her to marry you … *actually?*"

"Well, no, not yet, actually," I try to answer as cheerfully as I can, "but I am sure she will say 'Yes!'"

The woman stares at me with an incredulous look, as if I had just escaped from an asylum. Without another word, she gets up, turns, and walks off.

Looking down at the stage again, I see that Margot is gone now, and most of the audience is leaving as well. I repeat aloud to myself, "Not yet, actually, but I am sure she will say 'Yes!'" *[See inset.]*

Flash Forward

As I relived this past life memory, I recognized the soul who was Margot; she has become my first wife in this current lifetime.

In a repeat of history, she is still a gifted singer, and currently her name is Margaret, very similar to the name Margot. Similarities like this often happen from one life to the next.

Pursuing Margot

It took more than a week for Louis to arrange to meet Margot. She focused intensely on her singing career, and though she appreciated her admirers, she was careful not to get involved romantically. Her career came first.

Louis had to utilize all of his influence to meet her, mainly because of his reputation. By now, his days of wild living in Montmartre were common knowledge. Even though he was an art dealer, clearly he had crossed the line of propriety. According to the code of the well-heeled, it was acceptable to buy paintings from artists; it was, however, not acceptable to smoke opium with them while they painted.

In addition, Louis had little tolerance for the affectations of the wealthy, even though he was from an aristocratic family himself. His bluntness around "polite" society tended to get his name removed from invitation lists, not that he regretted this fact very much. However, he was now interested in overcoming his past enough to include Margot in his future.

Reluctantly, she agreed to meet him on social occasions when doing so did not conflict with her career. Over the next year, they came to know each other well and developed a comfort level with each other. Outwardly, each of them was very different, and yet they complemented each other. Margot was practical, grounded, and success-oriented, though she occasionally showed a fiery temper. She possessed a strictly no-nonsense approach to life.

Louis, on the other hand, loved much of life's lighter nonsense and actively sought it out. He was more romantic than she was, more mercurial, and more unpredictable. Overall, even though he was an art dealer, Louis had the temperament of an artist, although he was not one. By contrast, Margot, who was an artist, had more of the practical nature of an art dealer, even though she was not one. Getting along very well, much to Margot's surprise, they saw each other with increasing frequency.

A Few Months Later on the Seine River, Paris

Beyond the edge of the rowboat, among the blossoming water lilies, points of light dance on the rippling water. I let the rowboat glide for a moment, and now, I carefully turn both oars on their pivots and swing the blades into the rowboat. The oars make a slight clunking sound as they hit the wet wood of the boat. I take care that I do not get the Seine's greenish water on Margot's lovely pure-white dress or parasol. She can be easily peeved.

Still struggling with emotions, I do not say anything yet. Finally, I reach into the picnic basket and pull out a colorfully lacquered tin of candy. "Margot, my dear, I have discovered some delightful new treats from the New World. I hope you will find them to your taste." I pop open the lid and present them to her.

With a smile of anticipation, she leans forward and folds back the thin translucent paper that covers them. Leaning forward even more, she selects the middle piece of rich brown-and-white chocolate, ringed with a golden band that glitters in the noonday sun. Removing her white glove, she reaches out lightly with two fingers to touch the candy.

A slight frown forms on her brow, "Do they bind chocolates with hard wrappers these days?" Now, as full understanding hits her, she jerks back her hand as if the box contained a live eel!

"Louis! You promised you would not propose again." She indignantly crosses her arms, and her expression turns stormy. She refuses to look at me.

I plead, "Margot, I cannot help it. You know how much I love you!"

I reach for the chocolate, slide off the ring, and turn it so the setting shows. Set off by a dozen brilliant Peruvian emeralds, the flawless yellow diamond sparkles and flashes in the light. I hold out the ring for her to see. Without turning her head, she moves just her eyes to look at it, glances at me, and looks away again. I can tell she is weakening a little.

"You know I am deeply fond of you, Louis, but for now, my career is first. There will be enough time for a family later."

"But, Margot, my dear," I protest, "you can have both. I do not

Figure 4-56. "On the Seine with Margot." *[Reminds me of the incident; from Manet's "Boating," 1874. Reprinted from Meier-Graefe (1922).]*

ask you to give up your singing; you know I am your greatest fan. But I can help you greatly. Together, I believe we can do things that you cannot do alone. You say that you are happy while singing – and you say you are happy with me – so let us put the two together. Then, you shall be happy all the time. Please, Margot, I do not wish to live apart from you any longer."

She uncrosses her arms and turns to look at me fully. Her gaze softens, and a faint smile touches the corners of her mouth. "Oh, Louis, you never give up," she says with mock exasperation. After a slight pause, she says, "However, given my feelings for you, I shall reconsider it."

My heart pounds with excitement, and I move to kneel in front of her, rocking the boat precariously for a moment. Gingerly holding out the ring, I offer, "Please accept this in the meantime, Margot, as a token of my love for you."

She eyes the ring and me doubtfully, unsure of making even that commitment.

"Please," I beg her, placing one hand over my heart, "wear it without the slightest obligation to me. You may keep it no matter what your answer shall be, and I promise not ask you again."

"Louis, that is exactly what you said last time," she protests, looking at the ring for several long moments. "It is exquisitely beautiful." She looks up at me, a little unsure, and now gazes at the ring again. With a sigh, she holds out her left hand. Effortlessly, with singing in my heart, I slip the ring over her finger, praying inwardly that I do not go unconscious from excitement and fall into the Seine.

Second Thoughts

Louis' excitement was short-lived. A week later, Margot returned the ring, refusing to wear it and to make even that small commitment. Offering Louis some consolation, she did say that she would indeed marry him in time, but just not now. She would not accept the ring because of her career, so he would just have to be patient and wait. Louis nodded his head, knowing better than to argue with her at that moment, but he had a plan. Patience was not one of his stronger virtues.

Two Months Later

Late for the rehearsal, I hurry in from the foyer of the opera house. As I walk briskly down to the front row near the orchestra pit, I watch Margot rehearsing for a new opera. I had expected the hall to be nearly empty, but there are quite a few people here. There are many who idolize the singers and come to hear them whenever possible. I feel a bit nervous about the timing of my plan, but with a sigh, I dismiss my fears. Today is the day!

The conductor, perched on his stand, taps three times with his baton to ask for silence. There are nearly a hundred members of the chorus, and they gradually settle into place and give him their full attention. Margot stands quietly next to the conductor, ready to begin rehearsing her part.

Figure 4-57. The ornate grand foyer of the Opera Garnier. *[Photo taken in the 1890s. Courtesy of the Library of Congress.]*

Figure 4-58. "There are many who idolize the opera singers.'" *[Reminds me of the opera; from Mary Cassatt painting, "The Loge." Reprinted from Jewell (1944).]*

The orchestra and the chorus begin, and now, Margot comes in on cue. As she reaches the crescendo of the piece, her incredibly lovely, richly colored soprano voice fills the entire concert hall, reverberating with subtle undertones. A sudden thrill of excitement courses through my body. She has that same effect on many who hear her sing.

As she finishes, I am unable to contain myself any longer. I leap up, burst into applause, and race down towards the stage, interrupting everything. Margot, musicians, singers, and conductor all stop and stare at me. By now, Margot is used to my many shenanigans, though she does not tolerate some of them very well – like this one. Indignantly, she puts her hands on her hips and stares daggers at me.

Still clapping, I leap onto the stage, and approach her almost at a run, shouting out, "Wonderful, my dear! Simply wonderful!"

She looks as if she would like to slap me in the face, so I give her my most beguiling smile. I rapidly approach her, and just as I reach her, I suddenly drop to my knees, sliding the last few feet. Surprised and thinking that I must have tripped, she reaches down to break my fall. I gaze up at her with obvious admiration.

The entire hall, containing nearly a hundred people, is totally silent. There is not a sound. Everyone is motionless.

Before Margot can speak or react further, the conductor taps his baton three times on the podium. Surprised, Margot looks up. Without warning, the chorus and orchestra break into an unscheduled refrain. With a beautiful multipart harmony, the sopranos, altos, tenors, and basses blend their voices to sing the following:

Margot, will you hold this man,
Forever and a day?
Margot, will you take his hand?
Please say "Yes!" we pray.

The wonderful harmonious blend of a hundred voices fades to total silence again. Stunned but slowly regaining her composure, Margot looks at me, narrowing her eyes a little. With her mouth forming a slight smile, she begins slowly shaking her head back and forth. At first, I fear that she is refusing me once again, but she speaks in a stage whisper. "Louis St. Jacques, I cannot believe my ears. How on earth did you pull this off?"

Without waiting for an answer, she takes my hand and pulls me up to a standing position. Leaning forward, she whispers very quietly this time, "Louis, will you please stop proposing to me every other week?"

In a whisper, I respond enthusiastically, "Of course, my dear. All you have to do is say 'Yes!'"

Extending both hands to hold me at arm's length, she studies me for several seconds, and now shakes her head back and forth again with mild exasperation.

"May I take that for a 'Yes!'?" I plead hopefully.

She purses her lips a little, the way she does when she scolds me for some prank, and now she responds with that musical laugh of hers that never fails to weaken my knees.

Looking at the chorus, she speaks up so they can hear her clearly, "Since all of you have asked, then I must inform you that, because of the silly, childish actions of this man today …" she pauses to frown directly at me, as my heart drops, "the answer is … 'Yes!'"

The cast members break into thunderous applause, as I jump up to embrace her, feeling so overjoyed that I almost forget the next part. The conductor clears his throat several times over the noise to remind me. Recovering my composure, I nod to him solemnly. He taps his baton loudly three times, until everyone gets quiet again. Now he turns to me.

I extend my right palm, and with a magnificent flourish, the maestro touches it lightly with the tip of his baton. As he does so, he opens his closed fingers ever so slightly to allow a glittering

Figure 4-59. "Excitedly, I plan wedding details with Margot after the rehearsal." *[Reminds me of the meeting with Margot. Detail of Manet's painting "At Pere Lathuille's." Reprinted from Meier-Graefe (1922).]*

gold ring to rattle down the baton into my hand. I turn, and without waiting for Margot to reconsider, I slide it onto the ring finger of her left hand. As we embrace lovingly, the full chorus applauds one more time.

Now, with a radiant smile on her face, she asks me, "Are you happy, now, my dearest?"

Speechless with excitement, I can only nod enthusiastically.

"Good," she says sweetly with that angelic smile of hers, "now will you get out of this hall and let us finish rehearsing?"

18 Years Later in Paris (1914)

The sun has almost set. The chambermaid draws the curtains tighter to ease my eyes, shutting out all but a few rays of the last remaining light. As she leaves, she says, "The doctor will be here soon."

"I can hardly wait," I answer sarcastically. The bed is soaked from perspiration. "After he leaves, please return with some clean linens."

She bows and says "Yes, monsieur."

I respond very politely for the hundredth time, "Please do not bow. You know I do not wish it, and please do not call me 'monsieur.' You may call me 'Louis.'"

She has always been a little afraid of me, and she cannot get over it. "Yes, monsieur," she says, bowing as she leaves. For the hundredth time, I sigh and resolve not to talk to her about it again.

Figure 4-60. "I tell her, 'Please do not call me *monsieur*.'" *[Reminds me of the maid. Berthe Moriscot painting, 1881. Reprinted from Jewell (1944).]*

Figure 4-61. "The doctor listens patiently to my troubles." *[Reminds me of the doctor. Renoir painting, 1879. Reprinted from Jewell (1944).]*

A short time later, the doctor arrives. He has been my doctor ever since he helped me over my drug addictions, and he attended Margot at the birth of Adrienne, our only child. He and I know each other well; he has seen me at my worst, so there is no longer any need for pretense.

I slip on my spectacles with shaking hands, saying, "Hello, doctor." I do my best to be pleasant and to keep the session from becoming too serious. "Come to continue 'torturing' me, have you?"

"My dear Louis, it appears that I have not 'tortured' you enough yet," he answers with his most likeable smile. "Since you are still capable of speaking, I will have to try much harder."

We both delight in this verbal jousting. "Oh, I am sure you are up to the task."

He smiles, asking, "Just how is the patient today?"

"Well, let me see," I put my hand to my chin, as if considering the question. "My joints are aching; my head is throbbing; and my brain is boiling. Periodically, I shake as if the earth is coming apart; my skin is a lovely shade of yellow; I am leaking at the seams like Noah's Ark; the maid continues to bow. Why, everything is just *delightful*."

He smiles. "I marvel that your dry sense of humor has been unaffected," he says, as he pauses to feel my pulse. "Louis, we must talk seriously. This malarial infection and high fever are not responding to the treatments as well as I had hoped. I must be frank: I cannot be certain of success."

Still teasing him I reply, "My dear doctor, perhaps it is time for the 'lead cure.' Please go to the mantle above the fireplace. Get my dueling pistol and put me away like an old race horse."

He appears to consider the idea, "Hmm, tempting thought. Certainly, you shall have no lack of volunteers to do the deed."

I nod amiably, "No doubt. In truth, I will gladly do it myself."

He ignores any more of my gallows humor, and turns serious again, "Usually, Louis, the quinine keeps the parasites under control. However, it may be that you have an unusually virulent form of the disease. It is not common in Paris, though I have encountered it occasionally. It is quite likely that you contracted it on your last trip to Egypt – probably from the bite of a Nile mosquito. *[See inset.]*

"Our treatments usually work, but I have never seen anything like this – it resists all that I do. If you had not been so healthy, I fear that you would have succumbed long ago."

Egyptian Adventures

Louis' restlessness led to a life of adventures. On one of those, he traveled to Egypt to collect art treasures for sale to wealthy patrons in France.

On that trip, he also traveled to Nubia searching for gold. He found none, losing a small fortune to the locals instead, but he hardly cared -- the adventure was more important than gold.

After pausing again for a moment, he continues quietly, "It does not look promising, my friend."

"Mosquitoes? Let's see," I think back. "It certainly could have happened in Egypt – probably when I traveled from the Nile overland to the Nubian gold fields. Lots of mosquitoes – and big, too. Did I ever tell you about it, Doctor?"

Before he can stop me, I continue, "During the night, one of our Bedouins wandered outside. We found him in the morning, just a withered shell of bones and wrinkled skin. The mosquitoes had drained all of his blood. I tell you, we packed up as fast as we could and headed back to Cairo."

I glance up to see if he is listening. Ignoring his I-do-not-believe-this-one-bit expression, I get to the final part. "Doctor, I must tell you that on that trip, we accidentally solved one of the world's great mysteries – mummies. I am convinced that the priests just left the deceased Pharaoh outside overnight. By morning, the mosquitoes had turned him into a perfect mummy."

He screws up his face and his gaze meets mine. "Sadly, Louis, this disease has affected your brain so that you can no longer separate fact from fiction," he glances at me with a slight smile, "if you *ever* had such ability."

I chuckle, happy to tease him a little; I have few joys left. He continues, turning serious again. "We must try a stronger elixir, and I have prepared one, but I must tell you, Louis, I can only pray that it works. I am mystified by the tenacity of this disease."

I am puzzled, too, and weary of it as well.

"Over my lifetime, doctor, I have survived crocodiles, cobras, and calculating crooks. Now, however, I lie here on my derriere brought low by some *parasite*, by some mindless 'bug' that I cannot even see. Doctor, it makes no sense. Surely, you can see the irony in this. Has the great God-in-Heaven played some cruel joke on me?"

Looking away, the doctor answers softly, "Louis, I have no answer. I am not a priest or philosopher – I am only a physician – one who knows his many limitations well. I can do only what I can do." He turns to look at me again. "What I can do is to offer you a new treatment. It will be even more painful, but it may turn the tide of the disease or – it may do nothing at all. It is your choice alone to try it or not." *[See inset.]*

I look over at him, "If it tastes as bad as the last elixir, there shall be a race to see which kills me first, the bugs or the cure. Doctor, I am wagering on the

> **Malaria**
> This disease was a major problem in the 1800s, and physicians tried many different treatments, among them morphine and mercury. Doctors do not use either treatment today.
>
> Many patients who were treated with morphine became seriously addicted to the drug.
>
> The treatment using mercury is widely regarded today as having been far more deadly to patients than the malaria itself.

cure. By the way, what is in it, my friend, bat's wings? Frog's liver? Assuming frogs have livers, that is."

I cannot lighten his seriousness, and he replies, "It contains the same quinine that you have been taking. In addition, I have added morphine and finely divided mercury. It is said that the latter sometimes can have a pronounced effect on the parasites, but it is not without risk."

I consider what he says. "Doctor, as you know, I have never sought out a tame and pampered life; I have always taken risks. I have lived my life fully and with passion, like my friend Vincent. Using his life as my blueprint, I determined long ago to live my life without having tasteless 'wallpaper' on my walls."

The doctor looks puzzled at the last reference, but I continue anyway. "I do not compare myself to him; he lived his life in a larger arena, beyond mine. Like some heavenly comet, he was destined to flare brightly and burn out, leaving us in darkness again." My voice chokes for a moment and I clear my throat. "Doctor, my life was very different than his, but in my own small way, I have succeeded, and I am satisfied."

The doctor shifts position a little on the bed, still listening.

"Following Vincent's lead, I have pounded on the gates of Hell, and now I lie here, peering through the gates of Heaven. I am content to die now, if that is my fate. Having faced down ferocious crocodiles, I feel certain that Grim Death will not have any uglier face. If I am to go soon, I know that Margot will be well provided for."

My voice breaks a little, and I stop to compose myself. "But there is one thing – just one thing that is left undone …" My voice trails off into thought.

"And that is?" he says when my pause goes on too long.

I reach out and touch him on the arm. "Adrienne. My lovely daughter is to be married next month. She is seventeen, and I have promised to give her away. Is it possible to keep this wretched body alive until then?"

"My friend, there is an excellent chance for several more months, probably more, especially for such a tough old goat as you." He smiles and rests his big hand on my shoulder. "Shall we begin now?"

I nod and he hands me a bottle of his "magic elixir." I take it with an unsteady hand. "Drink it all quickly," he says,

Hearing the word "quickly," I understand what he means. I take two large gulps before I gag. It is terrible, worse than terrible. I make a face at him but say nothing. With great effort, I finish it all, coughing several times.

When I regain the ability to talk, I speak with a raspy voice, "Now I recall why I hate doctors, doctor." Having said that, I fear that, perhaps, I have overdone my joking. "Pardon me, sir. Please forgive me, for it is nothing personal. I like you extremely well as a person and value your friendship. It is only the doctor part of you to which I object," I explain earnestly.

"It is so good of you, sir, to clear that up for me," he says dryly. "I feel so much better now."

"My pleasure," I answer, with genuine pleasure.

With a light knock on the door, Margot and Adrienne enter the room. After kisses and greetings, they both look hopefully to the doctor for news of my condition, but I speak quickly before he can. "The doctor told me that I am doing extremely well, given the circumstances, and he said that – and I believe this to be an exact quote – 'In spite of this jungle fever, and judging by his sharp tongue, I believe we can expect another twenty years for the old goat.'"

Adrienne says in mock exasperation, "Daddy, you are incorrigible!"

The doctor turns to explain the new elixir to them, while, behind his back, I mimic drinking from the bottle, contorting my face, and puckering my lips in evident distaste. The two women try to suppress their laughs.

The doctor turns to catch my charade and says, shaking his head sadly, "There is one unfortunate side effect of this disease: some victims revert to their childhood."

Margot looks at me with a sweet smile and says innocently, "There is little evidence that Louis ever grew out of his." Everyone laughs in agreement.

I say happily, "You see, doctor, why I love her so: she sees me as I am and accepts me in spite of it." I blow a loving kiss to her.

Figure 4-62. "I always have been overwhelmed by Margot's loveliness." *[Reminds me of Margot. Detail of Manet's "Jeanne," 1882. Reprinted from Meier-Graefe (1922).]*

Adrienne steps closer to the bed. "You know, Daddy, the wedding is less than a month away. Will you be strong enough by then to give me away?"

I nod, smiling, "I would not miss it for the world."

As she leans towards me, moving in front of the window, the afternoon light from the fading sunset streams through, catching her long golden hair and lighting it up with the glowing halo of an angel.

Around her lovely neck, she wears a cream-colored antique cameo, tightly fastened with a black satin ribbon. The color of her delicate, high-collared, blue chiffon dress matches the radiant sky-blue color of her eyes. Her beauty is simply stunning. She is so innocent, and so like her mother at that age.

That old jealousy arises again, and I do not want to let her go, do not want to let a stranger have her. With two such lovely, creative, loving women in my life, I wish only to keep them near me always. *[See inset.]*

> **Flash Forward**
> As I relived this memory of my daughter in this past life, I recognized Adrienne; she incarnated as my high school sweetheart in this current lifetime, my first true love. I proposed to her, and we planned to be married, but it was not to be. As fate would have it, I "lost" her in both lifetimes, though for different reasons.

The morphine starts to take effect, and my speech becomes slurred. Seeing that I am getting drowsy, they turn to leave me to sleep. I wave weakly to all of them, thankful that a loving God sent such an abundance of love into my life. My physical pain is nearly gone now, masked by the morphine, and my mind drifts out, filled with visions of the grand wedding of my beloved only daughter.

During the night, the tiny, unseen invaders take full control of my body, spreading their poison. Before the new dawn, before my lovely ladies return, my body convulses uncontrollably, and my breathing stops.

It is time for me to go, and it is just as well, for I do not think I could have given Adrienne away. Now, someone else must do it.

"Good-bye, beloved Adrienne and Margot. Good-bye to both of you who have so blessed me with your love. I am so sorry to leave you this way. I tried, but I just could not stay any longer."

Figure 4-63 (above). Vincent's "The Sower," 1888. *[Reprinted from Faille (1939).]*

Figure 4-64 (left). Detail of Vincent's "Reaper with a Sickle," Sep. 1889. *[Reprinted from Meier-Graefe (1922).]*

Stepping out of the Body

The bedroom shimmers just a little, like some desert mirage and now vanishes, fading evenly into a vision of a field of freshly harvested wheat. Great rolls of hay lie scattered in rows all around me, brought in by the men of the fields. I stand in the middle of it all. Off in the distance, some field hands with a horse and wagon are still working. A warm, gentle breeze blows across my face.

Suddenly from behind me, I hear a familiar voice call out, "Louis! Hello, old friend!" I spin around to see Vincent sitting behind me in the field at his easel. As he stands up, I race over to hug him, exclaiming, "It is so good to see you, my brother. I was heartbroken when I lost you."

He says, happily, "You cannot lose an old friend like me. We just move away for a while. We will always meet again eventually in some other time and some other place."

After my surprise at seeing Vincent subsides, I notice that we are on a raised wood-plank floor about 10-feet square. Two tilted head-high walls, each with an open window, stretch along the back and join at the far corner. The room, if you can call it that, reminds me of his bedroom in Arles, except that it has no roof and has two walls missing. In the middle of the floor, a single chair sits alongside Vincent's easel.

"Is this real?" I ask him, doubtfully, motioning to the room with my hand.

"No," he answers cheerfully, "I created it for you so that you would feel at ease." *[See inset.]*

Shaking my head, smiling, I respond, "Am I supposed to feel at ease in a room with no roof and only two tilted walls?"

"Oh, well," he shrugs, "that part was for me. I never liked being under a roof."

I laugh, observing, "Same old Vincent – but is this the same old Earth?"

"Well, yes and no. They are real," he answers, pointing to the farmers out in the fields. "Those are Earth people. However, they cannot see us, since we are no longer wearing Earth bodies. They cannot see my lovely open house either, since it is not made of Earth stuff."

> ## Astral Worlds
> The physical world is the realm of matter, whereas the astral world, where we go after death, is the realm of thoughts. Events happen there much more rapidly. In fact, they move at the "speed of thought" even faster than the speed of light. Events appear to be much more fluid and dreamlike there, since, as a matter-of-fact, during our dreams, we actually visit the astral worlds.
>
> In the afterlife, if a soul thinks of something, then it usually appears instantly. Such was the case of Vincent's room. He thought of it, and it appeared for both of us to see.

After overcoming my joy at seeing my old friend, I ask, "What are you painting?" Curious, I begin to walk around behind the easel.

Vincent quickly holds out a hand to stop me. "You cannot look at it yet," he says hastily. "It is another portrait of you, and you must wait until I finish. Otherwise, you are such a harsh critic that if you look at it early, you will certainly say that it does not look like you, as you did in Arles. Just stand there for a few moments and be patient – if you can." He smiles at me knowingly.

He begins painting furiously with his brush moving at a frantic pace. Finally, overcome with curiosity, I lean just slightly forward and to the left to catch a glimpse of what he is doing.

"Will you be *still!*" he suddenly shouts at me.

He startles me for a moment, but now we both break into laughter. "It has been a while since I heard those words," I respond, still laughing.

As he goes back to work, I look at him directly to say with a slight smile, "Vincent, I hope you paint it better than last time. My eyes were tilted then, as you might recall."

With mock seriousness, he looks up to say, "Well, that was not my fault, Louis. You would not sit still then either. It was hard to tell exactly where you eyes were supposed to be. You kept moving them around!" We both laugh again.

Before long, he steps back from the painting, cocking his head a little to one side and now the other. "All right, it is finished," he announces.

Eagerly, I walk around the easel to look at the painting. There on the canvas, made with Vincent's typical swirling brush strokes, is a scene of a brilliant night sky filled with stars. However, unlike his earthly artwork, the stars on the painting twinkle brightly like real stars, and the pigment flows slowly around in ever-moving, multihued rivulets.

Intrigued, I bend closer to get a better look. "This time, it truly does not look like me *at all,*" I complain. "I am not anywhere any in it. It contains only stars."

"See, I knew you would say that," complains Vincent with a straight face.

"You are in there; you are just very, very small."

"Where?" I ask doubtfully, leaning closer.

"Pick a star," he says with that familiar chuckle.

Figure 4-65. "I complain that it does not look at all like me." *[Detail of Vincent's "Starry Night," June 1889. Reprinted from Elgar (1958).]*

Now it dawns on me – stars again – and we both have a good laugh. "All right, which one is your star?" I ask him.

"In a minute. You choose first," he says, as he puts his big hand on my shoulder. "Go ahead. Pick one."

Leaning closer to the liquid ever-changing canvas, I study the star-field carefully, finally pointing to a bright one that seems to call out to me.

"Nice choice," he says. Now, studying the painting, he points to a different one nearby. "That one is mine this time."

"So we will not be going together?" I ask, feeling a twinge of regret.

Straightening up, he says simply, "No, but we will meet again ... and again ... and again. We go way back." He pauses for a moment and says, "It will take a little while to remember your past lives, so I will try to tweak your memory. Do you recall, just before your overdose, how I got very excited about Buddhism and life-after-death?" As I nod, he continues, "I painted a few canvases with Japanese themes, you know, like the bridge in the rain. Do you remember that one?"

"Yes and there was the pear tree," I add. "They were all very different from any of your other paintings. I loved them all a lot."

"Do you know why? It was because we shared a lifetime in Japan, as Buddhist monks, of all things. In Arles, I did that self-portrait looking like a shorn monk contemplating the Eternal Buddha. I had a vision in my head of that one and painted it in just a few hours. I must say, though, that I do not look the same now as I did in that lifetime. Not too many red-haired monks in Japan!" He winks at me. *[See inset.]*

Figure 4-66. Vincent's "Blossoming Pear Tree," April 1888. *[Reprinted from Faille (1939).]*

Flash Forward
As I meditated on my former life with Vincent, I saw a vision of him as a Zen monk in this previous lifetime that he and I had shared.

Reawakening some of the experiences from that lifetime with him in Japan, I studied as a Zen Buddhist monk for several years in California, complete with robes and shaved head, much like Vincent in the painting. The lifestyle felt very familiar to me and was much more peaceful than my life as Louis had been!

Figure 4-67. Detail of Vincent's "Self-Portrait" as a monk, Sep. 1888. *[Reprinted from Tralbaut (1959).]*

I shake my head in amazement, "Monks! Well, now, there is a radical change. How in the world did we go from being meditative, ascetic monks to being hedonistic Parisians?" I ask laughing.

He responds, "I guess, dear Louis, that we decided we had too much tranquility in our lives and needed more trouble. Did you get enough trouble this time?" he asks with a mischievous smile.

I screw up my face and nod my head vigorously, "Enough for two lifetimes! In fact, I believe that in this lifetime, unlike you, I actually died *twice!*" He laughs good-naturedly.

Looking back at the star painting, I say a little wistfully, "I will miss you, old friend. You always add a touch of adventure and liveliness to any lifetime."

He smiles, "Time will pass quickly where we are going, much faster than here. I predict that we will meet again soon, my friend, and many times again after that."

He puts his hand on my shoulder affectionately, and I smile in return. My love for this great soul floods my heart and threatens to spill out as tears. To change the subject, I quickly look down at the canvas again, "What is it like where I am going? Do you know? Is it an earth world, a physical planet?"

"It is a heaven world," he says. "This has been an intense life for both of us, and now, we get a vacation, so to speak. It will not be difficult like Earth, but of course, we cannot stay there forever. We will choose to come back down to Earth again after that. Even though life on Earth is difficult, we can progress faster here."

He pauses for a moment as I study the canvas and continues, "By the way, even though we will be separated for a while, you will know me when we meet again. I will be the thin, grumpy man with red hair." He winks to show that he is teasing. Now, he says simply, "Time to go."

We look at each other for a moment, knowing that there is no more to say. Now, we silently hug each other, gripping each other in a powerful embrace, just two old friends who love and accept each other.

"Ready? All together now," he says, poising his finger over his own star. A little hesitantly, I reach out towards mine. Just before I do, Vincent says happily, "Bon voyage, my friend. Bon voyage!"

Figure 4-68. "I point to my star, and there is a flash of light!" *[Detail of Vincent's "Road to Provence." Reprinted from Meier-Graefe (1922).]*

I salute him with "*Au revoir, mon ami!* Until we meet again!" When our fingers contact the swirling pigment on the canvas, there is a blinding flash of light.

As the light dims a little, Vincent is gone, along with all trace of earth. I am out in space, surrounded by countless radiant stars, except I never saw starlight like this from earth. It shimmers and shines like a rainbow or like the aurora, and there is music with it, faint music that ebbs and flows to match the intensity of the light. The reddish stars make the lower bass tones, and the blue ones are treble. I am overwhelmed with the incredible beauty of it all.

Now, an angelic woman appears ahead of me, with flowing golden hair and robes of radiant white. Floating down towards me from out of the light of one of the brighter stars, she is smiling, luminous, and lovely … and very familiar. Stopping in front of me, she wavers slowly as if floating on the gentle waves of an invisible sea. Her voice is a flowing melody, and her words are lyrical:

Welcome back, my son.
Always know that you are Spirit.
You are not an earthbound body.
You never have been;
you never can be.

You have lived in many bodies
which all have crumbled to dust.
You, however, are still alive.
You always have been;
you always will be.

The truth is:
you are Spirit.

Ecstatic in her presence, the lifetime as Louis fades from my mind like some dream that never happened. "Who are you?" I ask simply.

She says, "In your last lifetime on earth, I was one of your spiritual guides, and I will be your guide in this world, as well. You have been like a son to me, a spiritual son."

Curious about this, I ask, "Have I ever been your actual son?"

"No," she says simply. "It has not been necessary for me to incarnate on physical planets. My work is only on the astral worlds, though I often work with those who have chosen the difficult mission of incarnating on worlds like Earth.

"With all the care of an earthly mother, though, I have watched over you throughout your lifetime there, unseen behind your troubles and pain. Like an earthly mother, sometimes I had to remain in the background and let you grow and experience life as you chose. It was not my task to prevent you from falling or being hurt, but I was always there afterwards to quietly help you turn your woes into wisdom, though often you were not aware of my presence.

"I was always there for you, never forsaking you, even though there were times when you turned away from the ways of truth and spirit. I will always be here for you, wherever you are, and whenever you need someone that cares about you."

She smiles at me lovingly, and her love and beauty are so overwhelming that I cannot say anything. My joy is so intense that my thoughts grow still, as I bask in her radiant love.

"Is there anything you wish to ask? Anything you need to know about your life as Louis?" she asks.

"No," I answer quietly, finding my voice.

She continues, "When you almost died that night with Vincent, you were not happy with your life. How do you feel about it now?"

"After I went back to the body, I did the best I could. I changed, and now I am satisfied," I reply.

Figure 4-69. Vincent's "Figure of an Angel," Sept. 1889. *[Reprinted from Faille (1939).]*

"Good. Are you ready to move on?" she asks, smiling radiantly.

I can only nod. Powerful feelings of love burst into my consciousness, like sparkling fireworks. Such a simple smile to produce such an overwhelming feeling. She holds out her hand to me, and I take it. I do not know her name, but I recognize who she is – someone who accepts me unconditionally, someone who loves me just as I am, without judgment. I return that love to her as much as I can in my own small way.

I do not know where we are going, but it does not matter. I would go anywhere with her – and so, I do.

Life Review & Analysis

GROUP-LINKS: In every lifetime, there are many connections to other souls in our past. Becoming aware of those connections in each lifetime is vital to a better understanding of our present circumstances. This is particularly true of interpersonal relationships, which typically have roots deep in the past. These connections are one of the reasons we say, "History repeats itself." Often, the same souls are the ones doing the repeating. Here are some from Louis' lifetime:

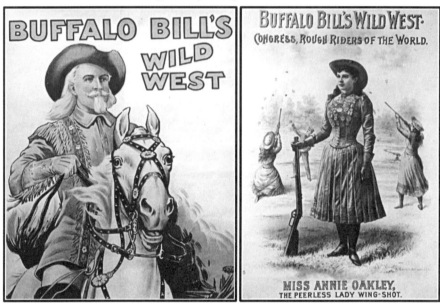

Figure 4-70. Posters of Buffalo Bill and Annie Oakley. *[Courtesy Denver Public Library, Western History Coll.; Salsbury, NS-245.]*

GROUP-LINK: "The Buffalo Bill Cancan," My Wild West Connection.

In the 1870s and 1880s, Louis read American dime novels about Buffalo Bill Cody, Annie Oakley, and Sitting Bull, reawakening his fascination with the Indians. In 1889, when Louis attended the Paris Exposition (the World's Fair), he was spellbound by Buffalo Bill's Wild West Show. Cody's shows, along with others like it, toured Europe from 1889 until the outbreak of WWI in 1914, which coincided with Louis' death.

In a link to the past lifetime as Sorrel Horse, Louis saw several members of Cody's show who had been at the Little Bighorn, including the following:

Figure 4-71. Wild West Show photo of Walks-under-the-Ground posing with Prince Louka, a Russian Cossack and fellow cast member. *[Ca. 1890, courtesy Denver Public Library, Western History Coll.; Salsbury, NS-141.]*

Walks-under-the-Ground (probably born circa 1840): He was one of the Lakota warriors that had hidden in the bushes alongside Sorrel Horse at Medicine Tail Coulee. When the troopers rushed the ford, Walks-under-the-Ground wounded Custer, thereby changing the course of the battle.

After the Indian Wars were over, Walks-under-the-Ground became a star performer in Buffalo Bill's show. He traveled to many cities in the U.S. and crossed by boat to Europe for a multi-city tour. Louis saw him in Paris in 1889.

Figure 4-72. Chief Iron Tail, along with the Indian Head Nickel. *[Photo courtesy Denver Public Library, Western History Coll.; X-31830. Coin photos courtesy of the US Mint.]*

Iron Tail (ca. 1850-1916): As war chief and aide to Sitting Bull at the Little Bighorn, he was deeply involved in the battle. He was well known to Sorrel Horse, since he was one of the top leaders of the boy's adopted tribe.

Buffalo Bill invited him to join the show when it toured Europe in 1889. His image was so striking that he was one of three Indians who were used as models for the Indian Head Nickel. Two Moons, who led Sorrel Horse in the final charge against Custer, was one of the other two models.

Figure 4-73. Early Texas oil field *[Ca. 1919. Courtesy of the Library of Congress.]*

GROUP-LINK: "'Texas Tea' for Two," my Oil Connection

When wildcatters first discovered oil in Texas, the news made international headlines. In 1894, Louis excitedly read newspaper reports about the discovery of a huge oil field under the city of Corsicana, Texas. By 1898, after nearly 300 wells had been drilled, the field was producing a staggering 50,000 barrels daily, which was a sizeable percentage of the entire world's output of oil at that time.

These discoveries created a worldwide sensation, fueling an international "oil rush." Seeing these headlines, Louis, who had always loved excitement, developed a strong desire to become an oil wildcatter. Nevertheless, despite his intentions to go to the oil fields of Texas, he never went. Instead, he invested in oil partnerships from a distance and profited from them.

However, those karmic desires did not die, and about 80 years later in my current lifetime, I became an oil well operator in Corsicana, Texas, the same city that Louis had read about so avidly. At one point, our company owned over 40 oil wells. One of them turned out to have been among the first sensational discovery wells that Louis had read about in France. After 80 years, the well was still producing oil profitably.

This incident is a prime example of how desires or actions in one lifetime can manifest in another one, sometimes compelling us to do things that seem totally out of character, such as, for me, becoming a Texas oilman. By recognizing these compulsions from the past, we can take control of them, giving us the choice either to undo them or to play them out, as we choose.

Lessons Learned

Recalling past life memories is useful only if one uses them to become happier and freer in the present lifetime. Reliving this lifetime as Louis brought up many powerful buried feelings:

- *Grief* over the suicide of Vincent.
- *Fear of dying* during the drug overdose.
- *Disdain* for pampered aristocrats, even though he was born one.
- *Lust for drugs and alcohol* coupled with *despair* from addiction.
- *Addiction to sex* with the prostitutes of Montmartre.
- *Frustration* over being rejected several times by Margot.

As I became aware of each of these feelings, I worked to undo them, using mostly the Sedona Method mentioned in Appendix A1. As I let go of all of these past highly charged memories, I felt instantly happier. Even though these memories were far in the distant past, they still had been affecting me on a hidden level. Undoing them has helped me to live more in the present moment. Anyone can do the same thing with past life recall.

As with any lifetime, there were good moments to go with the bad. Here are some of the positive things that Louis experienced:

- *Developing artistic inspiration* by being around the intensely creative Vincent van Gogh, as well as other artists.
- *Exploring nontraditional spirituality*, as expressed by Vincent and Paul, who were very religious in a unique way that inspired Louis.
- *Overcoming addiction* to drugs and sex.
- *Developing an egalitarian worldview* in which all men and women truly are equal in the eyes of God.
- *Experiencing deep love* for two beautiful and loving women – Louis' wife and daughter.

NOTE: Appendix A contains information about some simple yet very powerful spiritual techniques. They can free you from the undesirable effects of past lives and allow you to get the best out of your current life.

Alive 5 times

Testimonial: I personally use all three of the following techniques, and they work very well for me. They should work well for you, too. I highly recommend all of them, especially since none are difficult, and, in fact, all of them are quite enjoyable.

Disclaimer: Please note, however, that the organizations involved with these techniques do not necessarily endorse all of the concepts in this book. They may have their own way of explaining the physical world and the world of spirit.

Appendix A1: The Sedona Method ©

At the early age of 42, Lester Levenson was terminally ill. When he suffered a second heart attack, his doctors told him that he had only days to live. Sick, depressed, and unhappy, Lester went home to die.

It was the turning point of his life. His illness caused him to question his life to the very core of his being. That questioning led to startling discoveries about how to achieve lasting happiness and inner peace.

The process that he developed has become known to others as the Sedona Method. Totally cured, Lester taught his method to thousands of people for more than 40 years, allowing them to benefit just as he did.

The Method is an extremely simple but highly effective technique for "letting go," or "releasing," the mental and emotional blocks to abundance, health, happiness, and success. Using it allows anyone to enjoy a life that is happier, more productive, more satisfying, more loving, and more joyous.

Today, live seminars are presented in many of the principle cities in the U.S., as well as in Canada, Europe, and Australia. In addition, the Sedona Method Course is available on audiotape for use in the privacy of your home.

[Note: The Sedona Method is a generic technique that does not deal directly with past life recall; it deals with their effects. In fact, reincarnation is never mentioned in the course, even though the founder personally experienced past life recall many times. Nevertheless, the process is an extremely fast and powerful way to undo the negative effects of past lives, such as unwanted emotions, physical discomforts, etc.]

For a FREE AUDIO TAPE and to learn more about the Sedona Method, visit this website:
www.sedona.com/cgi-bin/protrack/link.cgi?910ST
Sedona Training Associates
60 Tortilla Drive, Sedona, AZ 86336
Phone: Toll free: (888) 282-5656; or (928) 282-3522
Books URL: www.lightrise.com/books

Lester's Amazing Story

(Courtesy of Sedona Training Associates)

I was born July 19, 1909 in Elizabeth, New Jersey into a middle-class family as a very shy person. I tried to do things the way they were supposed to be done – doing the right thing, getting a good education, and being the best in my field. My natural inclination was towards science, especially the science of the world, and of man himself. I graduated from Rutgers University in 1931 as a physicist, after which I worked 20 some years in physics and engineering.

I also went into various businesses, including restaurants, lumber, building, and oil, intertwined with engineering, wanting to make money– wanting to make it in the world. At that time, I did not know what I now know – that what I was seeking was actually the answers to life itself. And nothing that I had worked at would give me that answer. As the years went by, I became heavy with depression and with sickness. By 1952, I had been through constant illness – I even had jaundice three or so times a year. I had an enlarged liver, kidney stones, spleen trouble, hyper and hypoacidity, ulcers that perforated and formed lesions, and to top it off, I had 10 years of migraine headaches.

This all culminated in 1952 when I had my second coronary thrombosis. I was told I would not live much longer – that I might die any day and shouldn't make the effort to take so much as a step unless I necessarily had to. I was extremely fearful of dying, but I said to myself, "You're still breathing, Lester – there is still a chance."

An intense fear of dying overwhelmed me, the fear that I might drop dead any minute. This stayed with me for days. I went through a real, horrible, low, spinning period there, in the grip of intense fear of dying or of being a cripple for the rest of my life in that I wouldn't be able to be active. How could I take care of all that, and me? I felt that life would not be worthwhile any more. This caused me to conclude with determination, "Either I get the answers, or I'll take me off this earth. No heart attack will do it!" I had a nice easy way to do it, too. I had morphine the doctors gave me.

Well, I was always a smart boy, always made the honor roll. Even got myself a four-year scholarship to Rutgers University at a time when scholarships were very rare ... "But what does this avail me? Nothing! Here I am with all this brilliance, as miserable and scared as can be."

"Having lived 42 or so years, and having reached the end of the line without happiness, without health – all this knowledge you have accumulated is of no avail."

I had studied Watson's Behaviorism in the 30s and Freud's [works] in the late 30s and early 40s. I had studied the philosophies. I had studied logic. I studied economics. I studied all the major fields of man, and with all that knowledge there; I was at the end of the line. This made me realize that the accumulated knowledge of man was of no use.

Then I said, "Lester, you were not only not smart, you were dumb! Dumb! Dumb! There's something wrong in your intellect. With all your knowledge, you've come to this bottom end! Drop all this knowledge you've so studiously picked up on philosophy, psychology, social science, and economics! It is of no avail! Start from scratch. Begin all over again your search for the answers."

And with an extreme desperation and intense wanting out—not wanting to die, I began to question, "What am I? What is this world? What is my relationship to it? What do I want from it?"

"Happiness."

"Well, what is happiness?"

"Being loved."

"But I am loved. I know several very desirable girls with beauty, charm, and intellect who want me. And I have the esteem of my friends. Yet, I'm miserable!"

I sensed that the closest thing related to happiness was love. So I began reviewing and reliving my past love affairs, looking at the points where the little happiness that I had were. I began to pull up and dissect all my high moments of loving.

Suddenly, I got an inkling that it was when I was *loving* that I had the highest feeling!

I remembered one evening, a beautiful balmy evening, in the mountains when I was camping with Virginia. We were both lying on the grass, both looking up at the sky, and I had my arm around her. The nirvana, the perfection of the height of happiness was right there. I was feeling how great love for Virginia is! How wonderful is knowing all this nature! How perfect a setting!

Then I saw that it was my loving her that was the cause of this happiness! Not the beauty of the setting, or being with Virginia.

Then I immediately turned to the other side. Boy it was great when she loved me! I remembered the moment when publicly this beautiful, charming girl told the world that she approved of Lester, she loved Lester—and I could feel that nice feeling of approval. But I sensed that it was not as great as what I had just discovered. It was not a lasting feeling. It was just for the moment. In order for me to have that feeling continuously, she had to continue saying that.

So, this momentary ego approval was not as great as the feeling of loving her! As long as I was loving her, I felt so happy. But when she loved me, there were only moments of happiness when she gave me approval.

Days of further cogitation gradually revealed to me that this was correct! I was happier when I loved her than I was when I got that momentary ego-satisfaction when she loved me. Her loving me was a momentary pleasure that needed constant showing and proving on her part, while my loving her was a constant happiness, as long as I was loving her.

I concluded that my happiness equated to my loving! If I could increase my loving, then I could increase my happiness! This was the first inkling I had as to what brings about happiness. And it was a tremendous thing because I hadn't had happiness. And I said, "Gee, if this is the key to happiness, I've got the greatest!" Even the hope of getting more and more happiness was a tremendous thing, because this was the number one thing I wanted—happiness.

That started me on weeks and weeks of reviewing my past love affairs. I dug up from the past, incident after incident when I thought I was loving, and I discovered that I was being nice to my girlfriends, trying to get them to love me, and that was selfish. That was not really love. That was just wanting my ego bolstered!

I kept reviewing incidents from the past, and where I saw that I was not loving, I would change that feeling to loving that person. Instead of wanting them to do something for me, I would change it to my wanting to do something for them. I kept this up until I couldn't find any more incidents to work on.

This insight on love, seeing that happiness was determined by my capacity to love, was a tremendous insight. It began to free me, and any bit of freedom when you're plagued feels so good. I knew that I was in the right direction. I had gotten hold of a link of the chain of happiness and was determined not to let go until I had the entire chain.

I felt a greater freedom. There was an easier concentration of my mind because of it. And I began to look better at my mind. What is my mind? What is intelligence?

Suddenly, a picture flashed of amusement park bumper-cars that are difficult to steer so that they continually bump into each other. They all get their electrical energy from the wire screen above the cars through a pole coming down to every car.

The power above was symbolic of the overall intelligence and energy of the universe coming down the pole to me and everyone else, and to the degree we step on the gas do we use it. Each driver of the cars is taking the amount of energy and intelligence that he wants from that wire, but he steers his car blindly and bumps into other cars, and bumps and bumps.

I saw that if I chose to, I could take more and more of that overall intelligence.

And so I dug into that. I began to examine thinking and its relationship to what was happening. And it was revealed that everything that was happening had a prior thought behind it and that I never before related the thought and the happening because of the element of time between the two.

When I saw that everything that was happening to me had a thought of it before it happened, I realized that if I could grab hold of this, I could consciously determine everything that was happening to me!

And above all, I saw that I was responsible for everything that had happened to me, formerly thinking that the world was abusing me! I saw that my whole past life, and all that tremendous effort to make money and in the end, failing, was due only to my thinking!

This was a tremendous piece of freedom: to think that I was not a victim of this world. I saw that it lay within my power to arrange the world the way I wanted it to be; that rather than being an effect of it, I could now be at cause over it and arrange it the way I would like it to be!

That was a tremendous realization, a tremendous feeling of freedom!

I was so ill when I started my searching; I had one foot in the grave. And when I saw that my thinking was cause for what was happening to me, I immediately saw my body from my chin down to my toes as perfect. And instantly, I knew it was perfect! I knew the lesions and adhesions of my intestine due to perforated ulcers were undone. I knew everything within me was in perfect running order.

And it was.

Discovering that my happiness equated to my loving, discovering that my thinking was the cause of things happening to me in my life gave me more and more freedom. Freedom from unconscious compulsions that I had to work, I had to make money, and I had to have girls. Freedom in the feeling that I was now able to determine my destiny, I was now able to control my world, I was now able to arrange my environment to suit me. This new freedom lightened my internal burden so greatly that I felt that I had no need to do anything.

Plus, the new happiness I was experiencing was so great! I was experiencing a joy that I had never known existed. I had never dreamed happiness could be so great.

I determined: "If this is so great, I'm not going to let go of it until I carry it all the way!" I had no idea how joyous a person could be.

So, I began digging further on how to extend this joy. I began further changing my attitudes on love. I would imagine the girl I wanted most marrying one of my friends, or the boy I would want her to marry least, and then enjoy their enjoying each other. To me, this was the extreme in loving, and if I could achieve it, that would give me more of this wonderful thing that I was experiencing.

And so I worked on it. I took a particular fellow, Burl, and a particular girl, and I wouldn't let go until I could really feel the joy of their enjoying each other.

Then I knew I had it—or almost had it.

Later on, I had further tests of this in talking to people who were opposing me no end when I was trying to help them. I would consciously feel the greatest love for them when they were attacking me. And the joy of loving them was so wonderful, I would, without any thought, thank them so profusely for having given me the opportunity of talking with them, that it threw them into a dither.

Not that the world ever stopped pushing against me – it continued – but I was at a place where I could resolve things almost immediately. Having cleared out the negative fears, all the negative "I can not's," I would focus right on the answer to every problem and get it very quickly. And so, my whole life turned around from being depressed and sick, to being happy and in perfect health all the time!

One of the things that happened in this process was my identification with others. I saw that we are all related, that we are all interconnected – each mind is like a radio broadcasting and receiving station. That we are all tuned into each other unconsciously – that we are just not aware of it. That life was meant to be beautiful … meant to be happy all the time with no sorrow … and to be with perfect health. And so after reaching that high point of understanding in 1952, I wanted to help others discover what I discovered.

The glory is in knowing what you really are. It's a tremendous experience, it's an ecstasy, a euphoria. There are no real words to describe it because, well, we're in an age where these things are not experienced and therefore not understood, so how can there be words for things that are not understood?

There are no words to describe these feelings, they're so beyond present understanding. So you pick the words you know best to describe it and that's it. Paramhansa Yogananda uses the words "ever-new joy welling up every second," and that's a practical way of describing it. At first, it's a joy that spills over every second, just keeps pouring out—you feel as though you can't contain it.

Later on, it resolves itself into a very profound peace, the most peaceful peace you could ever imagine … the peace that passeth all understanding. It's a deep, deep peace. You move in the world, the body moves, but you have absolute peace all the time. Bombs could be dropping all around you and you have that perfect peace, regardless of what's going on.

I believe if I can do it, anyone can do it.

For a FREE AUDIO TAPE and to learn more about the Sedona Method, visit this website:
   www.sedona.com/cgi-bin/protrack/link.cgi?910ST
Sedona Training Associates
60 Tortilla Drive, Sedona, AZ 86336
Phone: Toll free: (888) 282-5656; or (928) 282-3522
Books URL: www.lightrise.com/books

Appendix A2: Meditation & Yoga

Paramahansa Yogananda
[Reprinted from Yogananda (1946).]

Paramahansa Yogananda was one of the first spiritual teachers to come from India to the West, bringing the message of Eastern spirituality to the materialistic West. Part of his mission was to show the basic harmony among all of the world's great religions.

Yogananda is well known for his book *Autobiography of a Yogi*, considered a rare spiritual classic. *[Excerpts are included below in this section.]* When it was first published in 1946, it was the first time that an authentic Hindu yogi had written his life story for a Western audience. Describing in vivid detail his many years of spiritual training under a Christlike master, Sri Yukteswar, Yogananda revealed a fascinating and little-known phase of modern India. The subtle but definite laws by which yogis perform miracles and attain complete self-mastery are explained with a scientific clarity.

There are colorful chapters on the author's visits to Mahatma Gandhi and to many other genuine Eastern saints throughout India. The section dealing with Yogananda's Western experiences includes a chapter on his great friend Luther Burbank and an account of the author's pilgrimage to Bavaria in 1935 to meet Therese Neumann, the amazing Catholic stigmatist.

In addition, Yogananda created *The Self-Realization Fellowship Lessons*, a home-study work-at-your-own-pace series, which gives systematic instructions in his methods of meditation and energization. I highly recommend these techniques, which are simple yet very powerful, allowing one to recharge the body with energy, to reawaken the mind's unlimited power, and to experience personal awareness of the Divine.

Where to get Yogananda's Lessons:
Web URL: www.paramahansayogananda.org/lessons/index.html
Self-Realization Fellowship
3880 San Rafael Avenue, Los Angeles, CA 90065-3298 USA
Phone: (323) 225-2471 (9am to 5pm PST)
Books URL: www.lightrise.com/books

Song of the Morning Yoga Retreat Center

Operated by Golden Lotus, Inc., the Retreat provides its visitors with a great place for relaxation and spiritual refreshment.

It was founded in 1970 by a highly advanced disciple of Paramahansa Yogananda, **Yogacharya J. Oliver Black** (below), who passed away in 1989 at the age of 96. Yogacharya and the beautiful woodland retreat have been sources of inspiration for thousands of visitors from all over the world.

Bob Raymer (right), Spiritual Director of Song of the Morning and a direct disciple of Paramahansa Yogananda, was ordained as a minister by Yogananda in 1951 to teach the science of self-realization. To be in Bob's presence is a rare opportunity to catch the true spirit of meditation, which goes far beyond a teaching or technique. Through his talks, presence, and gentle guidance, he serves as a catalyst for spiritual awakening in others.

The Clear Light Community is located on the same scenic forested land on which the Retreat is located. Leased lots for private homes are available, each of which has its own particularly beautiful characteristics. If you would like more information about living in a spiritually oriented community, contact Song of the Morning (as shown below). Tours are available by appointment.

Golden Lotus and Song of the Morning exist for the primary purpose of practicing and teaching yoga in all of its physical, mental, and spiritual applications. Yogananda's teachings are nonsectarian, are easily practiced, and offer practical solutions to the challenges of modern life.

To visit the Retreat or to be part of a Live-in Community, contact:
Song of the Morning Yoga Retreat Center
9607 Sturgeon Valley Road, Vanderbilt, MI 49725-9742
Phone: (989) 983-4107
Web URL: www.goldenlotus.org

[Photos and copy courtesy of Golden Lotus, Inc.]

Autobiography of a Yogi by Paramahansa Yogananda
(Reprinted from the original 1946 Edition)

> The following is an excerpt in which Yogananda relates a description of the astral or spirit worlds by his spiritual teacher, Yukteswar. As the story opens, Yukteswar had recently passed into spirit in March 1936. Yogananda had developed an intense longing to see his teacher again, and finally in June 1936, his wish was fulfilled.

Chapter 43. *The Resurrection of Sri Yukteswar*

Sri Yukteswar (1855-1936)
[Reprinted from Yogananda (1946).]

.... I was roused from my meditation by a beatific light. Before my open and astonished eyes, the whole room was transformed into a strange world, the sunlight transmuted into supernal splendor.

Waves of rapture engulfed me as I beheld the flesh and blood form of Sri Yukteswar! "My son!" Master spoke tenderly, on his face an angel-bewitching smile.

For the first time in my life, I did not kneel at his feet in greeting but instantly advanced to gather him hungrily in my arms. Moment of moments! The anguish of past months was toll I counted weightless against the torrential bliss now descending.

"Master mine, beloved of my heart, why did you leave me?" I was incoherent in an excess of joy....

"... I left you only for a little while; am I not with you again?"

"But is it you, Master, the same Lion of God? Are you wearing a body like the one I buried beneath the cruel Puri sands?"

"Yes, my child, I am the same. This is a flesh and blood body. Though I see it as ethereal, to your sight it is physical. From the cosmic atoms, I created an entirely new body, exactly like that cosmic-dream physical body which you laid beneath the dream-sands at Puri in your dream-world. I am in truth resurrected—not on earth but on an astral planet. Its inhabitants are better able than earthly humanity to meet my lofty standards. There you and your exalted loved ones shall someday come to be with me."

Alive 5 times

"As prophets are sent on earth to help men work out their physical karma, so I have been directed by God to serve on an astral planet as a savior," Sri Yukteswar explained. "It is called Hiranyaloka or 'Illumined Astral Planet.' There I am aiding advanced beings to rid themselves of astral karma and thus attain liberation from astral rebirths. The dwellers on Hiranyaloka are highly developed spiritually; all of them had acquired, in their last earth-incarnation, the meditation-given power of consciously leaving their physical bodies at death.

My mind was now in such perfect attunement with my guru's that he was conveying his word-pictures to me partly by speech and partly by thought-transference. I was thus quickly receiving his idea-tabloids.

"You have read in the scriptures," Master went on, "that God encased the human soul successively in three bodies—the idea, or causal, body; the subtle astral body, seat of man's mental and emotional natures; and the gross physical body. On earth a man is equipped with his physical senses. An astral being works with his consciousness and feelings and a body made of lifetrons.[1] A causal-bodied being remains in the blissful realm of ideas. My work is with those astral beings who are preparing to enter the causal world."

"There are many astral planets, teeming with astral beings," Master began. "The inhabitants use astral planes, or masses of light, to travel from one planet to another, faster than electricity and radioactive energies.

"The astral universe, made of various subtle vibrations of light and color, is hundreds of times larger than the material cosmos. The entire physical creation hangs like a little solid basket under the huge luminous balloon of the astral sphere. Just as many physical suns and stars roam in space, so there are also countless astral solar and stellar systems. Their planets have astral suns and moons, more beautiful than the physical ones. The astral luminaries resemble the aurora borealis—the sunny astral aurora being more dazzling than the mild-rayed moon-aurora. The astral day and night are longer than those of earth.

"The astral world is infinitely beautiful, clean, pure, and orderly. There are no dead planets or barren lands. The terrestrial blemishes—weeds, bacteria, insects, snakes—are absent. Unlike the variable climates and seasons of the earth, the astral planets maintain the even temperature of an eternal spring, with occasional luminous white snow and rain of many-colored lights. Astral planets abound in opal lakes and bright seas and rainbow rivers.

---

[1] Sri Yukteswar used the word prana; I have translated it as lifetrons. The Hindu scriptures refer not only to the anu, "atom," and to the paramanu, "beyond the atom," finer electronic energies; but also to prana, "creative lifetronic force." Atoms and electrons are blind forces; prana is inherently intelligent. The pranic lifetrons in the spermatozoa and ova, for instance, guide the embryonic development according to a karmic design.

"The ordinary astral universe—not the subtler astral heaven of Hiranyaloka—is peopled with millions of astral beings who have come, more or less recently, from the earth, and also with myriads of fairies, mermaids, fishes, animals, goblins, gnomes, demigods and spirits, all residing on different astral planets in accordance with karmic qualifications. Various spheric mansions or vibratory regions are provided for good and evil spirits. Good ones can travel freely, but the evil spirits are confined to limited zones. In the same way that human beings live on the surface of the earth, worms inside the soil, fish in water, and birds in air, so astral beings of different grades are assigned to suitable vibratory quarters.

"Among the fallen dark angels expelled from other worlds, friction and war take place with lifetronic bombs or mental mantric[2] vibratory rays. These beings dwell in the gloom-drenched regions of the lower astral cosmos, working out their evil karma.

"In the vast realms above the dark astral prison, all is shining and beautiful. The astral cosmos is more naturally attuned than the earth to the divine will and plan of perfection. Every astral object is manifested primarily by the will of God, and partially by the will-call of astral beings. They possess the power of modifying or enhancing the grace and form of anything already created by the Lord. He has given His astral children the freedom and privilege of changing or improving at will the astral cosmos. On earth a solid must be transformed into liquid or other form through natural or chemical processes, but astral solids are changed into astral liquids, gases, or energy solely and instantly by the will of the inhabitants.

"The earth is dark with warfare and murder in the sea, land, and air," my guru continued, "but the astral realms know a happy harmony and equality. Astral beings dematerialize or materialize their forms at will. Flowers or fish or animals can metamorphose themselves, for a time, into astral men. All astral beings are free to assume any form, and can easily commune together. No fixed, definite, natural law hems them round—any astral tree, for example, can be successfully asked to produce an astral mango or other desired fruit, flower, or indeed any other object. Certain karmic restrictions are present, but there are no distinctions in the astral world about desirability of various forms. Everything is vibrant with God's creative light.

"No one is born of woman; offspring are materialized by astral beings through the help of their cosmic will into specially patterned, astrally condensed forms. The recently physically disembodied being arrives in an astral family through invitation, drawn by similar mental and spiritual tendencies.

---

2   Adjective of mantra: chanted seed-sounds discharged by the mental gun of concentration. The Puranas (ancient shastras or treatises) describe these mantric wars between devas and asuras (gods and demons). An asura once tried to slay a deva with a potent chant. But due to mispronunciation, the mental bomb acted as a boomerang and killed the demon.

"The astral body is not subject to cold or heat or other natural conditions. The anatomy includes an astral brain, or the thousand-petaled lotus of light, and six awakened centers in the sushumna, or astral cerebro-spinal axis. The heart draws cosmic energy as well as light from the astral brain, and pumps it to the astral nerves and body cells, or lifetrons. Astral beings can affect their bodies by lifetronic force or by mantric vibrations.

"The astral body is an exact counterpart of the last physical form. Astral beings retain the same appearance which they possessed in youth in their previous earthly sojourn; occasionally an astral being chooses, like myself, to retain his old age appearance." Master, emanating the very essence of youth, chuckled merrily.

"Unlike the special, three-dimensional physical world cognized only by the five senses, the astral spheres are visible to the all-inclusive sixth sense—intuition," Sri Yukteswar went on. "By sheer intuitional feeling, all astral beings see, hear, smell, taste, and touch. They possess three eyes, two of which are partly closed. The third and chief astral eye, vertically placed on the forehead, is open. Astral beings have all the outer sensory organs—ears, eyes, nose, tongue, and skin—but they employ the intuitional sense to experience sensations through any part of the body; they can see through the ear, or nose, or skin. They are able to hear through the eyes or tongue, and can taste through the ears or skin, and so forth.[3]

"Man's physical body is exposed to countless dangers, and is easily hurt or maimed; the ethereal astral body may occasionally be cut or bruised but is healed at once by mere willing."

"Gurudeva, are all astral persons beautiful?"

"Beauty in the astral world is known to be a spiritual quality, and not an outward conformation," Sri Yukteswar replied. "Astral beings therefore attach little importance to facial features. They have the privilege, however, of costuming themselves at will with new, colorful, astrally materialized bodies. Just as worldly men don new array for gala events, so astral beings find occasions to bedeck themselves in specially designed forms.

"Friends of other lives easily recognize one another in the astral world," Sri Yukteswar went on in his beautiful, flutelike voice. "Rejoicing at the immortality of friendship, they realize the indestructibility of love, often doubted at the time of the sad, delusive partings of earthly life.

"The intuition of astral beings pierces through the veil and observes human activities on earth, but man cannot view the astral world unless his sixth sense is somewhat developed. Thousands of earth-dwellers have momentarily glimpsed an astral being or an astral world.

---

[3] Examples of such powers are not wanting even on earth, as in the case of Helen Keller and other rare beings.

~ ~ ~

"Communication among the astral inhabitants is held entirely by astral telepathy and television; there is none of the confusion and misunderstanding of the written and spoken word which earth-dwellers must endure. Just as persons on the cinema screen appear to move and act through a series of light pictures, and do not actually breathe, so the astral beings walk and work as intelligently guided and coordinated images of light, without the necessity of drawing power from oxygen. Man depends upon solids, liquids, gases, and energy for sustenance; astral beings sustain themselves principally by cosmic light."

"Master mine, do astral beings eat anything?" I was drinking in his marvelous elucidations with the receptivity of all my faculties—mind, heart, soul. Superconscious perceptions of truth are permanently real and changeless, while fleeting sense experiences and impressions are never more than temporarily or relatively true, and soon lose in memory all their vividness. My guru's words were so penetratingly imprinted on the parchment of my being that at any time, by transferring my mind to the superconscious state, I can clearly relive the divine experience.

"Luminous ray-like vegetables abound in the astral soils," he answered. "The astral beings consume vegetables, and drink a nectar flowing from glorious fountains of light and from astral brooks and rivers. Just as invisible images of persons on the earth can be dug out of the ether and made visible by a television apparatus, later being dismissed again into space, so the God-created, unseen astral blueprints of vegetables and plants floating in the ether are precipitated on an astral planet by the will of its inhabitants. In the same way, from the wildest fancy of these beings, whole gardens of fragrant flowers are materialized, returning later to the etheric invisibility. Although dwellers on the heavenly planets like Hiranyaloka are almost freed from any necessity of eating, still higher is the unconditioned existence of almost completely liberated souls in the causal world, who eat nothing save the manna of bliss.

"The earth-liberated astral being meets a multitude of relatives, fathers, mothers, wives, husbands, and friends, acquired during different incarnations on earth,[4] as they appear from time to time in various parts of the astral realms. He is therefore at a loss to understand whom to love especially; he learns in this way to give a divine and equal love to all, as children and individualized expressions of God. Though the outward appearance of loved ones may have changed, more or less according to the development of new qualities in the latest life of any particular soul, the astral being employs his unerring intuition to recognize all those once dear to him in other planes of existence, and to welcome them to

---

[4] Lord Buddha was once asked why a man should love all persons equally. "Because," the great teacher replied, "in the very numerous and varied life spans of each man, every other being has at one time or another been dear to him."

their new astral home. Because every atom in creation is inextinguishably dowered with individuality, an astral friend will be recognized no matter what costume he may don, even as on earth an actor's identity is discoverable by close observation despite any disguise.

"The span of life in the astral world is much longer than on earth. A normal advanced astral being's average life period is from five hundred to one thousand years, measured in accordance with earthly standards of time. As certain redwood trees outlive most trees by millenniums, or as some yogis live several hundred years though most men die before the age of sixty, so some astral beings live much longer than the usual span of astral existence. Visitors to the astral world dwell there for a longer or shorter period in accordance with the weight of their physical karma, which draws them back to earth within a specified time.

"The astral being does not have to contend painfully with death at the time of shedding his luminous body. Many of these beings nevertheless feel slightly nervous at the thought of dropping their astral form for the subtler causal one. The astral world is free from unwilling death, disease, and old age. These three dreads are the curse of earth, where man has allowed his consciousness to identify itself almost wholly with a frail physical body requiring constant aid from air, food, and sleep in order to exist at all.

"Physical death is attended by the disappearance of breath and the disintegration of fleshly cells. Astral death consists of the dispersement of lifetrons, those manifest units of energy which constitute the life of astral beings. At physical death, a being loses his consciousness of flesh and becomes aware of his subtle body in the astral world. Experiencing astral death in due time, a being thus passes from the consciousness of astral birth and death to that of physical birth and death. These recurrent cycles of astral and physical encasement are the ineluctable destiny of all unenlightened beings. Scriptural definitions of heaven and hell sometimes stir man's deeper-than-subconscious memories of his long series of experiences in the blithesome astral and disappointing terrestrial worlds."

"The physical karma or desires of man must be completely worked out before his permanent stay in astral worlds becomes possible," my guru elucidated in his thrilling voice. "Two kinds of beings live in the astral spheres. Those who still have earthly karma to dispose of and who must therefore reinhabit a gross physical body in order to pay their karmic debts could be classified, after physical death, as temporary visitors to the astral world rather than as permanent residents.

"Beings with unredeemed earthly karma are not permitted after astral death to go to the high causal sphere of cosmic ideas, but must shuttle to and fro from the physical and astral worlds only .... After each loss of his physical body, however, an undeveloped being from the earth remains for the most part in the deep stupor of the death-sleep and is hardly conscious of the beautiful astral sphere. After the astral rest, such a man returns to the material plane for further lessons, gradually accustoming himself, through repeated journeys, to the worlds of subtle astral texture.

"Normal or long-established residents of the astral universe, on the other hand, are those who, freed forever from all material longings, need return no more to the gross vibrations of earth. Such beings have only astral and causal karma to work out. At astral death, these beings pass to the infinitely finer and more delicate causal world. Shedding the thought-form of the causal body at the end of a certain span, determined by cosmic law, these advanced beings then return to Hiranyaloka or a similar high astral planet, reborn in a new astral body to work out their unredeemed astral karma.

"Now do you understand?" Master smiled so enchantingly!

"Yes, through your grace. I am speechless with joy and gratitude."

Never from song or story had I ever received such inspiring knowledge. Though the Hindu scriptures refer to the causal and astral worlds and to man's three bodies, how remote and meaningless those pages compared with the warm authenticity of my resurrected Master! For him indeed existed not a single "undiscover'd country from whose bourn no traveller returns"!

"The interpenetration of man's three bodies is expressed in many ways through his threefold nature," my great guru went on. "In the wakeful state on earth a human being is conscious more or less of his three vehicles. When he is sensuously intent on tasting, smelling, touching, listening, or seeing, he is working principally through his physical body. Visualizing or willing, he is working mainly through his astral body. His causal medium finds expression when man is thinking or diving deep in introspection or meditation; the cosmical thoughts of genius come to the man who habitually contacts his causal body. In this sense, an individual may be classified broadly as 'a material man,' 'an energetic man,' or 'an intellectual man.'

"A man identifies himself about sixteen hours daily with his physical vehicle. Then he sleeps; if he dreams, he remains in his astral body, effortlessly creating any object even as do the astral beings. If man's sleep be deep and dreamless, for several hours he is able to transfer his consciousness, or sense of I-ness, to the causal body; such sleep is revivifying. A dreamer is contacting his astral and not his causal body; his sleep is not fully refreshing."

I had been lovingly observing Sri Yukteswar while he gave his wondrous exposition.

"Angelic guru," I said, "your body looks exactly as it did when last I wept over it in the Puri ashram."

"O yes, my new body is a perfect copy of the old one. I materialize or dematerialize this form any time at will, much more frequently than I did while on earth. By quick dematerialization, I now travel instantly by light express from planet to planet or, indeed, from astral to causal or to physical cosmos." My divine guru smiled. "Though you move about so fast these days, I had no difficulty in finding you at Bombay!"

"O Master, I was grieving so deeply about your death!"

"Ah, wherein did I die? Isn't there some contradiction?" Sri Yukteswar's eyes were twinkling with love and amusement.

"You were only dreaming on earth; on that earth you saw my dream-body," he went on. "Later you buried that dream-image. Now my finer fleshly body – which you behold and are even now embracing rather closely! – is resurrected on another finer dream-planet of God. Someday that finer dream-body and finer dream-planet will pass away; they too are not forever. All dream-bubbles must eventually burst at a final wakeful touch. Differentiate, my son Yogananda, between dreams and Reality!"

This idea of Vedantic[5] resurrection struck me with wonder. I was ashamed that I had pitied Master when I had seen his lifeless body at Puri. I comprehended at last that my guru had always been fully awake in God, perceiving his own life and passing on earth, and his present resurrection, as nothing more than relativities of divine ideas in the cosmic dream.

"I have now told you, Yogananda, the truths of my life, death, and resurrection. Grieve not for me; rather broadcast everywhere the story of my resurrection from the God-dreamed earth of men to another God-dreamed planet of astrally garbed souls! New hope will be infused into the hearts of misery-mad, death-fearing dreamers of the world."

"Yes, Master!" How willingly would I share with others my joy at his resurrection!

"I leave you now, beloved one!" At these words, I felt Master melting away within my encircling arms.

"My child," his voice rang out, vibrating into my very soul-firmament, "whenever you enter the door of nirbikalpa samadhi[6] and call on me, I shall come to you in flesh and blood, even as today."

With this celestial promise, Sri Yukteswar vanished from my sight. A cloud-voice repeated in musical thunder: "Tell all! Whosoever knows by nirbikalpa

---

[5] Life and death as relativities of thought only. Vedanta points out that God is the only Reality; all creation or separate existence is maya or illusion. This philosophy of monism received its highest expression in the Upanishad commentaries of Shankara.

[6] In sabikalpa samadhi, the devotee has spiritually progressed to a state of inward divine union, but cannot maintain his cosmic consciousness except in the immobile trance-state. By continuous meditation, he reaches the superior state of nirbikalpa samadhi, where he moves freely in the world and performs his outward duties without any loss of God-realization.

realization that your earth is a dream of God can come to the finer dream-created planet of Hiranyaloka, and there find me resurrected in a body exactly like my earthly one. Yogananda, tell all!"

Gone was the sorrow of parting. The pity and grief for his death, long robber of my peace, now fled in stark shame. Bliss poured forth like a fountain through endless, newly opened soul-pores. Anciently clogged with disuse, they now widened in purity at the driving flood of ecstasy. Subconscious thoughts and feelings of my past incarnations shed their karmic taints, lustrously renewed by Sri Yukteswar's divine visit.

In this chapter of my autobiography, I have obeyed my guru's behest and spread the glad tiding, though it confound once more an incurious generation. Groveling, man knows well; despair is seldom alien; yet these are perversities, no part of man's true lot. The day he wills, he is set on the path to freedom. Too long has he hearkened to the dank pessimism of his "dust-thou-art" counselors, heedless of the unconquerable soul.

Where to get Yogananda's Lessons:
Phone: (323) 225-2471 (9am to 5pm PST)
Web URL: www.paramahansayogananda.org/lessons/index.html
Books URL: www.lightrise.com/books

Autobiography of a Yogi by Paramahansa Yogananda
(Reprinted from the original 1946 Edition)

> The following is an excerpt in which Yogananda describes his first experience of Cosmic Consciousness or union with God. All of the world's religions indicate that anyone, with the proper effort, can experience this state of ecstasy.
>
> As we pick up the story, Yogananda had previously abandoned his teacher, Sri Yukteswar, to run off into the Himalayas, seeking enlightenment. Now, seeing his error, he has returned sheepishly to his teacher's ashram.

Chapter 14. *An Experience in Cosmic Consciousness*

Yogananda and Yukteswar (1935)
[Reprinted from Yogananda (1946).]

"I am here, Guruji." My shamefacedness spoke more eloquently for me.

"Let us go to the kitchen and find something to eat." Sri Yukteswar's manner was as natural as if hours and not days had separated us.

"Master, I must have disappointed you by my abrupt departure from my duties here; I thought you might be angry with me."

"No, of course not! Wrath springs only from thwarted desires. I do not expect anything from others, so their actions cannot be in opposition to wishes of mine. I would not use you for my own ends; I am happy only in your own true happiness."

"Sir, one hears of divine love in a vague way, but for the first time I am having a concrete example in your angelic self! In the world, even a father does not easily forgive his son if he leaves his parent's business without warning. But you show not the slightest vexation, though you must have been put to great inconvenience by the many unfinished tasks I left behind."

We looked into each other's eyes, where tears were shining. A blissful wave engulfed me; I was conscious that the Lord, in the form of my guru, was expanding the small ardors of my heart into the incompressible reaches of cosmic love.

A few mornings later, I made my way to Master's empty sitting room. I planned to meditate, but my laudable purpose was unshared by disobedient thoughts. They scattered like birds before the hunter.

"Mukunda!" Sri Yukteswar's voice sounded from a distant inner balcony.

I felt as rebellious as my thoughts. "Master always urges me to meditate," I muttered to myself. "He should not disturb me when he knows why I came to his room."

He summoned me again; I remained obstinately silent. The third time his tone held rebuke.

"Sir, I am meditating," I shouted protesting.

"I know how you are meditating," my guru called out, "with your mind distributed like leaves in a storm! Come here to me."

Snubbed and exposed, I made my way sadly to his side.

"Poor boy, the mountains couldn't give what you wanted." Master spoke caressively, comfortingly. His calm gaze was unfathomable. "Your heart's desire shall be fulfilled."

Sri Yukteswar seldom indulged in riddles; I was bewildered. He struck gently on my chest above the heart.

My body became immovably rooted; breath was drawn out of my lungs as if by some huge magnet. Soul and mind instantly lost their physical bondage, and streamed out like a fluid piercing light from my every pore. The flesh was as though dead, yet in my intense awareness I knew that never before had I been fully alive. My sense of identity was no longer narrowly confined to a body, but embraced the circumambient atoms. People on distant streets seemed to be moving gently over my own remote periphery. The roots of plants and trees appeared through a dim transparency of the soil; I discerned the inward flow of their sap.

The whole vicinity lay bare before me. My ordinary frontal vision was now changed to a vast spherical sight, simultaneously all-perceptive. Through the back of my head, I saw men strolling far down Rai Ghat Road, and noticed also a white cow who was leisurely approaching. When she reached the space in front of the open ashram gate, I observed her with my two physical eyes. As she passed by, behind the brick wall, I saw her clearly still.

All objects within my panoramic gaze trembled and vibrated like quick motion pictures. My body, Master's, the pillared courtyard, the furniture and floor, the trees and sunshine, occasionally became violently agitated, until all melted into a luminescent sea; even as sugar crystals, thrown into a glass of water, dissolve after being shaken. The unifying light alternated with materializations of form, the metamorphoses revealing the law of cause and effect in creation.

An oceanic joy broke upon calm endless shores of my soul. The Spirit of God, I realized, is exhaustless Bliss; His body is countless tissues of light. A swelling glory within me began to envelop towns, continents, the earth, solar and stellar systems, tenuous nebulae, and floating universes. The entire cosmos, gently luminous, like a city seen afar at night, glimmered within the infinitude of my being. The sharply etched global outlines faded somewhat at the farthest edges; there I could see a mellow radiance, ever-undiminished. It was indescribably subtle; the planetary pictures were formed of a grosser light.

The divine dispersion of rays poured from an Eternal Source, blazing into galaxies, transfigured with ineffable auras. Again and again I saw the creative beams condense into constellations, then resolve into sheets of transparent flame. By rhythmic reversion, sextillion worlds passed into diaphanous luster; fire became firmament.

I cognized the center of the empyrean as a point of intuitive perception in my heart. Irradiating splendor issued from my nucleus to every part of the universal structure. Blissful amrita, the nectar of immortality, pulsed through me with a quicksilver-like fluidity. The creative voice of God I heard resounding as Aum, the vibration of the Cosmic Motor.

Suddenly the breath returned to my lungs. With a disappointment almost unbearable, I realized that my infinite immensity was lost. Once more, I was limited to the humiliating cage of a body, not easily accommodative to the Spirit. Like a prodigal child, I had run away from my macrocosmic home and imprisoned myself in a narrow microcosm.

My guru was standing motionless before me; I started to drop at his holy feet in gratitude for the experience in cosmic consciousness which I had long passionately sought. He held me upright, and spoke calmly, unpretentiously.

"You must not get overdrunk with ecstasy. Much work yet remains for you in the world. Come; let us sweep the balcony floor; then we shall walk by the Ganges."

I fetched a broom; Master, I knew, was teaching me the secret of balanced living. The soul must stretch over the cosmogonic abysses, while the body performs its daily duties. When we set out later for a stroll, I was still entranced in unspeakable rapture. I saw our bodies as two astral pictures, moving over a road by the river whose essence was sheer light.

"It is the Spirit of God that actively sustains every form and force in the universe; yet He is transcendental and aloof in the blissful uncreated void beyond the worlds of vibratory phenomena," Master explained. "Saints who realize their divinity even while in the flesh know a similar twofold existence. Conscientiously engaging in earthly work, they yet remain immersed in an inward beatitude. The Lord has created all men from the limitless joy of His being. Though they are painfully cramped by the body, God nevertheless expects that souls made in His image shall ultimately rise above all sense identifications and reunite with Him."

The cosmic vision left many permanent lessons. By daily stilling my thoughts, I could win release from the delusive conviction that my body was a mass of flesh and bones, traversing the hard soil of matter. The breath and the restless mind, I saw, were like storms which lashed the ocean of light into waves of material forms—earth, sky, human beings, animals, birds, trees. No perception of the Infinite as One Light could be had except by calming those storms. As often as I silenced the two natural tumults, I beheld the multitudinous waves of creation melt into one lucent sea, even as the waves of the ocean, their tempests subsiding, serenely dissolve into unity.

A master bestows the divine experience of cosmic consciousness when his disciple, by meditation, has strengthened his mind to a degree where the vast vistas would not overwhelm him. The experience can never be given through one's mere intellectual willingness or open-mindedness. Only adequate enlargement by yoga practice and devotional bhakti can prepare the mind to absorb the liberating shock of omnipresence. It comes with a natural inevitability to the sincere devotee. His intense craving begins to pull at God with an irresistible force. The Lord, as the Cosmic Vision, is drawn by the seeker's magnetic ardor into his range of consciousness.

I wrote, in my later years, the following poem, "Samadhi," endeavoring to convey the glory of its cosmic state:

Vanished the veils of light and shade,
Lifted every vapor of sorrow,
Sailed away all dawns of fleeting joy,
Gone the dim sensory mirage.
Love, hate, health, disease, life, death,
Perished these false shadows on the screen of duality.
Waves of laughter, scyllas of sarcasm, melancholic whirlpools,
Melting in the vast sea of bliss.
The storm of maya stilled
By magic wand of intuition deep.
The universe, forgotten dream, subconsciously lurks,
Ready to invade my newly-wakened memory divine.
I live without the cosmic shadow,
But it is not, bereft of me;
As the sea exists without the waves,
But they breathe not without the sea.
Dreams, wakings, states of deep turia sleep,
Present, past, future, no more for me,
But ever-present, all-flowing I, I, everywhere.
Planets, stars, stardust, earth,
Volcanic bursts of doomsday cataclysms,
Creation's molding furnace,
Glaciers of silent x-rays, burning electron floods,
Thoughts of all men, past, present, to come,
Every blade of grass, myself, mankind,
Each particle of universal dust,

Anger, greed, good, bad, salvation, lust,
I swallowed, transmuted all
Into a vast ocean of blood of my own one Being!
Smoldering joy, oft-puffed by meditation
Blinding my tearful eyes,
Burst into immortal flames of bliss,
Consumed my tears, my frame, my all.
Thou art I, I am Thou,
Knowing, Knower, Known, as One!
Tranquilled, unbroken thrill, eternally living, ever-new peace!
Enjoyable beyond imagination of expectancy, samadhi bliss!
Not an unconscious state
Or mental chloroform without willful return,
Samadhi but extends my conscious realm
Beyond limits of the mortal frame
To farthest boundary of eternity
Where I, the Cosmic Sea,
Watch the little ego floating in Me.
The sparrow, each grain of sand, fall not without My sight.
All space floats like an iceberg in My mental sea.
Colossal Container, I, of all things made.
By deeper, longer, thirsty, guru-given meditation
Comes this celestial samadhi.
Mobile murmurs of atoms are heard,
The dark earth, mountains, vales, lo! molten liquid!
Flowing seas change into vapors of nebulae!
Aum blows upon vapors, opening wondrously their veils,
Oceans stand revealed, shining electrons,
Till, at last sound of the cosmic drum,
Vanish the grosser lights into eternal rays
Of all-pervading bliss.
From joy I came, for joy I live, in sacred joy I melt.
Ocean of mind, I drink all creation's waves.
Four veils of solid, liquid, vapor, light,
Lift aright.
Myself, in everything, enters the Great Myself.
Gone forever, fitful, flickering shadows of mortal memory.
Spotless is my mental sky, below, ahead, and high above.
Eternity and I, one united ray.
A tiny bubble of laughter, I
Am become the Sea of Mirth Itself.

~ ~ ~

Alive 5 times

Sri Yukteswar taught me how to summon the blessed experience at will, and also how to transmit it to others if their intuitive channels were developed. For months, I entered the ecstatic union, comprehending why the Upanishads say God is rasa, "the most relishable." One day, I took a problem to Master.

"I want to know, sir—when shall I find God?"

"You have found Him."

"O no, sir, I don't think so!"

My guru was smiling. "I am sure you aren't expecting a venerable Personage, adorning a throne in some antiseptic corner of the cosmos! I see, however, that you are imagining that the possession of miraculous powers is knowledge of God. One might have the whole universe, and find the Lord elusive still! Spiritual advancement is not measured by one's outward powers, but only by the depth of his bliss in meditation.

"Ever-new Joy is God. He is inexhaustible; as you continue your meditations during the years, He will beguile you with an infinite ingenuity. Devotees like yourself who have found the way to God never dream of exchanging Him for any other happiness; He is seductive beyond thought of competition.

"How quickly we weary of earthly pleasures! Desire for material things is endless; man is never satisfied completely, and pursues one goal after another. The 'something else' he seeks is the Lord, who alone can grant lasting joy.

"Outward longings drive us from the Eden within; they offer false pleasures which only impersonate soul-happiness. The lost paradise is quickly regained through divine meditation. As God is unanticipatory Ever-Newness, we never tire of Him. Can we be surfeited with bliss, delightfully varied throughout eternity?" ....

"That is true; but He is also near and dear. After the mind has been cleared by Kriya Yoga of sensory obstacles, meditation furnishes a twofold proof of God. Ever-new joy is evidence of His existence, convincing to our very atoms. Also, in meditation one finds His instant guidance, His adequate response to every difficulty."

"I see, Guruji; you have solved my problem." I smiled gratefully. "I do realize now that I have found God, for whenever the joy of meditation has returned subconsciously during my active hours, I have been subtly directed to adopt the right course in everything, even details."

"Human life is beset with sorrow until we know how to tune in with the Divine Will, whose 'right course' is often baffling to the egoistic intelligence. God bears the burden of the cosmos; He alone can give unerring counsel."

Where to get Yogananda's Lessons:
Phone: (323) 225-2471 (9am to 5pm PST)
Web URL: www.paramahansayogananda.org/lessons/index.html
Books URL: www.lightrise.com/books

Appendix A3: "Reflection" and the Kinniburghs

Donna Kinniburgh has worked full-time in the spiritual field for over 20 years. During that time, she has provided thousands of personal and public sessions as a channel for the group Reflection.

Reflection says that they are a large group of entities that are not now in physical bodies; they have lived many lives in many different professions gaining a vast amount of experience. The group is composed of the Spiritual Guides of both Donna and Steve, with others added to the group as the situation requires.

Reflection speaks through the physical form of Donna Kinniburgh while she is in "deep trance." This is the deepest form of channeling whereby the conscious mind of Donna is completely withdrawn during a reading. Consequently, the conditioning, programming, and belief system of the medium, which so often taint channeled information, are bypassed so that purer data is provided.

Reflection's purpose is to give information and to advise, not to tell us exactly what to do. Their mandate is to empower others to be their own leaders. They do this in a direct and non-judgmental way, allowing for and never violating an individual's free will.

As a group, the guides are growing spiritually, too, so they see their own spiritual quest as supplying the vital information and tools required to expand our individual awareness and to aid us in realizing more of our true selves, physically, mentally, emotionally, and spiritually.

Readings from Reflection offer several advantages: (1) if you have not yet fully developed your own intuition, you can get an answer easily; or (2) you can get answers if your own intuition is not working clearly and you are stuck.

Reflection's guidance was particularly useful in exploring and double-checking the past life memories used in this book. Throughout the writing process, they provided many exciting new details and fresh avenues to explore.

To get a reading/consultation from Reflection:
Rainbow Lady Communications
P.O.Box 7038, Dacre, Ontario, Canada K0J 1N0
Phone: (613) 649-8245
Web URL: www.rainbow-lady.com/index1.htm

> **Steve Kinniburgh** is a former professional firefighter who now makes a full-time career out of his lifelong interest in the spiritual and metaphysical realm.
>
> He has been a Deep Trance Director for more than 20 years, directing and training other professional mediums and teaching Trance Mediumship (channeling) through courses and workshops. Steve has directed over 13,000 private and public readings.

The following are definitions and explanations of various aspects of reincarnation and spirituality from Reflection in their own words:

Akashic Record

The Akashic Record, as it has been referred to by many schools of thought, is one name that was provided by a particular medium known as Edgar Cayce to describe the etheric memory patterns or experiences that do exist in the "Universal Unconscious Mind." Another school of thought would refer to the Akashic Records as the "Group Mind," or the "Sea of Unconscious." This is the blueprint of thought and memories of experiences in detail of various lifetimes that entities do choose. This is stored in an etheric or a conceptual universe where [the] corporeal does not exist, but [rather] would be *"thought forms,"* which is energy that does not occupy space.

Alternate Reality

Indeed, an alternate reality is a life or experience whereby individuals choose a life at the same place or space, yet in a different time continuum to experience the various different facets of a life. For example, one may choose a life as a chef preparing food and serving to a patron in a restaurant. Yet in a different time frequency, indeed, the experience could be that the chef would be on the receiving end of the food, as the customer, and the receiver in the first scenario would be the chef ....

Yet also in that very same time continuum, there could be other multiple alternate lifetimes with even just slight change. These personas would look exactly as you do when looking in the mirror in a visual sense but be exploring different actions of the same type of scenario. These types of lifetimes explain statements such as "experiencing the many parts of you."

Other lives (time)

Humanity has a tendency to believe that lives begin and end in a linear perspective, for this is what the individual would perceive as their passage through time. Time itself, from the soul's perspective, is an illusion and [is] created by individuals to measure their experiences and to keep track of their action in the physical plane.

Time is perceived from our perspective as a circle in motion or that of a "wheel." … Envision the hub of a wheel being the vantage point of the soul, and the outer rim of the wheel being the viewpoint of the human element or being.

The spokes of the wheel would be the many different entries into the physical and the returnings to the soul and spiritual plane…. From the physical beings' perspective, they would view time in a very shortsighted pattern and, therefore, would believe in a beginning and an ending.

As lives do exist in one moment of your perception of time and history and are, in fact, simultaneous, therefore the term "past lives" or "future lives" is an illusion and is not applicable. We would refer to lifetimes of experience as "Other Lives," all happening at the same moment in reality.

As you go through an experience, be aware at that very moment that you are exploring your life, there are many other lifetimes occurring at the same time that you would occupy [in] a different space…. Life itself is indeed living [in] the moment, and, as you go through your pattern of life, building and balancing karma, you are balancing karma in other lifetimes as you experience your perspective of "time," you see.

Karmic Connections

Karma is the process in which entities would practice learning of the self by balancing issues be these considered pleasurable or awkward lifetimes. Karma is the act of balancing, and when two or more individuals come together and impact each other with an action or an experience, they would be "karmically connected" indeed. When two individuals fall in love, they are karmically connected and are learning about the self through the other to balance karma. Perhaps in another lifetime, they had "fallen" into hate, or yet in another time frame, they could have "fallen" into lust. We use the word "falling" because oft times when entities are karmically connected, they feel as if they are out of control. Therefore, they would perceive this connection to be of a "falling" sensation.

Yet when one understands karma as a whole, they would feel more in control rather than less, you see. Karma is not the paying back of a debt, but rather a balancing factor.

Soul Fragments

The soul chooses to enter into the physical reality to learn of the life experience and sometimes chooses to fragment itself into various aspects or personalities at the same time of your history in different physical bodies. Each of these personas would be part of the same soul .... To gain an experience, for example, say, [in] 1929, [the soul] would choose a lifetime on the North American continent to examine life in that time period. Another fragment of that soul may enter into a life in 1929 [to] explore a life in Africa ... so that the soul could understand itself through these life experiences. One life in that same time period may be one of abundance, and the other may be one of lack, you see. Just as [a person could give] birth to twins, triplets etc., the soul [can] fragment itself into various different energy forms of life as well .... Yet the soul fragmentations would have very different physical appearances and choose very different life paths.

Soul Mates

Many people have used the term "soul mate" loosely without understanding its totality. Return to the basic thoughts or words: the "soul" first and the "mating" second. It is the mating of the souls, [though] the souls are not with a gender .... It does not necessarily mean a marital contract of relationship. It could, but not always.

The act of "soul mating" is whereby two or more souls exchange data through the process of integration, which has been explained previously, and make an agreement to enter the physical reality to help each other gain the maximum experience .... They may soul travel with each other through different time continuums, gathering and strengthening their individuality as ... individual souls. Soul mates may be brother and sister, parent and child, two good friends, coworkers, indeed, teachers and students of any given profession within and outside of the spiritual realm of teaching, and as well, could be intimate love relationships depending upon the individual needs and requirements of the soul.

Often times, [they] have very opposite experiences which is why they integrate to share them, and hence, the term opposites attract. Be mindful, as well, that even those one would consider a foe (though to [us], foes are nonexistent) could be considered soul mates. Why? Because they may teach you the most and impact each other the greatest. These would be the life lessons that you may not forget, you see.

Kindred Spirit

A Kindred Spirit [represents the] ultimate of understanding and acceptance [but does] not necessarily [mean an] intimate connection. The Kindred Spirit is the entity that you may never see for many years and when you return together again it is like no time has passed. These are those that you can depend upon without agenda. No matter what the circumstances are, these are the individuals that you can call at four in the morning and say, I need to talk or I need help. Those who would be considered best friends in this capacity could be of this nature. Kindred spirits do not hold grudges but ... they may agree to disagree. They may not necessarily hold committed intimate love relationships. Yet, in some of these types of relationships, the kindred spirit aspect does exist but with other types of soul energies present as well. There can be one or more aspects in any of these connections, [you] understand.

Twin Flame

Indeed, twin flames are exactly this. The flame being the passion. Individuals who come together with a high degree of physical attraction or passion but would not have anything else in common. They would remain together until they can no longer accept each others "heat," if you will. Indeed, those are the old flames that you remember, as there is a great deal of passion and [you] would long to rekindle with, yet you would find that the intensity would be so great that you would burn each other out. The term "two ships passing in the night" could describe twin flames, yet twin flames oft times appear to be [the] love that you cannot get out of your system but know you cannot stay together or live together too long. Sometimes this is the first love.

Soul Partners

Soul Partners are two individuals who would hold many of the aspects with the other terms we would identify. Soul Partners appear to be soul mates, would have kinship, would hold passion, would have a sense of commitment for the same cause .... Soul partners have agreements, and as well, this would include the agreement to disagree. They would hold true to their commitment.

Other comments [on Karma]

It is important to note when one is dealing with karma, the more individuals become threatened, disillusioned, angry or hurt, the more they will repeat the action until they understand the connection. You will find as well, in karmic connections of all varieties, [that] you will draw to you individuals of similar astrological signs at specific periods of life to learn the various different facets of these connections, and when you become non-reactive to a particular sign, then you have the understanding and acceptance, and balance occurs.

336

God and Life Continues

This channeled session with Reflection was held on November 1, 1999. These abbreviations are used throughout:

QUE: Questioner
REFL: Reflection

QUE: How do you access your answers to questions?

REFL: We have access to and tap into universal knowledge and spiritual experience from a multitude of lifetimes. Hence, when a particular question is asked, all those of us who would have understanding on the subject would give their opinion. We would examine the entire circumstance, put all the pieces of the puzzle into place, and come to a unanimous agreement by consensus. Indeed, we would view into the subconscious mind of the individual, you see, without violating the subconscious choices of the persona. We would research the data found in what some would call the Akashic Records or what some others may refer to as "Group Mind Consciousness," being the records of all experiences of all lifetimes in all realities. We would draw information from this and present it for the entities to review and to assist themselves.

QUE: Of all the extant religions on earth today (e.g., Buddhism, Hinduism, Yoga, Islam, Christianity, Spiritualism, etc.) which teachings are closest to the truth as you see it? Why?

REFL: Indeed, all religions hold "truth." As we have stated, "truth" is multifaceted, but to answer the query most clearly, of course, it would be "Spirituality" which may not necessarily mean the religion of "Spiritualism." The term "religion" simply means, indeed, "a belief that is practiced religiously or habitually" until it becomes a lifestyle. Indeed, know that if any organized religion does not hold the spiritual essence of "unconditional love" and judges the belief of another, then the foundation is shaky. Some religious bodies preach one thing and do the other. One will not find spirituality by practicing on one day of the week. Those who would walk in the path of their own words and would not judge or criticize but practice harmony, be closer to the spiritual essence of what some would call God, others Buddha, some Allah, and many other names of reference. If each be claiming theirs alone is the true path, and indeed, if they have need to prove their belief so adamantly to others, then it may be themselves they wish to convince. The spiritual essence cannot be owned by one religion but is individual and given and accepted, indeed, most freely.

QUE: Describe the nature of the One or All That Is. Is it merely a force that creates, but does not interfere in the affairs of humankind, or is it a personal God who does intervene? If the One intervenes, under what circumstances does It do so and in what form? Are you personally in touch with the One? Can we also be?

REFL: Indeed, the "One" is a good word for and, as well, a description of that which is referred to as God. God usually implies a male reference whereas the One is the duality of both genders and all. The One, if you will, is, indeed, or can be described as a force of nature that is in every aspect of your being. The One, indeed, is intelligent and wise, practical; the One is a force, or power, indeed, that protects when required without interference and only intervenes to give direction, allowing for freedom. The One allows for choice and opportunity, indeed, and is a personal One or, to use the familiar term God/Goddess, if you will, that does not judge or interfere. 'Tis only the personality of the self that judges and interferes.

We, as Spiritual Guides, are connected to you and to that which are called "Angels" which are connected to that which you refer to as the One which is also connected to you, therefore, we, you, they, and all are connected. 'Tis liken to a chain, each link is important to the whole or the One and therefore is one, you see. Indeed, the One is not significant only to that of the planet Earth; therefore, ownership of the One does not exist. Know that the One is beyond your known Universe. All can be in touch with the One by practicing the description of the One that we have provided and by working towards unconditional love so that ye can walk as one in the path with all other parts of the One, side by side, not attempting to lead nor to follow but to be!

QUE: So, in your estimation, God does not interfere but adds the energy that we need to create our reality, is that right?

REFL: That is correct, think as yourselves as the arms and legs of the Godhead or the One or God—[as means for] the One's experiences in the physical.

QUE: What is the nature of the typical dying process? What usually occurs during the death process? Are the "tunnel," the "Being in white light," and life review processes described in the "near death experience" literature accurate? Do we sleep for a while, awaken in our astral body, and move to a vibration appropriate to our level of spiritual development or what?

REFL: Indeed, when individuals leave the physical that some refer to [as] the "casting off of clay," after they have gone through the five stages of transition in their physical bodies, they would go through what is called an absorption process. In that, indeed, their spiritual essence, the spirit being which provides the life force or the spark that operates the physical body, would be absorbed into the subconscious mind or portion, indeed, where all is clear and understood ….

They are greeted by whatever spiritual beliefs that give them comfort. Now, if for example, one has had a very strong upbringing in their life, such as "Christianity" being one belief, indeed, and followed the path of say, Jesus the Christ, spiritual guides would give this as a reference to ease the transition and to bring comfort and to avoid the shock of the letting go. They would be met with that which would provide the security. All would be greeted with known factions of their reality such as loved ones that have crossed over previously to assist.

During this process, they would, in fact, feel themselves engulfed in what has been described as a white light. But this is not a white light that one could actually see from a visual point of view. For it is a light or an energy that embraces and, indeed, purifies and is that which is called "pure love," unconditional love, being that which humanity does not yet know in its entirety.

This feeling is so powerful and so welcoming that individuals follow the light with joy and bliss. The only way to describe this light so that you would in part understand is "pure bliss" and even bliss is not understood in your reality.

A period occurs where entities view their physical reality and would take notes, so to speak, without emotional connection or, shall we say, indeed, that they are removed from the emotional limitations yet they would remain in their previous vibration to observe. Liken [it] to watching a movie and witnessing themselves going through the life process; note again that time here doth not exist.

They would, in fact, not be comforted by the grieving process. For there is not the ability to communicate but if they could, they would wish to tell their loved ones, "Do not weep for me, but rejoice instead."

Indeed, then they would move to the next stage of "witnessing." From this they would be greeted with options to remain on the vibrational state of the spiritual to learn of another aspect of life of which we call "spiritual guidance." Some would choose to incarnate; some would not.

QUE: When we pass to the afterlife, what sort of activities do we engage in? Is there sex in the afterlife? Are there soul mates and soul twins? What are the different levels of vibration there? How do we decide to reincarnate?

REFL: "Afterlife" is a good term to use because it is a life without [the] corporeal, and in fact, there are entire planets that would have life forms without the physicality but would be pure energy. For that is what we are in the spiritual domain, individual sparks of pure energy, and these energies would hold a multitude [of] experience in a multitude of lifetimes.

There are certain activities or actions, if you will, that be done (now these words that we use here are applicable to your physical reality, but there is no other way to describe this). Some choose to interact with a physical being as a Spiritual Guide; sometimes it is a loved one they have left behind, that is struggling with issues [for which] that entity can provide direction or encouragement. Some others would be in similar roles but rather than in a direct guiding state, they would be considered similar to your interns or apprentices, observing [and] going from one entity to another. Know that it's a learning state always.

Some would choose to gather and collect information to sort. Think of this as a tremendously large database, that of the Akashic Record, for lack of a better term, the record of all times, and realize that there are no limits here.

Some would choose to study only that of childlike sparks of energy; others would choose a variety of life studies. The activities are always to observe and absorb knowledge, and the greatest joy, so to speak, is to sort that which has been learned and to review the lessons. For if one entity does realize [that] some issue was not mastered, then a parallel life might be opted for to complete that understanding.

QUE: Could you comment on the question of sex in the afterlife, twin souls, soul mates etc.?

REFL: Indeed, now again, the word "sex" itself in your physical reality and the word "intercourse" mean to communicate in the physical with the intent to provide pleasure and to create [more new bodies]. Correct?

In the Spiritual Realm vibration, or the afterlife as you call it, or shall we state "after physical life," the same process does occur, but it is lacking the physical to provide the so-called pleasure. It is an energy transfer, and in this energy transfer is the experience of bliss! Soul mates choose, while they are in the spiritual experience, or "after physical life," to integrate. This is what we would think of as our sexual type of experience ….

Integration is a blending of the spiritual experiences just as intercourse is the blending of the physical experiences. The decision to incarnate is dependent upon what lessons are required. Know, as well, one does not have to incarnate to learn a lesson, one can incarnate simply because, indeed, they enjoy living in the physical reality. And the greater purpose of physicality is to "enjoy."

QUE: Many who live on the planet today either wish or would like it to be their last experience because of the traumas that they experience and problems they have or because it is a type of spiritual landmark to say that or hear that. What are your comments on this?

REFL: Indeed, for those who have a strong desire for that concept, there are several psychological reasons for this. One is that they have difficulty accepting their life choices and because they are taught to see life as being painful rather than gainful. They see living as work and drudgery and not pleasure and they wish to leave. That is one reason. Yet another is because by believing or thinking it is their last life, they give themselves some sort of feeling of power or that they are more evolved and there you have the "level" thinking again.

Alive 5 times

QUE: Religions such as Yoga and Buddhism teach that it is possible for us to achieve enlightenment (i.e., nirvana, samadhi, satori, etc.) while in this life. Is this true? If so, please describe the process and how to achieve it.

REFL: Indeed, number one, it is true. Know this first, and the moment that you stop "trying" is the moment you will experience it. Because, you see, when you reach for something outside of yourself, it will be like the carrot held on a stick in front of a mule. We [suggest you] go back to being childlike and ... to being in the present moment.

Work on being non-judgmental and work towards loving unconditionally, starting by loving the self, as one cannot love or know love if it does not exist within, indeed. If you concentrate on being the best of who you are, not better than, not less than, but being as much as ye can be and enjoy it, then you are taking the steps towards bliss, nirvana, samadhi, satori, etc. Meditation alone will not bring you there, action will.

QUE: Is there life on other planets in the universe? If so, have we made contact with them? Are some of them among us now on earth? What are their intentions and plans?

REFL: Yes to most of this. There are life-forms on other planets, your governments have made contact with them and have had for many of your years, since the '40s-'50s of your time span. Indeed, their intentions depend upon the groups involved.

Indeed, know that these are not all magical beings that will swoop down, gather up the children of humanity, and whisk them away to a safe haven. Indeed not! These are physical beings, scientists, communicators, negotiators, ambassadors, and yes, indeed, militants and some benevolent and spiritually focused, some researchers, [and] galactic travelers to name but a few.

There is not one group alone. Some [of their] intention, a most important fact, is to be of assistance without interfering [with] the planet, yet not to save the Earth but by so doing assist themselves. This is a universal mission. The Vegan Alliance's intention is to work in conjunction with humanity. For some others, indeed, that we refer to as the renegades, 'tis not the case but 'tis for their own survival only. We have much information on this, which cannot be answered in this query alone. [Note: there is more about this on the website.]

QUE: There are many so-called New Age prophecies regarding the new millennium, catastrophic earth changes, and the ascent of humankind to a higher stage of spiritual being. Can you confirm or deny any of these prophecies and, if so, what is the source of your knowledge?

REFL: There has been much overplaying of the millennium issues. Yes, indeed, there is and shall be disruptions but not [a] world catastrophe or shutdown. Be aware of this first!

As to the prophecies, these have been stated as probabilities. For many a seer from the earlier period of the Christ time frame to Michel de Notredame [*Nostradamus*] to Edgar Cayce, so on and so forth, have foreseen the Earth shifts and changes of time, based on humanity's unchanging attitudes. This is one source of our own knowledge, as well, from this pattern and from observing the path of humanity and its development as a race. 'Tis not all destructive, you see, but it is human nature to focus on, indeed, disaster rather than to see the successes that have occurred.

QUE: As an addition to that, most people's pace of life is so fast and so quick these days more out of necessity than out of want. How does one get back to that silence, that stillness, and become aware of what's around you?

REFL: Surrender! It is that simple. Indeed, individuals do not take time to enjoy a baby's smile. They take it for granted. All babies smile, they would think, but that baby is smiling at you, and that is special. Stop for a moment and appreciate the individual shape of leaves. Note that no two are the same, as everything in nature is individual, [just] as you, too, are part of nature and unique unto yourself.

If you stop a moment and fret over the fact that it may be snowing in your part of the world, you begin to think about shoveling snow and the inconvenience. Stand outside, stick out your tongue, and taste a snowflake. Indeed, when was the last time you smelled the leaves in autumn? Not just the leaves as a whole. Practice smelling the individual leaves. You will note that there are individual fragrances in all leaves be it autumn, spring, or summer.

Have you ever looked at [the] color of a raindrop [or] remembered when you were a child sitting and watching an anthill in wonderment? You have time to do many things that are of lesser importance though [they] may [seem] important to you at the time. Indeed, you have time to shout at an inconsiderate driver on the highway. If you have time for this, you have ample time to admire the sunset, as you sit impatiently waiting for the traffic jam at rush hour to begin moving.

Too much focus is on anger, indeed, and not on joy. Put things into perspective. Worry and stress serve no purpose, but [rather they] create "dis-ease" of the physical, whereby the body is not at ease with the self. The term "to worry themselves to death" is quite accurate. Focus on your *life* instead.

To get a reading/consultation from 'Reflection:'
Phone: (613) 649-8245
Web URL: www.rainbow-lady.com/index1.htm

A Word of Caution about Most Other Mediums

Over the last 30+ years, I have worked with dozens of mediums, several of whom were internationally known. However, not one of them was as accurate or as helpful as Reflection and the Kinniburghs. If you plan to use a psychic, I recommend that you give them a call.

Finding a good medium is difficult these days because of the many charlatans. In addition, just because a spirit guide gives you advice, it does not mean that it is spiritually correct. For example, the souls who were Stalin and Hitler presumably are still in the spirit worlds. If they did not tell you who they had been, would you like to receive spiritual advice from them? Maybe not.

If you plan to use some other medium, I offer several cautions:

(1) **Are they truly spiritual?** True spirit guides will never build up your ego. Instead, they will try to help you get free of it. Therefore, if a guide tells you that you are better than other people or are somehow specially chosen, watch out. A true spiritual guide will not talk that way.

(2) **Do they talk to you as an equal?** Be wary if guides begin to tell you how great they are, claiming, for example, that they are something like the "Most High Emissaries of the Supreme Grand Galactic Council of Exalted Ones." True spiritual guides will not grandly build themselves up that way or talk down to you – they consider all beings equal, including plants and animals. They will talk to you as one close friend to another.

(3) **Do they want you to develop your own intuition?** True guides will not suggest that you slavishly follow their advice. They want you to be happy and free, not enslaved. True spiritual guides will help you to develop your own inner intuitive contact.

(4) **Do they claim to be omniscient?** Where I was able to verify known facts, I found that even the best guides are sometimes wrong—about 25% of the time. They are not omniscient and will not claim to be, although being right 75% of the time is extremely good. If you get advice from a guide, just keep in mind that it may be wrong; then try to verify it with your own intuition. Follow the advice only if it feels right to you

In summary, getting advice from guides such as Reflection can be extremely useful if approached with discrimination. Sometimes, we get "stuck in the mud," so to speak, and can use a wise detached viewpoint for getting on track again. Overall, we are better off using our own inner intuition if possible, but sometimes we just cannot do it on our own. Getting wise words of counsel from spirit often can help us get back on track.

Appendix B: Waking Up:
Miracles and other Realizations.

After the age of 15, I began to have some odd "supernatural" experiences that presaged what would come later in life. This appendix briefly describes a few of them.

1965—Age 19: Experience with life after death

I was cramming for a college test, and my aunt offered to let me stay in their guest cottage—a three-room cabin, dating back to the Civil War era.

The floor was made of wooden boards that were not well supported, and they creaked whenever I walked over them. As I put in long hours studying, I often heard creaking noises from the wood frame and floor of the house, though I dismissed the noises as just the house "settling."

One night the noises were particularly loud, and I began to notice that the noises followed a pattern as if someone were walking around. I began to get a very powerful sense that I was not alone. Then, the floorboards started to creak in the other room, and the noise came right into the room I was in, moving around my chair. With a sweaty, trembling hand, I leaned over and touched the floor as the creaking passed. I distinctly felt the floorboards sink about 1/8 inch as the creaking passed by me, and then rebounded as the creaking passed.

Feeling a little afraid, I wondered if I should get out of the house, but my curious mind took over. I asked, *What is going on here? Could these really be ghosts?* The instant I thought that, I had a waking vision of the room. I could see the actual room with my eyes open, but superimposed over it, I saw the figures of four people, transparent and bluish-colored. I could see them clearly, but I could also see the walls of the present-day room through their bodies.

My intuition told me that they were one of the original families who lived in the house – mother, father, and two children – and that they were still "living" there. They didn't seem know they were dead! The family members were not very aware spiritually and seemed confused about whatever had happened to them. The father was vaguely aware that I was in "their" house and was a little irritated by my presence, but they all tolerated it and simply ignored me like an uninvited houseguest. They just went on with their own business.

The next time the father walked toward me, I conducted a "test." I leaned over to feel the creaking floor. As before, it dipped as he walked by, except that I could see him this time. This time was very different, though. He walked right *through* my head and shoulders as I leaned over! A slight tingling moved through me as he passed by, similar to the "pins and needles" you feel when your leg goes to "sleep."

I was a little bit afraid all right. This was all new to me, but I was consumed by curiosity, and it didn't seem that they could hurt me. After all, I reasoned, one of them just walked through me with no damage. But from that time on, there was no more creaking and no more ghost family. They never came back, or that is, I never sensed them again.

The next day, I told my aunt about what had happened. As I went into detail, her smile got stiff and frozen on her face. It was clear that she didn't feel comfortable at all with the idea of ghosts in her house, so I gave her an abridged version, after which all she said was, "That's nice, dear," and promptly forgot all about it ... but I didn't. I was determined to find out more.

1965—Age 19: Experience with astral travel

In college, I majored in psychology and decided to experiment with self-hypnosis. My brother gave me a book on the subject, along with a biofeedback device to help attune my brain wave frequency, which supposedly made it easier to be hypnotized. From the start, I became much more relaxed using the device and began to use it during meditation. Then, I turned to astral travel, i.e., moving out my body by imagining that I was floating above it. It worked and I had some mild experiences that indicated that something unusual was going on.

About that time, I was dating a local girl named Jennie, and during Thanksgiving break, while I was home away from her, I decided to try the out-of-body technique. I relaxed and imagined moving out of my body, traveling up through the ceiling, drifting over the Florida landscape, enjoying the beautiful moonlit evening, and then arriving at the house where Jennie lived with her parents. I imagined walking right through the closed front door, down the hallway, and into her bedroom. Next, I imagined sitting down on the bed to watch her sleeping. Then, suddenly, I popped back to my mother's house. The journey was over. I put it out of my mind and thought nothing more about it.

Later, on returning to college, the first time I met Jennie again, she immediately said, "I have to tell you something strange that happened. Over Thanksgiving, I was sleeping when I woke up suddenly. I looked down the hallway because I knew someone was coming, but I couldn't see anybody. I felt an invisible "presence" come over to my bed and sit down. I became terrified, jumped up out of bed, ran into my parents' room, and slept with them for the rest of the night."

I was stunned – she had just described exactly what I had "imagined" under self-hypnosis. When I told her about it, she began to look at me differently, clearly afraid of what had happened. Her reaction really surprised me, that she – the only person I knew who was sensitive to the process – didn't want to talk about it. I was confused, elated, surprised, hurt, and excited all at the same time. Things were never the same between us after that and we drifted apart. However, I was determined to find out more about what had happened.

None of my friends or professors could explain what had happened, or, for that matter, could even accept it, so I began a quest to understand and master the ability. This was the first time that I *knowingly* left the body, though now I understand that we all do it every night – "dreaming." The only difference is that I had stumbled across a way to do it consciously.

1966—age 20: Meditation Vision

As I learned more about spirit-travel, I developed serious confusion about the direction of my life. I was in my senior year and was about to graduate from college with a degree in Psychology and Drama. I had wanted to be a psychiatrist/doctor in the mold of Jung and Freud, the acknowledged fathers of psychiatry. I had already interviewed at Harvard Medical School for admission, and the registrar had indicated that I would gladly be accepted.

Not long afterward, I came across a quote by Jung, who, when asked if he would go into psychiatry again, said no, he would have studied yoga. And Freud, when asked the same questions, replied no, he would have studied psychic phenomenon. I began to reason that if the two greatest psychiatrists would not study psychiatry again, then why should I? So I was tempted to go study yoga and psychic phenomenon, just as Jung and Freud had wanted to do. My dilemma was whether to stay in college or to leave and pursue these studies.

Standing on the beach in Florida near my college, I closed my eyes and prayed for some help with my confusion. Not knowing what to do, I resolved to stay there all night if necessary in order to get an answer. After several hours of agonizing over the problem, suddenly I began to feel better and my mood began to lift.

With eyes closed, I saw an inner-vision of the beautiful curve of the beach stretching out ahead of me, just as if my eyes were open. Then, beginning right in front of me, I saw a footprint appear in the sand and become lit with golden light, even though there was no visible foot to cause the print. Next, another print formed and another, all appearing along the beach – a series of several dozen glowing footprints. Then, one of the most melodious and lovely voices I have ever heard spoke to me, saying, "Follow me." Shivers of joy ran up my back, and goose bumps stood up on my arm. I had my answer.

I could not see who had spoken, but I was deeply grateful and deeply satisfied. The voice had given me the answer I needed as clearly as could be, and with deep compassion. I had gotten an answer from someone who knew exactly what I needed, someone who cared about me and gave me a much-welcome answer.

Within a few days, even though I was in my senior year, I took a sabbatical from college and headed off on a new quest – to find answers that could not be found from my professors. I never returned to my old college, though I did finish my degree several years later. Only a short time after hearing "Follow me," and seeing golden footprints in the sand, I was on my way to the Golden State of California on a religious/spiritual quest to find more answers.

1968—age 22: Answers from Spirit

With a wild leap of faith, I quit my job working in a Zen Buddhist retreat, broke up with my girlfriend, and moved from San Francisco to Los Angeles on what I hoped would be the next step of my spiritual journey. However, now that I had arrived, I wasn't so sure I was doing the right thing. I didn't know anyone and had no place to stay, no car, and almost no money. As I walked down the street looking for a place to stay, doubts began to race through my mind. *What am I doing here? Maybe I've made a mistake. Maybe I've come to the wrong place. Should I stay or go back to San Francisco?*

At that moment, I noticed an old homeless man across the street walking the other way. He clearly had not bathed in a long time and was seriously drunk, staggering along the sidewalk. Homeless just like him, I watched him, thinking I wasn't much better off that he was – except for my recent bath. Then as if I had just shouted out his name, he suddenly looked over at me.

With a great big wide smile on his face, he pointed to me, shouted, "YOU!" and started running across the street towards me. Instantly, I became afraid that he would mug me or worse, hug me, and I looked around for some escape. Before I could figure out what to do, he came right up to me. Shaking a dirty finger in my face, wearing a strangely happy-crazy smile, he said, "You! You have come to the *right* place!" Then he let out a loud, crazed belly laugh and wobbled off down the street laughing all the way.

I had to laugh with him – I was delighted at the message and the unusual messenger. I said an inward thanks to a benevolent Universe, which can use the mind of a homeless drunk to deliver a message to someone too confused to hear it directly.

1968—age 22: Self-regression and Understanding Incarnation

I had been taking months of courses to learn how to regress to a past-life. In one session, the following recall came up of my present lifetime:

I was hovering around in the hospital operating room watching my mother give birth to my body. I could tell she was very sick. I knew she had malaria and was close to death, but the doctor could not diagnose the problem. I tried to tell him from spirit, but his earth ears and mind could not hear me. I was angry and frustrated with him. Because of this experience, I have never liked doctors this life very much.

In spite of my mother's serious illness, she finally gave birth. While she did, I hovered around the birth table, until, at the moment of birth, I entered the body. Recalling my own birth, I understood that the soul does not really take possession of the new body, until the very first breath is taken. The body does not contain a soul until that moment, even though it is technically alive.

1968—age 22: *Visit to the Other Side*

My grandmother had died the year before. We had been very close and she was one of my favorite family members. I hadn't been able to visit her before she died, so I decided to visit her in the spirit world. I meditated, concentrated on her, and found her. Her world looked just like our own, with grass, trees, and bushes, except the colors were more vivid and feelings were much more intense.

Roses were her favorite flowers and I saw many wild rose bushes nearby. She was with a group of friends, and when I called to her, she came over to see me. She was glad to see me, but I could sense that there was a difference. She was friendly, but not the way it had been on earth. When I wondered why, I realized intuitively that sometimes, when a soul's body dies in the physical world, they "wake up" in the spirit world much like we wake up from sleeping. When they do, their earth experiences fade like a night dream, as if they never happened. She recognized me as a friend, but I don't think she remembered much of her last life – it had mostly faded away. She politely said, "It's so nice to see you again, but if you will excuse me, I should get back to my friends." Satisfied that she was doing well, I said good-bye.

1968—age 22: *A waking-vision of my life's direction*

Later that year, while I was in Southern California, I was at another crossroads. Over recent years, I had studied deeply and intensely with various teachers of all of the world's religions, including Buddhism, Hinduism, Christianity, Islam, Judaism, and many other "isms" and "ologies." I had found people who really knew some answers, unlike my college professors. I knew that studying spirituality was the right path for me at the time, but was confused about the direction of my life for the future; part of me just wanted to run away to a monastery and meditate on a mountaintop. I had already spent months in a Zen Buddhist monastery, and I liked it. However, another part of me wanted to follow the example of Albert Schweitzer and others who got married and lived a spiritual life while performing their worldly duties.

So, to find what to do next, I "went to mountain," specifically San Bernardino, California, where there is a huge cross on a hill. I climbed the rocky hill and sat below the cross, touching it. I prayed to Jesus and the Masters as intensely as I possibly could, determined to stay until I got an answer. For hours, I alternately prayed, sobbed, called out, meditated, demanded, and pleaded for an answer, but none came.

Finally, I felt the confusion suddenly lift from my mind. As if unseen hands had touched me, my head was turned so I would look down on the beautiful, luxuriant, green valley next to the mountain on which I sat. The same flowing, melodious voice that I had heard on the beach in Florida said, "Go down into the green valleys among men." I had my answer – no mountain top seclusion for me this lifetime. With a heartfelt inner "Thank you," I turned and walked down the mountain back into the world of men and women. I knew that life on a mountaintop was not my path this lifetime.

Within the year, I became a minister of a nondenominational, ecumenical religious group, remaining in the world, and I am still a minister today, although retired.

1986—age 40: Inner Voice and a Physical "Miracle"

I was driving to Phoenix to attend a spiritual awakening class and was really looking forward to the class. Suddenly, steam began to roll from under the hood. Driving slowly to the next gas station, I looked under the hood and discovered a 2 inch long split in the rubber hose into the radiator. A steady, powerful jet of steam was pouring out of the split that passed totally through the wall of the hose.

The more water I added, the more steam poured from the split. I shut the engine off, knowing that the tow to a mechanic would take hours, and that I would miss the class. As I thought about it, I began to surrender to Divine Will. I just "let go and let God," thinking, if this is the way this day is supposed to be, then so be it.

A deep sense of inner peace came over me, and then an inner voice said softly, "Drive to Phoenix. You will have three days to repair it."

I started the car and was amazed that no steam escaped. Inspecting the hose, I could see a tiny line where the crack used to be, as if the rubber hose had been somehow welded shut. With a silent thanks to the Divine, I got in the car, drove the two hours to Phoenix, and made it to the class on time.

Within the three days, I had the hose repaired. The mechanic was amazed that I had made it to Phoenix at all. He showed me the crack by flexing the hose – the 2 inch crack extended entirely through the rubber. He stuck his finger right through it and refused to believe that it had been possible to drive the car at all. I just smiled. I knew that Divine Law supersedes the "Law of Rubber Hoses."

Alive 5 times

Appendix C: Chart of Major Soul-Players

Soul Group Relationships: One theme this book explores is the relationship with other souls who incarnate as the players on our life's stage. For many reasons, souls tend to incarnate in groups, so that the same souls meet up lifetime after lifetime.

The following table summarizes how my soul, in different incarnations, encountered a dozen other key souls in my soul group. Interrelationships vary considerably along with gender (marked with (F) or (M)). All twelve have been in three or more of my soul's last five lives, including the current one.

	Present: Allen Eastman	Meera, shaman	John Hogans, soldier	Sorrel Horse, Lakota	Louis St. Jacques
#1	**(F) Mother**	(M) Suitor	(F) Nurse at Gettysburg	(M) Clan Sub-Chief	(F) Dancer and model
#2	**(M) Father**	(M) Spanish soldier	(M) Soldier; not at battle	(M) Trooper; not at battle	(M) Doctor
#3	**(M) Brother**	(F) Sister	(M) Brother, James	(M) Older friend	(M) French field hand
#4	**(F) Grand-mother**	(M) Shaman-teacher	(F) Black woman	(F) Lakota woman	——
#5	**(M) Cousin, JB**	——	(M) Rebel soldier	(M) Lakota boy	(M) Art dealer
#6	**(M) Cousin, BB**	(M) Chief's son	(M) Rebel soldier	——	(F) High society lady
#7	**(F) Cousin, PB**	——	(M) Union solder	(M) Friend, Whirlwind	(F) High society lady
#8	**(F) Wife, Andrea**	(F) Shaman, nearby tribe	(F) Female family friend	(F) Mother	(F) Mother
#9	**(F) Ex-wife, PW**	——	(F) Wife	——	(F) Wife
#10	**Current spirit guide**	Spirit guide	——	Spirit guide	(M) Father
#11	**(M) Mentor, OB**	(F) Mother	(M) Friend and mentor	——	(M) Starving painter
#12	**(M) Friend, AJ**	(M) Tribes-man	——	(F) Sister	(F) Dancer

350

All of the souls listed above have incarnated many times with me, changing relationships and gender often. Though each lifetime is different, sometimes there are threads of similarities that run through many of them, mainly because a soul will have certain interests that will continue from lifetime to lifetime until they play out and get replaced by other interests.

Let's look at two of the souls above to see how group incarnation works. Most of the details below were not included in the main stories because of space constraints, so they are brief mini-stories in themselves.

SOUL #1, My Current Mother: This soul is close to me spiritually, more so than others in my immediate family are. She is very compassionate, inquisitive, and adventurous, traits that run through the last few lives I shared with her.

Meera: In the lifetime with Meera in the 1700s, she was not my mother, instead playing a different role. This soul was male then and was an early suitor of Meera, who was not at all interested in marriage, even though she eventually married Whale-Slayer. Even though he was a rejected suitor, nevertheless he remained a close friend to Meera and took a great interest in her development as a shaman.

Hogans: In that life, this soul changed gender to female and incarnated in the rural South. John did not know her early but eventually encountered her as an Army nurse after the Battle of Second Manassas. John was seriously wounded in August 1862 and was not able to return to duty until November of that same year. During that time, she felt a special attraction to John, nursing him back to health and caring for him as a mother would. Though he did not see her again after that, she played a crucial role in saving his life.

In my current lifetime, this soul, as my mother, visited the Gettysburg battlefield, where she had powerful feelings of sadness and felt an odd sense of *déjà vu*. Not surprising, since she had been there about 100 years earlier.

Sorrel Horse: This soul changed gender again in this incarnation, returning to become a clan sub-chief in Sitting Bull's tribe. Older than Sorrel Horse, he served as his mentor and spiritual teacher, especially since Custer's men had killed his parents at Washita. Sitting Bull was more like Sorrel Horse's surrogate grandfather, while this soul was more like a surrogate father

Louis: In this lifetime, this soul, who likes adventure and new experiences, changed gender again to incarnate in Paris. Louis met her in the cabarets of the Montmartre district, where she was a dancer and artist's model. During this life, she struggled with the allure of alcohol, sex, and drugs, as Louis did, and on occasion, she offered friendly help to Louis in dealing with his own addictions, finally overcoming her own as well. She and Louis did not know each other for long in this life, but their close relationship was like that of a loving brother and sister.

SOUL #8, My Wife Andrea: This soul has interests in spiritual matters, alternative healing, gemstones, and essential oils, all of which have spanned several lifetimes. Today she is part owner of a distribution company that markets aromatherapy and natural health products internationally. In all of these lives, she has chosen to be female, though she has been male other times.

Meera: In that life, this soul was born into a nearby tribe, where she became the tribe's shaman-woman. She was older than Meera, so Meera looked up to her for guidance during her own training. In addition, being female, she had a different perspective than the male shaman in Meera's own tribe. Wise in the ways of healing the body using natural means, she brought these same abilities into the present.

Hogans: A female friend of John's, this soul had a crush on John from an early age but never let him know. On the other hand, John loved her like a sister and never thought of her as a potential wife. When John married Rose, she was hurt but never showed it, and her loving nature led her to want only the best for both of them. She never married, choosing to live at home and help care for her large family of brothers, sisters, nephews, and nieces.

As often happens during war when violent emotions affect the spiritual climate, disease epidemics spread across the war-ravaged South. She died during one of these, shortly before John was shot at Appomattox. She was one of the spirit friends who waited along with Rose when John crossed into spirit.

Sorrel Horse: As the Cheyenne mother of Sorrel Horse, this soul died during the Battle of Washita when he was young, but she was a major influence on him during their short time together. Though she was not formally a medicine-woman, nevertheless, she showed great skill in herbal healing and in using earth minerals to cure her family and neighbors, using abilities that have spanned several lives. After her body died, she continued to influence Sorrel Horse as a guide from the spirit world, and when Sorrel Horse crossed over into spirit, she was the first one to greet him.

Louis: This soul returned to become Louis' mother, though she chose a very different role for herself that time. She had the difficult jobs of dealing with a dictatorial husband and a wayward son, two jobs that required a lot of patience and equanimity. In that lifetime, she experienced great wealth and social standing, which she accepted and enjoyed, while at the same time not looking down on others who had not chosen the same situation. In fact, part of her envied the freer and less demanding lifestyle of Louis' friends in Montmartre.

This Parisian lifetime was in great contrast to the simple, rural lifestyle she had led as a Cheyenne woman, but she adapted well and was equally at ease in both settings. Louis's father loved her very much, as did Louis, so that when she died at a relatively young age a few years after the overdose, Louis's father was devastated to be without her. He died soon afterward, I believe, of heartache over losing her.

> **Note:** *Some of the books listed below are available for a discounted price through www.lightrise.com/books*

Appendix D: Bibliography

Resources for Reincarnation and Spirituality

Dwoskin, Hale, and Levenson, Lester. *Happiness Is Free: And It's Easier Than You Think!* Sedona Press, 2002.

Newton, Michael Duff. *Journey of Souls: Case Studies of Life Between Lives.* Llewellyn Publications, 1994.

Newton, Michael Duff. *Destiny of Souls: New Case Studies of Life Between Lives.* Llewellyn Worldwide, Ltd., 2000.

Stevenson, Ian. *Children Who Remember Previous Lives: A Question of Reincarnation.* McFarland & Company, 2000.

Stevenson, Ian. *Twenty Cases Suggestive of Reincarnation.* University Press of Virginia, 1980.

Stevenson, Ian. *Where Reincarnation and Biology Intersect.* Praeger Publishers, 1997.

Weiss, Brian. *Many Lives, Many Masters.* Fireside, 1988.

Weiss, Brian. *Meditation: Achieving Inner Peace and Tranquility in Your Life.* Hay House; Book and CD edition, 2002.

Weiss, Brian. *Mirrors of Time: Using Regression for Physical, Emotional, and Spiritual Healing.* Hay House; Book & CD edition, 2002.

Yogananda, Paramahansa. *Autobiography of a Yogi.* Self Realization Fellowship Pub., 1979.

Yogananda, Paramahansa. *Man's Eternal Quest.* Self Realization Fellowship Pub., 1982.

Yogananda, Paramahansa. *Whispers from Eternity.* Self Realization Fellowship Pub., 1998.

Introduction Section

Foucher, A. (Alfred). *The beginnings of Buddhist art, and other essays in Indian and Central-Asian archeolog.* Paris: P. Geuthner; London: H. Milford, 1914 and 1917.

Jewett, Sarah Orne. *The story of the Normans, told chiefly in relation to their conquest of England.* London: T. Fisher Unwin, 1887.

North, Leigh. *Predecessors of Cleopatra.* NY: Broadway Publ. Co., 1906.

Lifetime #1: Meera and the Makah

Asahi Shimbun. "Team looks for nutty animal behavior to predict quakes." (www.asahi.com). *November 2, 2002.*

Atwater, Brian F. *"Holocene Earthquakes in Western Washington,"* USGS Project No. 7460-12080. (www.wou.edu/las/physci/taylor/g473/waseis1.htm). U.S. Geological Survey, 1998.

Gunther, Erna. *Indian Life on the Northwest Coast of North America.* Chicago: The University of Chicago Press, 1972.

353

Halliday, Jan, Globe Correspondent. *"Life among the Makah Tribe."* Sunday Boston Globe, page M1, August 15, 1999.

Kirk, Ruth, with Richard D. Daugherty. *Hunters of the Whale, an Adventure in Northwest Coast Archaeology.* New York: William Morrow and Company, 1974.

Library of Congress. (http://memory.loc.gov)

Makah Nation website. (www.northolympic.com/makah). November, 2002.

National Archives and Records Administration. (http://www.archives.gov)

National Oceanic and Atmospheric Administration/Department of Commerce, photos. (http://www.photolib.noaa.gov)

Oregon Dept. of Geology and Mineral Industries, *"Penrose Conference 2000, Great Cascadia Earthquake Tricentennial, Program Summary and Abstracts".* Special Paper 33.

(http://geohazards.cr.usgs.gov/pacnw/paleo/greateq/conf.html)

Reagan, Albert B. *"Some Additional Myths of the Hoh and Quileute Indians."* Utah Academy of Sciences, Arts, and Letters, Vol. XI, 1934.

Reflection. *Tape Recordings of Intuitive-Trance Sessions covering my Past Lives.* 2002.

Tomczak, Matthias. *Introduction to Physical Oceanography, Version 2.* (www.es.flinders.edu.au/~mattom/IntroOc/notes/lecture10.html) Sept., 2000.

Washington State Department of Ecology. *Shoreline Aerial Photos.* http://apps.ecy.wa.gov/website/coastal_atlas. Seattle, WA, 1992-1997.

Washington State University & National Park Service. *Ozette archaeological project research reports.* Edited by Stephan R. Samuels. Pullman, [Washington] Dept. of Anthropology, Washington State University, 1991-

Wright, Robin K, editor. *A Time of Gathering: Native Heritage in Washington State.* Seattle: Burke Museum; Seattle and London: Univ. of Washington Press, 1991.

University of Washington Libraries. (http://content.lib.washington.edu/all-collections.html)

Lifetime #2: John Hogans and the Civil War

Adams, Cecil. *Did the U.S. Civil War create 500,000 morphine addicts?* (http://www.straightdope.com/classics/a990709.html). Chicago: Chicago Reader, Inc., July 9, 1999.

Anderson, Ken. *The Coincidence File: Synchronicity, Morphic Resonance or Pure Chance?* Blandford Press, June, 1999.

Calkins, Chris M. *The Battles of Appomattox Station and Appomattox Court House.* Lynchburg, VA: H. E. Howard, Inc., 1987.

Gallman, J. Matthew, general editor; edited by David Rubel and Russell Shorto. *The Civil War chronicle : the only day-by-day portrait of America's tragic conflict as told by soldiers, journalists, politicians, farmers, nurses, slaves, and other eyewitnesses.* New York : Crown Publishers, 2000.

Greene, William B., 1843-1879. *Letters from a Sharpshooter : the Civil War letters of Private William B. Greene, Co. G, 2nd United States Sharpshooters (Berdan's) Army of the Potomac, 1861-1865 / transcribed by William H. Hastings.* Belleville, Wis.: Historic Pub., 1993.

Hamilton, Joseph Grégoire de Roulhac. *The life of Robert E. Lee for boys and girls.* New York, Houghton Mifflin Company, 1917.

Hendrickson, Robert. *The Road to Appomattox.* New York: J. Wiley, c1998.

Jones, J. William. *Personal reminiscences, anecdotes, and letters of Gen. Robert E. Lee / by J. William Jones.* New York : D. Appleton, 1875.

Library of Congress. (http://memory.loc.gov)

Macdonald, John. *Great battles of the Civil War.* New York: Collier Books; New York: Maxwell Macmillan International, 1992.

Murray, Alton J. *South Georgia Rebels.* St. Marys, Georgia: Alton J. Murray, Pub., 1976.

MyTrees.com. (www.kindredkonnections.com/).

Nichols, G. W. **A Soldier's Story of His Regiment (61st Georgia) and Incidentally of the Lawton-Gordon-Evans Brigade, Army of Northern Virginia.** Kennesaw, GA: Continental Book Co, 1961.

Reflection. *Tape Recordings of Intuitive-Trance Sessions covering my Past Lives.* 2002-2003.

Schroeder, Patrick A. *The Confederate Cemetery at Appomattox.* Virginia: Patrick A. Schroeder Publications, 1999.

Wert, Jeffry D. *Custer, the Controversial Life of George Armstrong Custer.* New York: Simon & Schuster, 1996.

Wert, Jeffry D. *General James Longstreet : the Confederacy's most controversial soldier: a biography.* New York: Simon & Schuster, 1993.

Lifetime #3: Sorrel Horse and Custer

Brady, Cyrus Townsend. *Indian Fights And Fighters : The Soldier And The Sioux.* New York : McClure, Phillips & Co., 1904.

Camp, Walter M. *Custer in '76.* Provo: Brigham Young Univ. Press, 1976.

Connell, E.van S. *Son of the Morning Star.* SF, CA: North Point Press, 1984.

Curtis, Edward S. *The North American Indian.* 1907-1930.

Dixon, Joseph K., Dr. *The Vanishing Race.* NY: Bonanza Books, 1913.

Fox, Richard A. *Archaeology, History, and Custer's Last Battle.* Norman: University of Oklahoma Press, 1993.

Goble, Paul and Dorothy. *Red Hawk's Account of Custer's Last Battle.* New York: Pantheon Books, 969.

Godfrey, Edward Settle. *An account of Custer's Last Campaign and the Battle of the Little Big Horn.* Palo Alto: Lewis Osborne, 1968.

Graham, W. A. *The Custer Myth: a source book on Custeriana.* Harrisburg, PA.: Stackpole Co., 1953.

Grinnell, George Bird. *The Fighting Cheyennes.* New York: Charles Scribner's Sons, 1915.

Hardorff, Richard G. *Cheyenne Memories of the Custer Fight.* Lincoln and London: University of Nebraska Press, 1995.

Hardorff, Richard G. *Hokahey! A Good Day to Die.* Lincoln and London: University of Nebraska Press, 1993.

Hardorff, Richard G. *Lakota Recollections of the Custer Fight.* Lincoln and London: University of Nebraska Press, 1991.

Inman, Henry. *The old Santa Fé trail; the story of a great highway.* New York, Macmillan, ca. 1897.

Library of Congress. (http://memory.loc.gov)

Marquis, Thomas B. *Keep the Last Bullet for Yourself.* New York: Two Continents Publishing Group, Ltd., 1976.

Marquis, Thomas B. *Wooden Leg, a Warrior who fought Custer.* Lincoln: University of Nebraska Press, 1931.

McGaw, Jessie Brewer. *Chief Red Horse tells about Custer: the Battle of the Little Bighorn.* New York: Elsevier/Nelson Books, 1981.

McLaughlin, J. *My Friend the Indian.* Seattle: Salisbury Press, 1970.

Miller, David Humphreys. *Custer's Fall.* New York: Bantam Books, 1957.

National Archives and Records Administration. (http://www.archives.gov)

Neihardt, John G. *Black Elk Speaks.* Lincoln: U of Nebraska P, 1961

'Reflection'. *Tape Recordings of Intuitive-Trance Sessions covering my Past Lives.* 2002-2003.

Remington, Frederic. *Drawings by Frederic Remington.* New York, R.H. Russell; London, Lawrence & Bullen, 1897.

Remington, Frederic. *Pony tracks.* New York, Harper & Brothers, 1895.

Remington, Frederic. *The way of an Indian.* New York, Fox, Duffield & Company, 1906.

Scott, Douglas D., et al. *Archaeological Perspectives on the Battle of Little Bighorn.* Norman: University of Oklahoma Press, 1989.

Stands in Timber, John and Liberty, Margot. *Cheyenne Memories.* New Haven and London: Yale University Press, 1967.

Taylor, William O. *With Custer on the Little Bighorn : a newly discovered first-person account.* New York: The Penguin Group, 1996.

Tillett, Leslie. *Wind on the Buffalo Grass.* New York: Thomas Y. Crowell Company, 1976.

Turning Bear, James. *James Turning Bear collection.* Montana State Univ., Bozeman campus. (http://www.montana.edu/wwwfpcc/tribes/index.html)

Utley, Robert. *Custer and the Great Controversy.* Pasadena, CA: Westernlore Press, 1980.

Viola, Herman J. *It Is a Good Day to Die.* NY: Crown Publishers, 1998.

Viola, Herman J. *Little Bighorn Remembered.* NY: Times Books, 1999.

Welch, James. *Killing Custer.* NY: W. W. Norton & Company, 1994.

Wert, Jeffry D. *Custer, the Controversial Life of George Armstrong Custer.* New York: Simon & Schuster, 1996.

Winch, Frank. *Thrilling lives of Buffalo Bill, Col. Wm. F. Cody, last of the great scouts and Pawnee Bill, Major Gordon W. Lillie (Pawnee Bill) white chief of the Pawnees.* New York, S.L. Parsons & co., inc., c1911.

Lifetime #4: Louis and the French Artists

Elgar, Frank. *Van Gogh, a study of his life and work.* NY: Praeger, 1958.

Esswein, Hermann. *Henri de Toulouse-Lautrec.* München : R. Piper, 1912.

Faille, J. Bernard de la. *Vincent van Gogh.* New York, N. Y.: French and European publications, 1939.

Hiatt, Charles. *Picture posters; a short history of the illustrated placard.* London, G. Bell; New York, Macmillan, 1896.

Hulsker Jan, *Vincent and Theo, a Dual Biography.* Ann Arbor Holland, 1990.

Jewell, Edward Alden. *French impressionists and their contemporaries represented in American collections.* New York, The Hyperion Press; Random House, distributors, 1944.

Jewell, Edward Alden. *Vincent Van Gogh.* New York, The Hyperion Press and Duell, Sloan, and Pearce, 1946.

Library of Congress. (http://memory.loc.gov)

Meier-Graefe, Julius. *Edouard Manet.* München, Piper, 1912.

Meier-Graefe, Julius. *Vincent Van Gogh : a biographical study.* London : The Medici Society, 1922.

Morice, Charles. *Paul Gauguin.* Paris, H. Floury, 1919.

National Archives and Records Administration. (http://www.archives.gov)

'Reflection'. *Tape Recordings of Intuitive-Trance Sessions covering my Past Lives.* 2002-2003.

Pickvance, Ronald. *Van Gogh In Arles.* New York, 1985.

The Vincent van Gogh Gallery, (http://www.vangoghgallery.com/index.html)

Tralbaut, Marc Edo. *Van Gogh; a pictorial biography.* New York, Viking Press, ca.1959.

Index

absinthe, 228, 233-236, 242, 244, 246-248, 256, 262-263, 270
Adrienne, daughter, 293, 295-297
afterlife, 298, 340-341
akashic records, 333, 337
angel, 303
Appomattox, 85-87, 103, 105-108, 111-112, 114-115, 130-132, 160, 352
Arles, France, 250, 252, 256-259, 261-264, 267, 275-276, 280, 298-300
assassination, 131-135, 137, 139-144
astral travel (see soul travel)
astral worlds, *xix*, 100, 129, 298, 303, 317-324, 328, 338, 345
Autobiography of a Yogi, 315, 317, 326
Beltway Sniper, *xvi*
Benteen, Capt. Frederick, 164, 171-172, 189, 205
Black, J. Oliver, 316
bliss, 326-331, 341
Booth, John Wilkes, 132-133, 135, 141-143
Boyer, Mitch, scout, 175, 177-178
brothel, 262, 267, 270, 275
Buddhism, *xv*, 300, 337, 343, 348
buffalo, 109, 153-154, 163, 165-166, 169, 171-172, 174, 178, 194-198, 200, 203, 205-206, 208, 212-213
cavalry, 102, 105, 109-110, 112, 145, 148, 160, 164, 172-173, 189, 191, 219
Cemetery Ridge, 182-183
Cheyenne, 110, 147, 151-152, 159-160, 169-170, 173, 179, 182-184, 202, 352
Christianity, *xv*, 337, 348
CIA, 139, 141-142
Claudette, 239-247
Cody, Buffalo Bill, 177, 304-305
Colby, William, 139
colony, artists', 250, 256, 261, 266
Colt pistol, 91
Community, Clear Light, 316
Confederate, 84, 86, 88, 94, 105-106, 108-109, 111-112, 115, 131-132, 138, 140, 142-144

Conqueror, King William I, *vi, vii*
Cosmic Consciousness, 326-331, 341
Coup Boys, 181, 183-184, 186
coup, count, 150-156, 159, 162-163, 167-168, 183, 185-186, 188, 190, 192-193
Cox, Col. Samuel A., 132, 135, 140
Crazy Horse, 139, 153, 157, 159, 179, 183, 216
crossing over, 205
Custer, Gen. George A., *xxi-xxii,* 110-113, 127, 145, 147-148, 159-160, 162, 164, 166, 171-178, 181-189, 193, 214, 218-219, 305, 351
Daddy Hogans, 80-83, 119-130
dancers, wedding, 42-45
Dealey Plaza, Dallas, 133, 136, 143
death vow, 38
Dentalium shells, 36
doctor, 117, 142, 177, 268, 277, 292-296, 350
dream world, 39, 129, 255-256, 317
Dreamball, drug, 255-256, 270
drugs, 117, 142, 244, 247, 263, 270, 293, 307, 351
earthquake, *xviii,* 6-7, 13, 16, 23, 77
enlightenment, 326-331, 341
environmentalist movement, 76
exile, 71-72, 75
flashbacks *vi, viii-xi, xiii, xviii,* 73
fords, river, 169-176, 178-179, 181-182
gangrene, 117
Gauguin, Paul, 222, 227-235, 247, 256, 258, 260-270, 275-276, 282
Geronimo, 139, 215-216
ghosts, *x,* 99-100, 123, 344-345
Golden Lotus Retreat, 316
Gordon's Bull, 89
Grant, Gen. U. S., 86, 102, 106, 112, 118, 139, 148
grassy knoll, Dallas, 141-142
grave, Vincent's, 278-280
Great Spirit, 9, 12, 19, 21-22, 24-25, 30-31, 35, 37-39, 58, 60, 62-64, 68, 70-71, 74, 148, 209, 214

harmonica, 93-94, 102

harpoon; harpooner, 32-36, 38, 46-47, 52-54

Hays, Pvt. Gideon, 85, 87-88, 90, 95-96, 107

heaven, 100, 125, 234, 281, 295, 301, 319, 321-322

Hinduism, *xv*, 337, 348

Ho Chi Minh, 139, 216

Hoover, J. Edgar, 138

hospital, 92, 115-119, 121-122, 124, 126, 270, 275-277

Hunt, H.L., 135, 140

hypnosis, *x, xix,* 131, 346

incarnate (see reincarnation)

Islam, 338, 349

James Hogans, brother, 92, 121-123, 129-130

Japan, 250, 300, 339, 348

Jesus, *xv*

JFK (see also under Kennedy), 134-136, 139-143

Johnson, Pres. Andrew, 137, 139, 142, 216

Johnson, Pres. Lyndon, 137, 216

Judaism, *xv,* 348

karma, *xv-xvii, xix, xxi,* 75, 112, 133-135, 140-141, 144, 157, 177, 193, 215-217, 274, 306, 318-319, 322-325, 334-337

Kennedy, Jacqueline, 136

Kennedy, Pres. John F., 131, 133-136, 140, 142-144

Kennedy, Robert, 140-141

kindred spirits, 336

King, Martin Luther, 140-141, 144

Kinniburgh, Donna and Steve, *xix,* 332-333

Lakota, *xviii, xxi,* 109-110, 112, 127, 147-148, 151, 153, 157, 159-161, 166, 168, 170, 183, 215, 219, 305, 350

Lee, Gen. Robert E., 79, 85-87, 91, 101-102, 104-106, 112, 118, 132, 144

letting go of the past, 309

Levenson, Lester, 309-314

life after death, *x,* 300, 344

Lincoln, Mary Todd, 136

Lincoln, Pres. Abraham, 131-136, 138-144, 216

Lindbergh, Charles, 134

liquefaction, sand, 12, 23

Little Bighorn, *xviii,* 147-148, 150, 164, 170, 182, 208, 214, 219

Mafia, 141-142

Makah tribe, 3-7, 23, 40, 76

malaria, 293-294, 347

Marc Antony, 218

Margot, wife, 285-297

marriage, 33-37, 40-48

Medicine Tail Coulee, 170, 172-173, 179, 181-182, 189

meditation, *xviii-xix,* 80, 129, 133, 315-316, 318, 323-324, 329-331, 341, 345-346

monk, Buddhist, 300

Morning-Song, daughter, 49-50, 52, 54-55, 58-63, 68, 71

morphine, 117, 294-295, 297

near-death experience, 269-276

nirvana, 326-331, 341

Oakley, Annie, 304

oil, Texas, 306

Opera Garnier, 283-285, 288-290

opium, 116-118, 233, 235, 244, 246-248, 255, 273

orca, 13, 16, 18, 26-31, 42-43, 61-62, 65-66, 68-69, 71, 74-75

Oswald, Lee Harvey, 142

out-of-body experience, *x,* 30, 100, 346

overdose, drug, 276, 300

Ozette, village, 5, 8, 23, 36, 47

Papa St. Jacques, 222-228, 232, 235, 241, 257-258, 266-267, 277

past life regression, *x, xviii*

Paul, Apostle, *xv*

Pinkerton, Allan, 138

portrait of Louis, 264-265

potlatch, 40-42

quest, spiritual, 24-31

Raymer, Bob, 316

rebirth, 55, 318, 347-348

Reflection, *xix,* 80, 133, 137, 140-141, 144, 177, 186, 188, 216, 218, 263, 265, 274, 332-343 reincarnation, *x-xxiii,* 55, 76, 80, 109, 117, 126-127, 133-144, 147, 161, 177, 215-218, 297, 303, 309, 318, 321, 325, 339-340, 347, 350-352

releasing the past, 309

religion, *x, xv,* 315, 326, 337, 341, 348

Reno, Maj. Marcus, 164-165, 170-171, 182-183, 205, 214

Rey, Dr., 269, 274, 276-277

Rosetta (Rose) Johns, 84, 91-93, 97-102, 118, 123-124, 129-130, 145, 352

Rue Lepic, 248-249

salmon vision, 25-31

samadhi, 324, 326-331, 341

satori, 326-331, 341

sea lions, 9, 12-14, 18, 58-64

Sedona Method, *xviii,* 77, 309

self-realization, 313, 316, 324-326

shaman, 3, 7, 13, 21, 24, 31, 34-35, 40, 46, 49, 58-59, 65-67, 70-71

shells (see Dentalium)

Sings-on-the-Wind, 21-31, 40, 49-58, 67-68, 74-75

Sitting Bull, 151, 153-155, 159, 168, 179-180, 184-185, 195, 201-203, 304, 351

Song of the Morning Retreat, 316

soul fragments, 335

soul groups, *xii, xxi,* 76, 131-144, 215-219, 304-306, 350-352

soul mates, 335, 339-340

soul partners, 336

soul travel, *x,* 335, 346

soul, *vii, x-xi, xiii-xiv, xix-xxiii,* 21, 30, 55, 80, 123, 126-127, 147, 160-161, 205, 221, 239, 274, 286, 298, 318, 321, 327-331, 334, 347-348

Spaniards, 57

spirit (see also soul), *viii-xiii, xx,* 15, 23-24, 30-32, 49, 55, 65, 67, 70, 74-75, 100, 120, 123, 126-128, 208, 303, 317, 338, 347-348, 352

spirit guide, *xix,* 14-15, 19-22, 24-31, 302-303, 332, 338-339, 343, 350

spirit warning, 15

spiritual test, 75

Spivey, Cpl. Ervin, 87-91, 93-96, 102, 106-114

stagecoach, 257-259, 278

Stands First, 185-188

Suicide Boys (see Coup boys)

sweat lodge, 24, 30, 38

Swim-Fast (sea lion), 61-64

Thunderbird Spirit, 7-8, 10, 21, 58, 68, 70

totem, 25, 31, 43, 65, 68-69, 71, 74-75

Toulouse-Lautrec, Henri de, 222, 227-228, 230-233, 235-239, 242-243, 247, 276, 280, 357

trance, *xix,* 62, 144, 186, 324, 332-333

Travel-Far, son, 58, 68, 71

trigger, *ix, xviii,* 60, 68, 166, 198

Tsues, village, 3, 5, 8-9, 18, 32, 58

tsunami, *xviii,* 7, 16, 23

twin flames, 336

van Gogh, Theo, 221, 228, 230, 232, 234, 247-249, 254, 256, 265, 275-276, 279-280

van Gogh, Vincent, 221-282, 298-302

Vietnam War, 137, 139-140, 215-218

vision, spiritual, *xvi, xviii,* 24-30, 50-52, 55-57, 65, 67, 74-76, 94, 154, 159, 203, 269-274, 276, 298-301, 326-328, 344-349

Wakan Tanka, 148, 159, 166-167, 180, 184-185, 195, 198-199, 202, 206-209, 212-213

Walks-under-the-Ground, 169, 176-177, 305

wedding, 40-49

Whale Spirit, 7-8

whale, 50-52, 75

Whale-Slayer, husband, 33-49, 52-58

Whirlwind, 149-163, 183, 188, 193, 198-199, 206, 209-213

Winchester rifle, 153-156, 173, 176

wounds, 92, 113-116, 160, 176-178, 180-183, 189-190, 192-193, 198-203, 207, 214, 218, 275, 305

Yankees, 85-91, 95-97, 104-114

Yellow-Hair (see also Custer), 159-162, 176-180, 184-186, 188

Yellowstone National Park, 199-200, 204, 211

yoga retreat, 316

yoga, 198, 315-316, 329, 331, 337, 341, 346

Yogananda, Paramahansa, 314-317, 324-326